An Invitation to Environmental Sociology

Sociology for a New Century

A Pine Forge Press Series

Edited by Charles Ragin, Wendy Griswold, and Larry Griffin

Sociology for a New Century brings the best current scholarship to today's students in a series of short texts authored by leaders of a new generation of social scientists. Each book addresses its subject from a comparative, historical, and global perspective, and, in doing so, connects social science to the wider concerns of students seeking to make sense of our dramatically changing world.

Forthcoming:

AN INVITATION TO ENVIRONMENTAL SOCIOLOGY

MICHAEL MAYERFELD BELL
Department of Sociology
Iowa State University
Ames, Iowa

PINE FORGE PRESS
Thousand Oaks • *London* • *New Delhi*

For information, address:
Pine Forge Press
A Sage Publications Company
2455 Teller Road
Thousand Oaks, California 91320
E-mail: sales@pfp.sagepub.com

Printed in the United States of America

00 01 02 03 10 9 8 7 6 5 4 3 2

Library of Congress Cataloging-in-Publication Data

Bell, Michael Mayerfeld, 1957-
      Invitation to environmental sociology / by Michael Bell.
           p. cm. — (Sociology for a new century)
      Includes bibliographical references and index.
      ISBN 0-7619-8509-3
      1. Environmentalism. 2. Environmental responsibility.
  3. Environmental ethics. I. Title. II. Series.
  GE195.B46 1998
  363.7—dc21   97-45255
                                              CIP

Production Coordinator: Windy Just
Copy Editor: Stephanie Prescott
Proofreader: Lisa Auer
Designer: Lisa S. Mirski
Typesetter: Stacey Denney
Cover Designer: Ravi Balasuriya
Print Buyer: Anna Chin
Artist: Jennifer Rezek

For my father,
Moses David Bell (1923-1996)
Writer, scholar, teacher
Washtub-bass player extraordinaire
A lover of people and the land:
He fished without hooks

BRIEF TABLE OF CONTENTS

⋮ DETAILED TABLE OF CONTENTS

ABOUT THE AUTHOR

Michael Mayerfeld Bell lives in Ames, Iowa, where he teaches environmental sociology and social theory at Iowa State University. He is the author of two previous books, *Childerley: Nature and Morality in a Country Village* (1994) and *The Face of Connecticut: People, Geology, and the Land* (1985), both of which won national awards. On the weekends, he plays fretted things (guitar, banjo, and mandolin) with two local folk groups, the Pretty Good Band and the Barn Owl Band.

ABOUT THE PUBLISHER

Pine Forge Press is a new educational publisher, dedicated to publishing innovative books and software throughout the social sciences. On this and any other of our publications, we welcome your comments, ideas, and suggestions. Please write or call us at:

Pine Forge Press
A Sage Publications Company
2455 Teller Road
Thousand Oaks, CA 91320
(805) 499-4224
Fax: (805) 499-7881
E-mail: sales@pfp.sagepub.com

Visit our new World Wide Web site, your direct link to a multitude of online resources: http://www.sagepub.com/pineforge

Sociology for a New Century offers the best of current sociological thinking to today's students. The goal of the series is to prepare students, and—in the long run—the informed public, for a world that has changed dramatically in the last three decades and one that continues to astonish.

This goal reflects important changes that have taken place in sociology. The discipline has become broader in orientation, with an ever growing interest in research that is comparative, historical, or transnational in orientation. Sociologists are less focused on "American" society as the pinnacle of human achievement and more sensitive to global processes and trends. They also have become less insulated from surrounding social forces. In the 1970s and 1980s sociologists were so obsessed with constructing a science of society that they saw impenetrability as a sign of success. Today, there is a greater effort to connect sociology to the ongoing concerns and experiences of the informed public.

Each book in this series offers a comparative, historical, transnational, or global perspective in some way, to help broaden students' vision. Students need to be sensitized to diversity in today's world and to the sources of diversity. Knowledge of diversity challenges the limitations of conventional ways of thinking about social life. At the same time, students need to be sensitized to the fact that issues that may seem specifically "American" (for example, the women's movement, an aging population bringing a strained social security and health care system, racial conflict, national chauvinism, and so on) are shared by many others countries. Awareness of commonalities undercuts the tendency to view social issues and questions in narrowly American terms and encourages students to seek out the experiences of others for the lesson they offer. Finally, students also need to be sensitized to phenomena that transcend national boundaries, economics, and politics.

It is a sometimes awkward fact that "society" doesn't just function in empty space, with groups being simply units lurching around in conflict, or cooperation. Society takes place—so far, and not exclusively even now—on a planet where things like water, soil, weather, plants, minerals, and animals operate as resources for and limits upon groups' ambitions, objects of their competitions, and touchstones of their philosophical and moral inquiries. In his rich account of the material, ideal, and practical issues raised by this awkward fact, Michael Bell manages to cover the tremendous variousness of topics in environmental sociology while at the same time investing his treatment with a personal passion rarely seen in sociological texts. *An Invitation to Environmental Sociology* is more than an invitation; it is a seduction. Readers will be challenged by the complexity of environmental puzzles Bell poses, informed and therefore intellectually enabled to make their own private and public choices, and inspired to care about the social footprints on the planet.

—Wendy Griswold

As I sit down to write the preface to this book, having finished the main text a few weeks ago, I'm reflecting on a peculiarity of book-writing. The preface of a book is usually the last section an author writes, even though it appears at the book's beginning. This may seem an odd practice—to end by beginning—but I believe it to be a sound one. At least, the practice seems very appropriate to one of the main messages of this book: Social and environmental interactions are best understood as a kind of ecological dialogue, a never-ending conversation in which one interchange leads to another, and every ending is a new beginning.

Given the current difficult state of our environmental affairs, I find hope in this open-ended sense of potential. We *can* change, particularly if we act as a *we*, as a community that invites into the conversation all its social and environmental constituents. Thus the title of my book: *An Invitation to Environmental Sociology*.

The title is also drawn from an engaging little volume that appeared over thirty years ago—Peter Berger's *Invitation to Sociology*. Check the sociology section of nearly any used bookstore in North America, and a battered paperback copy is almost sure to be there. (Some students, of course, sell back *all* their course books, good and bad.) In that book, Berger sought to extend "an invitation to an intellectual world that I consider to be profoundly exciting and significant," and over three decades of sociology students have accepted that invitation. In this book, I try to extend a similar invitation, but to an intellectual world that is at once more specialized and far more encompassing than sociology: environmental sociology. My prose, I fear, is not as engaging as Berger's, and I know this book could not be described as "little." Nevertheless, my intent has been to offer a work in what I hope is an equally welcoming spirit. We all need to be involved in this great, though often troubled, conversation of environment and society.

It has been a rare pleasure to work with a publisher like Pine Forge Press that supports both engaging and challenging writing. Many textbooks try to present the "medium" view of an academic field—or worse, a smoothed-over view—in an effort to create a text that goes down easy. Scholarly works, although they may take a strong and novel position, are generally written in language accessible to only a small club of experts. Neither approach inspires broad public interest and participation in the life of the mind. Pine Forge Press, through the *Sociology for a New Century* series and other publications, supports authors who seek to transcend the traditional boundary between the textbook and the scholarly monograph, offering works that are readable and accessible to students but nonetheless original and intellectually challenging syntheses of academic fields.

In other words, while I hope my book is accessible and interesting to students, I also offer it as a work of scholarship. The principal scholarly contribution of the book is the concept of ecological dialogue, a concept that I believe can serve as one useful framework for understanding environmental sociology. But I do not present ecological dialogue as the last word on the subject of environmental sociology. Rather, I can only hope that the concept stimulates students and other readers to consider closely the issues of environmental sociology and to contribute to reasoned discussion about them. That will be enough. Let the end of this book lead to many more new beginnings. Thus we may find that changing social and environmental interactions is not only possible, but that we've already done it.

....

This was not an easy book to write. When Wendy Griswold, one of the two editors of the *Sociology for a New Century* series, first approached me about writing, I had just finished teaching a course on environmental sociology in the spring of 1995. The course had gone well, and I had detailed lecture notes field-tested in the heat of the classroom. Putting together a book should be a matter of little more that writing up those notes in a more coherent form, I thought. Six months should do it. Two years later . . . As many have discovered, the more closely one considers the issues of environmental sociology, the more one realizes one has not considered them closely enough. Seeking guidance, I read through hundreds of books and articles. (The literature on social and environmental interactions is huge, as befits the scope and importance of the topic.) In the end, many of the chapters bear little resemblance to what we covered in that spring, 1995 course.

But through all the delays and deadlines stretched to the breaking point, Pine Forge's visionary publisher, Steve Rutter, remained a rock of gently prodding patience. I owe an enormous amount to his guidance, encouragement, and sense of what this book could be. I feel lucky to have worked with him. Thanks, Steve.

I am also grateful for Wendy Griswold's confidence in asking me to write this book. As well, her critical eye (and gifted tongue) guided me into making many improvements over my first tentative draft, and also gave me the self-assurance to try again. Thanks, Wendy.

These two made the most central contributions, but many, many others lent a hand at various crucial moments. I was fortunate enough to have from Pam Ozaroff the most detailed and thought-provoking critique imaginable for what was then the first two chapters of the book. Becky Smith gave the entire manuscript a detailed reading at a later stage and made many helpful suggestions. Copy editors terrify me, but Stephanie Prescott went through the manuscript with as sensible and sensitive a pencil a writer could wish for (if I may dangle a preposition at her). Jennifer Rezek did a marvelous job, I think, in creating illustrations with character and presence. And Windy Just, the production manager at Pine Forge, handled with good cheer and unwavering aplomb my many delays and dribbled mailings of illustrations and re-edited manuscript. Thanks Pam, Becky, Stephanie, Jennifer, and Windy.

Much of the book was written while I was a visiting fellow at the Centre for Rural Economy of the University of Newcastle-upon-Tyne in the fall of 1996. The Centre's staff—Eileen Curry, Philip Lowe (the director), Chris Ray, Hilary Talbot, Rachel Woodward, and Martin Whitby—provided me with peace and intellectual stimulus in just the right proportions. But that fellowship (in every sense of the word) would not have been possible had not my department chair back at Iowa State, Will Goudy, worked a bit of magic to get me the necessary leave from my normal duties. Thanks Eileen, Philip, Chris, Hilary, Rachel, Martin, and Will.

There are still others to acknowledge. I had the privilege of working with three undergraduate research assistants at various times while I was writing the book—first Lucas Rockwell at Iowa State, then Kate Entwhistle at the University of Newcastle, and finally Jake Peterson back at Iowa State again. Lucas in particular went way beyond the call of duty, bringing me articles I hadn't known to look for and critiquing an early draft of chapter one. My good friends Ram Guha and Eric Pallant (who, unfortunately, have never met) read chapter one as well, and helped me avoid some dangers I had gotten into. Pine Forge also arranged for six anonymous reviewers of the manuscript at various points in its genesis. They are: Marilyn Aronoff, *Michigan State University*; Richard Coon, *Carroll College*; Anne Martin, *Edmonds Community College*; Valerie Gunter, *University of New Orleans*; Ted Napier, *Ohio State University*; Robert Schaeffer, *San Jose State University.* I thank them heartily for their constructive comments.

And then there are my students in that spring 1995 course in Environmental sociology, as well as Margaret Munyae, my splendid teaching assistant in the course. All these—and more—can find the influence of their words and spirits in these pages, and I am thankful for their generosity and insight.

But my greatest thanks go to my family. My wife Diane Bell Mayerfeld proved to be, once again, an invaluable editor and my closest intellectual colleague. Whenever I was stuck on a passage or confused about the argument

I was trying to make, raising the problem with Diane almost always led to a ready solution or redirected my thinking such that I discovered one soon enough. She also provided far more emotional support than any spouse could reasonably expect. I honestly cannot imagine how this book ever would have been completed without her many-splendored presence in my life.

And thanks as well to Sam, our son, who with generally good humor put up with several missed rides in the skiff, the grouchiness of a dad who stays up too late, and a sense that time was becoming a commodity we spend instead of a river in which we dabble our toes together. Our family could do with a lot more toe dabbling. And now that this book is complete, I think we'll find ourselves doing just that. I can hear the splashing already.

MMB
November 3, 1997
Ames

The author gratefully acknowledges from the following sources permission to republish, in modified form, portions of his earlier work: In Chapter 2, "The Ghosts of Place", *Theory and Society* (forthcoming); in Chapter 3, "The Dialectic of Technology: Commentary on Warner and England", *Rural Sociology*, 1995, 60(4); in Chapters 5 and 6, Childerley: Nature and Morality in a Country Village, 1994, University of Chicago Press; in Chapter 7, Stone Age New England: A Geology of Morals, from Creating the Countryside: The Politics of Rural and Environmental Discourse, Melanie Dupuis and Peter Vandergeest, eds., 1996, Temple University Press; in Chapter 8, "The Dialogue of Solidarities, or, Why the Lion Spared Androcles", *Sociological Focus*, (forthcoming).

The author gratefully acknowledges from the following sources permission to republish: Cover, *I and the Village* by Chagall, The Museum of Modern Art, New York; *The Discovery of Honey* by Piero di Cosimo, Worcester Art Museum; A Medieval illustration of an Ox-drawn moldboard plow, The Folger Shakespeare Library; *Lake and Mountains*, The Gallery of Ontario; *The Price of Global Warming*, Worldwatch Institute; *Dying Forests*, World Resources; *Accelerating Treadmills*, Worldwatch Institute; *World Grain Production*, Worldwatch Institute; *Harvard Forest Dioramas for 1740, 1830, and 1850*, Fisher Museum; *Ecological Modernization*, Worldwatch Institute; *A Warming World*, Worldwatch Institute; *CO2 on the Rise*, Worldwatch Institute.

CHAPTER 1

Environmental Problems and Society

Without self-understanding we cannot hope for enduring
solutions to environmental problems, which are
fundamentally human problems.

-Yi-Fu Tuan, 1974

"Pass the hominy please."

It was a lovely brunch, with fruit salad, homemade coffee cake, a great
pan of scrambled eggs, bread, butter, jam, coffee, tea—and hominy grits.
Our friends Dan and Sarah had invited my wife and me and our son
over that morning to meet some friends of theirs. The grown-ups sat
around the dining table, and the kids (four in all) careened from their
own table in the kitchen to the pile of toys in the living room, and often
into each other. Each family had contributed something to the feast
before us. It was all good food, but for some reason the hominy (which
I had never had before) was the most popular.

There was a pleasant mix of personalities, and the adults soon got
into one of those excited chats that leads in an unreproducible way
from one topic to another, as unfamiliar people seek to get to know
each other a bit better. Eventually the inevitable question came my
way: "So what do you do?"

"I'm an environmental sociologist."

"Environmental sociology. That's interesting. I've never heard of it.
What does sociology have to do with the environment?"

The point of this book is to answer that question, a question I'm
often asked—and in a more complete way than the two-minute
answers that the dynamics of casual conversation generally allow. But
let me begin with the two-minute answer.

Environmental sociology is the study of community in the largest
possible sense. People, other animals, land, water, air—all of these are
closely interconnected. Together they form a kind of solidarity, what we

have come to call *ecology*. As in any community, there are also conflicts in the midst of the interconnections. Environmental sociology studies this largest of communities with an eye to understanding the origins of, and proposing solutions to, these all-too-real social and biophysical conflicts.

Environmental problems are not only problems of technology and industry, of ecology and biology, of pollution control and pollution prevention. They are also social problems. Environmental problems are problems *for* society—problems that threaten our existing patterns of social organization. Environmental problems are as well problems *of* society—problems that challenge us to change those patterns of organization. It is people who create environmental problems, and it is people who must resolve them. And for that we need, among other disciplines, sociology.

One of sociology's most basic contributions to the study of environmental problems is to point out the pivotal role of social inequality. Not only are the effects of environmental problems distributed unequally across the human community, social inequality is also deeply involved in causing those problems. Social inequality is both a product and a producer of pollution, overconsumption, resource depletion, habitat loss, risky technology, and rapid population growth. As well, social inequality influences how we envision what our environmental problems are. And most fundamentally, it can even influence how we envision nature itself, for inequality shapes our social experiences and our social experiences shape all our experience.

Which returns us to the question of community. Social inequality cannot be understood apart from the communities in which it takes place. We need, then, to make the study of community the central task of environmental sociology. Ecology is often described as the study of natural communities. Sociology is often described as the study of human communities. Environmental sociology is the study of both together, the single commons of the earth we humans share, sometimes grudgingly, with others—other people, other forms of life, and the rocks and water and soil and air that support all life. Environmental sociology is the study of this, the biggest community of all.

A PANORAMA OF THE BOOK

That's the two-minute answer. But clearly the topic of environmental sociology is vast. Not even a book the length of this one can cover all of it, at least not in any detail. In the pages to come, we will take a series of field trips into this vast landscape, pausing here and there for a closer look at various significant features of the terrain. Rather than attempting some sort of sociological aerial photography, the book intensively investigates a few topics on the ground and occasionally scales a high overlook for a panoramic view. Such an approach, I believe, will lead to the most balanced understanding of environmental sociology.

For the most part, this first chapter presents several such panoramic views—of environmental sociology, of the environmental predicament, and, in this section, of the book itself. After this introduction, the book falls into three parts:

The Material: how consumption, the economy, technology, development, population, and biophysical resources shape our environmental situation.

The Ideal: how culture, ideology, moral values, and social experience influence the way we think about and act toward the environment.

The Practical: how we might solve environmental conflicts, taking both the material and the ideal into account.

Of course, it is not possible to fully separate these three topics. This is, in fact, one of the most important truths that environmental sociology has to offer, I believe. The parts of the book represent only a sequence of emphases, not rigid conceptual boundaries. A number of themes running throughout the book help unite the three parts:

- The central role of social inequality in environmental conflicts
- The dialogic, or interactive, character of causality in environmental sociology
- The interplay of material and ideal factors
- The connections between the local and the global
- The power of the metaphor of community for understanding these social and ecological dynamics

By approaching environmental sociology in this way, I hope to bridge a long-standing dispute among scholars about the relationship between environment and society. *Realists* argue that environmental problems cannot be understood apart from the threats posed by society's current ecologic relations. They believe that social scientists can ill afford to ignore the material truth of environmental problems. *Constructionists* do not necessarily disagree, but they emphasize the influence of social life in how we conceptualize those "threats" or the lack of those "threats." Constructionists focus on the ideological origins of environmental problems—including their very definition *as* problems (or as nonproblems). A realist might say, for example, that the ozone hole is a dangerous consequence of how we currently organize social life. A constructionist might say that in order to recognize the danger—or even the existence—of the ozone hole, we must wear the appropriate ideological and cultural eyeglasses. Simply put, realists and constructionists disagree over whether the purpose of environmental sociology is to understand environmental problems or environmental "problems."[1]

Fundamentally, the realist-constructionist debate is over *materialist* versus *idealist* explanations of social life. The tension between materialist and idealist explanations is itself a centuries-old philosophical dispute, one that perhaps all cultural traditions have grappled with in one way or another. There is an ancient fable from India that expresses the tension well. A group of blind people encounter an elephant for the first time. One grabs the tail and says, "An elephant is like a snake!" Another grabs a leg and says, "An elephant is like a tree!" A third grabs an ear and says, "An elephant is like a big leaf!" To the materialist, the fable shows how misinformed all three blind people are, for a sighted person can plainly see how the "snake," "tree," and "big leaf" connect together into an elephant. To the idealist, the fable says that we all have our ideological blindnesses, and that there is no fully sighted person who can see the whole elephant—that we are all blind people wildly grasping at the illusive truth of the world.

The approach to this ancient debate that I will take is that the material and the ideal dimensions of the environment depend upon and interact with each other. What we believe depends on what we see and feel, and what we see and feel depends on what we believe. It is not a matter of either/or; rather, it is a matter of both/together. I will term this mutual interdependence *ecological dialogue*. Throughout the book I will consider the interplay, the constant conversation, between the material and ideal dimensions of this never-ending dialogue. (See Exhibit 1.1.)

Let me also make it clear that this book takes an activist position with regard to environmental problems and the way we think about them. We often look to scholars to provide an unbiased perspective on issues that concern us, and we sometimes regard an active commitment to a political position as cause for suspicion about just how scientific that perspective is. Yet, as many have argued, it is not possible to escape political implications.[2] Everyone has concerns for and interests in the condition of our world and our society. Such concerns and interests are what guide us all every day, and scholars are no different from anyone else in this regard. Nor should they be any different. Such concerns and interests are not necessarily a problem for scholarship. On the contrary, they are the whole reason for scholarship.

This does not mean that anything goes—that any perspective is just as academically valid as any other because all knowledge is only opinion and we are all entitled to our own opinion. Scholarship is opinion, of course, but it is a special kind of opinion. What scholarship means is being critical, careful, honest, open, straightforward, and responsible in one's opinions— in what one claims is valid knowledge. One needs to reason critically and carefully, to be honest about the reasons one suggests to others, to be open to the reasons others suggest, to be straightforward about one's political reasons, and to be responsible in the kinds of reasons one promotes. Being honest, open, and straightforward with each other about our careful, critical reasons is the only academically responsible thing to do.

Exhibit 1.1 Ecological Dialogue.

Therefore, it is best for me to be straightforward about why I think environmental sociology is an important topic of study: I believe there are serious environmental problems that need concerted attention, and soon. And I believe environmental issues are closely intertwined with a host of social issues, most of them at least in part manifestations of social inequality and the challenges inequality poses for community. Addressing these intertwinings, manifestations, and challenges is in everyone's interests. We will all benefit, I believe, by reconsidering the present state of the ecological dialogue.

Such a perspective, particularly the focus on social inequality, coincides more closely with the current politics of the left than the right. Yet issues of the environment cut across traditional political boundaries, as chapter 6 will discuss. The evidence and arguments that I offer in this book should be of interest to anyone committed to careful, critical reasoning. In any event, we should not let political differences stop us from engaging in dialogue about ecological dialogue.

Nevertheless you, the reader, should be aware that I indeed have a moral and political perspective and that it unavoidably informs what I have written here. Keep that in mind as you carefully and critically evaluate what is in this book. But it is also your scholarly responsibility to be open to the reasoning I present and to have honest reasons for disagreeing.

THE ENVIRONMENTAL PREDICAMENT

Let us now turn to some of the reasons that lead many to believe there is cause for considerable concern about the current condition of the ecological dialogue: the challenges to *sustainability, environmental justice*, and the *rights and beauty of nature*. These, the three central environmentalism issues, will already be well known to some readers. Still, it is appropriate to pause and review them here, as these considerations underlie the rest of the book.

Sustainability

How long can we keep doing what we're doing? This is the essential question of sustainability. The length of the list of threats to environmental sustainability is, at the very least, unnerving. True, much is unknown, and some have exaggerated the dangers we face. Consequently, there is considerable controversy about the long-term consequences of humanity's continuing transformation of the earth.[3] But much is known, and some have underestimated the dangers involved. It is therefore prudent that we all pay close attention to the potential challenges to sustainability.

Global Warming. Perhaps the greatest uncertainty (and controversy) surrounds an issue that poses one of the greatest potential environmental threats: global warming. There is considerable evidence that the world is heating up. When averages are calculated for the entire globe, the twelve warmest years on record (through 1996) have all occurred since 1980.[4] And the trend is upward: The 1970s were hotter than the 1960s, the 1980s were hotter than the 1970s, and the 1990s are shaping up to be hotter yet.[5] In every year since 1977, the annual average world temperature has been at least 15 degrees Celsius (59 degrees Fahrenheit), a level hardly ever reached in the past two hundred years.[6]

Exhibit 1.2 A warming world: Average surface temperature of the Earth, 1866–1996.

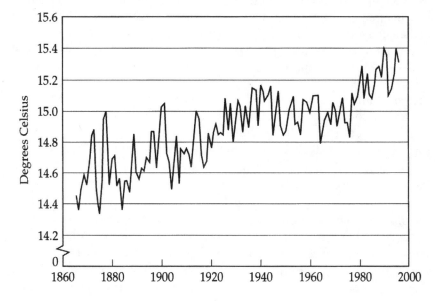

Source: Brown et al. (1997).

These weather records show that there was a grain of truth to an earlier generation's stories about having to walk to school through three feet of chilling snow, barefoot and uphill both ways. Eighteenth- and nineteenth-century images of the whole town out for a skating party or of the Dutch skating to work on frozen canals are more than merely romantic. It really was colder back then. Winters were longer, blizzards were stronger, and glaciers used to come down farther out of the mountains. There are even reports that Long Island Sound, the body of salt water between Long Island and the Connecticut coast, occasionally would freeze over and people would drive fifteen miles across the ice with a team and wagon. That hasn't happened in 150 years.[7]

If this warming trend continues over the next 100 years, say most climatologists and oceanographers, we will see some major environmental changes. Climatic zones will shift, rainfall patterns will change, and weather conditions will become more variable. In addition, sea level will rise between five and fifteen feet as glaciers and the ice caps melt and as ocean water heats up and expands. (Ocean water will not heat up and expand by much, but the incredible volume of water in the oceans means that even a slight expansion leads to a considerable rise in sea level.)

The predicted consequences would be dramatic, to say the least. Some forests may die off because of newly unfavorable growing conditions. Some urban areas will experience increased drinking water shortages and heat waves. Warmer temperatures and changes in rainfall patterns could increase the incidence of disease, as the new conditions would likely be more hospitable to mosquitoes, ticks, rodents, bacteria, and viruses. The incidence of damaging storms is also likely to increase. Extensive regions of low-lying coastal land (where much of the world's human population lives) would be under water. Whole countries, such as the low-lying Pacific island nations of Tuvalu and Kiribati, might disappear beneath the waves. (Not surprisingly, the governments of Tuvalu and Kiribati have been vocal proponents of worldwide controls on the emission of greenhouse gases.)[8]

The consequences for agriculture would be complex. Some prime agricultural areas will likely be stricken with drier conditions. For example, farmers in Iowa, the leading corn-producing region in the United States, might have to switch over to wheat and drought-tolerant corn varieties, which would mean overall declines in food production per acre.[9] On the other hand, some regions will likely receive more rain. Yet many of these regions do not have the same quality of soil as, say, Iowa. To add to the complexity, carbon dioxide (the gas implicated as the principal cause of global warming, as I'll discuss in a moment) can stimulate plant growth, perhaps compensating for decreased rainfall. However, this stimulation may not result in increased crop yields because of other limiting factors, such as low rainfall, poor soil conditions, and the biology of plant development. No one really knows what the overall effects would be.

Nevertheless, it's scary stuff. Indeed, some say the predictions are already coming true. Health officials worry that we are seeing an increase in heat waves, such as the spell of days over 100 degrees between July 13 and 15, 1995, that has been blamed for at least 733 deaths in Chicago—or the 116-degree heat waves that killed 35 in the south of Spain and 400 in India in 1995.[10] (At the time of this writing, 1995 is the hottest year on record.) As well, warmer world weather has been implicated in the resurgence of cholera in Latin America in 1991 and pneumonic plague in India in 1994 and in the outbreak of a hantavirus epidemic in the U.S. Southwest in 1994. Scientists are wondering if global warming is a factor in about ten other diseases that resurged or reemerged in the 1990s.[11] There are already indications that we are seeing an increase in devastating storms and hurricanes, and the insurance industry is worried that there has been an upsurge in claims as a result. Nineteen ninety-six was the worst year on record for weather-related insurance claims—they totaled a whopping $60 billion. (See Exhibit 1.3.) By comparison, weather-related claims for all of the 1980s totaled $17 billion.[12] On a possibly more positive note, regions north of 45 degrees north latitude turned greener between 1981 and 1991. These areas are greening up about a week earlier in spring, staying green a few days longer in the fall, and experiencing about a 10 percent increase in plant growth, perhaps stimulating crops in the long run.[13]

Exhibit 1.3 *The price of global warming: Economic losses from weather-related natural disasters worldwide, 1980–96.*

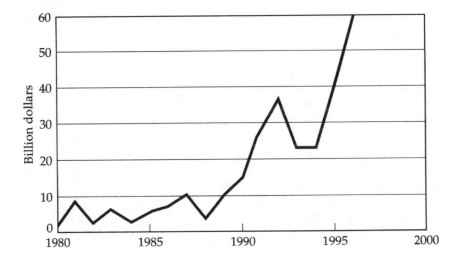

Source: Brown et al. (1997).

Not all climatologists agree that we are seeing the first stages of human-induced global warming, though most do.[14] There can be little doubt, though, that the world has been heating up of late.[15] The questions most dissenters ask are why and whether it will continue. Perhaps such variations in world climate are normal processes of nature. The sun could be putting out more radiation than it used to, for example. There is evidence to suggest that the world climate goes through cycles of warm and cold. Around 1000–1300 C.E., the global climate was warm enough that the Vikings settled southern Greenland and established farms.[16] But the next 500 years were much colder. Glaciers all over the world advanced down mountain valleys, and the Vikings had to abandon their quixotically named Greenland. Climatologists call these years the "Little Ice Age." Similar centuries-long periods of sustained cooling preceded this recent one.

Some scientists have suggested that these periods, as well as shorter-term cycles in the global climate, are due to variations in the workings of the sun.[17] The sun does experience cycles in its activity, such as the 11-year sunspot cycle, and recent studies suggest this could account for some of the global warming trend. Some scientists say solar variation could account for almost all of the warming—but most do not.[18] So little is known. Direct evidence about solar radiation in any time beyond the most recent past does not exist, of course. And almost all scientists agree that the 11-year sunspot cycle (which can be measured) is not significant enough (or long enough) to explain a 150-year trend.

Moreover, this most recent Little Ice Age was a particularly short one. If the past is any guide, it ended a couple of centuries too soon.[19] As the United Nations Intergovernmental Panel on Climate Change, representing scientists from 120 countries, wrote in 1996, "The balance of evidence . . . suggests a discernable human influence on global climate."[20]

We do know, however, that levels of carbon dioxide in the atmosphere have been steadily increasing since about the time the Little Ice Age ended. In the mid-nineteenth century, the atmosphere was about 280 parts per million carbon dioxide; today the figure is 340 parts per million and rising. This jump closely correlates with the coming of the industrial revolution. Fossil fuels and trees are great banks of carbon, and burning is a process of oxidization that releases energy. The energy moves the machines of industry, and the oxidized carbon joins the atmosphere. We now burn huge amounts of fossil fuels—coal, oil, natural gas, and peat—to stoke the fires of industrial technology. And we have cleared much of the world's forest land to grow crops for a rapidly expanding population. As a result, we have sent a vast quantity of oxidized carbon, mainly in the form of carbon dioxide, into the sky.

Increasing levels of carbon dioxide are significant because of what climatologists call the "greenhouse effect." The energy we get from the sun travels here in the form of light, not heat. When sunlight reaches the earth's surface, some of that energy is absorbed and converted into heat. This heat then radiates back out. Our atmosphere lets much of this radiant heat energy pass into outer space, but, like the glass on a greenhouse, blocks the passage of some of it. No problem here. The greenhouse-like effect of the atmosphere keeps the world in its usual temperature range of 0 to 100 degrees Fahrenheit. If our atmosphere didn't trap some heat, the earth would be as cold as the moon. But heat does not pass through carbon dioxide as easily as it passes through some of the other constituents of the atmosphere. Thus, extra carbon dioxide increases the amount of heat trapped by the atmospheric greenhouse, as if someone had closed off the vents at the apex of the greenhouse roof.

You could also think of increased carbon dioxide as acting like an extra blanket on a warm night, gradually stifling the planet. I say "on a warm night" because even without carbon dioxide, the ecological processes that led to the last Little Ice Age should be ending their cooling effect on the global climate along about now, judging by past climatic cycles. Thus, we could be on the verge of seeing two major warming trends working together—the cyclical rebound from the Little Ice Age (that's the warm night) in combination with increased heat-trapping gases (the extra blanket)—leading to an Industrial Warm Age. We could be on the verge of many centuries of generally lousy sleeping weather—and things much, much more ominous than that.

Exhibit 1.4 CO₂ on the rise: Atmospheric concentration of carbon dioxide, 1764–1996.

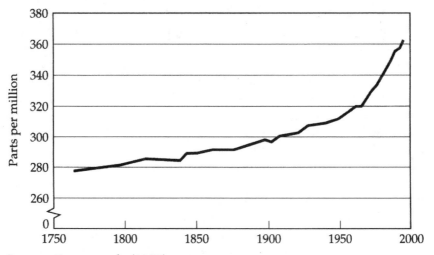

Source: Brown et al. (1997).

No one knows for sure. There is no way to prove absolutely the connection between the increasing global temperatures of the last 150 years and rising levels of carbon dioxide and other atmospheric gases that have a similar greenhouse effect (most notably methane). But a majority of climatologists are convinced that the connection probably exists. The United Nations Intergovernmental Panel on Climate Change recently projected that average global temperature will rise 1.5 to 4.5 degrees Celsius during the next century as a result of added greenhouse gases.[21] In addition, another recent study suggested that changes in solar radiation could add another half degree— the "warm night" again.[22] This is an enormous average increase when you consider that an average drop of only 6 degrees Celsius caused the ice ages—

not the Little Ice Age (that took a drop of only 2 degrees Celsius) but the big ones, the ones that periodically covered half of North America and Europe with a mile or more of ice.[23] Climate is a touchy thing; a few degrees average change can make quite a difference.

At the very least, the connection between global warming and greenhouse gases is something to think about on a hot summer night as you ponder whether you should crank the air conditioner up another notch, causing your local utility to burn just that much more carbon-based fuel to generate the necessary electricity.[24] You could be making matters worse.

The Two Ozone Problems.   There are several other threats to our atmosphere—threats which, while perhaps not quite as drastic in their potential consequences as global warming, are much more certain. And they are plenty drastic enough for considerable concern. Two of these threats involve ozone, although in quite different ways.

Ozone forms when groups of three oxygen atoms bond together into single molecules, molecules chemists signify as O_3. Most atmospheric oxygen is in the form of two bonded oxygen atoms, or O_2, but a vital layer of the O_3 form in the upper atmosphere helps protect life on the earth's surface from the effects of the sun's ultraviolet radiation. Ultraviolet light can cause skin cancer, promote cataracts, damage immune systems, and disrupt ecosystems. Were there no ozone layer in the upper atmosphere, life on Earth would have evolved in quite different ways—if indeed it had begun at all. In any event, current life forms are not equipped to tolerate much more ultraviolet radiation than the surface of the Earth currently receives. We badly need the upper atmosphere ozone layer.

In 1974, two chemists, Mario Molina and Sherwood Rowland proposed that chlorofluorocarbons, could be reacting with the ozone layer and breaking it down. "CFCs," as they are called, were widely used at the time as refrigerants, as propellants in aerosol cans, and in a number of manufacturing processes. Molina and Rowland predicted that CFCs could ultimately make their way into the upper atmosphere and attack the integrity of the ozone layer. In 1985, scientists pouring over satellite imagery of the atmosphere over Antarctica discovered (almost accidentally) that the ozone layer over the south pole had, in fact, grown dangerously thin.

Many studies later, we now know that this "ozone hole," as it has come to be called, is growing in overall size. We also know that it changes in size with the seasons, has a mate over the north pole, and stretches to some degree everywhere on the planet except the tropics. In fact, it's really not a hole—it is more accurate to say that, outside the tropics, the ozone layer is *thinning*, particularly over the poles. At times, the layer thins to less than 50 percent of the levels observed in the 1970s.)[25]

Just as there is no "proof" that increased atomospheric carbon dioxide causes global warming, there is also no proof that CFCs are causing the thinning of the ozone layer. But the drama of Rowland and Molina's prediction (although even they had underestimated the degree of thinning), the seriousness of the likely consequences, and measurements that consistently show ultraviolet radiation on the increase have galvanized the world into unusually cooperative action.[26] In 1987, the major industrial countries signed the first of a series of agreements, known as the Montreal Protocol, to reduce the production of CFCs. As a result of these agreements, CFC production in these countries ended on December 31, 1995, and will end throughout the world after 2005. By 1994, annual CFC production had already fallen to 295,000 tons—down from a high of 1,260,000 tons in 1988.

It will be many decades until the thinning is repaired, however. The ozone-damaging chlorine that CFCs contain remains resident in the atmosphere for some time, and the HCFCs (hydrochlorofluorocarbons) industrial countries are turning to as a substitute until 2030 also damage the ozone layer to some extent. (Unfortunately, HCFCs are also a potent greenhouse gas and could significantly increase global warming.) Scientists expect that conditions in fact will not improve until early in the next century.[27]

But the reduction of CFC production is nevertheless an astounding success story—not least for Rowland and Molina, who received the 1995 Nobel Prize in chemistry for their work, along with Paul Crutzen for his important earlier studies of the ozone layer. Given the unusual level of international cooperation that led to the Montreal Protocol, it is particularly appropriate that this Nobel Prize went to a Mexican (Molina), an American (Rowland), and a Dutch scientist (Crutzen).

Much less progress, however, has been made on resolving the other ozone problem: ozone at ground level. Hardly a city in the world is free of a frequent brown haze above which only the tallest buildings rise. Ozone is the principal component of this brown smog that has become an unplesantly familiar feature of modern urban life.

Ground-level ozone forms when sunlight glares down on a city's dirty air. As a result of combustion, cars and factories discharge large volumes of a whole array of nitrogen oxide compounds. NO_x (pronounced "knocks") is the usual term for this varied nitrous mixture. In sunlight NO_x reacts with atmospheric oxygen to produce ozone. If the day is warm and still, this ozone will hug the ground. Because it needs sunlight to form, scientists often call the resulting haze "photochemical smog."

Exhibit 1.5   *Late afternoon air pollution settles in the hills behind New Haven, Connecticut.   The air pollution from major cities often seeps out into the surrounding countryside.*

Photo: Mike Bell

Although we need ozone up high to protect us from the sun, down low in the inhabited part of the atmosphere, ozone burns the lung tissue of animals and the leaf tissue of plants. This can kill. It is hard to come up with precise figures, but current estimates are that photochemical smog and other forms of outdoor air pollution cause 50,000 to 188,000 premature deaths in the United States every year; worldwide, the figures are probably four times as much.[28] Smog alerts have become an everyday feature of big city life in all industrial countries. Walking and bicycling are increasingly unhealthful and unpleasant—driving people even more into thier cars and causing even more smog. Mexico City is the worst; unhealthy levels of ozone, as defined by the World Health Organization, occur there over 300 days each year.[29] When it drifts out of the city into the countryside, smog also reduces crop production and damages forests. According to a 1994 study, drifting smog can cause a 5 to 10 percent reduction in crop yields in affected areas, and worldwide is responsible for yield reductions on the order of a few percent—not an insignificant amount in a hungry world.[30]

To put the matter simply, there's too much ozone down low, not enough up high, and no way to pump ozone from down here to up there.

Particulates and Acid Rain. Big cities and their surrounding suburbs also face the hazard of fine particulates in the air. In contrast to the brownish color of photochemical smog, fine particulates envelop cities with a whitish smog. Most of these particulates are tiny pieces and droplets of sulfates formed during the burning of sulfur-containing fuels, such as the coal used for electric generation. Automobile emissions also contribute significantly to fine particulate pollution. These particles are microscopic—the definition of "fine particulates" is particles 2.5 microns (1/40 the diameter of a human hair) or smaller in size—and they penetrate deeply into lung tissue when we breathe them in.

According to a 1991 study by the U.S. Environmental Protection Agency, some 60,000 Americans a year suffer premature death because of fine particulates.[31] Another study found that in American cities with the most fine particulates, residents are 15 to 17 percent more likely to die prematurely.[32] Fine particulates smaller than 10 microns in diameter, those we now know to be the most dangerous ones, at the time of this writing remain unregulated.[33]

And then there's acid rain. This is an issue that has largely dropped from sight, after a flurry of concern in the 1970s and early 1980s over sharp declines in the populations of some fish and frogs and extensive signs of stress and die-back in many forests. But acid rain is still falling from the sky, despite substantial efforts to reduce acidifying emissions of sulfur dioxide and NO_x (pollutants that have other dangerous impacts, as we have seen). These pollutants combine with water in the atmosphere to acidify rain, resulting in widespread damage to plants and animals—particularly in areas with normally acidic conditions, where ecosystems have less capacity to buffer the effects of acid fallout. The situation is especially severe in northern Europe, where over 90 percent of natural ecosystems have been damaged by acid rain.[34] (See Exhibit 1.6.)

Technological improvements, international treaties, and domestic legislation have all contributed to a sharp decline in sulfur emissions in most countries. But we have made little overall progress in reducing nitrogen emissions. Industry's nitrogen emissions have been reduced, but these advances have been overwhelmed by increased emissions from automobiles and trucks as the world comes to rely ever more on these highly polluting forms of transportation. For example, in the United Kingdom in 1980 industrial emissions of nitrogen were about equal to those of cars and trucks—roughly 880,000 metric tons versus 840,000 metric tons. By 1992, cars and trucks were emitting more than twice the amount that industry did—1,400,000 versus 700,000 metric tons—and the combined amount had gone up.[35] Worldwide, the overall decline in sulfur and nitrogen emissions has been slight.[36]

Acid rain is still a big problem.

Exhibit 1.6 Dying forests: European woodlands either moderately or severely defoliated or dead, 1994, due to acid rain and other pollutants.

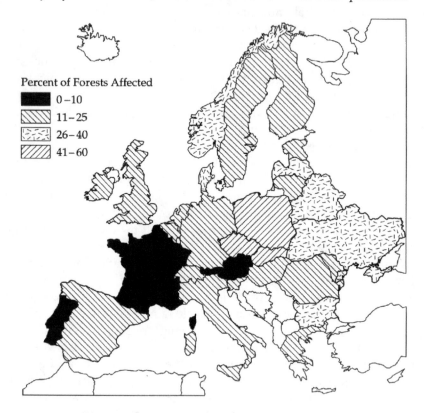

Source: World Resources Institute (1996).

Threats to Land and Water. There's a well-known saying about land: They aren't making any more of it. The same is true of water. And in a way, there is less of both each year as the expansion of industry, agriculture, and development erode and pollute what we have, reducing the world's capacity to sustain life.

Consider soil erosion in the United States. Soil erodes from American cropland sixteen times faster than it can form anew through ecological processes.[37] Despite decades of work in reducing soil erosion, largely in response to the lessons of the Dust Bowl, it still takes a bushel of soil erosion to grow a bushel of corn.[38] The Conservation Reserve Program, implemented by the U.S. Congress in 1985 and reauthorized in 1996, resulted in significant improvements by offering farmers ten-year contracts to take the most erodable land out of production. Many farmers have also switched to much less erosive cropping practices. Consequently, soil lost to water erosion dropped from

1,700 million tons each year to 1,150 million tons, and soil lost to wind erosion dropped from 12 tons per hectare to 11 tons.[39] But those numbers are still way too high, most observers in and out of agriculture agree.

Elsewhere, the situation is equally grim. Soil erosion exceeds replacement rates on a third of the world's agricultural land. Worldwide, about 10 million hectares of farmland must be abandoned each year because of soil degradation—that's an area about the size of West Virginia.[40] True, fertilizers can make up for some of the production losses that come from eroded soils, at least in the short term, but only at increased cost to farmers and increased energy use from the production of fertilizer and the application of it to fields—and increased water pollution as the fertilizer washes off into streams, rivers, and groundwater.

Soil erosion is only one of many serious threats to farmland. For example, irrigation often waterlogs poorly drained soils. Irrigation can also salinize soils, as most irrigation occurs in parched regions where abundant sunlight evaporates much of the water away, leaving salts behind. Rising water tables from the clearing of land are doing the same thing in Australia. Once the land is cleared of its native woodland and bush, rates of transpiration—the pumping of water through the leaves of plants, enabling plants to "breathe"—slow down. Water tables in the dry wheat belt of western Australia are rising by up to one meter a year, waterlogging these poorly drained soils and salinizing them through evaporation. One estimate suggests that 33 million hectares of land have been degraded by salinization in Australia, resulting in an annual loss of $200 million (in Australian dollars) worth of farm production.[41]

Irrigation of cropland, combined with the growing thirst of cities, is leading to an even more fundamental problem: a lack of water. By the time it reaches the ocean in the Gulf of California, the Colorado is probably the world's most famous nonriver, for not a running drop remains after the farms and cities of the United States and Mexico have drunk their fill. Further development in the regions dependent on the Colorado will require water from other sources—and it is not obvious where those generally dry territories can easily find other sources—or greatly improved efficiency in current water use.

In the Murray-Darling Basin of Australia, the country's richest agricultural region, the story is much the same. Now only a fourth of the water that enters the basin's rivers is still there by the time the Murray reaches the sea, and the comparative trickle of water that remains is salty and prone to bacterial blooms and fish kills.[42] Perhaps the most dramatic example of overuse of water sources is the Aral Sea in central Asia. Once the world's fourth-largest freshwater lake, diversion for irrigation has reduced its surface area by 46 percent and its water volume by 69 percent. Salinity has tripled, former fishing ports lie miles inland, thousands of square miles of lake bottom have turned to desert, the original fish are gone (as well as half the bird and mammal species), and the region's economy has collapsed.[43]

Not only surface water, but ground water too is being rapidly depleted. Overirrigation can lead to rising water tables and the waterlogging of soils in some regions, but the more general problem is *falling* water tables from the depletion of ground water stocks. Around the world, extraction of ground water for cities and farms is exceeding replenishment rates. In the dry Great Plains of the United States, farmers pump the famous Ogallala Aquifer eight times faster than it recharges from precipitation, endangering 15 percent of U.S. corn and wheat production and 25 percent of U.S. cotton production; the taps have already been turned off in many places, as the water table has dropped as low as 6,000 feet below the surface of the land.[44] In some regions, the lowering of water tables is causing major land subsidence. Downtown Mexico City has dropped 10 feet. Some parts of the Central Valley of California have dropped 25 feet.[45]

In coastal areas, overextraction leads to a problem closely related to falling water tables: the invasion of seawater into ground water aquifers. Ten percent of wells in Israel have already been abandoned for this reason, and many more will soon have to be given up.[46] In the Indian state of Gujarat, half the hand-pumped wells are now salty, and 90 percent of all wells show declines in water levels.[47]

Much of the freshwater that remains is badly polluted. "The amount of water made unusable by pollution," Donella Meadows, Denis Meadows, and Jorgen Randers have noted, "is almost as great as the amount actually used by the human economy."[48] In fact, we are very close to using, or making unusable, all the easily accessible freshwater—freshwater that is close to where people live (as opposed to rivers in the Arctic, say) and which can be stored in rivers, lakes, and aquifers (as opposed to the huge amounts of freshwater lost to the sea during seasonal floods, which cannot be easily stored.)[49] The remaining margin for growth in freshwater use is disturbingly narrow.

Cleaning up water pollution is one way to increase that vital margin, and industrial water pollution has diminished in many areas, particularly in the wealthier countries. We have also made progress in controlling agricultural water pollution. But we still have a long way to go. Since 1950, farmers across the world have upped their use of commercial fertilizers eight-fold and their use of pesticides thirty-two-fold.[50] The resulting runoff continues to threaten the safety of many drinking water supplies and has had severe impacts on the ecological viability of many lakes, rivers, and streams. We all need something to eat and something to drink, but our efforts at maintaining food production through the use of pesticides and commercial fertilizers are putting us in the untenable position of trading one for the other.

Or are we trading them both away? In addition to the threats to agricultural production due to soil erosion, salinization, waterlogging, and water shortages, we are also losing considerable amounts of productive farmland to the expansion of roads and suburbs, particularly in the wealthiest nations. Cities need food; thus, the sensible place to build a city is in the midst of productive agricultural land. And that is just what people have done for centuries. But the coming of the automobile has made possible (although not inevitable) the sprawling forms of low-density development so characteristic of the modern city. The result is that cities now gobble up not only food but also the land it is grown on. The problem is worst in the United States, which has both a large proportion of the world's best agricultural land and also some of the world's most land-consuming patterns of development. Some 56 percent of U.S. farm production (measured in dollar value) and 87 percent of fruit and vegetable production comes from urban counties or from counties adjacent to urban counties. Each year, 2.7 million acres of this land is lost to development, equal to 8 percent of U.S. cropland every ten years.[51] You work out the math from here.

Then factor into the calculation the effects of global warming, photochemical smog, and acid rain on crop production. Add some major issues I have not even mentioned: increased resistance of pests to pesticides, declining response of crops to fertilizer increases, the tremendous energy inputs of modern agriculture, loss of genetic diversity, desertification due to overgrazing, pesticide residues in food. No wonder that increases in agricultural production are showing signs of falling behind increases in human population. Although corn yields per hectare continue to climb, much as they have for decades, wheat and rice yields are flattening out.[52] Plus there are more people to feed. The result is that, after decades of steady increases, world grain production per person per year has declined from the historical high of 346 kilograms in 1984 to 319 kilograms in 1996, despite the record harvest of that year.[53]

The land fares ill, and there is less to eat and less to drink.

Environmental Justice

On the morning of January 4, 1993, 300,000 Ogoni gathered together in protest. The protesters waved green twigs as they listened to speeches by Ken Saro-Wiwa, a famous Ogoni writer, and others. With such a huge turnout, the Ogoni—a small African ethnic group, numbering only half a million in all—hoped that finally someone would pay attention to the mess that Shell Oil Company has made of their section of Nigeria. Leaking pipelines. Oil blowouts. Disrupted field drainage systems. (Much of Ogoniland has to be drained to be farmed). Fish kills. Water so polluted that even wearing clothes washed in it causes rashes. Meanwhile, the profits have flowed overseas to Shell and over to the notoriously corrupt Nigerian military government. The Ogoni have gotten only the pollution.[54]

Such open protest by the relatively powerless is a courageous act. And for the Ogoni, the consequences were swift and severe. Over the next two years, Nigerian soldiers oversaw the ransacking of Ogoni villages, the killing of about 2,000 Ogoni people, and the torture and displacement of thousands more.[55] Much of the terror was carried out by people from neighboring regions whom the soldiers forced or otherwise enticed into violence so that the government could portray the repression as ethnic rivalry.[56] The army also sealed the borders of Ogoniland, and no one was let in or out without government permission. Ken Saro-Wiwa and other Ogoni leaders were repeatedly arrested and interrogated. Finally, the government trumped up a murder charge against Saro-Wiwa and eight others and, despite a storm of objection from the rest of the world, executed them on November 10, 1995.[57]

What happened to the Ogoni is a vivid example of a common worldwide pattern: those with the least power get the most pollution.

What happened to the Ogoni is also an outrage, as virtually the entire world (aside from Nigeria's ruling generals) agrees.[58] This outrage is a vivid example of another of the three central issues of environmentalism: the frequent, and tragic challenges to environmental justice. There is a striking unevenness in the distribution of environmental benefits and environmental costs—in the distribution of what might be termed *environmental goods* and *environmental bads*.[59] Global warming, sea-level rises, ozone depletion, photochemical smog, fine particulate smog, acid rain, soil erosion, salinization, waterlogging, desertification, loss of genetic diversity, loss of farmland to development, water shortages, water pollution—these have an impact on everyone's lives. But the well-to-do and well-connected are generally in a better position to avoid the worst consequences of environmental problems—and, often, to avoid the consequences entirely.

Who Gets the Bads?   Take the hazardous waste crisis, for instance. Wealthy countries are now finding that there is more to disposing of garbage than simply putting it in a can on the curb. One response has been to pay others to take it. We now have a lively international trade, much of it illegal, in waste too hazardous for rich countries to dispose of at home.

There has been considerable protest about this practice. In 1988, Nigeria even went so far as to commandeer an Italian freighter with the intent of loading it up with thousands of barrels of toxics that had arrived from Italy under suspicious circumstances and shipping it back to Europe. After a heated diplomatic dispute, the waste—which in fact turned out to originate in ten European countries and the United States—was loaded on board the *Karin B.*, a West German ship, and sent back to Italy. But harbor officials in Ravenna, Italy, where the waste was supposed to go, refused the load because of vigorous local opposition to it. The *Karin B.* was later refused entry in Cadiz, Spain, and banned from French and British ports, where it also tried to land. Months later it was finally accepted into Italy.[60]

In 1989, in response to diplomatic crises like these, 105 countries signed the Basel Convention, which is supposed to control international toxic shipments. Yet loopholes are large enough, and enforcement lax enough, that these shipments still go on.

Nor do international conventions control domestic companies like COINTERN of Mexico, which dumped 20,000 tons of illegal waste near the Mexican town of Gualdalcazar between 1989 and 1993. Nor do international conventions stop foreign companies from merely relocating their most hazardous production practices to countries desperate for the jobs—like Metalclad Inc. of Illinois, which purchased the Guadalcazar site, promising to clean up the dump, but only if the Mexican government would allow Metalclad to reopen the dump afterward.[61] The people of Guadalcazar will still have to put up with a toxic dump.

Toxic wastes are typically local in their effects, and it is typically the local communities that are least politically empowered—whether because of class, race, ethnicity, nationality, or rural location—that receive the bulk of them.[62] So too for the siting of hazardous industrial facilities. These are realities painfully well known to the people of Bhopal in India, Love Canal and Prince William Sound in the United States, Minamoto in Japan, and the thousands of communities subjected to lesser-known local toxic disasters. Although individually smaller, these disasters are collectively just as—if not more—significant than the better-known ones.[63]

Toxic wastes have an impact not only where people live but also where they work. Consider the cumulative effects of pesticides and toxic chemicals on those who work with them every day. Many of our industrial practices expose workers—generally those on the production line, as opposed to those in the front office—to environmental hazards. Increasingly, the wealthy countries are exporting these kinds of jobs overseas, where workers have less choice over their conditions of employment, and then importing the goods back home (but still scooping up the profit in between). Exporting hazardous jobs does not lessen the degree of environmental inequality involved, however. Indeed, the inequality often increases because of lax environmental regulation in poorer countries.

But all this seems to take the place far away—until a toxic disaster happens in your own community. The growing placelessness of the marketplace makes it easy to overlook the devastating impact untempered industrialism can have on the daily lives of the farmworker applying alachlor in the field and the factory worker running noisy machines on a dirty and dangerous assembly line. When we shop, we meet a product's retailers, not the people who made it, and the goods themselves tell no tales.

• •

SOCIAL ACTION CASE STUDY
THE ENVIRONMENTAL JUSTICE MOVEMENT IN THE UNITED STATES

In 1987, the United Church of Christ's Commission for Racial Justice released the first of two controversial reports. Based on studies of zip codes, the reports concluded that African Americans and other people of color were two to three times as likely as other Americans to live in communities with commercial hazardous waste landfills.[1] Over a dozen other studies have found that the distribution of air pollution, solid waste dumps, and toxic fish, as well as hazardous waste facilities, corresponds with either race, social class, or both. For example, 3 percent of all whites and 11 percent of all minorities in the Detroit region live within a mile of hazardous waste facilities—a difference of a factor of nearly four.[2]

Findings like these helped galvanize the emergence in the early 1990s of the *environmental justice movement*. Originally a largely grassroots movement of local activists concerned about pollution in their neighborhoods, environmental justice now has a prominent place on the agenda of most national and international environmental organizations. Environmental justice has become one of the central civil rights issues in the United States and elsewhere, helping create a political climate for change.[3] The U.S. government has taken these issues quite seriously and has undertaken several self-studies. As a result, in 1992 the U.S. Environmental Protection Agency admitted that it may sometimes have been discriminatory in its siting and regulatory decisions, and in 1994 President Clinton signed Executive Order 12898, which requires all federal agencies to work toward environmental justice.[4]

The U.S. hazardous waste industry also responded to this new climate by funding a study, but with rather different results. In 1994 a team of University of Massachusetts sociologists—with funding from WMX Technologies, the country's largest handler of toxic wastes—published a report that contradicted earlier findings of pervasive environmental racism.[5]

Like the United Church of Christ study, the University of Massachusetts study was based on a national survey, but instead of zip codes used census tracts (a smaller unit) to define communities. The University of Massachusetts census tract results showed no nation-wide correspondence of toxic waste sites with race and no nationwide correspondence with poverty, although they did nonetheless find a relationship of toxic waste sites with blue-collar neighborhoods.[6] The University of Massachusetts researchers argued that the contradictory results of their study were due to the finer-grain analysis that census tracts provide.

These results unleashed a storm of debate, in part because the study had been sponsored by the waste industry itself. Of course, the source of sponsorship should not in itself be cause for rejecting either the University of Massachusetts study or the United Church of Christ study. But the University of Massachusetts study was arguably biased in favor of the toxic waste disposal industry. For example, the University of Massachusetts study excluded rural areas, and many toxic waste landfills are in poor rural regions with a high percentage of minority residents—such as Emelle, Alabama, a mainly African-American community where WMX Technologies operates the largest toxic waste landfill in the United States.

More studies are under way, and the debate continues. In any event, almost every study of the distribution of environmental hazards shows a strong relationship with social class. But whether by race or by class, such biases are a challenge to the environmental justice we all have a right to enjoy.

Notes
1 Goldman and Fitton (1994).
2 Mohai and Bryant (1992).
3 Boerner and Lambert (1995).
4 Heiman (1996) and Goldman (1996).
5 Anderton et al. (1994)

• •

Who Gets the Goods? Environmental justice also concerns patterns of inequality in the distribution of environmental goods. These patterns are usually closely associated with inequality in the distribution of wealth. Thus, those who are concerned about environmental justice often point to the huge inequalities in average income between countries.

Here are the numbers, based on gross national product per capita in 1995 in U.S. dollars.[64] The average annual income in the world is $4,880. In the

United States, the world's richest nation, it is $26,980. (A few other countries have higher average annual incomes, with Switzerland's $40,630 at the top, but the lower cost of living in the United States makes it the richest nation in buying power.) The average income in the world's 24 wealthiest countries is $24,930. By contrast, the forty-nine poorest nations (out of the 133 nations for which we have reasonably complete economic information) average just $430, hardly more than a dollar a day. Mozambique has the lowest average annual income: just $80. Ethiopia is second lowest: just $100. True, the cost of living is unusually low in Mozambique and Ethiopia. That $80 annual income in Mozambique buys about what $810 buys in the United States. But even $810 is not very much. And because Ethiopia's cost of living is higher than Mozambique's, that $100 annual income in Ethiopia buys only about what $450 buys in the United States, making Ethiopia the world's poorest nation.[65] Imagine living on so little.

Moreover, despite the many advances in technology and the change to a more market-oriented world economy, income inequality has dramatically increased in recent decades. In 1960, the richest fifth of the world's countries commanded thirty times as much of the world's income as the poorest fifth—a figure that, in most people's view, was bad enough.[66] Today, the richest fifth of countries command sixty-one times as much of the world's income as the poorest fifth. Those in that bottom fifth live on just 1.4 percent of the world's total income.[67] (See Exhibit 1.7.)

One could try to put the matter in more positive terms and point out that the percentage of the world's population living in poverty is roughly the same today as it was in 1960, perhaps indicating that things really haven't gotten any worse. But the *number* of people living in poverty has doubled with the doubling of the world's population since that time, and the difference between top and bottom has widened dramatically.[68]

With this wealth, the average person living in one of the world's industrial countries consumes three times as much grain, fish, and fresh water; six times as much meat; ten times as much energy and timber; thirteen times as much iron and steel; and fourteen times as much paper as the average resident of a developing country. And that average person from an industrial country uses eighteen times as much in chemicals along the way.[69] These consumption figures are lower than the sixty-one to one income differential because the comparison here is between the roughly 20 percent of the world that lives in industrial countries and the roughly 80 percent who don't—not the richest fifth of countries and the poorest fifth. If the 60 percent in the middle were removed from the calculations, the consumption gap for many of these items would probably reach or exceed the sixty-one to one ratio of wealth. (Some, however, would not—even a very wealthy person can eat only so much grain, fish, and meat.)[70]

Exhibit 1.7   *The champagne glass of world wealth distribution: The fifth of world population from the world's richest countries receives about sixty-one times the income of the fifth of world population from the poorest countries, or about 85 percent of the total world income. When calculated on the basis of the richest fifth of persons from all countries versus the poorest fifth from all countries, the ratio of income disparity rises to 150 to 1.*

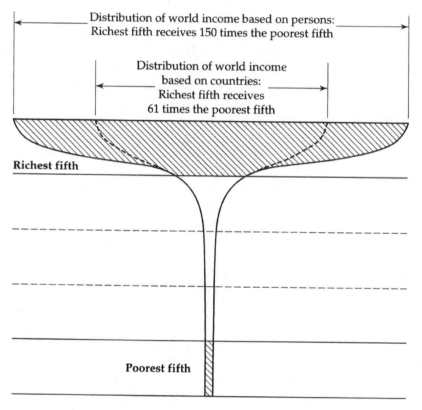

Distribution of world income based on persons:
Richest fifth receives 150 times the poorest fifth

Distribution of world income
based on countries:
Richest fifth receives
61 times the poorest fifth

Richest fifth

Poorest fifth

Source: UNDP (1994) and Korten (1995).

The consequences of these differentials are serious indeed. Nearly 800 million people in the developing countries suffer malnutrition, about 18 percent of the total world population. Thirty-four percent of the children in the developing countries are underweight for their age, a figure that reaches as high as 66 percent in Bangladesh, one of the world's poorest nations. Because of rampant malnourishment, adults face a reduced capacity to work and children grow up smaller, have trouble learning, and experience lifelong damage to their mental capacities.[71]

Many of the world's poor find it difficult to protect themselves from environmental bads. All told, one billion of the world's 5.7 billion people do not have shelter that adequately protects them from such environmental hazards as rain, snow, heat, cold, filth, and rats and other pests. One hundred million have no shelter at all.[72] Moreover, the world's poor are more likely to live on steep slopes and in low-lying areas which are prone to landslides and floods. More than a billion lack access to safe drinking water.[73] The poor are also typically relegated to the least productive farmland, undermining their capacity to provide themselves with sufficient food (as well as income). Compounding the situation are the common associations between poor communities and increased levels of pollution and toxic waste and between poverty and environmentally hazardous working conditions. Considering these stark facts, it comes as no surprise that people live an average of fifteen years longer in the wealthiest countries than in the poor countries, despite great advances in the availability of medical care.[74]

These international differences are exacerbated by substantial levels of inequality *within* countries. Typically, the income differential between the richest 20 percent and poorest 20 percent within a country is somewhere between five to one and ten to one. In about 20 countries, the ratio is even higher, in some cases a lot higher. The situation is most extreme in Botswana, where the richest fifth command 47.4 times the income of the poorest fifth. Ratios higher than twenty to one apply as well to Brazil, Guatemala, Panama, Tanzania, and Honduras.[75]

The United Nations Development Programme keeps track of what it calls the Human Development Index (the HDI), a widely used measure of quality of life that combines figures on longevity (life expectancy), knowledge (schooling and literacy), and standard of living (purchasing power per capita). It, too, shows widespread differences within countries (as well as between countries.) For example, the HDI for Chinese living in Beijing is double that of Chinese living in Tibet. The HDI of South African whites is double that of South African blacks.[76] The HDI in the Bendel region of Nigeria—which contains Lagos, the capital—is four times higher than that in the Borno hinterlands, where life expectancy is 20 years less.[77]

Substantial within-country inequality is also a feature of rich nations.[78] In the United States, the richest fifth of the population commands 13.4 times as much income as the poorest fifth—the most unequal ratio among the rich countries.[79] By comparison, the income ratio in Japan, Germany, Sweden, and Holland is in the range of four to one and five to one, with all the other rich countries lying somewhere between these ratios and the U.S. figure.[80] Interestingly, this situation represents a historical reversal. In the 1920s (the first decade for which these figures are available) the United States was one of the most economically egalitarian countries, giving America the image of the land of opportunity. In comparison, most European countries, such as Britain, were more wealth-stratified at the time.[81]

Within-county differences in income have a substantial impact on the quality of life of the poor even in rich countries. A 1988 study revealed that half a million Americans could be found in any given week eating in soup kitchens, living in shelters, or sleeping in the street.[82] Three million Europeans are homeless, 10,000 in Paris alone.[83] In Britain, somewhere between 200,000 and 500,000 people have no permanent address, according to a 1991 census, most of them young people between eighteen and thirty-five.[84] Thirty million Americans are chronically malnourished, half of them children and three-quarters of them people of color.[85] The HDI for white Americans is 12 percent higher than it is for black Americans, and life expectancy for American whites is nearly six years longer.[86]

Inequality within countries means that the sixty-one to one ratio of income between the richest fifth and poorest fifth of countries understates the level of global inequality. If the richest 20 percent of the world population from all countries, rich and poor, were put together, their income would total *150* times that of the poorest fifth of the world's population.[87] (See Exhibit 1.7)

As Tom Athanasiou has observed, ours is a "divided planet."[88]

The Rights and Beauty of Nature

"A thing is right when it tends to preserve the integrity, stability, and beauty of the biotic community. It is wrong when it tends otherwise."[89] These are probably the most famous lines ever written by Aldo Leopold, one of the most important figures in the history of the environmental movement. His words direct our attention to a broader sense of our community and, in a way, to a broader sense of equality and inequality. Understood in this broad way, environmental justice concerns not only the rights of humans but also the rights of nonhumans—of animals, plants, and even the land. Leopold also directs our attention to a word that is certainly one of the hardest of all to define but is no less significant for that difficulty: beauty. (Indeed, the diffulty of defining beauty may be much of what makes it so significant.)

Exhibit 1.8   The hole in the gene pool: Percentage of known species threatened in the U.S.

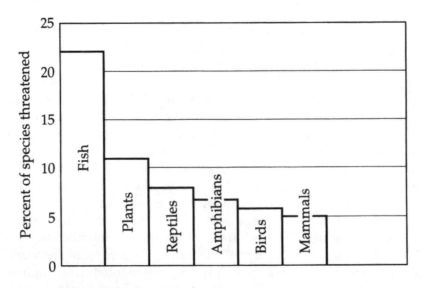

Source UNEP (1997.)

Threats to the integrity, stability, and beauty of the biotic community are manifold. Take the loss of species. For example, of the 9,600 known species of birds, 6,600 are currently in decline. A thousand of these are threatened with extinction and many have already gone—the passenger pigeon, the dodo, and the ivory-billed woodpecker are only some of the best known. Estimates of extinction for all species vary widely because we still do not have a good count of how many there are, or ever were. Many species are still unknown or already survive in such low numbers that they are hard to study. But even the low estimates are staggering. Biologists place the current rate of extinction for all species at between 4,000 and 36,000 each year— somewhere between one every ten minutes and one every ninety minutes.[90] That means it is likely that another species went extinct since you began reading this chapter. When we add in the extinction of subspecies and varieties, the decreasing diversity of planetary life is even more dramatic.

Of course, species have always come and gone, as Charles Darwin famously observed in his theory of natural selection. But the rate of these losses has greatly increased since the beginning of the industrial revolution. Some have disappeared because of habitat loss, as forestlands have been cleared, grasslands plowed, and wetlands drained and filled. Some have suffered from pollution. Some have found themselves with no defenses against animals, plants, and diseases that humans have brought, often unintentionally, from other regions of the world. The earth is a single, gigantic preserve for life, and we have not been honoring its boundaries and protecting its inhabitants.

The loss of species is an instrumental issue of sustainability. The leaking global gene pool means a declining genetic resource base for the development of new crops, drugs, and chemicals. In addition, most ecologists suspect that decreased diversity destabilizes ecosystems, ecosystems that we too need to survive. But the ethical and aesthetic impact of the loss of so many forms of life may be as great, if not greater.

Exhibit 1.9   The human footprint in ten countries: Percentage of land area converted from natural ecosystems.

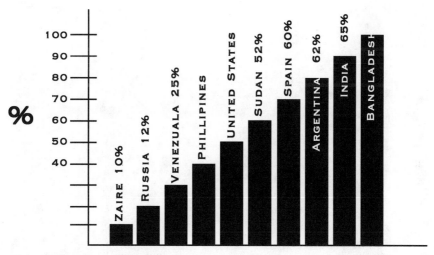

Source: Brown et al. (1997).

The loss is not only one of forms of life but also forms of landscape. Take deforestation, an issue that has received much attention recently. The world has lost one-third of its original forestland, and the rate of loss has been accelerating since 1950.[91] Particularly worrying is the high rate at which we are losing tropical forests, a relatively new problem. Nearly 750,000 trees are cut in tropical forests every hour.[92] Fifty-six percent of the world's original tropical forests are now gone.[93]

Deforestation presents a challenge for sustainability. The loss of trees promotes global warming as trees are converted into atmospheric carbon dioxide and forest habitat is converted into agricultural land. Yet deforestation also has an aesthetic impact, destroying the beauty of forests and the spiritual value of wooded wilderness. Forests are often replanted, of course, but at only one-sixth the rate of deforestation.[94] And most of these replanted forests are poor substitutes for the woods they replace— the ecological equivalent of exchanging the paintings in the Louvre for a permanent display of engineering blueprints.

There's another loss too—the disappearance of a kind of quiet intimacy with the earth, the sense of being connected to the land and to each other through land. It is a common complaint that modern technology removes us from contact with a greater, wilder, and somehow realer reality. This removal, it should be said, has been the whole point of modern technology, but some have come to wonder whether our lives are emptier because of it. A romantic concern, perhaps: But do we want a world without romance?

Exhibit 1.10 *The beauty of nature: Sunset on the Connecticut coast.*

Photo: Mike Bell

And finally, there's the question of our right to make such great transformations in the world. Nothing lasts forever, of course. Over millions of years, even a mountain is worn away by erosion. Wind, rain, ice, and changes in temperature constantly sculpt the land, and the shape of earth's surface constantly changes as a result. But geologists now recognize humans to be the most significant erosive force on the planet.[95] Agriculture, forest cutting, road building, mining, construction, landscaping, and the weathering effects of acid rain—all these have resulted in enormous increases in the amount of sediment that rivers carry into the oceans. We wield the biggest sculptor's chisel now. Perhaps it is our right. If so, then it is also our responsibility.

Although I have not covered the question of the rights and beauty of nature in much detail, let me conclude here. These issues are certainly no less worthy of our consideration than those of sustainability and environmental justice, it seems to me. But I'm exhausted just thinking about the others, and I imagine you are too. Maybe that's the most difficult environmental problem of all. There are so many of them.

THE SOCIAL ORGANIZATION OF ENVIRONMENTAL PROBLEMS

Yet, these matters seemed quite remote at that lovely brunch as we loaded up our plates with fruit salad, coffee cake, scrambled eggs, bread, butter, and those great hominy grits. Remote but ironic. Here I was amid a group of three families whose incomes, although not unusually high by Western standards, are sufficient to command a brunch that two centuries ago would have been seen as lavish even by royalty. And what was I doing? Once I had finished explaining environmental sociology, I was reaching for seconds.

My point is not that there is something wrong with pigging out every once in a while. Nor is it that consumption is necessarily a bad thing. (To live is to consume.) Rather, I tell this story to highlight how social circumstances can lead to the sidelining of concern and action about environmental consequences.

Everything we do has environmental implications, as responsible citizens recognize today. The adults at the brunch were genuinely interested in my explanation of environmental sociology for just that reason. But the currents of social life quickly washed over the momentary island of recognition and concern that my explanation had created. (One does not dwell long on any topic at a party.) Soon we were all reaching for more of the eggs from chicken-factory hens; the fruit salad with its bananas raised on deforested land and picked by laborers poorly protected from pesticides; the coffee cake made with butter and milk from a dairy herd likely hundreds of energy-consuming miles away; the grits made from corn grown on an Iowa farm at the price of one bushel of soil erosion for one bushel of grain. Meanwhile, the conversation moved on to other matters. And soon we guests would be getting into our cars and driving home, spewing smog and greenhouse gases all along the way.

A completely ordinary brunch. But do you refuse to invite friends over because you cannot easily get environmentally friendly ingredients for the dishes you know how to prepare? Do you refuse a host's food because it was produced in an environmentally damaging and environmentally unjust manner? And do you refuse an invitation to brunch because the buses don't run very regularly on a Sunday morning, because a 20-minute ride in the bike trailer in below-freezing weather seems too harsh and long for your 5-year-old, and because no one nearby is coming to the party to carpool with? Do you refuse, especially when you have your own car sitting in the driveway, as is almost certainly the case in the United States?

Likely not.

What leads to this sidelining of environmental concern and action is the same thing that manufactures environmental problems to begin with: the *social organization of daily life*—how we as a human community institute the many structures and motivations that pattern our days. Caught in the flow of society, we carry on and carry on and carry on, perhaps pausing when we can to get a view of where we're eventually headed, but in the main just trying to keep afloat, to be sociable, and to get to where we want to go on time. Our lives are guided by the possibilities our social situation presents to us and by our vision of what those possibilities are—that vision itself being guided in particular directions by our social situation. That is to say, it is a matter of the social organization of both our material conditions and the ideas we bring to bear upon them. Yet the environmental implications of those conditions and those ideas are seldom a prominent part of how we socially organize our situation. Instead, that organization typically depends most on more immediate presences in our lives: Other people.

We need, I believe, to consider the environment as an equally immediate (and more social) presence in our lives. That does not mean to be always thinking about the environmental consequences of what we do. As an environmental sociologist, I cannot expect this—especially when I don't always think about environmental consequences myself. People have lots and lots of other concerns. Nor should it be necessary to think constantly about environmental consequences. Rather, what is necessary, is to think carefully about how we as a community organize the circumstances in which people make environmentally significant decisions. What is necessary is to create social situations in which people take the environmentally appropriate action, even when, as will often be the case, they are not at that moment consciously considering the environmental consequences of those actions. What is necessary is to reorganize ourselves so what we daily find ourselves doing compromises neither our social nor our environmental life.

The challenge of environmental sociology is to illuminate the issues such a reorganization must consider.

PART I

THE MATERIAL

CHAPTER 2

Consumption and Materialism

I buy, therefore I am.

-Graffiti seen in New Haven, Connecticut, mid-1980s

Wladziu Valentine Liberace did not lead a modest life. At the time of his death in 1987, the famous Las Vegas entertainer owned more than thirty cars, including a Model A Ford, an English taxi, and two Rolls Royces. One Rolls was covered in mirrored tiles. The second was painted in patriotic red, white, and blue, and he would sometimes start his shows by driving it onto the stage. Liberace made his money playing the piano. He had eighteen of these, including ones played by Chopin, Brahms, Schumann, Liszt, and Gershwin—not to mention a vast collection of miniature pianos. Onstage, Liberace favored long capes, dazzling jewelry, and lots of gold lamé. One of his capes reportedly weighed more than one hundred pounds, and the Neptune costume that he wore at the 1984 World's Fair in New Orleans weighed two hundred pounds. It took forty-seven trunks to stow all the outfits he took on tour. (Liberace liked changing clothes.) The Liberace Museum of Las Vegas needs three buildings to display it all.[1]

We are not all Liberaces. Nor would we likely be even if we all earned $50,000 a week, as Liberace did at the height of his career. Few of us are so unabashedly materialistic. But it is certainly the case that, aside from the desperately poor, nearly everyone consumes more than is necessary to survive, and some of us a lot more. Yet we are not satisfied.

Why? What do we want it all for? This is an important sociological question, for it relates to all three of the central issues of environmentalism: sustainability, environmental justice, and the rights and beauty of nature. Can society and the earth sustain a world of Liberaces? Can some people consume like Liberace without impoverishing others and without damaging nature?

One common answer to the question of why we consume so much more than we need is that people are greedy. In the words of Mahatma Gandhi, "The world has enough for everybody's need, but not enough for everybody's greed."[2] There is much wisdom in Gandhi's aphorism. Better sharing of the world's resources would go a long way toward resolving the three central issues of environmentalism, and this is a theme that subsequent chapters will continually return to.

But Gandhi was also implying something else, both in this statement and in the way he lived his remarkable life: It is possible to change our feelings of "greed," if we make an effort to do so. "Greed" is socially highly variable. There are those who make $50,000 a week and give quite a bit of it away. (Even Liberace gave some away.) There are also people who truly have no interest in such wealth. The variability of greed indicates that it is not an immutable natural fact. How we arrange our social life can markedly influence the character of the "greed" we feel within ourselves. The kinds of goods that our "greed" desires vary markedly across time and culture. It is also important to see that the motivations behind the pursuit of material pleasures are complex.

This chapter begins the exploration of the material dimensions of environmental sociology by considering the *social psychology of consumption* and the complex and variable pleasures that underlie it.

THE MATERIAL BASIS OF THE HUMAN CONDITION

We have bodies. We need to eat, we need shelter, and we generally need some kind of clothing. Certain inputs and outputs are essential to all living bodies, which means that no body can exist without interacting with its environment. As Karl Marx, the controversial nineteenth-century philosopher observed, "The worker can create nothing without *nature*, without the *sensuous external world*. It is the material on which his labor is manifested, in which it is active, from which and by means of which it produces."[3] But can there be any controversy here? Who could long deny— and yet still live—that we must produce our livelihood from what Marx called the "sensuous external world," or what is commonly termed today the "environment"? (By "sensuous" Marx meant what we learn of through our senses.)

Marx also observed that "the mode of production of material life conditions the social, political and intellectual life process in general."[4] In other words, there are many ways that societies can arrange material production from the environment, and these arrangements have great consequences for how we live, even how we think. Our ecology is our economy, and our economy is our society.

You don't have to be a Marxist to appreciate the centrality of material forces in social life. Marx's basic idea is as widely accepted as any idea probably could be. Bill Clinton—an occasional liberal, perhaps, but certainly no Marxist—put it well with the famous motto of his 1992 U.S. presidential campaign: "It's the economy, stupid."

Ecological Dialogue

But we must be wary of the simplistic clarity of a purely materialist perspective. *Material* factors always depend upon *ideal* factors. The converse is equally true. Our ideals are shaped by the material conditions of our lives, and our material conditions are shaped by our ideals. You can only do what you can do. But what you can do is as much a matter of what you know, believe and value—all ideal factors—as it is a matter of what your material circumstances are. Moreover, what your material circumstances are depend in large measure on what you know, believe, and value. And what you know, believe, and value depends on your material circumstances. It's a *dialogue*—a constant interplay of factors that condition and influence each other, a never-ending conversation between the material and ideal dimensions of social life.[5]

The concept of dialogue provides an alternative to the mechanical, hammer-and-nails notion of causality that the social sciences for many years attempted to borrow from that ultimate materialist science, physics. In social life, causality is rarely, if ever, a one-way street, and the material is rarely, if ever, all that is involved. (In fact, mechanical materialism probably isn't even good physics, as a number of prominent physicists have recently argued.)[6] Rather than a mechanical realm of linear causes and effects, social life is an interactive phenomenon in which causes cause effects and effects effect causes, blurring the boundary between them. When we call something in social life a "cause" or an "effect" we are intellectually, and artificially, arresting this constant interplay for a moment. A material cause or effect and an ideal cause or effect are all mere "moments" in the endless *ecological dialogue*. (See Exhibit 1.1.)

Social analysis does have to enter the dialogue somewhere, though. In this part of the book we enter the ecological dialogue from the material side of things. In the next part, we will enter from the ideal side. Although we enter the dialogue from these different sides, these different moments, in each chapter of each part we will be inevitably drawn over from the material to the ideal and from the ideal back to the material. But we do have to start somewhere.

The Hierarchy of Needs

One of the most famous explanations of the relationship between the material and the ideal is psychologist Abraham Maslow's theory of the *hierarchy of needs*. This hierarchy, Maslow argued in a 1945 paper, is relatively fixed and universal across cultures.[7] At the bottom of the hierarchy are the "basic needs," beginning with a foundation in physiological needs and moving up to needs for safety, belongingness and love, esteem, and self-actualization. Above the basic needs are additional needs for knowledge and understanding and for aesthetic satisfaction. (See Exhibit 2.1.)

Why this hierarchy? Isn't knowledge and understanding, for example, a pretty basic need? Maslow argues that some needs have to be satisfied before we will direct our efforts toward others and that these are therefore the most basic. When a person's "belly is chronically full," wrote Maslow, "at once other (and higher) needs emerge and these, rather than physiological hungers, dominate the organism. And when these in turn are satisfied, again new (and still higher) needs emerge, and so on."[8]

Maslow made several key observations about the hierarchy of needs:

- Our efforts to gratify the hierarchy of needs are both conscious and unconscious, but more often unconscious.
- Any one action may be directed at several needs simultaneously.
- Most people's needs are never more than partially satisfied, but their lower needs have to be relatively satisfied before they can move on to the higher ones.
- We sometimes undervalue a lower need after it has been met for a while, but we typically can do so only temporarily. Maslow gave the example of a person who quits a job rather than lose self-respect and yet after six months of starving is willing to take the job back even if it means losing self-respect.
- Those who gain the opportunity to work on the higher needs tend to engage in more socially beneficial behavior. As Maslow put it, "the higher the need the less selfish it must be. Hunger is highly egocentric . . . but the search for love and respect necessarily involves other people."[9]

The hierarchy of needs is an intuitively compelling theory. Think how hard it is to study on an empty stomach. If you are not in good shape, it isn't sensible to try to climb a mountain. Place a book and a piece of bread in front of a starving person and there is little doubt which that the person will reach for. The intuitive appeal of Maslow's theory suggests that it speaks to a widely shared understanding of human motivation, which probably accounts for much of the theory's popularity: It feels right to many of us.

Exhibit 2.1 Maslow's hierarchy of needs.

"higher needs" (ideal needs)

Aesthetic
Knowledge and Understanding

Self Actualization
Esteem

Belongingness and Love

"basic needs"

Safety

Physiological

"lower needs" (material needs)

The theory is not without problems, though. First, a case can be made that we do not experience our needs as a hierarchy. Rather, we tend to act on whatever need is currently least well met or most under threat and that we are in a position to do something about.[10] Students may study so hard that they forget to eat. People in poor shape sometimes climb mountains anyway. There are starving people—for example, those fasting for a political cause—who will refuse the bread and take the book. Similarly, we may find that the higher needs, like the lower, can be only temporarily ignored and undervalued. That person who took back a demeaning job after six months of starving may well quit once again to regain self-respect, even if it means more starving.

Second, the theory lacks a sense of dialogical interplay between the more material and the more ideal needs. If, because of my aesthetic judgment, I do not like the meal before me, I will not eat very much, even if I was initially hungry. I may "lose my appetite," as we sometimes say. Thus my aesthetic ideal need can lessen the strength of my physiological, material need. Material needs also shape our aesthetic ideals, however. If I am very hungry, I may decide that the food really does not taste so bad after all, even if it is something I usually don't like. In other words, there is a dialogic interaction between my state of hunger and my aesthetic sensibilities concerning what is good food.

Third, Maslow's theory could be seen as condescending to non-Westerners. The higher needs—self-actualization, the pursuit of knowledge, aesthetics— are also the achievements we stereotypically associate with the degree of "civilization" and "development" of a country or a people. Poor people in "developing" countries who must concern themselves more with the lower needs lead a lower form of existence, or so the theory could imply. The hierarchy of needs is therefore flattering to Westerners, who typically see themselves as being more developed and more civilized than non-Westerners. Part of the appeal of Maslow's theory, then, may be Western hubris.

And fourth, and perhaps most important for this chapter, Maslow's theory cannot account for why we consume more material stuff than we need. According to the hierarchy of needs, no one should overconsume. Because their "lower" needs are satisfied, all wealthy and well-fed people should be composing symphonies, writing poetry, and volunteering for Oxfam. Sometimes, of course, wealthy and well-fed people do these "higher" things. But very often they buy more shoes, more clothes, another TV, and sometimes a mirror-tiled Rolls Royce instead.

The Original Affluent Society

In fact, we moderns are the real materialists, perennially concerned with the "lower" needs, argued the anthropologist Marshall Sahlins in his classic 1972 essay "The Original Affluent Society."[11] We who are so rich are far more preoccupied with material things than any previous society. Thus, in a way, maybe we're not particularly rich, suggests Sahlins, even in comparison to hunter-gatherers, who are usually regarded as the poorest of the poor. In his words, "By common understanding, an affluent society is one in which all the people's material needs are easily satisfied."[12] Sahlins argues that hunter-gatherers eat well, work little, and have lots of leisure time, despite living on far less than modern peoples. And not only are the material *needs* of hunter-gatherers easily satisfied by their manner of living, but their material *wants* as well—because they don't want much. Hunter-gatherers are thus the world's original rich, for they are rich in terms of meeting their "lower" needs and their "higher" ones too.

Time-allocation studies conducted by anthropologists with the few remaining (and fast-disappearing) hunter-gatherer societies show that it does not take long to gather and hunt. Typical adult hunter-gatherers work two to five hours a day. In that time they secure a diet that compares very well with our own in calories, protein, and other nutrients. This leaves quite a bit of the day open for hanging around the campfire chatting and visiting, singing songs, exchanging information, telling stories, making art objects— thus satisfying the "higher" needs for belongingness, love, esteem, self-actualization, knowledge, and aesthetics. Nearly everyone in hunter-gatherer societies is some kind of artist. Anthropologists have long been impressed by the incredible richness of "primitive" sculpture, costumes, music, folktales, and religion and have filled many a museum and library shelf with evidence of these.

Of course, hunter-gatherers do have to move periodically when the hunting and gathering gets thin. Many early observers, particularly missionaries, took this constant movement as a sign of shiftiness and the great amount of leisure time as a sign of laziness. They thought hunter-gatherers should settle down and do something productive, like raising crops. But here's what one hunter-gatherer told a visiting anthropologist: "Why should we plant when there are so many mongomongo nuts in the world?"[13] As Sahlins put it, arguing the hunter-gatherer's case, the biblical "sentence of 'life at hard labor' was passed uniquely on us."[14]

Perhaps most confounding to modern observers is the apparent disregard in which hunter-gatherers hold material goods, despite their seeming poverty. Here's how one anthropologist described the attitude toward possessions of the Yahgan Indians of South America:

> Actually, no one clings to his few goods and chattels which, as it is, are often and easily lost, but just as easily replaced. . . . A European is likely to shake his head at the boundless indifference of these people who drag brand-new objects, precious clothing, fresh provisions, and valuable items through thick mud, or abandon them to their swift destruction by children and dogs. . . . Expensive things that are given them are treasured for a few hours out of curiosity; after that they thoughtlessly let everything deteriorate in the mud and wet.[15]

Why don't the Yahgan bother to put things away in clean and dry places? Not because they have no clean and dry places or have no time to construct them. Rather, hunter-gatherers have their own version of the law of diminishing returns, says Sahlins. The returns from hunting and gathering dwindle after a while as nearby game, roots, and berries are gradually harvested. So the group has to up and move. They have to carry with them what they want to keep, though. But if you can remake what you need wherever you go, and if the pace of your work life is gentle enough that you have plenty of time to do this remaking, and if you enjoy this remaking as a communal and artistic activity anyway, why trouble yourself to haul it? And why care much about what happens to things after they are used?

Consequently, hunter-gatherers do not bother with an institution like private property. Individuals do not amass goods and commodities, and what goods and commodities there are in the community are equitably distributed and communally held. If you make a particularly nice bow and your neighbor breaks it hunting or your neighbor's child breaks it playing, there's no need to fuss. Now you have an excuse to sit around the fire and make another one, even nicer. We who worry ceaselessly about goods and commodities live by the great economic motto of "waste not, want not." The great economic motto of the hunter-gatherer is, as Sahlins wrote, "want not, lack not."[16]

But the hunter-gatherer life is not an Eden that the rest of us have been thrown out of. It has its struggles. People have to move often and keep their population low. Excess infants and those too old or too sick to make it to the next place must be killed or must go off alone into the bush to die so as not to harm the group. It's their "cost of living well," as Sahlins says. This trade-off may sound grim, but compare it to the many tragedies of our own lifestyle: stress, repetitive and meaningless work, far less leisure, individualistic isolation bred by economic competitiveness, and other tragedies that we each might list.

The hunter-gatherer's cost of living well may still sound grim. But Sahlins's point remains: You do not have to have a lot of money or goods to live well— to lead a life that affords a focus on the needs Maslow termed "higher"— and thus to be rich. As Sahlins says, "The world's most primitive people have few possessions, but they are not poor. . . . Poverty is a social status. As such it is the invention of civilization."[17]

Using Maslow's hierarchy as a measure, it is we moderns who may be the poorer, for we must spend so much more of our time in work, securing our physiological and safety needs. Wealth, that most basic measure of material well being, depends on how you look at it.

CONSUMPTION, MODERN STYLE

One of the great modern sins is being late. Reputations are sullied, grades sunk, and jobs and friends lost through lateness. Consequently, lateness is something that modern people are perpetually anxious about. Most of us wear watches, constantly check them throughout the day, and regularly synchronize our readings with the community standard which is broadcast on TV and radio and displayed on the clock on the wall and on the computer.

And we often inquire of others what their watches read. "What time do you have?" we ask, meaning the reading on the person's watch. Being moderns, we can easily guess at the other meaning—how *much* time the person has: very little.

But if timekeeping devices can be found on the wall, the computer, the television, and the wrists of so many of our associates, why bother to wear one ourselves? (Indeed, I no longer do, although I sometimes carry one in my pocket.) If you are in any social setting where precise time needs to be kept, chances are a timepiece of some sort is there already.

About twenty years ago I learned why people wear watches nevertheless. I was working as a geologist in the Talamanca Mountains of Costa Rica in the middle of a dense rainforest some three days' walk from the nearest road. (I was mapping the rock formations for an American mining company, a job I later came to regret because of the environmental and social implications of what I was doing—but that's a story for another time.) Our supply helicopter had suffered a minor crash that decommissioned it for awhile, and we had to trade for food with the local Bri-Bri Indians. The Bri-Bri in that area, and at that time, maintained a mixed economy of hunting, gathering, and limited agriculture. The missionaries had been through, so local people owned radios and wore modern-style clothes, and a few times a year they mounted trading and shopping expeditions to town. They knew what money was and much of what it does.

One local man who traded with us even sported a watch. He would often ask me what time it was and, upon receiving the answer I gave from my watch, check down at his own. (I still wore a watch in those days.) After a few days of these exchanges, thinking to make a little small talk, I asked to have a look at his watch, mentioning that it appeared to me to be quite a nice one. I was shocked to discover that in fact it was broken, missing a hand. It clearly had been inoperable for some time.

"How ignorant these people are!" a coworker exclaimed when I told him the story later. But rather than being a sign of his ignorance, this man's broken watch was a sign of his sophistication. He understood perfectly well what a watch was really for: a status symbol. He could tell time just fine anyhow—that is, he was completely competent to temporally coordinate his activities as well as his local community required. Living in a latitude where the day length and path of the sun across the sky hardly change throughout the year, he had only to check the sky. Although he had no need for a functioning watch, his sophistication had given him another need, however. It had given him an awareness of something he never knew before: that he was "poor" and that others might consider him even poorer unless he took some conspicuous measures to give a different impression.[18]

The Leisure Class

A century ago, Thorstein Veblen argued that this form of sophistication is what lies behind modern materialism. In his 1899 book, *The Theory of the Leisure Class*, Veblen argued that most of modern culture revolves around attempts to signal our comparative degree of social power through what he famously termed *conspicuous consumption*, as well as through *conspicuous leisure* and *conspicuous waste*.[19] It is not enough merely to be socially powerful. We have to display it. Power in itself is not easy to see. We consume, we engage in leisure, and we waste in conspicuous ways to demonstrate to others our comparative power. In other words, we demonstrate our power by demonstrating our material wealth, because wealth is the surest indicator of power in modern life.

There is an important environmental connection here. Veblen argued that conspicuous consumption, leisure, and waste are convincing statements of power because they show that someone is above being constrained by the brute necessities of material life and the environment. Because of your wealth and position, you do not have to engage in productive activities yourself. You can command the environment through your command of other people, a command made possible by wealth and social position. Environmental power thus indicates social power.

Let me give a few examples of each form of consumption. By conspicuous consumption Veblen had in mind visible displays of wealth, such as expensive homes, cars, clothes, computers, boats, and the like, as well as sheer volume of consumption. The material visibility of these displays shows one's social ability to command a steady flow of material goods from the environment. Such display is, I think, well known to all of us.

Conspicuous leisure is often more subtle. By this term, Veblen meant the non-productive consumption of time, an indication of distance from environmental needs—productive needs—and thus a sign of wealth. The most obvious example is a long vacation to a faraway and expensive place, two weeks at a Club Med hotel, say. But Veblen also had in mind social refinements, like good table manners, which require sufficient time free from productive activities to master. Maintaining a pristinely clean home is a similar demonstration of time free from productive necessities. Wearing the clothing of leisured pursuits—sports shirts, jeans, running shoes, backpacks—as daily wear is another form of conspicuous leisure, for such clothes suggest that a person regularly engages in nonproductive activities. Choosing forms of employment that are far removed from environmental production, such as being a lawyer or a corporate manager, is a particularly important form of conspicuous leisure, Veblen suggested. He noted that most high-status and well-paid jobs are far removed from environmental production, which is why he referred to the wealthy as the "leisure class"—not just because the wealthy have more leisure time.

By conspicuous waste Veblen meant using excessive amounts or discarding something rather than reusing it or repairing it. Examples might be buying the latest model of a consumer item and throwing out the old, running a gas-guzzling power boat at top speed, or routinely leaving food on your plate. Those who can afford to waste in these (and countless other) ways thus demonstrate their elevation above material concerns.

Veblen also pointed out that the leisure class engages in *vicarious consumption*, *vicarious leisure*, and *vicarious waste*—that is, consumption, leisure, and waste that others engage in because of your wealth. The vicarious can be highly effective statements of social and environmental power. Veblen had in mind here everything from parents who dress their children in expensive clothes and send them to college with a new car and credit card to male business executives who insist that their wives refrain from productive employment.

Veblen's terms overlap (as do probably all categorical distinctions about social life). For example, wearing leisure clothes can be simultaneously a form of conspicuous leisure and conspicuous consumption; designer jeans and name-brand running shoes are far from cheap, and everyone knows that. The occasional fashion for ripped jeans, which emerged for a while in the late 1960s and reemerged for a while in the early 1990s, is a form of conspicuous waste: Who but the wealthy could afford to deliberately rip their clothes and be so confident about their social status as to wear them in public? Thus, the same pair of designer jeans could be a form of conspicuous consumption, conspicuous leisure, and conspicuous waste.

In a way, all modern materialism can be reduced to waste. Conspicuous consumption is wasteful, and leisure is a waste of time. As Veblen put it, modern society is guided by "the great economic law of wasted effort"—a theoretical, and satirical, dig at utilitarian economics and its idea that modern life is guided by ever-increasing efficiency.[20]

I'd like to highlight two important ecological implications of Veblen's analysis. The first stems from the relative subtlety of conspicuous leisure. Conspicuous consumption and conspicuous waste are generally much more visible. But it is hard to put a price tag on good table manners, a clean home, or time spent watching television. Nor do friends and associates see you when you are away on your winter holiday. Perhaps that is part of the reason why tourists are so fond of bringing back home gifts, throw-away knickknacks, and a tan. These visible symbols of a vacation trip allow you to turn inconspicuous leisure into conspicuous consumption and conspicuous waste.

The greater visibility of consumption and waste is ecologically significant because leisure is potentially less environmentally damaging. Spending time with family and friends, reading books (particularly books borrowed from friends or the library), taking a walk, riding a bike—leisure activities like these consume fewer resources than spending your salary on the latest bit of loud and colorful plastic. Leisure is not always less environmentally damaging, however. It depends on how you engage in it. For example, travel—particularly travel by air and automobile—consumes energy and creates pollution. But in general, consuming or wasting time is less environmentally damaging than consuming or wasting things.

The second and more important environmental implication of Veblen's work is the competitive and comparative character of conspicuous consumption, leisure, and waste. To be conspicuous, you have to exceed the prevailing community norm. As long as others are also attempting to signal their social power through conspicuous consumption, leisure, and waste, the levels required to make a conspicuous statement of power continually rise. Therefore, the environmental impacts from conspicuous consumption, leisure, and waste also continually rise.

To summarize Veblen, through wealth we signal our power over the environment and thus over society. When we can engage in conspicuous consumption, leisure, and waste, we feel socially powerful. But as this is a comparative and competitive matter, we must continually up the ante of conspicuous signals of wealth and power. As a result, we moderns are motivated in our environmental relations not by a hierarchy of needs but by a hierarchy of society.

Positional Goods

Although Veblen's theories do have their limitations, as I'll come to, let us first explore the ideas of a scholar whose work bears a close affinity with Veblen's: the economist Fred Hirsch.

Why do we experience so much scarcity in the world? Hirsch argued that scarcity is due not only to physical limits in the supply of goods but also to social limits. Conventional economics tells us that when many people want something of which there is not very much, shortages are likely as demand exceeds supply. Hirsch, on the other hand, argued that people often want something precisely because it is in short supply. The supply and demand of a good are not independent phenomena, with the price set at the point where they meet; rather, there can be important interactions between supply and demand. Hirsch argued that, for some goods, demand will go up as supply goes down and that demand will go down as supply goes up. As Hirsch put it, "An increase in physical availability of these goods . . . changes their characteristics in such a way that a given amount of use yields less satisfaction."[21]

The point is, scarce goods create an opportunity for conferring status and prestige upon those who gain access to or possession of them. As Mark Twain wrote, describing the famous white-washing scene in *The Adventures of Tom Sawyer*, "[Tom] had discovered a great law of human action, without knowing it—namely, that in order to make a man or boy covet a thing, it is only necessary to make that thing difficult to attain."[22]

Hirsch called such difficult-to-attain things *positional goods*, goods whose desirability is predicated at least in part on short supplies, limited access, higher prices, and consequent social honor.

The notion of positional goods helps us understand why some goods and not others become the objects of conspicuous consumption. Goods that have a short supply, or can be made to have a short supply, are most likely to take on positional importance. One example of such a good is lakefront property. The amount of shoreline on lakes is limited by the physical landscape and the expense of reengineering that landscape. Hirsch argued that, although we rarely admit it to ourselves, part of the desirability of such property is the fact that there is so little of it—particularly in places that have a good climate and are relatively close to cities. The same is true of country cottages. If everyone lived in the countryside, it would not be the countryside; nor would it be so desirable.

Moreover, said Hirsch, the owners of positional goods may deliberately attempt to limit access to these goods, increasing their own positional advantage. An illustration of what Hirsch had in mind are some political movements to preserve the countryside, such as the two-acre-minimum lot sizes that many American exurban communities instituted in the 1970s and 1980s. Local proponents argued that two-acre lots would limit development and thereby protect wildlife habitat and preserve rural character. Hirsch would say that such zoning provisions provided a means for exurban residents to pull up the drawbridge behind them, even though they might not admit such a motivation to others or even to themselves. I might add that, in fact, two-acre zoning accelerates the deterioration of habitat and rural character by increasing the amount of land consumed by any new development. It is environmentally far more effective to concentrate development in a few areas and leave the bulk of it open.[23] Two-acre zoning does, however, ensure that only those wealthy enough to afford a lot of that size will move in, protecting the social honor of the exurban landscape.

The concept of positional goods also helps us understand the social pressures that sometimes result in the extinction of valued species of plants and animals. If a species is particularly valued, one might expect that those who appreciate it would do everything possible to protect it. The reverse is very often the case.

For example, on September 3, 1996, a joint operation of undercover police and the Royal Society for the Prevention of Cruelty to Animals seized 107 rhinoceros horns from a long-term storage garage in Kensington, England, the largest haul of such horns ever recovered. The horns were from both white and black rhinos. With a combined population of fewer than 10,000 (2,400 black rhinos and 7,500 white rhinos, according to the World Wildlife Fund) these are both perilously endangered species.[24] Hunting rhinos and trade in rhino horn is now banned by international convention and extensive efforts have been made to preserve their habitat and to protect the animals from poachers. But a few of those who value the rhinoceros are not participating in these efforts. Rhino horn remains a favored ingredient in some Chinese traditional medicines, particularly as an aphrodisiac, and is also still a respected accoutrement of masculine pride in Yemen, where rhino horn is used to make the handles of jambiyya daggers.

In fact, as rhino horn becomes harder to come by, its positional value increases for those able to gain access to jambiyyas and rhino horn aphrodisiacs. As the supply goes down, the desirability of rhino horn goes up, creating enormous economic pressure to carry on the poaching of rhino from wildlife reserves (and the stealing of rhino horns from the walls of old hunting lodges) until there is not a single rhino left. The 107 horns in that Kensington garage had an estimated street value of $4.3 million.[25] The current price on a rhino's head is thus approximately $40,000. This price will only increase as the supply of rhinos goes down through poaching and, perversely, through the establishment of wildlife reserves and international treaties to protect them.

Hirsch's analysis of positional goods can also be extended to our concepts of beauty. If scarcity makes something desirable, then, in a way, scarcity makes something beautiful. The most beautiful countryside is rarely the most ordinary. The most admired forms of wildlife are rarely the most common. This suggests to me a tragic point. Destroying some of the environment can sometimes make the rest of it seem more beautiful.

GOODS AND SENTIMENTS

A Veblenesque portrait of social motivation is a familiar form of social critique in modern life, and it can have a certain intuitive appeal, particularly when one is in a cynical frame of mind. Most of us have, I imagine, leveled Veblenesque charges at those around us—at least in our minds—reducing the behavior of others to greedy, competitive, self-serving display. We can easily imagine others having these motivations because, I believe, we have often sensed them in ourselves.

But there is more to people than a will to gain power and to show off. Many sociologists have long contended that ascribing all human motivation to *interest*, the desire to achieve self-regarding ends, is too narrow a view. As humans, we are equally motivated by *sentiment*, the desire to achieve other-regarding ends revolving around our norms and social ties.[26] It is wise, though, to maintain a critical outlook on the sentimental side of human motivation, lest we be seduced by the potential flattery of such an interpretation of social behavior. I will try to maintain such a critical outlook in the pages that follow.

The Reality of Sentiments

We can get a handle on the sentimental side of motivation for acquiring goods by looking at the way we "cultivate" meaning in objects, to use the language suggested by Eugene Rochberg-Halton.[27] One of the principal sources of the meanings we cultivate is the network of our social ties. The goods we surround ourselves with show not only how we set ourselves apart from others—Veblen's point—but also how we connect ourselves to others. They are talismans of community.

We all can give many personal examples; here is one of mine. For many years, until it wore out completely, one of my favorite T-shirts was from a softball team I used to play on, the Slough Creek Toughs. (We were all geology students, and the team name came from the name of a rock formation, the Slough Creek Tuff.) It was neither a particularly clever name nor a particularly nicely designed shirt, but the shirt brought back pleasant memories of good times with friends from long ago. This shirt was not an emblem of the "old boy" network of my student days, for I have since changed professions from geology to sociology, and it has been years since I saw any of the team's former members. Perhaps there is some social advantage in the conspicuous leisure of wearing a T-shirt, but it is hard for me to see what social advantage I gained in wearing that particular, rather plain and obscure, T-shirt. I think what I gained was simply a chance to express a sentimental connection to others.

Not all social scientists would agree that such an interpretation is justified, though. An important theoretical tradition, long established in economics but also in other social sciences, argues that all we ever do is act on our interests, as best we understand our interests and the possibilities of achieving the desires that stem from them. This is often called the theory of *rational choice*. Veblen's theory of the leisure class is an important forerunner of this tradition. A close parallel is the theory of the selfish gene in evolutionary biology. Rational choice theory would argue that I had lots of self-serving reasons to keep wearing that old T-shirt. For example, I might wear it because one of my interests is to have a good opinion of myself, and one route to such a good opinion is the self-flattery of believing myself to be motivated by more than self-interests. In this view, sentiments are thus a self-serving fiction.

The rational choice perspective yields many fruitful insights. But it is also extraordinarily materialist in approach. As I will argue throughout this book, theories of social life that emphasize either the material or the ideal generally turn out, on close inspection, to be unbalanced. Although we cannot discount the accuracy of a purely materialist or purely idealist perspective out of hand, a case can usually be made for the equal importance of the other side of the dialogue.

Let me try to make such a case here.[28] Consider the rational choice view that sentiments are a self-serving fiction. Now it may be true that sentiments always have self-interest behind them. But that is not how you and I experience sentiments, at least not always. We experience our sentiments as sentiments—as feelings of concern, affection, empathy, and affection for others; as commitments to common values and norms; and frequently as the lack of these feelings and commitments (such lacks being equally manifestations of our sentiments). Thus we may at times give up or refuse material gain because we experience concern for, and commitment to, the interests of others. We may also hold dislikes for others and their values that run contrary to our potential for material gain—refusing a high-paying job with an unpleasant boss in an environmentally damaging industry, for example.

Now perhaps there is always some hidden agenda of self-interest behind such refusals of personal material gain. But if we do not consciously experience interests behind our sentiments, we must then be basing our conscious decision making at least in part on other criteria. In other words, as long as the agenda of self-interest really is truly hidden—hidden even from the self—sentiments will be important sources on their own of what it pleases us to do.

In any event, as I have elsewhere written, there is simply "no way of knowing that that hidden agenda always exists, for, after all, if it does exist, it is often hidden."[29] But what we can know is what experience tells us does exist: that we have conscious orientations toward material goods that are both self-regarding and other-regarding, both materialist and idealist, both interested and sentimental.

Hau: *The Spirit of Goods*

One aspect of the sentimental experience of material goods is what the Maori people of New Zealand traditionally called the *hau*, the social spirit that attaches to gifts.[30] A Maori wise man, Tamati Ranaipirir, once explained the *hau* to a visiting anthropologist this way:

> Let me speak to you about the *hau*. . . . Let us suppose that you possess a certain article and that you give me this article. You give it to me without setting a price on it. We strike no bargain about it. Now, I give this article to a third person who, after a certain lapse of time, decides to give me some things as a payment in return. . . . It would not be fair on my part to keep these gifts for myself, whether they were desirable or undesirable. I must give them to you because they are a *hau* of the gifts that you gave me. If I kept these other gifts for myself, serious harm might befall me, even death. This is the nature of the *hau*, the *hau* of personal property, the *hau* of the gift, the *hau* of the forest. But enough on this subject.[31]

Hau is the Maori word for both "wind" and "spirit" much as the Latin word *spiritus* means both "wind" and "spirit," and it is probably not accidental that two such widely separated cultures should have such a parallel. All peoples recognize that there can be a kind of palpable, yet intangible, presence in things. For Tamati Ranaipirir that presence was the interconnected *hau* of personal property, gifts, and the life-giving forest. This interconnected *hau* watched over the movement of goods through the community to make sure each gift was reciprocated. In a way, the soul of the person who gave the gift—that soul being connected to the wider soul of the forest—lingered on within the gift, even after it had been subsequently given to someone else. As the anthropologist Marcell Mauss observed, "this represents an intermingling. Souls are mixed with things; things are mixed with souls."[32] Through this mixing, as Mauss also observed, the tangibility of gifts brought a Maori group together, causing them to recognize and to celebrate something intangible: their sentimental connections.

Think about it. Articles we receive as gifts have a very different influence on our behavior than articles we buy for ourselves. The same is true for any good that we come to appreciate not just for its instrumental purpose (if it even has one) but for the association we make between that good and a person or persons. We moderns still mix souls with things.

The wedding ring I wear on the fourth finger of my left hand is an example. It has no instrumental purpose, and only modest material value. And yet if some experimentally inclined social scientist was to offer me an absolutely identical ring, plus 100 dollars, I would refuse the trade. I would refuse it for $1,000 and probably for $10,000—though at this level I am less sure! But even if I weaken at such a figure, my ring, I believe, remains more than a cold, material object to me.

What makes my wedding ring more than a material object to me is my sentimental sense that it has a *hau*, in this case the *hau* of two souls joined in marriage. Similarly, my old Slough Creek Toughs T-shirt contains the *hau* of that softball team. Although I could go to the store and buy an endtable for my living room that is not as stained and wobbly as the one my grandfather made, no store sells end tables that embody the *hau* of my grandfather. All of us, I imagine, could point to similar spirited articles of social sentiment among our own possessions.

Goods are thus not merely objects of social competitiveness and social interest. They are also the means by which we remind ourselves, and indeed even create, the web of sentimental ties that help support our feelings of social communion. In the words of Mary Douglas and Baron Isherwood, material possessions serve our interests, "[b]ut at the same time it is apparent that the goods have another important use: they also make and maintain social relationships."[33]

Sentiments and Advertising

Most goods today, however, do not have a *hau*. In this age of the global economy and the shopping mall, most of the goods that surround us were made by people we will never meet, bought from people we do not know, and chosen primarily because of price and convenience. We care about these purchased goods because of how they serve our interests. They are socially empty, or nearly so.

Companies routinely try to persuade us that their wares are not socially empty, however. Advertisers routinely appeal to sentiments to pitch products, and it is instructive to examine the techniques they use. The agenda behind sentimental appeals is very often not so hidden.

The principal form of advertising is price advertising. With so many purchasing options available it is not easy to persuade consumers to spend their cash on a particular product. Moreover, people do have considerable resistance to ads; people know that ads are manipulative propaganda.[34] From the glitzy "blowout clearance sale with unbelievable values" to the simple statement of object and cost that is the norm in classified ads, advertisers have long found that price is the single most effective means of generating sales.[35]

But price advertising does have limits to its effectiveness, particularly when a rival is advertising a similarly low price. In addition, emphasizing the monetary aspect of a transaction reminds the potential purchaser that the principal interest of the seller is similarly financial, undermining consumer trust in the quality of the good. So, in order to divert attention from the fact that in reality the seller is out for our money, advertisements routinely try to appeal to our sentiments.

One popular technique is to claim that a product is being offered for sale out of concern for *you*. Here's a sample newspaper ad in this *you* genre:

TRULY EXCEPTIONAL SERVICE STARTS WITH CAREFUL LISTENING

It is why your Republic Account Officer makes sure to obtain a precise picture of your financial goals, time frame, risk acceptance, and other key factors. He keeps these constantly in mind as he looks after your interests.

So year after year, you can count on us for the exceptionally complete, timely and personalized service that makes Republic truly unique.[36]

After the banner, the words you or yours appear in every sentence. But whose interest does a Republic Account Officer really look after?

In addition to service, advertisements attempt to bestow a feeling of concern for the *you* through claims to offer choice and individualized products. "Double the size and even more choice," reads an ad for a new branch of Marks and Spencer, Britain's largest retailer. "Have it your way at Burger King," went a popular slogan of a few years ago—a remarkable claim for a company that sells food made on an assembly line. Specialty shops make a related pitch by seeking the business of only a select group of customers with particular needs. "The Choice for Big or Tall Men," runs the slogan for High and Mighty, a men's clothing store in a large shopping mall in Newcastle, England. Ads like these evade the mass produced, machine-made, *hau*-less origin of modern goods by saying, "See, we care enough about you to provide just your size and color and taste. Mom herself couldn't have done it better at her sewing machine at home."

You advertising may exhibit supposed sentiments on the part of merchants, but of course it also appeals directly to the buyer's status and power interests. Statements about the merchant's commitment to every wish of the *you* entice the buyer with a romance of the customer's high status and power over the merchant. Indeed, after price, status is likely the principal theme of advertisements. "The finest watch in the world will only be worn by exceptional people," runs an ad for Audemars Piguet. "Compromise shouldn't enter your vocabulary, let alone your garage," puffs a recent ad for Volvo. A store name like High and Mighty is another effort to cash in on status. Status advertising is particularly characteristic of ads for clothing and luxury goods. Similarly, companies often boast of their own reputations as the "best in the business," not only to proclaim the quality of their products but also to establish a status enticement to "shop with the best."

Few of us like to feel that we are mainly motivated by a desire for social status, however. Whether or not we are only fooling ourselves about our sentimental concerns, thinking purely in terms of status and interest does leave one feeling a bit hollow, and probably thinking as much of the advertiser. So ads very often try to convince us that the product on offer is not just for status display, but for displaying love too.

Christmas advertising is notorious for this. Dad (it is usually Dad) hands his college-age child the keys to the gleaming car in the background, as the music swells. Happy children play with this year's new toy rage while Mom (it is usually Mom) looks on contentedly. Similar "hooks" appear in other seasonal ads, particularly those for the Hallmark holidays invented by the advertisers, and most popular in the United States: Mother's Day, Father's Day, Secretary's Day, and the like. Veblen would argue that the real motive behind buying your child the latest piece of expensive plastic junk is vicarious consumption, and I believe it would be hard to deny the common existence of such a desire. Yet vicarious consumption is far more likely to be psychologically palatable if we experience it as, at least in part, an expression of sentiment. The dialogical converse also applies: We are more likely to consume vicariously through those for whom we have strong sentimental ties.

Ads often portray a more generalized sentimentalism too, placing a kind of good-for-the-world, friendly, family-values frame around the item on offer. "Get Together" proclaims an ad for Nokia cellular phones opposite a photograph of a seven-hands handshake. "It's nice to meet you" runs an ad for LG Semicon, along with a photograph of some of the company's chip designers. "It took you a long time before you could walk. Air France will save you some when you want to fly," reads the caption of a photo of a father's hand helpfully reaching down to a toddler. Here as well, *you* is a prominent theme in the advertising copy.

Green Advertising

A new form of sentimental hook is green consumerism. Companies like The Body Shop (cosmetics), Ben and Jerry's (ice cream), Celestial Seasonings (herbal tea), and Working Assets (socially responsible financial services) demonstrate that they are concerned about more than profit through the environmental and social good works they support. They also make a sentimental appeal to the guilt we feel over our own consumptive habits.

The catalog of Seventh Generation, an American mail-order firm that sells "products for a healthy planet," is an example. It is full of expensive *you* products, personal care items that could hardly be deemed essential but are made with organic cotton, recycled rubber, and the like. Environmentalists might be pleased to see that Seventh Generation promotes the use of organic and recycled products, but there must be some disappointment in seeing them pitch items like $185 silk comforters ("the luxury of silk" reads the photo caption), a $298 runner-style door mat ("a runner for special homes" says this caption), or a $1,595 king-size mattress made from organic cotton (the twin-size is just $950).[37] The message is that you can consume conspicuously and still be an environmentalist. Indeed, you can be conspicuous about your environmental consumerism. Sentiment itself becomes display.

The environment is also a common theme in the ad campaigns of major corporations, particularly oil companies, automobile manufacturers, pesticide firms, and other industries with spotty environmental records. "Green-washing" is what critics call it, and perhaps with some justice.[38] "It's nice to know the environment also impacts the auto industry," comforts the headline of an ad for Saturn cars. Opposite the headline is a photo of "the Saturn plant, as seen from just inside our white picket fence" which surrounds the company's new Spring Hill, Tennessee, facility. And instead of the looming, metal-sided building one expects, the photo shows a pasture, a lake, and three children playing, one with a cute little scrape on his nose— another sentimental hook. The ad copy describes how much Saturn recycles, how the company has kept most of the land it acquired for the facility in farming, and how it has landscaped the site so that the automobile plant is hidden from view. Other companies' ads boast about how they make large contributions to environmental campaigns, sign their managers up for two-day short courses in environmental protection run by Greenpeace, and support campaigns such as Britain's "Young Ethical Entrepreneur of the Year," which runs slogans like "You don't have to harm the environment to make money."

In this age of widespread support for environmental concerns, a green halo is good for a corporation's image. To be sure, some of the things that corporations do to acquire that halo truly may help to resolve environmental problems. It is a good thing that Exxon contributes money to the coffers of the Nature Conservancy, that The Body Shop allows customers to recycle their bottles, that Ben and Jerry's supports the local dairy farms of Vermont, and that corporations in general are learning that, in fact, it is possible to make money in more benign ways. We should not lose sight of the environmental significance of green business practices. But we should also recognize that good environmental citizenship makes a corporation's sentimental appeal to consume all the more potent.

Exhibit 2.2   The uncertain relationship between happiness and material consumption.

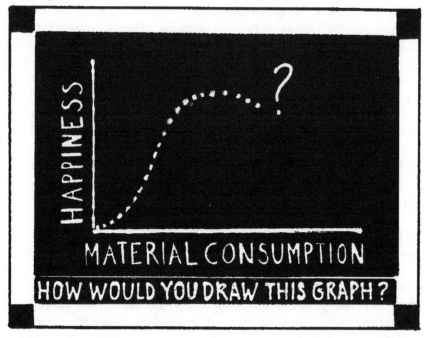

GOODS AND COMMUNITY

Why are appeals to our sentiments so potent? Social scientists have long observed the way the individualism of modern life has weakened the ties of community. We feel the lack of these ties, even though we may not consciously recognize it. So we try to buy community, the psychologist Paul Wachtel has argued. We try to buy a feeling of community in the goods we purchase for ourselves and the goods we buy for others, and we try to gain status within our community through the goods we display. Goods, then, are a substitute for social needs. In Wachtel's words,

> Faced with the loneliness and vulnerability that come with the deprivation of a securely encompassing community, we have

sought to quell the vulnerability through our possessions. When we can buy nice things, we can look around and see our homes well stocked and well equipped, we feel strong and expansive rather than small and endangered.[39]

Moreover, suggests Wachtel, a vicious circle is in operation: The more we lose community, the more we seek to find it through goods—and the more we seek the wealth to attain these goods, the more we immerse ourselves in the competitive individualism of the modern economy, thus undermining community. Meanwhile, the environment is undermined as well.

The Time Crunch

Part of the problem is simply a lack of time. The hunter-gatherer life of leisure is lost to us, and perhaps to our overall benefit, but with it went the abundant opportunity for interaction with our families and communities.

Loss of time got really out of hand in the early years of the industrial revolution. In 1840, the average worker in the United Kingdom (the first country to experience widespread industrialization) put in 69 hours a week.[40] By the 1960s, in response to widespread protest over these conditions, the average workweek had fallen to half that throughout the industrialized world. Many observers foresaw the coming of a society that had hardly any need for work as improved machines replaced the drudgery of early industrialism and as a new sense of a social contract between workers and employers ensured that time demands remained reasonable.

Yet in the United States the length of the workweek is now back on the upswing, and the trend seems to be spreading throughout Europe.[41] Rising competitiveness in a globalizing economy combined with low job security provides a powerful incentive for workers to acquiesce to employers' demands for long hours. The economist Juliet Schor estimates that the average American worker in 1987 was putting in 163 more hours of work a year than in 1967, the equivalent of a month of 40-hour work-weeks.[42] Simultaneously, paid time off—vacation, holidays, sick leave—had slipped back by several days, despite already being at levels far below most European countries where paid vacation alone is commonly 4 to 5 weeks, by law, even for low-paid workers.[43]

Schor suggests that this time crunch may be much of the reason why consumerism is so pronounced in the United States. Americans are trapped in what Schor calls the cycle of *work-and-spend*: They must maintain a highly consumptive lifestyle in order to be able to put in all those hours at work. The clothes to wear to work, the several cars most households need to get there, the time-saving home conveniences and prepared food—these are the unavoidable costs of holding down a job, or the two or three jobs many Americans now work. This work-related consumption in turn increases the amount of time spent shopping; second to watching television, shopping is the fastest growing use of time in the United States.[44] The result is even less time for other pursuits— like spending time with family, eating meals together, visiting with the neighbors, and participating in local voluntary organizations, all activities which surveys show have fallen off in the United States since the 1950s.[45] With everyone doing so much consuming, the pace of competitive display ratchets up, leading to yet more need for work. More than the people in other wealthy countries, Americans find themselves working and spending, working and spending, rather than enjoying the vacation time they don't have anyway.

The time crunch propels environmental damage along with consumerism. The raw materials to support this high level of consumerism have to come from somewhere. Moreover, with so little vacation time, Americans have less opportunity to use leisure as a status symbol, generally a less environmentally damaging form of conspicuous display than consumption and waste.

Similar trends are underway elsewhere, for example in Britain where work hours, shopping, and television watching are all up, while participation in voluntary organizations is down.[46] Although consumerism is most pronounced in the United States, other wealthy countries are not far behind. Indeed, as several social critics have commented, it appears that, aside from television, shopping is now the industrialized world's leading recreational activity.

Increases in productivity per worker have been such that people in all the wealthy countries could be working far, far less. For example, Schor has calculated that in the United States everyone could work a four-hour day, or only six months a years, and still have the same standard of living that prevailed in 1948.[47] But the people of no country have chosen such a course. Perhaps we have not been allowed to choose such a course, and perhaps we have not allowed ourselves to choose it. Probably, and dialogically, both are true. Nevertheless, we work and we spend and we simultaneously drift further away from one another, as we increase our rate of environmental consumption.

Consumption and the Building of Community

The rhetoric on consumerism and its relationship to the loss of community can easily get overheated, though. To begin with, although we are frequently critical of grabs for social status and social power, few would deny their central importance to social-psychological health. All of us need some status and power within our communities. Indeed, we are critical of unequal distributions of status and power because these needs are important to everyone. The granting of status and the power with which it is closely associated is something we expect from our communities. Moreover, that granting and that expectation help build our commitment to our communities.

Consumption can also enhance community, despite all the competitive individualism it can promote. Consumption can have a kind of festive air about it. Christmas gatherings, wedding ceremonies, and birthday parties have some of the hallmarks of potlatch—festivals of community in which we strengthen social ties through gift exchange—as anthropologists have argued.[48] Some *hau* exists even in the consumer society. And in addition to circulating *hau* through gifts, we make community through the goods we consume in common. Reciprocal exchanges and what Douglas and Isherwood called *consumption matching* can bring us together.

But Douglas and Isherwood carried this argument too far when they wrote that, "consuming at the same level as one's friends should not carry derogatory meaning. How else should one relate to the Joneses if not by keeping up with them?"

Must we really keep up materially with someone to relate to him or her socially? This is, no doubt, quite a common approach to fellowship.[49] But such an attitude quickly divides a society into class-bounded patterns of community. Note that Douglas and Isherwood did not suggest that one should lower one's consumption level to that of, say, the Collinses as a way to find community. When we engage in consumption matching, we nearly always attempt to match those above us in status. In other words, consumption matching is rarely only about building community.

Just as it would not be accurate to ascribe all consumption to competitive display, it is not accurate to ascribe it all to reciprocity and fellowship, as Douglas and Isherwood do. Both motivations can exist together. The consumption of goods generally represents a double message, a complex mix of competition and community, interest and sentiment. This complexity leads to considerable ambiguity in the meaning one person can read from another person's consumptive act. This ambiguity, to be frank, is often socially useful when we engage in a little *you* advertising of our own.

THE TREADMILL OF CONSUMPTION

Meanwhile, the cycle of competitive and communal consumption accelerates. As one tries to keep up with the Joneses, the Joneses are trying to keep up with the neighbor on the other side, and up the line to Liberace, the Rockefellers, the Bass family, Queen Elizabeth, the Sultan of Brunei, and Bill Gates. And Bill Gates, the Sultan, and the Queen are constantly looking back over their shoulders.

Although the desire for more—more money, more stuff—is pervasive, level of wealth has little to do with a sense of happiness, at least beyond a certain minimum. A 1982 study in Britain found that unskilled and partly skilled workers, the bottom of the pay scale, were indeed less happy than others (measured by asking if a respondent was "very pleased with things yesterday"). But skilled manual workers from the lower middle of the pay scale were actually slightly happier than better-paid, nonmanual, professional workers.[50] Several American studies have found that the poor are least happy but that the wealthy are only slightly more satisfied with their standard of living than are others.[51]

A cross-national comparison from 1960 revealed the same pattern. (I have encountered no more recent figures.) In the fourteen countries compared, people in India and the Dominican Republic, two nations with extensive poverty, did indeed express the least personal happiness, and by a considerable margin. Yet the three happiest countries were Cuba, Egypt, and the United States, three countries that differ substantially in wealth per capita.[52] People in countries like Nigeria, Panama, and the Philippines described themselves as only slightly less happy than Israelis and West Germans, who are far wealthier on the whole.

There is also no certain link between economic growth and increasing happiness. For example, the percentage of Americans who report themselves as "very happy" peaked in 1957 and has not recovered, despite continuous national economic growth since that time.[53] Even in happy, wealthy America, the link of increased wealth to life satisfaction is not clear (except for the poor).

The lack of this link is something of a paradox, given all the effort put into wealth accumulation. It is the paradox of a positional economy. Levels of consumption are constantly devalued as, through general economic growth, more people attain them. Because this constant devaluing affects everyone on the economic ladder equally, no one is made substantially happier than anyone else by moving up a rung, aside perhaps from the very poor. Consequently, economic advancement in an expanding economy has little to do with differences in overall happiness. You only gain in this comparative game when you are fortunate enough to advance in comparison to others, and by definition that advance must be limited to a few. We can not all be like Bill Gates—there isn't that much money in the world and likely never will be.

Exhibit 2.3 The teachings of world religions and major cultures on consumption and materialism.

Religion or Culture	Teaching and Source
American Indian	"Miserable as we seem in thy eyes, we consider ourselves . . . much happier than thou, in this that we are very content with the little that we have." (Micmac chief)
Buddhist	"Whoever in this world overcomes his selfish cravings, his sorrows fall away from him, like drops of water from a lotus flower." (Dhammapada, 336)
Christian	"It is easier for a camel to go through the eye of a needle than for a rich man to enter into the kingdom of God." (Matthew 19:23-24)
Confucian	"Excess and deficiency are equally at fault." (Confucius, XI.15)
Ancient Greek	"Nothing in Excess." (Inscribed at Oracle of Delphi)
Hindu	"That person who lives completely free from desires, without longing . . . attains peace." (Bhagavad-Gita, II.71)
Islamic	"Poverty is my pride." (Muhammad)
Jewish	"Give me neither poverty nor riches." (Proverbs 30:8)
Taoist	"He who knows he has enough is rich." (Tao Te Ching)

Source: Durning (1992)

Yet still we try. We can all be like the Collinses, but although consumption may be an act of community, there is more to it than that. So we try to be like Bill Gates instead. Meanwhile, Bill Gates has gotten even richer. The result is no end to our wants and little improvement in our satisfaction, despite increased consumption of goods. This whole process of moving materially ahead without making any real gain in satisfaction can be termed the *treadmill of consumption*.[54] (I'll discuss a parallel treadmill, the treadmill of production, in the next chapter.)

• •

SOCIAL ACTION CASE STUDY
THE SIMPLICITY MOVEMENT

Looking around at their friends and neighbors, most Americans recognize the extraordinary materialism of contemporary daily life—and, perhaps surprisingly, they don't like it. In a 1995 national survey, 95 percent of the respondents agreed that "most Americans" are "materialistic," and 82 percent agreed that Americans consume far more than they need to. They didn't like the competition that comes with over-consumption. "The Joneses is killing me," lamented a man in a focus group associated with the survey. And they didn't like the environmental destruction that materialism leaves in its wake. Some 93 percent of the survey's respondents agreed that "the way we live produces too much waste," and 91 percent agreed that "we focus too much on getting what we want now and not enough on future generations."[1]

So why aren't Americans doing something about it? They may be beginning to. Since about 1990, a wide array of groups have sprung up dedicated to plain living, frugality, "down-shifting," and living lightly on the Earth—what is increasingly called the "simplicity movement." At its peak, 100,000 people subscribed to Amy Dacyczyn's newletter *The Tightwad Gazette*, a weekly devoted to spending less and living more. Nearly a half million have bought her books detailing the arts of dumpster-diving and yard-sale surfing, and how Dacyczyn clothes her children on $50 a year and feeds her family of eight on $50 a week. Dacyczyn grew tired of editing the *Gazette* and closed it in 1996, but a big batch of similar newsletters have sprung up to replace it: the *Frugal Gazette*, *Use Less Stuff*, the *Miser's Gazette*, the *Something for Nothing Journal*, among others.

These popular newsletters and books emphasize saving money and taking pride in reusing old things. Other strands of the simplicity movement stress the social and environmental benefits of simple living. Cecile Andrews of Seattle is a leading advocate of "voluntary simplicity," choosing a lifestyle that is more in tune with the environment and more out of tune with competitive consumerism. Through her writings and lectures, she has been promoting the idea of "simplicity circles," local discussion groups in which people support each other through the transition away from consumer culture. Then there's the Center for a New American Dream (CNAD), founded in 1997. CNAD places particular emphasis the environmental importance of simple living, in addition to the social importance. CNAD seeks "to fundamentally change North American attitudes about the sustainability of a high-consumption, 'throw-away' culture," a long-term goal that they liken to earlier campaigns to change public attitudes toward smoking and toward nuclear power.[2] And in rural Ohio, the Center for Plain Living has begun publishing *Plain*, a largely hand-printed magazine that draws on the simple wisdom of the Old-Order Amish and other plain people. It takes up such topics as bartering, horse-power, leading a TV-free life, home work, midwifery, and localism, describing how these can be integrated into life in the 1990s.

Consumerism was supposed to be a sign of freedom. That's what we were all told. But it can also leave you trapped on the treadmill of consumption, consuming more and being satisfied less. Thus, millions are rediscovering an old truth: It's a gift to be simple—a gift to yourself and, because of the social and environmental consequences, to the wider community as well.

Notes

1 Merck Family Fund (1995).

2 CNAD's web site, www.newdream.org.

• •

Moreover, at one level or another, most of us are aware that money and goods are not happiness—even in the United States, that paragon of consumerism. A 1989 Gallup Poll asked Americans to rank what was most important to them, and "having a nice home, car, and other belongings" came out last among nine options.[55] A 1995 survey I helped conduct among Iowa farmers (who, as a group, are sometimes accused of being concerned more about having a big new tractor than about the social and environmental implications of their farming practices) showed a similar result.[56] These kinds of responses, which are common throughout the world, have been shaped by cultural values every bit as deep as consumerism. Virtually all the world's major philosophical traditions counsel that money is neither the route to happiness nor saintliness, as Exhibit 2.3 shows.

Sometimes, however, it takes a shock to put things, pun intended, in proper perspective. On a late flight across the country a few years ago, I got to talking with a flight attendant about a recent tragedy in her life: Six months previously her home had burned to the ground. Although no one was hurt, the house was a total loss. "How awful!" I exclaimed.

"No, not really," she replied. "Friends and family immediately came to my husband and me, giving us a place to stay, helping us clean up and salvage what we could, loaning us money, getting us back going again."

She paused, and reflected. "It taught me what is really important, and that's people. It's not your things."

Similar reactions are well known to social scientists who study the social consequences of disasters.[57] Major disasters in which many of one's friends and family suffer or even die are deeply troubling to the survivors, but disasters that take property and not lives—as can happen, for example, in floods that rise slowly enough for residents to evacuate—can actually leave people feeling better some months after the event.[58] The clean-up efforts bring people from behind the doors that usually separate them and join everyone together in a common endeavor. Unburdened of their possessions, they rediscover their community, without the ambiguity of the double message of goods.

Which suggests something significant, I think: Not only do we consume more than we need, we also consume more than we want.

Exhibit 2.4   Treadmill of Consumption: Even as consumption increases, satisfaction often remains elusive.

CHAPTER 3

Money and Machines

> We are becoming the servants in thought, as in action, of
> the machine we have created to serve us.
>
> -John Kenneth Galbraith, 1958

An ordinary day, nothing special. You get up, glare at the clock, flick on the radio for a weather forecast. A fatuously excited announcer is exclaiming about the fabulous once-in-a-lifetime sale this weekend at Loony Lucy's, a local computer discount store. Hit the switch. Maybe the weather channel on the cable would be better. Where's the remote? The screen comes to life just as the forecaster finishes with the segment on world weather, and the picture fades to a shot of a lush tropical beach, empty except for a lone sun umbrella emblazoned with a commercial logo you don't recognize. "Have you ever . . ." the voice-over begins. Who cares? Click. You look out the window to gauge for yourself if it's going to rain today, and you notice the company van from your neighbor's carpet cleaning business in her driveway. Her car must still be in the shop. "Our machines mean clean," the van's side panel promises. Jeans are fine for today, you decide. You reach for the unfolded pair from the pile of clean clothes you haven't put away yet. "Levi's" reads the label on the right rear pocket. (Nice jeans.) Four ads already and you haven't even made it out of the bedroom.

The last chapter described how the materialism of modern life is propelled by social-psychological desires for status and social connection. But these desires are not fixed, and they can be manifested in many different ways. The organization of social life shapes the desires we experience in daily living, and their manifestations. This chapter explores the economic and technologic basis of social organization and how, through interaction with culture and social-psychology, economic, and technologic factors help create the material motivations of modern life.

The inescapable presence of advertising, even in our bedrooms, is an obvious example of how technology and economics shape our motivations. Yet there is a need here for dialogical caution. Economics and technology are often construed as imperatives. As Stephen Hill has written, "The *experience* of technology is the experience of apparent inevitability," a statement that applies equally well to the experience of the economy.[1] Contrary to that experience, a constant theme of this chapter is that technology and the economy are not imperatives. We do have control over them, even as they have control over us. We can resist their influence and frequently do. We can resist the technologies of advertising.[2] We can switch off the radio and the TV; we can lobby for social controls on the amount and form of advertising on them. But simply by being present as something to resist or to succumb to, ads—and technology and the economy more generally—nevertheless unavoidably shape the conditions in which we form our desires and motivations.

The shaping of motivation by economics and technology is of particular importance in understanding why we consume so much more than we need. The current arrangement of the economy and the current use to which we put our technologies tend to encourage not only consumption but *growth* in consumption and thus in the economy. Economic growth, as many have observed, has become the most widely considered thermometer not only of economic health but of the social and political health of nations. As David Korten has written, "Perhaps no single idea is more deeply embedded in modern political culture than the belief that economic growth is the key to meeting most important human needs."[3] A rise or fall in economic growth is always headline news, and politicians constantly gear their efforts toward encouraging growth—in part because growth serves many powerful economic and technologic interests and in part because growth has become a central cultural value. Economic growth is a dialogical matter of both material interests and cultural ideals.

It is important to recognize that economic growth (and consumption too, for that matter) does not in itself lead to environmental damage. As the environmental economist Michael Jacobs has observed, certain forms of economic growth, such as investment in companies that promote the use of green technologies, may in fact be beneficial to the environment.[4] However, the structure of economic interests does tend to overwhelm efforts to direct economic growth in ways that do not damage the environment. The pressure for economic growth tends to shift environmental considerations off our collective and individual agendas. Economic growth can take such a hold over our lives that issues of sustainability, environmental justice, and the rights and beauty of nature fade from concern.

A further theme of this chapter is the relationship of economic growth to economic inequality. Without economic inequality, motivations for keeping up with the Joneses through conspicuous consumption disappear, because we are all equal to the Joneses. Understanding the origins of economic inequality is thus another central problem of social organization for environmental sociology to consider.

THE NEEDS OF MONEY

In most of the world, money is now the principal means of arranging for one's material needs and wants, and in much of the world it is virtually the only means. Thus the prudent person maintains a good supply of money, if possible. Money is useful stuff. Money is power. Because money is so powerfully useful, most of us wish for more of it rather than less.

In order to have money, though, you have to keep it moving—to keep it mobile through the economy. Stuffing it in a mattress, even a very secure one, is a rather shortsighted practice. Because of inflation, money left by itself decreases in value. Also, the uncertainties of the market lead us to nurture our money so that we are not left short. For instance, the possibility that employers may decide to downsize keeps nearly everyone at some degree of economic risk. Another source of risk is the business cycle, the seemingly inevitable tendency of any nation's economy to take a periodic downturn, increasing unemployment and other forms of economic stress. Consequently, almost everyone with any accumulation of money seeks to build with it a cushion that will at the very least retain, if not increase, its size and comfort. For these reasons alone—putting aside for the moment the common desire for simply having more—those with money invest, preferably in a way that offers high returns.

The inclination to seek high returns resonates throughout the economy. A bank can offer good interest rates only because of its own success in investing its depositors' money in loans, stocks, bonds, and other monetary instruments with strong returns. If the bank fails to offer competitive interest rates, it will lose depositors and possibly be forced to close. We often choose to improve on the rate of return banks offer by investing (if we have the time and sufficient capital) in stocks, bonds, and other financial markets. Managers of mutual funds and individual investors, like banks, seek a high rate of return for these investments. Mutual fund managers want to keep customers, and individual investors want to make it worth their time to play the market themselves. Even if an individual invests in socially and environmentally responsible stocks, bonds, and mutual funds, the tendency is to seek the highest rate of return possible from those opportunities.

Those of us with no savings—perhaps most especially those of us—usually look to increase our stock of money as well. We sell our labor power, auctioning it to the highest bidder. We seek to purchase goods—even positional goods—at low prices. And sometimes we trade work and goods informally to avoid depleting our scarce cash stocks.

In other words, nearly all of us find ourselves continually seeking more money—even to hold our economic place—which almost unavoidably leads us to assume the motives of the market: Seek the highest returns for labor and capital, and minimize costs. Sell high, buy low. The needs of money become our needs too.

This *generalization of the market* has the important consequence of promoting political interest in economic growth. If everyone is to have more wealth at the end of the year than at the beginning of the year, the economy must grow. This is simple math. Most politicians therefore see economic growth as a potential way to maximize the number of people who have been made wealthier—and thus, they hope, to maximize votes. Consequently, virtually all modern governments seek to maximize economic growth.

But there are no guarantees that growth will increase everyone's wealth, let alone that it will increase everyone's wealth equally. Growth in overall wealth may well be accompanied by growth in inequality. Indeed, without mechanisms for constantly releveling the playing field, an increase in inequality is probably an unavoidable consequence of growth. Even if everyone gains at least some wealth, the trend toward inequality will persist as the wealthy can almost always take better advantage of investments, labor auctions, and other economic opportunities—an economic version of what the sociologist Robert Merton once called the "accumulation of advantage."[5] Thus, although in the short term economic growth may help resolve political conflict, as many politicians hope, in the long term economic growth may only exacerbate it.

Nevertheless, country after country continues to seek political salvation in economic growth. Environmental concern usually remains on the political sidelines, bumped aside by the political momentum for economic growth, and economic inequality compounds as countries increasingly bump releveling mechanisms to the sidelines as well.

THE TREADMILL OF PRODUCTION

The momentum toward economic growth, economic inequality, and environmental sidelining is greatly heightened by the competitive pressure for production faced by firms and by the disadvantaged position of workers in this competition.

To maximize profits—a common desire and, because investors have to be repaid and retained, a common need of business—each firm tries to produce more goods more cheaply than the others. Merely making a profit isn't good enough. A firm continually needs to maximize its profits or investors will withdraw their support and put their resources in a firm that does. (Employee-owned and employee-financed firms can often shelter themselves from the maximizing pressure of investors, however.) As the environmental economist Richard Douthwaite has written, "It is not just that firms like growth because it makes them more profitable: they positively need it if they are to survive."[6] Repaying and retaining investors requires economic success on a scale of months, quarters, and years, diverting attention from longer-run issues like the environment.

Firms are interested in more than just repaying and holding on to their investors, however. They are also interested in profit for themselves. Owners and management usually decide to put as much profit as they can in their own pockets, after paying their debts, paying for needed reinvestment in the business, and paying employees enough to keep them coming to work. Thus it is a virtually universal pattern, although by no means economically necessary, that employers get paid more than employees. (Indeed, it is a virtually universal pattern in both nonprofit and for-profit institutions that those who have the most control over budgets are generally the highest paid.)

In sum, the tendency of uncontrolled market forces is for increased production, increased environmental consequences, and increased inequality.

A Widget Treadmill

Say I'm a widget maker. To set myself up in widget making, I probably had to borrow quite a bit of money. Machinery, land, buildings, labor—all these have to be paid for, often before the business is itself generating sufficient returns to cover these costs. Over time, the loans have to be repaid, which requires paying back more than the value of the loan. (Creditors want their profit too.) If I raised capital through selling stock, those investors have to be repaid as well, and at a level of return that attracts their investment in the first place. In short, I'm under a lot of pressure to make a profit.

Let's say I am a good widget maker, though, and I have managed to figure out a way to keep my production high enough, my costs low enough, and my market big enough that the books are balanced. And let's say that I am doing well enough to take home a good profit for myself, not just for my creditors and investors.

But I am not the only widget maker. You make widgets too. Like me, you are also interested in profit, perhaps even a bit more interested in it. Maybe your house is not as big as mine, and your car is not as fancy. Maybe your workers have asked for a raise, and you do not want to take it out of your own paycheck, however large it may be. Maybe your suppliers have just raised their prices. Maybe your shareholders are putting pressure on you, threatening to dump your stock in favor of a more profitable enterprise. Maybe all of these things. So you try a bold move. You agree to pay your workers a bit more, but only if they agree to a new kind of widget-making machine that increases your factory's output considerably but requires fewer workers to run it. You work out a deal whereby the workforce shrinks over time through retirement. No current employees lose their jobs, you are paying higher wages, and yet your labor bills fall over time. Prices drop as your new widgets flood the market, but because your output is now so high, your profits go up nevertheless. Sounds great for your company.

Meanwhile, I've got to find a way to deal with these lower prices. My investors are increasingly dissatisfied, but I'm stuck with my old widget-making machine and my old rate of output. Your new widget-making machine is patented, and you've put a very high price on the rights to the technology. So I call up some local government officials and politicians and ask to have some labor and environmental laws relaxed. Otherwise, I tell them, I will have to close my plant or move it elsewhere. I have always been a good contributor to the political party in power. Besides, the region needs jobs. The politicians agree and relax the laws. Meanwhile, I pressure my workers into accepting a pay cut in order to keep the plant open. Because the new labor laws have undermined their bargaining position, they accept.

This solution works fine until the government in your area also relaxes the labor and environmental laws affecting your company. (You are a good campaign contributor as well.) Now I have to try something else. I have already pinched my workers as far as they will go, and they are ready to strike. The government is cracking down on illegal foreign workers, and I can't find cheaper labor anywhere else. I have also pinched my creditors as far they are willing to go before they call in their loans and shut me down. My mood is grim.

Then one of my engineers calls to say that she thinks she has a way to increase production even more, if I can just acquire the capital to put into place the even better widget-making machine that she has just dreamed up. Although the new machine will use a rather toxic chemical, that should be okay under the newly loosened environmental laws. The idea is intriguing, but I fear that this plan will so flood the market with cheap widgets that prices will drop even further. I still will not climb out on top.

Then I hear that the national government is mounting a summit on free trade with a formerly hostile power, and I sign on as an industry representative. The deal concludes favorably, and I suddenly have a new market for widgets. I install my engineer's new widget makers in all the production lines, having used the promise of a new market to attract the necessary capital, and things are looking great. Pollution has increased quite a bit, and the workers are still upset about their low pay, but I am turning a profit once again.

Then the widget makers in that formerly hostile country start feeling pinched, and they pass the pinch on to their own national government and their own engineers and their own laborers. They also send industrial spies into my plant to figure out what I am doing. Since free trade works both ways, pretty soon their widgets are coming over here. My profit drops, but I am still alright because I was able to pay off some loans before the foreign widgets started coming in. I consider reinvesting in a still-faster version of my new widget-making machine, but I decide to sit tight to see what you do.

You are desperate. You threaten your workers with a pay cut, and they counterthreaten with a strike. You try boosting prices and mounting an ad campaign that promotes the supposedly higher quality of your widgets. But the campaign is a bust, orders drop, and some of the backlog of widgets in your warehouse develops rust. Your reputation for quality, in fact, goes down.

So you are faced with two general choices. One is to cut your losses and shut down your factory. This move would lower the overall output of widgets and raise prices, to the benefit of your competitors—like me—who are still making widgets. This would be emotionally hard for you to take, though. The other choice is to try to attract new creditors, to come up with a new invention, to win more concessions from your workers, to discover another new market, to talk to your local government about loosening more laws or about giving you a tax break, or to find some other means of keeping the money coming in and the products going out. But if you choose the latter course, the foreign competitors and I will probably try to respond in kind, which will increase overall production, lower prices, and raise economic pressures once again—all the while diverting attention from environmental considerations.

In broad outline, this is a familiar and endlessly repeated story in industry after industry. Through competition and increased production, returns to capital—profit—decline over time, creating what the environmental sociologist Alan Schnaiberg and others have termed the *treadmill of production*.[7] It's a process of mutual economic pinching that gets everyone running faster but advancing only a little, if at all, and always tending to increase production and to sideline the environment.

Exhibit 3.1 The Treadmill of Production: Mutual economic pinching keeps us always struggling to increase production, often with little regard for social and environmental consequences.

The Struggle to Stay on the Treadmill

But there are limits to how fast people—and competing companies—can run; you can only work so hard. The common adjustment mechanism is for someone to be forced off the treadmill—to choose the first option—lowering production to some kind of equilibrium with costs and prices. This is an outcome that everyone on the treadmill resists, however. The second option, making competitive adjustments, tends to be favored—at least initially. Eventually someone does get forced off the treadmill, though. But the struggle to find new customers that goes on before someone gets forced off usually means that the market expands in the process. The common result is fewer, bigger businesses—monopolization—and a higher level of overall production, often much higher. Meanwhile, those who are forced out of the market often switch to making different products or delivering different services, increasing the overall level of production of the economy by creating new treadmills.

As firms struggle to stay on the treadmill, they cut back where they can. The results are usually job losses and increased economic inequality as well as further disregard for environmental consequences. The social conditions of industrialism have generally given workers less control over cutbacks than management, owners, and shareholders. The worldwide democratic revolution of the last couple of centuries still pretty much stops at the boardroom door. By constantly pointing to the threats posed by the treadmill of production, and by pointing to the hungry pool of unemployed people, management is able to win the consent of workers to take home less than an equal division of a company's profits.

Not only do firms struggle to stay on the treadmill, but people do too. Those who lose their jobs may one day find new employment, but they are often forced to accept positions lower on the economic ladder than they previously enjoyed, if they are to have a position at all. The unemployment caused by the treadmill of production may be temporary (or may not be), but it also provides another opportunity for maintaining unequal distribution of income across a corporation, and thus across society at large.

In recent years, the ability of workers to bargain for more of the treadmill's proceeds has slipped even further, leading to declining incomes, despite overall economic growth.[8] Consequently, rates of corporate profit have regularly exceeded the economic growth rate. Typical rates of corporate profit are currently in the range of 2 to 12 percent, while typical rates of economic growth are in the range of 1 to 3 percent.[9] This differential is possible only if some are getting less than others. It is thus a measure of the extent to which the pressures of the production treadmill have been turned into an opportunity for the rich to get richer.

Meanwhile, the environment continues to be largely ignored.

Development and the Growth Machine

The dynamics of the treadmill also have an important spatial dimension, which leads to the constant conflicts over development that are familiar to local communities everywhere.

As the sociologists Harvey Molotch and John Logan have observed, local businesses have an interest in local economic growth: Investment is often relatively fixed in space. Buildings, land, machines, and a well-trained workforce are hard to move around, and firms try to create as much economic activity as possible for these fixed investments. Consequently, business leaders almost universally advocate pro-growth policies that increase the circulation of capital through their local area. Although local business leaders are often in competition with one another, one thing they can usually agree on is increasing the size of the local economic pie. And to the extent that local business can persuade local government of the importance of increasing local economic activity, growth becomes a leading cause of political leaders as well.

The result is that cities and towns act as what Logan and Molotch termed a *growth machine*, dedicated to encouraging almost any kind of economic development—frequently with little regard for environmental consequences or the wishes of affected neighborhoods. Local people have spatially fixed investments of a different sort, and because of them conflict with business interests often arises. Logan and Molotch call these local investments the *use values* of a place: homes, strong neighborhoods, supportive networks of friends and family, feelings of identification with the local landscape, aesthetic appeal, a clean and secure environment. Business, on the other hand, is interested in the *exchange values* of places, the ways that places can be used to make money. The use values that local people gain from a place are often incompatible with the exchange values business can gain—Maintaining open land for a park versus using that land for a housing development is an example from my own town.

And when there is conflict, the pro-growth business interests typically win, as they did in the conflict over the park in my town. Neighborhood groups tend to be far less organized than local business associations and are usually less able to influence the political process. Moreover, neighborhoods may feel divided allegiances between what is happening in some other neighborhood and their own economic interests, sometimes leading to not-in-my-backyard politics as opposed to not-in-anybody's-backyard politics. In the face of such divided interests, local governments tend to follow the pro-growth policies of the more united, better-organized business community.

A further result of the politics of the growth machine is an environmental conflict in the tasks we set for local government. On the one hand, government is expected to promote economic growth; on the other hand, it is expected to monitor and regulate environmental impacts.[10] Sometimes this dual role results in well thought-out development projects that promote economic growth without compromising the local environment. But, depending on the outcome of the political process, it can also turn government into an economic fox that guards the environmental chicken coop.

The "Invisible Elbow"

Adam Smith, the eighteenth-century founder of modern economic theory, envisioned that individual competitive decisions would guide us all toward prosperity by increasing production and efficiency. He suggested the famous image of the "invisible hand" to describe this process. The treadmill of production, however, makes the economy act like what Michael Jacobs has described as the "invisible elbow."[11] Even if the goal is merely to hold one's place on the treadmill, economic actors are involved in a constant jostle. Although this jostling is often unintentional—Jacobs says it is usually unintentional—both people and the environment get compromised in the process. "Elbows are sometimes used to push people aside in the desire to get ahead," Jacob writes. "But more often elbows are not used deliberately at all; they knock things over inadvertently. Market forces cause environmental degradation by both methods. Sometimes there is deliberate and intended destruction, the foreseen cost of ruthless consumption. But more usually degradation occurs by mistake, the unwitting result of other, smaller decisions."

The elbowing effect that Jacobs describes is more technically described by economists as *externalities*, economic consequences that are external to economic decision makers. Externalities may be divided into two broad types. Increased inequality and pollution are examples of *negative externalities*, external effects that we as a group do not want. There may also be *positive externalities*, external effects that we as a group do want, such as more efficient production though competition or, conceivably, an economic arrangement in which private decision making promotes greater equality and less pollution. The problem with Smith's image of the invisible hand is its rosy suggestion that the treadmill's market competition leads only to positive externalities. Jacobs's invisible elbow points out that negative externalities are also common consequences of the treadmill.

Externalities are not necessarily invisible, though, as Jacobs also points out. As we rush along the treadmill, we may be well aware of some of the consequences of flying elbows. The *visibility of externalities* is enormously significant for our social decision making. The ability to see and appreciate an externality, whether positive or negative, is the first step toward creating the social conditions that promote the former over the latter. If we are unaware of something, we are certainly unlikely to direct our actions with that something in mind. Creating this visibility is a political act of considerable social and environmental importance.

Factory Farms for Iowa Hogs

The controversial expansion of "factory farms" for hogs in Iowa illustrates well the politics of treadmills, the spatial conflicts of a growth machine, and the visibility of externalities.

Iowa is regularly the United States' leading producer of corn, and in some years the leading producer of soybeans as well. But unless you have a huge farm, it is hard to make a living raising only corn and soybeans. Decades on the treadmill of production have cut profit margins to the breaking point for many Iowa farms. Consequently, many of them have long been converting their cheap grain into something more valuable: pork. For years this worked quite well, as wholesale pork prices routinely ran some 20 to 30 percent above farmers' costs. Iowa became the country's leading pork producer, accounting for some 25 percent of the nation's total production.[12]

Exhibit 3.2 A large-scale hog confinement facility in Hamilton County, Iowa: Such "factory farms" for livestock are becoming increasingly common throughout the industrialized world, despite concerns about their implications for human health, animal health, economic justice and the environment. Note this facility's attempt to ward off criticism through use of patriotic symbolism.

Photo: Helen D. Gunderson

Eventually, though, large investors learned of this windfall. Since about 1992, several large corporations—Premium Standard, Decoster Farms of Iowa, Murphy Family Farms, Heartland Pork, and Iowa Select, among others—have been erecting huge hog production facilities in Iowa or contracting with local farmers to do it for them. "Hog lots" or "large-scale hog confinements," as they are often called, raise hogs indoors in vast metal buildings. Commonly 3,000 to 5,000 hogs are raised at a single site, divided among several buildings. The biggest facility in Iowa can handle 26,000 animals.[13] Feeding, watering, and waste removal are handled by machine, and sprinkler systems keep the hogs cool in the hot Iowa summers. Grain is trucked in from surrounding elevators and farms. The hogs never see the light of day.

Aside from size, factory farms for hogs actually represent little in the way of technological innovation. Iowa farmers have been using hog confinement systems since the mid-1970s, albeit on a much smaller scale. Thousands of Iowa farms have small "confinement units," largely built by the farmers themselves; each of these farms raise up to a few thousand animals a year using techniques similar to those of the larger corporate confinements. Even the scale is not all that new. Large-scale hog confinements have been in use in Europe since the 1970s, particularly in Denmark and the Netherlands. Some "contract growers" even established a few large-scale hog confinements in Iowa in the 1970s and 1980s, although these were still considerably smaller than the massive units that are currently sprouting in rural Iowa.

The massive scale of the new confinements has touched off a heated debate in Iowa about their social and environmental consequences. The environmental problems mostly relate to the vast quantities of manure the big hog factories produce. Hogs are big animals and they do little but eat in these facilities. A confinement with 10,000 hogs produces the equivalent effluent of a city of about 40,000 humans. The new large-scale hog confinements, however, have not erected the equivalent sewage treatment systems. Instead, the manure flows into artificial lagoons where it is stored until it can be applied as fertilizer to surrounding fields.

Using manure as fertilizer is generally a good thing; properly handled, it turns a waste product into a resource. But when so much manure is concentrated on a single site, proper handling becomes very difficult. Manure lagoons often leak into groundwater and streams, causing fish kills and water pollution. Sometimes the lagoon walls collapse, resulting in massive manure spills. Iowa experiences several major spills each year. Also, for convenience, the manure is generally applied to the fields closest to the lagoons, often at rates far above what the crop and the soil can absorb—again resulting in water pollution.

Another side effect is a terrific smell, sometimes strong enough to drive neighbors from their homes when the wind is wrong. Hog manure is pungent stuff, but the manure in storage lagoons is particularly strong because of the anaerobic bacterial activity promoted by the airless conditions in a big lagoon. The anaerobic smell of hog manure now pervades the Iowa countryside and even wafts into town, especially when the large-scale confinement operations pump out their lagoons and apply the manure to the fields.

The social controversy centers around the threat that the big operations pose to Iowa's roughly 21,000 smaller hog farmers. The market for Iowa pork is not endless, and farmers, rural communities, and their advocates worry that the large-scale operations will force prices down and drive a lot of Iowa farmers out of business. Indeed, during the winter of 1994–1995, the price farmers got for hogs dropped to less than twenty-eight cents a pound—far below the forty to forty-three cents a pound considered the average break-even point for Iowa hog farmers. Prices later recovered, but thousands of small farms were driven out of hog production during the market crash.

The corporate hog producers argue that the big operations create new jobs for those who work in them. Small farm advocates counter that big operations destroy more livelihoods than they create, that the new jobs are lower paid, that independent farmers are being converted into nonunionized workers, and that communities will ultimately suffer. Moreover, there have been a number of charges of exclusionary links between meat packers and the large-scale hog producers, shutting out small farms from sales and forcing them to accept lower prices.[14]

Still other issues are the human health effects of the meat and the humaneness of the production method for the animals themselves. Is it right, critics ask, to raise animals completely inside, where they are given almost no room and where they know no world other than concrete and metal? To raise animals in such close confinement, the big operations must mix feed with a "maintenance dose" of antibiotics that helps prevent the rapid spread of disease among the animals in the confinement barns. Outbreaks are still frequent, however, and so the animals often receive larger doses. Many health advocates and some scientists worry that the meat from confinements harbors antibiotic-resistant, food-borne bacteria because the constant presence of antibiotics selects for drug-resistant strains of bacteria.[15] Dosages are so high that antibiotics may also persist in the meat we eat, worry some other health advocates (but fewer scientists, at least thus far) so that consumers inadvertently administer antibiotics to themselves when they eat factory pork and other industrially raised meats.[16] The constant presence of antibiotics in the human body may also select for drug-resistant bacteria, the argument goes, thus weakening our ability to control all bacterial diseases, not merely food-borne ones.[17]

The social and environmental consequences of large-scale hog confinements are classic examples of the negative externalities of a production treadmill. Through political debate, these externalities have become socially visible, generating considerable controversy and conflict. Often people have found their allegiances divided, particularly when they, relatives, or friends are receiving some economic benefit from a big hog lot. Rural communities have been split. In one small Iowa town that I am familiar with, some people stopped speaking to each other in church and took to shaking their fists at the passing pickup trucks of locals who supported large-scale hog confinements. There was even a protest on the town green. These are not actions undertaken lightly in small towns.

The acrimony over these issues eventually prodded the state government to take some action. The Iowa governor established a commission, Iowa State University began hosting an annual conference on livestock odor, and the state legislature pondered new laws. The lobbying was intense. David Yepson, a prominent Iowa political commentator, called it "the hottest issue in Iowa."[18]

As of 1997, it would be safe to say that large-scale hog confinement interests have pretty much won the debate, at least for the time being. In 1995, the Iowa legislature passed a law imposing some mild environmental regulations on lagoon building and manure spreading as well as requiring that new hog lots be at least 1,000 feet from any homes. The legislature also required hog lot owners to pay into a special fund for cleaning up the sites of abandoned hog lots, should they later move on. But the legislature also banned what it described as "nuisance lawsuits" against the facilities and reaffirmed that localities do not have a right to regulate hog lots on their own, thus taking away the main legal tools that communities might use to stop the construction of hog lots.[19]

Basically, the hog lot operators got what they wanted. The protection against nuisance suits and local regulation gave the industry great latitude in building large-scale confinements. The environmental legislation introduced some constraints, but in exchange these rules gave the industry a way to demonstrate that it was being a "good neighbor" by following the standards set by government. And the main externalities remain external. Currently under state law, hog lot operators do not have to pay for the smell and the social inequality they create, nor for any water pollution they cause. (There have been a few fines leveled for fish kills caused by major spills, however.) These costs are passed along to local water users, the neighbors who must deal with the smell, and the government agencies that provide the social services— unemployment compensation, job training and job placement, welfare, and possibly substance abuse prevention—that may be needed for people who have lost their jobs and farms.

Part of the reason the large-scale confinement operators have thus far won the debate is because of their success in making a couple of political arguments. First, the large operators pointed to the rapid development of large-scale hog confinements in North Carolina, America's second largest pork production region, since the late 1980s. While North Carolina has been gaining market share in pork production, Iowa, although still number one, has been losing ground in most years. Second, the Iowa hog lot companies argued that their production would be essential for holding on to meat packing, another important Iowa industry. In essence, they argued, large-scale hog confinements are an economic imperative for Iowa.

The opponents of large-scale confinements—a loose coalition of small-farm, community, and environmental advocates—also tried to use North Carolina's experience to their political advantage. Between 1989 and 1995, North Carolina saw about 7,000 small hog farms (farms with fewer than 1,000 hogs) go out of business as about 700 large-scale hog farms (farms with 1,000 or more hogs) came in. By 1995, 94 percent of North Carolina hogs were on the large-scale farms. In contrast, in 1995 Iowa was still raising 53 percent of its hogs on farms with fewer than 1,000 animals.[20] Large-scale hog confinements, in other words, would mean the death of small, family-scale farms, a cultural issue of considerable importance in Iowa as well as an issue of economic justice. Moreover, hog lot opponents argued, small Iowa farms have been keeping the meat packing business going just fine for years.

Meanwhile, the search for new markets is on. Trade missions have been shuttling off to Southeast Asia, trying to find new markets for Iowa pork among the burgeoning economies of that part of the world. Iowa governor Terry Branstad himself has gone along, another example of government picking up the tab for the treadmill of production. Some small producers have been experimenting with nonconfinement systems of rearing hogs (which some Iowa farmers, in fact, had never stopped using) and marketing the result as a "natural" product among consumers concerned about health, animal welfare, and the environment. A substantial market for such meat has already developed in Europe and shows signs of developing in the United States and Canada.[21] At the time of this writing, however, the governor had yet to mount any trade missions on behalf of such a product.

• •

SOCIAL ACTION CASE STUDY
EXXON VALDEZ AND THE CERES PRINCIPLES

Big companies can have big economic elbows. After the supertanker *Exxon Valdez* ran aground at 12:04 a.m., March 24, 1989, the people of Prince William Sound, Alaska came to know this all too well. Within hours, over ten million gallons of Alaskan crude poured into the sound, creating a 3,000-square-mile oil slick that eventually washed up on over 1,200 miles of shoreline. Hundreds of thousands of birds and thousands of aquatic mammals such as seals and sea otters died. Disruption of the microbial life cycles led to disruptions in salmon runs, likely contributing to the many years of abysmal fishing that the region has recently suffered. Despite the two billion dollars Exxon subsequently spent cleaning up the mess, this spill was nevertheless one of the worst environmental disasters of recent decades.[1]

It was also a social disaster of considerable proportions for the five communities on Prince William Sound. All five are what environmental sociologists term *natural resource dependent communities*—communities whose economy and culture largely revolve around the harvesting of a natural resource such as timber, minerals, or, in this case, fish. Although no people died as a direct result of the Exxon Valdez spill, much about their communities did, so socially dependent were they on the ecological health of the sound. Even years after the spill, affected communities experienced high levels of social disruption, family tension, work-related problems, and feelings of stress—two to three times the stress levels in a comparable fishing community unaffected by the spill.[2]

Exxon paid out over a billion dollars settling legal claims from the spill, much of it to the residents of affected communities. But, as Kai Erickson observes, when the basis of your cultural and economic ties is suddenly largely gone—when annual fish runs drop to quarter of their former levels, when people find the pattern of their lives so drastically changed, and when it seems that the normal rhythms of nature itself can no longer be counted on—money is only a poor substitute.[3]

However, despite all the environmental and social devastation, something good has come out of the *Exxon Valdez* spill. In 1989, shortly after the spill, a group of 165 environmentalists, economists, and managers of socially responsible investment funds founded CERES, the Coalition for Environmentally Responsible Economies. Under the leadership of Joan Bavaria, president of a Boston-based investment research firm, and Denis Hayes, organizer of the first Earth Day, CERES proposed a set of ten guidelines for environmentally sound business practices.[4] Formerly known as the Valdez Principles in recognition of the event that precipitated them, the guidelines are now usually called the CERES Principles. Companies that sign the principles commit to:

1. Protecting the biosphere
2. Practicing sustainable use of natural resources
3. Reducing, recycling, and safely disposing waste
4. Using energy wisely
5. Reducing risky practices
6. Selling only products that are safe
7. Fully compensating for any harm caused to people and the environment
8. Disclosing any damaging incidents

9. Hiring environmental managers and appointing an
   environmental member to the board of directors
10. Publishing an annual audit of environmental practices

These are tough principles, given the state of much current business practice. But hundreds of companies have signed on, including General Motors, Bethlehem Steel Corporation, and Sun Company, a major oil refiner. In the words of Robert H. Campbell, CEO of Sun Company, "Environmental protection and economic growth can be compatible, and both are absolutely essential for the well-being of this nation."

Maybe the elbows are finally starting to come down.

Notes
1 Picou et al. (1992).
2 Picou et al. (1992) and Picou and Gill (1996).
3 Erickson (1994).
4 Keiner (1991).

• •

THE SOCIAL CREATION OF TREADMILLS

Despite the air of inevitability that often pervades economic discussions, it is human actors that direct the course of economic development. As the controversy over large-scale hog confinements in Iowa demonstrates, the treadmill of production is fundamentally a social process—the outcome of the interests of various social actors, the power that those actors have, and the level of their concern for the interests of others.

The Treadmills Inside

The treadmill of production also depends upon how we understand our interests—that is, upon the ideas and sentiments we bring to bear on our lives. In other words, there is an important ideal dimension to the treadmill of production.

For example, our productivist mentality depends in part on our sense that hard work is a moral virtue—a historically recent notion of virtue, in fact. (Chapter 5 will consider the origin of this notion of virtue in some detail when we explore the theories of the sociologist Max Weber.) We usually regard laziness as somehow immoral, even when working harder will only secure far more wealth than we physically need. In other words, we work hard not only to maintain our footing on the treadmill of production but also because we have internalized the notion that hard work is virtuous.

The idea that hard work is virtuous is particularly pronounced in the United States and Japan, as many have commented. The prevalence of this attitude is likely part of the reason vacation time is typically about two weeks a year in these two countries. Japanese and American workers have not fought harder for longer vacations in part because doing so would seem culturally inappropriate, which in turn perpetuates the cultural inappropriateness of long vacations. Meanwhile, both countries fall ever deeper into the cycle of work-and-spend, discussed in chapter 2.

In other words, the treadmill of production is not just an external pressure that we have no choice but to conform to; it is also a pressure that comes from within. At some level, most of us actually want to work hard—although probably not as hard as the treadmill of production often requires.

Given the speed increasingly required to stay on the production treadmill, it is probably materially advantageous that most of us are committed to the idea that hard work is a virtue. This advantage does not mean, however, that external forces determine internal ones. The relationship between external forces and internal forces is a dialogical one. True, hard work helps one stay on the treadmill, but hard work also leads to an acceleration of the treadmill—thereby creating conditions that will encourage people to work harder. Internal social factors such as a person's values thus support and are supported by external social factors like the economic speed of a production treadmill. The treadmill within and the treadmill outside create each other.

The interplay between the pressures of the external and the internal is equally characteristic of the treadmill of consumption. Like the virtue of hard work, the desire for *more* is something that nearly all of us from time to time feel inside to one degree or another. And yet these wants of consumption are based on material standards which, because of competition, are continually going up. The desire for *more* is thus both an internal source and an external product of the treadmill of consumption—another dialogue between the ideal and the material dimensions of social life.

The Dialogue of Production and Consumption

The treadmill of production and the treadmill of consumption are also dialogically interconnected. Increasing the pace of one treadmill increases the pace of the other. But also, the desire to increase the pace of one treadmill depends in part upon the social conditions created by the other.

Exhibit 3.3 *Interconnected treadmills. Production encourages consumption and consumption encourages production. Each propels the other.*

For example, the desire to consume *more* is propelled by both the treadmill of consumption and the treadmill of production through the relationship between *more* and profit. Because you need profit to survive on the production treadmill, the treadmill of production encourages people to regard profit as a virtue. But in order to demonstrate your success in attaining the virtue of profit, you need to consume *more*. You need to buy a BMW or its moral equivalent. Of course, consuming *more* is a desire that, because of the consumption treadmill, you likely already had. We want profit to consume just as we consume to demonstrate profit. It's a dialogue—although perhaps not one well calculated to support sustainability, environmental justice, or the rights and beauty of nature.

Hard work is another internal treadmill that is propelled by both production and consumption. Hard work keeps us going on the production treadmill, as the section above describes. But it also keeps us going on the consumption treadmill by helping us to rationalize inequalities in consumption. God helps those who help themselves, we often hear. Perhaps the real theological help is moral: relieving guilty consciences through the message that it's alright to consume *more* as long as you worked for it.

The internal treadmills of *more* and of hard work, then, dialogically connect the treadmills of production and consumption. Of course, you cannot have production without consumption and vice versa—at least not for long—as classical economics readily recognizes. But classical economics typically treats production and consumption as if they were separately generated phenomena, balanced by price. That balancing is often the only acknowledgment of dialogical interconnections. But what a fully dialogical approach suggests is that production and consumption do not merely balance each other; they create each other.

Moreover, the treadmills of production and consumption do not just mutually condition internal values like hard work and the desire for more. They also dialogically organize the external circumstances in which we have these values. Here is where economic inequality plays its most important dialogical role. The inequality created by the treadmill of production helps create the conditions under which the Joneses are constantly rising above us, fueling the treadmill of consumption. That fueling in turn creates the opportunity for further acceleration of the production treadmill, and its frequently unequal economic outcomes. It's a vicious dialogical circle: The production treadmill creates inequality, which creates the consumption treadmill, which creates more inequality and a further speeding of the production treadmill, thus keeping the whole cycle whirling ever faster.

Exhibit 3.4 Accelerating treadmills: Rising gross world product, 1950–96.

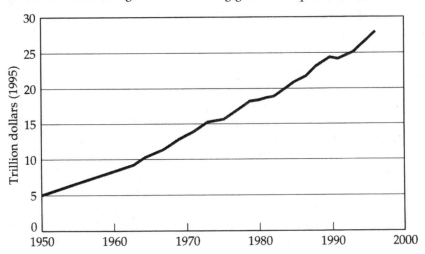

Source: Brown et al.

The Social Creation of Economics

We can summarize the usual results of the dialogue between the treadmill of production and the treadmill of consumption as follows:

- Decline in rates of economic return
- Bargaining with labor
- Bargaining with the state
- Search for new markets
- Fewer workers and more investment per unit of production
- Monopolization
- Increased production
- Social inequality
- Reinforcement of the desire for *more* and the virtue of hard work
- Reinforcement of the treadmill of consumption
- Conflicts over development
- Sidelining of environmental concerns

None of these outcomes are inevitable. As Alan Schnaiberg, John Logan, and Harvey Molotch have reminded us, treadmills are political. That is, treadmills result from the actions of human agents pursuing what they take to be their interests and sentiments. If we do not like the result, it must be because we have not fully understood what our interests and sentiments truly are or because the current distribution of power has prevented us from attaining our true interests and sentiments.

To achieve the outcomes we desire, we must first recognize the *social creation of economics*. The pinching pressures of the treadmills of production and consumption encourage us to think of the economy as something outside of us over which we have little control, as an external structure to which we must submit. And true, the economy has power over us. But we also have power over it. The economy is a result of countless individual decisions, as classical economics has long taught, with effects that present themselves as external structures. Yet it is precisely the fact that the economy begins with real human agents that makes it dialogically possible to direct the economy—by changing the circumstances in which we make our individual decisions.

Those economic circumstances are the result of bargaining between social actors such as the state, labor, and management. They are the result of legal precedents, of moral judgments, and of power relations within society. They are the result of the invisibility of externalities and the current limits to our imagination. Economies create societies, but societies create economies. Through bargaining between competing interests, through the selective involvement of the state, through the dynamics of the distribution of social power, through the moral visions of those involved, we shape the economic structures that shape us.

THE NEEDS OF TECHNOLOGY

"Not another call! I'll never get this lecture written!" I groaned as I reached for my ringing office phone. "Hello. This is Mike Bell," I said, hoping my impatience wouldn't show in the tone of my voice.

"I'm glad I reached you, Professor Bell," came a pleasant middle-aged male voice.

"Well, I hope I can be of some help," I replied, trying to sound interested.

"I hope so too," he quipped, and we both laughed. "You were recommended to me as a speaker for a conference I'm organizing on how local communities can adapt to technological change."

I was warming up to him. Still, he said "*can* adapt," I noted to myself. I wonder if what he really means is *should* adapt.

"That sounds interesting," I cautiously replied. "Who is sponsoring the conference and whom do you expect to attend?"

"I'm the development coordinator for several towns in the northern part of the state, and we're trying to put together an evening program for local people about hog lots. Are you familiar with the issue?"

"Oh sure," I said. "Of course." I live in Iowa, and you'd have to be a complete recluse to avoid hearing about the controversy.

"Then you'll appreciate the importance of the conference," my caller continued. "The problem is, people don't like change. But hog lots are coming, and coming fast. So we'd like you to talk about how communities can adapt to them."

I thought for a moment. It did sound like he meant *should*, not *can*. Finally, I replied, "This sounds like an important conference. I'd be happy to speak. But I'd like to speak not just about how communities can adapt to technological change. I'd also want to discuss how technologies can adapt to people. After all, it is people that invent technology."

Now it was his turn to say "That sounds interesting." Then he added, "I'll have to discuss it with our planning board, though. I'll get back to you."

A week later he called again, a bit more curt. "The board decided that it would like to keep the focus on how communities should adapt," he said. "Thanks very much for your willingness to participate, but . . ."

Can adapt had indeed become *should* adapt. He said it himself.

Technology as a Dialogue

I tell this story to introduce another of the central dialogues of environmental sociology, the *dialogue of technology*.[22] People often point to technology as one of the great motors of social change. One of the truisms of modern life is how much we have been changed by our technologies. The automobile, the tractor, the airplane, electronic media, birth control, the computer, the atomic bomb—these are all frequently cited examples of the role of technology as a social actor, as an independent agent of social change. Technology is also often seen as central to the pinching demands of the production treadmill. Indeed, we are often asked to accept the fact that more change will be coming in our lives because of technology. As my caller suggested, we had better be prepared for it, like it or not.

Our cultural training as Western modernists may make it particularly hard to see technology as an ecological dialogue, as an interplay between the material and the ideal, the external and the internal—as something that conditions our lives at the same time that we condition it. The metaphor of the machine, with its vision of sequential and linear causality, has become our master metaphor of technology. The word *technology* itself immediately conjures up images of machines. But a dialogical conception more accurately describes what technology is and does. A dialogical conception helps us to see that, like the economy, technology is not a mechanical imperative—unless we allow it to become one. Technology, too, is a social creation as well as a force that shapes the forms our social creativity takes.

For critics and supporters alike, there is great rhetorical attractiveness in a deterministic view of technology. In an attempt to energize us into action against a form of technology, critics sometimes portray it as a grim juggernaut that is rolling over our lives.[23] On the other hand, supporters like my phone caller often claim that there is little we can do once the Pandora's box of technology has been opened and that we had better make way for the changes that are bound to result. "Get big or get out" was the dictum of U.S. Secretary of Agriculture Earl Butz in the 1970s, explaining why American farmers had no choice but to buy bigger tractors and bigger farms.

Thus, fear-mongering is used by both sides. The logic of neither argument holds up, however. If technology is an uncontrollable juggernaut, then there is no point in asking us to try to resist it: We can't. If technology is an unclosable Pandora's box, than there is no need to ask us to make way for it: It is coming anyhow. Both arguments, in fact, logically depend on our having at least some control over technology.

As sociologists Keith Warner and Lynn England argue, technology is more than mere machines: Technology is all the techniques we have for gaining our desired ends. The knowledge of how to work a computer is just as much technology as the computer itself. Technology is the "how-to" of life, Warner and England write.[24] As such it is not the sole product of external forces—juggernauts and Pandora's boxes. Technology is something that human agents create. Plenty of human choice is involved.

But once we have made those choices, we will find that our future options have gained not only new possibilities but new limits. In other words, technology is not only a *how-to*, it is also a *have-to*. Humans make technology, and technology makes humans. Technology shapes the conditions of our lives and thereby helps direct the kind of choices we will feel compelled or inclined to make in the future. Technology does indeed structure our lives, but it is we who make that structure and pattern our lives accordingly. *Technology is political.* Technology is thus not a mechanical structure but a *social structure*, a form of social organization that we control as it controls us.

TECHNOLOGY AS A SOCIAL STRUCTURE

The automobile is an increasingly prevalent example of technology as a social structure. The automobile industry produces 36 million cars every year, and the world fleet now stands at just under 500 million.[25] Nearly every household in Canada, the United States, and Australia has at least one, and half of American households have two or more. The United States has nearly as many registered vehicles as people (190 million cars and trucks for 250 million people, as of 1990).[26] Vehicle-to-people ratios are lower in other countries, but rising rapidly. Only 20 percent of Japanese households had cars in 1970, but 72 percent did in 1988. Comparable figures apply to most of Europe. In France, 20 percent of households now have two or more cars.[27] Many poorer countries are also seeing big increases. In 1979, the roughly one billion people of China had only 150,000 cars; by 1996, they had 2.7 million.[28] Car sales in India increased by 40 percent in 1994 alone.[29]

The consequences are catastrophic. Over 40,000 people die in traffic accidents each year in the United States, nearly as many as died during the entire Vietnam War and far more than die of AIDS each year. Cars annually injure 3.6 million. For those over the age of one and under the age of thirty-five, traffic accidents are the leading cause of death in the United States. The death rate per capita from automobile accidents is even higher in Portugal, Estonia, and Latvia, roughly double the U.S. figures. Worldwide, nearly half a million people die each year in traffic accidents, and many tens of millions more are injured.[30] Millions of other animals also die each year because of traffic. In Britain, one study found that roads claim the lives of tens of millions of birds a year.[31] Comparable losses no doubt occur in all automobile-dominated countries.

Exhibit 3.5 The social and environmental impact of the car.

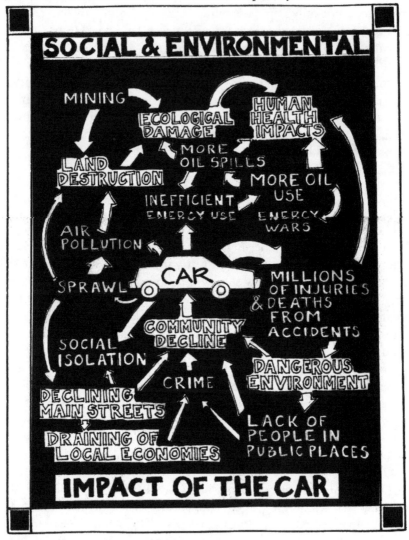

Cars and trucks remain serious polluters, despite efforts to clean up emissions. Growth in the use of cars and trucks has wiped out much of the gain from emission controls, and most large cities remain enveloped in smog and fine particulates. In Britain, according to a government study, automobile exhaust kills 10,000 people a year.[32] Cars and trucks are also important contributors to global warming and acid rain; according to one estimate, some 15 percent of greenhouse gas emissions come from automobile tailpipes.[33] Motor vehicles also have substantial indirect environmental impacts through the mining required to supply vehicle manufacturers with raw materials, the oil spills and other toxic waste disasters associated with keeping the fuel coming, and the consumptive patterns of land use with which cars and trucks are associated. Road noise can also affect the reproductive success of many wildlife species.[34]

Traffic has a huge impact on the quality of places. Traffic is noisy and dirty and turns even quiet streets into potential sources of death for us and our children. Cars bring out the worst emotions in drivers. Inside their wheeled cocoons, drivers commonly experience fury over slight infringements on the social decorum of traffic. "Road rage" is what the media call it. Drivers cut each other off, zoom close past bicycles, and accelerate right up to jay-walking pedestrians, threatening all with death and maiming. Streets are a major means by which we encounter the wider community. Through their danger, noise, and dirt, automobiles have made our daily encounters with one another hazardous and unpleasant. By terrorizing public life in these ways, cars contribute to the erosion of social commitment.

Why, then, are cars so popular? The standard answer is because cars are so convenient. Cars vastly increase our personal mobility, it is often said. They are an incredibly flexible and relatively inexpensive form of transportation. They protect travelers from inclement weather. They reduce physical labor. Cars, it is claimed, are simply a better way of getting around. To be sure, traffic is sometimes a problem, and so too is parking; but, goes the standard answer, bigger roads and parking lots can take care of these annoyances. And of course, we also gain a certain amount of personal pride and romance from owning an automobile, leading to what Americans term their "love affair" with the "dream machine." The pride and romance are understandable when one considers the superiority of automotive transport. Right?

The Social Organization of Convenience

At the center of this familiar argument about the benefits of cars is the image of technological choice, of opportunity, of convenience, of cars as a better how-to. Taking a bus or a train, by contrast, is so inconvenient. It is no wonder that people across the world are adopting the car as soon as they have opportunity.

But the convenience of cars is not a mere matter of a machine that makes our lives easier. A dialogical understanding of technology points to the *social organization of convenience*—the way that we often set up our lives around a particular technology so that it becomes difficult to do things any other way. A dialogical understanding of technology thus points to the common transformation of a how-to into a have-to. If we allow the alternatives to disappear, it indeed becomes hard to do things any other way—which is precisely what has happened with cars.

Yet the transformation of a how-to into a have-to is by no means inevitable, as cars also show. It depends on how we spend our money and allocate our resources. Supporters of the car often point to the substantial government subsidies given to public transportation. Private transportation, the argument goes, pays its own way through gasoline taxes and highway tolls. But a 1992 study by the World Resources Institute challenges this view by pointing to the hidden subsidies which cars receive—costs which are paid out of general revenues, not automobile-specific taxes.[35] In the United States alone, such subsidies total $300 billion every year.

Some $68 billion of the hidden subsidies for cars goes to road and highway services. Highway patrols; parking enforcement; police work in tracking down stolen vehicles and responding to accidents; and street maintenance—these are very expensive car-related services. Another $13 billion goes to road and bridge construction and repair not covered by gas taxes and other user fees. Road maintenance—snow removal, patching, pavement marking, litter removal, grass cutting on the sides of highways—adds another $12 billion not covered by user fees.

One of the largest hidden subsidies is for parking. Approximately 86 percent of Americans commute to work by car, and 90 percent of them find a free parking space when they get there. The average annual cost to business of one free parking space is $1,000 per year, taking into account what it costs to build and maintain a parking lot and the lost opportunity of developing that land for something else. The same is true for the "free" parking spaces provided by shops. These costs are passed along to customers through higher prices. Of course, drivers help pay for those prices when they shop, and all of a company's employees who drive to work get the same subsidy for parking. But anyone who arrives at work or at a store by some other means is also paying for those spaces and is being denied what amounts to a salary bonus and a price discount for the car drivers—to the tune of $85 billion per year.

Motor vehicle accidents cost the United States $358 billion a year. Most of this cost is borne by drivers through their own insurance. But some $55 billion is not, largely because of the medical costs incurred by the pedestrians and bicyclists who are involved in accidents.

Additional hidden costs include the price of military intervention to keep oil flowing from places like the Middle East and the cost of air pollution on health, crops, and buildings. These figures are hard to pin down, but the World Resources Institute study estimated them at roughly $60 billion.

The $300 billion in hidden subsidies for cars and trucks works out to 15 cents for each of the two trillion miles Americans drive each year. If a vehicle gets twenty-five miles to the gallon, the annual subsidy works out to $3.75 per gallon. Per vehicle, the subsidy is $1,579 a year—which, if the car lasts ten years, will probably add up to almost as much as the owner paid for it.[36] No wonder Americans drive so much.

The hidden subsidy for the automobile is a classic example of an externality, costs that the economic actor does not directly bear. Hidden subsidies are more than economic matters, though. They are also political matters. Powerful lobbies—such as the American Automobile Manufacturers Association, American Automobile Association, the American Petroleum Institute, and the various road-building associations—do what they can to keep these subsidies flowing in ways that benefit their industries.

During the 1930s and 1940s, General Motors went one step further. Using a company called National City Lines (NCL), a firm it set up for this purpose, General Motors went around the United States buying up the country's vast network of electric streetcar lines. GM then proceeded to convert these lines to buses, figuring that buses would not be as effective at countering demand for automobiles and that GM could sell buses in the meantime. Firestone Tire and Rubber, Phillips Petroleum, Standard Oil, and Mack Truck agreed with this strategy. These companies purchased much of the stock of NCL and helped finance its bus lines with sweetheart supplier contracts.[37]

In the 1970s, the U.S. government successfully brought suit against NCL for antitrust violations. But the damage had been done. The streetcar rails had been ripped up, and roadways had been expanded in their place. As a lawyer representing NCL at the trial put it, "This was all part of a very reasonable corporate strategy to develop a market."[38] Economically reasonable—but illegal.

The history of cars thus shows how we often socially organize (and sometimes socially manipulate) the convenience of a technology so that it comes to seem the most appropriate way to do things. The pattern of our lives, from where we live and work and shop to how we arrange our family life, from the kinds of things we expect from government to the kinds of things we expect of our neighbors, all come to revolve around and thus reinforce the convenience of the car. In this way, the convenience of a car comes to be what Robert K. Merton termed a "self-fulfilling prophecy."[39] As Merton observed, if we decide a thing is true and plan accordingly, very often it turns out just that way.

The Constraints of Convenience

But convenience also constrains. To say something is convenient is to say that we find our lives constrained so that some other thing is not convenient.

Again consider the car. We drive because, on the assumption that people own cars, we have allowed the location of common destinations to become decentralized. We drive because the bus now comes only every thirty minutes and the train once an hour, and maybe not at all. We drive because even if the schedules for the bus or the train fit our own, they probably do not go where we need to go, given that land use has become decentralized. We drive because little provision for bicycles has been built into the streets, because sidewalks are nonexistent or unpleasantly close to a thundering stream of traffic, and because the places we now have to go are so far away. There is no freedom in a car. We drive because this how-to really has become a have-to.

My point is not that we would have more freedom with more buses and trains, trams and light rail, bicycle lanes and sidewalks. If we were to organize our lives so that these technologies were the most convenient ways to get places (as they in fact still are in parts of some cities, mainly in Europe), we would still find our lives constrained. We would, for example, find it most inconvenient to use a car. Roads would be narrower, far less parking would be available, and land use would reflect the denser and more centralized patterns that make walking and public transport "convenient."

But although such a reorganization might not bring us any more freedom and convenience, it would not bring us any less either. And the pattern of convenience that public transportation, walking, and traditional town planning brings could in fact cost far, far less—less pollution, less land and energy consumption, less community alienation, and less loss of life.

TECHNOLOGICAL SOMNAMBULISM

Why, then, do we accept the increasing dominance of cars, despite their considerable social and environmental impacts, when more benign alternatives are readily at hand? The same question could be asked of other technologies and habits of doing things. "The interesting puzzle in our times," Langdon Winner has written, "is that we so willingly sleepwalk through the process of reconstituting the conditions of human existence"— a phenomenon Winner called *technological somnambulism*.[40]

In this section I'll briefly take up three answers to this puzzle: the phenomenology of technology, the culture of technology, and the politics of technology.

Phenomenology

Phenomenology means the manner in which we experience everyday life, and one of the central experiences that phenomenologists have long emphasized is *routinization*. If you stop to think about it, even the simplest tasks of everyday life are extraordinarily complex. We need ways to simplify what we do, and making routines is a common way.

Alfred Schutz, the founding figure in this area of sociological research, liked to use the example of walking out to the street corner to place a letter in a mailbox. This simple task is filled with presumptions about how the world works: The postal service will pick up the letter. Postal workers know how to read in the language I have used. The person I am sending the letter to knows how to read this language. There is such a thing as letter writing, and the post office and the person to whom I am writing understand that. There is such a thing as a postal service. There is such a thing as a mailbox, and there is no hungry monster at the bottom of the mailbox, waiting to eat the letter. In order to get to the mailbox, I need to get up, put my feet forward, cross the room, open the door, walk down the hallway, get my coat, put it on, open the outer door, step outside before I close it, close it, walk to the street, and so on.

If one did stop to think about all the presumptions involved every step of the way, one would likely never reach the door. Instead, through accumulated experience, we establish a series of little routines—*recipes of understanding*—that we can call upon without having to think the whole thing through each time.

The metaphor of recipes is quite appropriate; routinization is exactly what a cook's recipe allows. Say I have just found out that a friend is having a birthday and I decide to bake a cake as a surprise. It is four in the afternoon and the cake needs to be ready by seven if the surprise is going to work out. But how do I bake a chocolate cake, and what kind of chocolate cake should I bake? I certainly do not have time to experiment much, so I reach for my family's favorite recipe for chocolate cake, a recipe I have followed many times before and I know is likely to please. I bake the cake in time, and it is a big hit—because, through my use of a recipe of understanding, I had routinized the process of baking a chocolate cake.

Making use of any form of technology—and mailing letters and baking cakes are both forms of technology—requires a similar process. I know a little bit about how my computer works, although far from everything. But if I stop to think about all that I know every time I urge my fingers to strike the keyboard, it would take me all day to write this sentence, if not longer. I know that my computer works and, given the time constraints I have, I must usually be content to proceed with no more than that tacit confidence— technological sleepwalking.

But suppose a lightning bolt were to strike the building I'm in and send a charge through the electric lines that melts some essential bit of my computer's innards? (In fact, that happened to me once.) How could I keep on writing? I'm quite good about backing up computer files, but many of my files are stored only electronically. Until I got my own machine working again, or bought a new one, I would have to borrow a computer from someone else to read my diskettes. If one were available, I'd probably still have to contend with software I'm not quite used to. Still, despite these annoyances and economic barriers, I would only reluctantly resort to pen and paper, because doing so would force a major reorganization of my work habits.

The point I'm trying to establish is that our technological routines tend to lock us into continuing those routines and into trying only new routines that mesh well with our older ones. If something disturbs our technological sleepwalking, we will likely do all we can to walk around the disturbance, reclose our eyes, and return to pleasant walking slumber. And if this tactic fails, we may suddenly awake in a startled panic, having lost our confidence in the secure ordering of our experience.

The threat of broken technological routine was widely experienced in the United States during the gasoline shortages of the 1970s. The Arab oil-producing states of the time instituted a cartel to limit production, resulting in much higher prices and widespread gasoline shortages. Local governments instituted various rationing strategies, such as alternating "odd" and "even" days for buying gas, depending on whether a car's license plate ended in an odd or even number. In the Washington, D.C., area, motorists were prohibited from buying less than five gallons of gas, to prevent hoarding through topping off tanks. In a car-dominated society, this rule produced near-hysteria. A neighbor of my in-laws, who live near Washington, D.C., drove around the block for an hour one day, trying to empty her tank enough to be able to buy five gallons of gas.

The result of this panic attack in the middle of the technological night was not a United States with more public transportation and more centralized land use. Rather, the result was a United States that will go to war to keep the oil flowing and the cars rolling, as the Gulf War later demonstrated. Routinization follows the patterns of technology we have socially organized as the convenient way to do things. And once these routines are in place, they reinforce the same patterns of social organization that gave rise to them in the first place.

Culture

The same kind of dialogical momentum underlies the relationship between technology and culture.

We perceive all technological knowledge through the cultural lenses we use to make sense of our world. These lenses provide our technological means with technological meaning. Without culture, without meaning, we would not know what to do with our technological means. Yet technological means help shape technological meaning. The means available to us mold our contours of choice and thus our sense of the possible. By structuring the character of experience, means affect and sometimes even justify our cultural ends. We love cars in part because cars are now the main way we have to get around. Means become meaning.

Not only does technology shape culture, however; culture also shapes technology. Should we come to believe that cars are ugly, dangerous, and environmentally and socially destructive (a change I think may be under way) we may decide to reorganize our lives so that cars are less necessary. We may invent new technology to fit our new cultural aims. Meaning becomes means. Should we maintain a cultural commitment to what we see as the beauty, freedom, and pleasure of cars, we will be unlikely to seek alternatives—an outcome that equally represents the cultural shaping of technology.

Technological progress is one widespread example of the dialogue of means and meaning. On the one hand is our cultural faith in progress: We have gained so much in organizing our lives around technological change, who could dispute its value? We therefore ask for more new and wondrous technological means. On the other hand is our continuing effort to discover such new and wondrous means: We have given up so much in organizing our lives around technological change, how could we go back now? We therefore find ourselves compelled to entrust our lives to the future benefits of further technological change. To do otherwise would take an enormous realignment of our cultural commitments, a rude awaking from our technological sleepwalk.

Signs of such a realignment of meaning are, however, increasingly apparent—in part because of problems with the means. Pollution, danger, increasing social inequality, and the loss of traditional forms of beauty were never mentioned in the technological promise, and yet they have all occurred. (Chapter 7 discusses in detail the cultural realignments that have resulted from this broken promise.)

Technology has broken the promise of progress in another way too, one less often recognized. Surprising as this claim may at first seem, there has in fact been little significant technological change in the last thirty years. At least there has been little change of the magnitude predicted only a few decades ago, as the social critic Jean Gimpel has observed.[41] Consider the heady forecasts of the glorious technological future, so widespread in the 1950s and 1960s. A best-seller of 1968 predicted that by the year 2000 we could see, "the use of nuclear explosives for excavations and mining—permanent lunar excavations—artificial moons and other methods for lighting large areas at night—human hibernation for relatively extensive periods (months to years)—commercial extraction of oil from shale—effective desalination on a large-scale—life expectancy extended to 150 years—immortality?"[42]

The more minor of these miracles—desalination, extraction of oil from oil shale, the use of nuclear explosions in mining—are certainly technically feasible today, although oil shale and nuclear mining would have considerable environmental impacts. But the rest of it remains ludicrous.

Such predictions were clearly oversell, and most people at the time certainly knew they were. Nevertheless, it is striking to contemplate how few of the basic technologies of modern, middle-class comfort and convenience date from the last thirty or forty years. The train, the car, the bicycle, the airplane, the jet engine, the radio, the television, photography, movies, the phonograph, the telephone, central heating, air conditioning, indoor plumbing, hot running water, washing machines, gas and electric stoves, refrigeration, vacuum cleaners, antibiotics, sterile medical procedures, radiological treatment of cancer, the Pill—these all date from before 1960, most from before 1950. (See Exhibit 3.6.) Aside from the computer, there has been no new technological invention that has substantially reorganized the pattern of daily life and its conveniences.

And even the computer has not yet lived up to many of its promised changes. There are still secretaries and filing cabinets. We are far from achieving the much ballyhooed "paperless office;" in fact, paper consumption has seen explosive growth because it is now easier to churn out multiple drafts of everything. (Computers have done that much.) Although there is a bit of "telecommuting," most people still work in offices separated from their homes. True, E-mail is often handier than "snail mail," and cash machines do save a bit of time. True, word-processing and graphics programs do make clean-looking reports, posters, and résumés available to anyone with a halfway decent computer and printer. (Note, however, that the standards for decent looking printed matter have changed, requiring a level of perfection for routine documents that no one would have expected twenty years ago, thus wiping out any savings in the work necessary to produce something adequate.) But do these changes amount to the kind of major change in the rhythms of daily life associated with, say, the telephone, the automobile, and the television?

"Not yet, perhaps, but such change is coming," might be the response. Such a response only underscores the quasi-religious faith we still have in technological progress. As Lewis Mumford, probably the greatest critical scholar of technology, put it, "If anything was unconditionally believed in and worshipped during the last two centuries, at least by the leaders and masters of society, it was the machine."[43] The computer (along with the CD player, the microwave oven, the cell phone, and other minor modern gadgetry) is thus a culturally essential miracle for maintaining our technological faith.

In other words, it is not because of technical efficiency alone that we are adopting the computer. Our cultural faith in technological progress has dialogically propelled us to reorganize ourselves around the computer as much as the existence of the computer has alerted us to the possibility of such a reorganization.

Exhibit 3.6 There is nothing new about modern conveniences, as this ad from a 1930 issue of National Geographic shows. The basic technologies and associated patterns of the modern lifestyle have been in place for decades. Recent technological innovations have made relatively little difference to the way we live.

Politics

Technology is political, as I earlier noted. The political character of technology is made plain both by instances of active manipulation of the market through lobbying for subsidies and by instances of popular resistance to technological structures such as the environmental justice movement. Technological politics can also be passive and tacit, though. Technology is political even when we are sleepwalking. Because of routinization and romance—because of the phenomenology and culture of technology—we tend to uncritically promote particular technological structures and their social interests, sleepwalking a political order into place.

A decision to organize your life around a certain technology draws you into becoming one of its political supporters. Once you have bought your house in the car-dependent and car-worshipping suburbs, you have organized your life in such a way that you are likely to promote continued car use. If gas prices rise or your car becomes old and unreliable, you cannot easily switch to another means of transport. You will likely find yourself paying the higher gas prices and buying a new car—as well as clamoring for better parking and new highways to bypass the traffic caused by all your neighbors' cars. You will likely find yourself maintaining a place in the line of social interests that lead to the subsidies for the automobile, as well as the automobile's social and environmental consequences, a line that stretches from you to the local garage to the automobile manufacturers to the road builders to the oil companies.

Technological somnambulism is technological politics. Because of it, we may ironically find ourselves in the frequent position of promoting technological interests we wish we did not have.

THE NEEDS OF NEITHER

People have a common tendency to externalize the economy and technology—to treat them both almost as forces of nature. We speak of economic and technical changes as being driven by efficiency, subtly implying that these changes follow the thermodynamic laws of physics regarding the conservation of energy. It would be unnatural to reject them, we seem to be telling ourselves. In a parallel way, we speak of these changes as being driven by convenience, suggesting again a kind of external objectivity to the course of technical and economic development. We must therefore adapt to these imperatives, we probably all find ourselves thinking at least occasionally, and live as best we can with their social and environmental consequences.

But neither the economy nor technology is an imperative. Neither has needs. They often appear to us as external structures, as forces over which we have little control, as ends to which we must give way. But for all their objective status as facts of the market and of science, money and machines are our own creations, a part of human culture. It is we who have the needs. What Lewis Mumford said of technology applies equally to the economy: "The machine itself makes no demands and keeps no promises: it is the human spirit that makes demands and keeps promises."[44] Technology and the economy take the shape that they do only in response to human demands, promises, and broken promises. There are no imperatives but our own.

Once set into motion, however, the mills of technology and the treadmills of production and consumption become social structures that shape our needs and interests, just as those needs and interests dialogically shape the mills and treadmills to begin with. We are quickly lulled into the routines and cultural desires organized by these structures. We find ourselves dropping off into both technological and economic somnambulism.

Yet the dialogical influence that the economy and technology have over us should not be a cause for despair. In fact, in that influence lies hope. By changing the conditions under which we find ourselves making the decisions that we do, we can reinforce our movement toward the ends we truly desire. All we need to do is wake up and decide where we really want to go.

CHAPTER 4

Population and Development

God forbid that India should ever take to industrialization
after the manner of the West. The economic imperialism
of a single tiny island kingdom [England] is today keeping
the world in chains. If an entire nation of 300 million
[India] took to similar economic exploitation, it would
strip the world bare like locusts.

-Mahatma Gandhi, 1928

Thomas Malthus's *An Essay on the Principle of Population*, originally
published in 1798, is assuredly one of the most controversial works of
all time. The book's basic argument is that, unless checked in some way,
population growth tends to continue until it runs up against
environmental limits, causing poverty, hunger, misery, and resource
scarcity. The eventual result is a population crash.[1]

Although Malthus's ideas seem like common sense, you could etch
glass with some of the critics' reactions. Friedrich Engels termed
Malthus's theory a "vile and infamous doctrine," a "repulsive blasphemy
against man and nature," for it implied that the poor, through their
alleged inability to control their reproduction, were to blame for their
own poverty.[2] Others have called Malthus's theory "racist," for it
seemingly places the bulk of blame for environmental problems on poor
countries, and thus on people of color.[3] Still others, most notably
economists confident about the ability of human ingenuity in a free
market economy to overcome just about any problem, have labeled
Malthus's views "nonsense."[4]

There truly is a lot to object to in Malthus's ideas as well as in many
of the later applications of his argument. Yet his book continues to be
the basic point of departure for discussions of the relationship between
population, development, and the environment. Two hundred years
later we are still arguing about Malthus because, despite the

inadequacies of his book, it also forcefully states a basic incontrovertible truth: The world is only so big. It offers only so much room for development and only so many resources for people to consume.

The idea that we might face limits does not mesh comfortably with the modern spirit of constant growth. It represents a direct challenge to the treadmills of production and consumption around which we have organized so much of our lives. Much of the objection to Malthus can be understood as an ideological reaction to this challenge.

But Malthus also presented his theory of the relationship between population and environment in a deterministic way—as something which is inevitable, beyond our control. In the previous chapter I argued against a deterministic view of the economy and of technology. Malthus's critics are right that we should not accept a deterministic view of population and the environment either.

Neither can we ignore the influence that the environment does indeed have on society, however. The relationship between society and the environment is a dialogue; each shapes, but does not determine, the other. We need to avoid both the deterministic outlook of crude Malthusian arguments and the anything-goes outlook of crude anti-Malthusian arguments. The goal of this chapter is to tread our way through the problems of Malthusianism and anti-Malthusianism and to come to a balanced understanding of the dialogic relationships between population, development, and the environment.

THE MALTHUSIAN ARGUMENT

Many of the world's leading environmental thinkers argue that, despite his errors and overstatements, we still need to pay attention to the basic point of Malthus's thesis: the environmental and social threats posed by *exponential growth* in population, or growth that is constantly compounding.[5] Malthusians—those who agree with at least this much of Malthus—point out that, because of compounding, a constant rate of population growth leads to accelerating effects. Since the annual rate of growth also applies to the additional increments of previous years, not only will the number of people added each year go up, but the rate of the rise will constantly accelerate.

It's like a savings account. A deposit of $100 at a constant 10 percent annual interest rate will increase year by year from $10, to $11, $12.10, $13.31, $14.64, and so on. Each annual increment is larger by a wider margin than the one before because the interest is applied to an ever-increasing total. Because of compounding, the size of the increments can go up even if the growth rate falls somewhat, although the increments will eventually begin to drop if the growth rate falls sufficiently. Compounding is great news when you're trying to make money, but the situation is rather gloomier, say Malthusians, when we consider the appetite of a growing population in a finite world.

The rate of world population growth is in fact falling. The peak came in the 1960s when the world population was growing at an annual rate of over 2.0 percent.[6] By the early 1990s, the rate had fallen to 1.48 percent.[7] We therefore have little cause for alarm, say some.

Exhibit 4.1 History of world population growth.

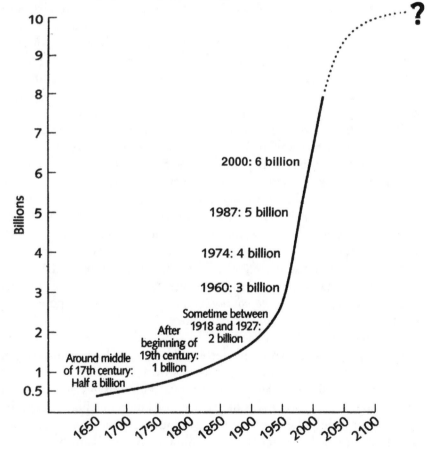

Source: Crosette (1996) and Independent Commission on Population and Quality of Life (1996).

Not so, respond Malthusians. Because of compounding, the size of new increments to the world's population has increased, even though the growth rate has declined. Today's slower growth rate is applied to a bigger population, so the world's average annual population increase has nevertheless jumped from around 50 million a year in the 1950s to around 70 million in the 1960s to approximately 82 million a year in the 1980s and early 1990s.[8] The time it took to add a billion people to the world therefore also sped up. It took fourteen years to go from 3 billion to 4 billion between 1960 and 1974. It took only thirteen years to get to 5 billion in 1987.[9]

Over 90 percent of the world's current population growth is taking place in poor countries.[10] Growth in rich and middle-income countries is far slower. In Japan and twenty-four European countries the growth rate is close to zero, ranging from plus to minus 0.3 percent a year.[11] In thirty-one poor countries, however, population growth is currently 2.5 percent or more a year.[12] This may not seem a substantially higher rate, but the power of compounding can be surprising. A country that maintained a 3 percent rate of growth for one hundred years would see its population increase nineteen-fold.[13] In a country like Tanzania, which had 30 million people and a 3 percent growth rate in 1995, the population would grow to 570 million in 2095—larger than all but two countries today, India and China.

It is important to distinguish between a population's rate of growth and its level of *fertility*, the average number of children born to women in a population. Between 1980 and 1995, the world fertility rate dropped from 3.7 children to 2.9 children. In poor countries the rate dropped from 6.3 to 5.0, and in rich countries it dropped from 1.9 to 1.7.[14] But a drop in fertility does not necessarily translate into fewer numbers of children born each year. Earlier high levels of growth often result in a population with a large proportion of young adults in the prime of their childbearing years. Lower fertility levels may thus result in just as many, or even more, births—an effect demographers term *population momentum*. Because of population momentum, it may be many years before a decline in fertility leads to a slowdown in population growth.

Still, demographers expect that fertility declines will eventually result in a drop in the size of annual additions to the world population. Some recent estimates in fact suggest that the size of annual additions has already begun to fall and that the world may not reach a population of 6 billion until the year 2000 or slightly afterward—thirteen or fourteen years after the previous billion was reached.[15] (Some of the recent fall, however, is attributable not to fertility declines but to high rates of AIDS deaths in sub-Saharan Africa and to sharp declines in life expectancy in the former Soviet Union due to economic dislocation.) The United Nations now predicts that world population will top out at between 9 billion and 12 billion sometime late in the twenty-first century.[16]

Many Malthusians worry that we will still have too many people, even if population growth eventually levels out. Because of the treadmills of production and consumption, a constant population may still have an increasing appetite for material resources. Moreover, the same logic of compounding applies to consumption and production: A constant rate of growth means not only increasing effects but accelerating effects. Currently, population growth compounds this compounding: Increases in population come on top of accelerating per capita consumption and production. But even if world population eventually stabilizes, environmental impacts may continue to compound.

The implications of compounding growth need to be considered carefully. On the one hand, growth in consumption, production, and population does not necessarily degrade the environment—at least theoretically. In fact, population growth itself has no environmental consequence at all. Any environmental impacts depend on what is being consumed and what is being produced by those increased numbers of people and on how they go about their consuming and producing.[17] Improved technology and social organization could possibly compensate for any potential impacts and even leave the environment in better shape than it was to begin with. We could, after all, decide to send a good bit of the human population to another planet someday, if we gain the necessary technological means.

On the other hand, although there are no theoretically necessary environmental outcomes, there are some theoretically likely environmental outcomes of our current forms of consumption, production, and population growth. Consider climate change, air and water pollution, deforestation, loss of habitat and biodiversity, soil erosion, soil impoverishment, per capita declines in food availability, shrinking water supplies, social differences in the distribution of environmental goods and bads. Challenges to the three central environmental issues—sustainability, environmental justice, and the rights and beauty of nature—are already well under way. Moving to another planet to escape the pollution of ours is not currently a realistic option (and in my judgment would be sad reason for planetary pioneering even if it were). We need, therefore, to be "taking population seriously," according to Frances Moore Lappé, a long-time critic of Malthusian arguments who might not be expected to hold such a view.[18]

In the remainder of this chapter, I will review the three main categories of criticisms of Malthusian arguments: *inequality critiques, technologic critiques,* and *demographic critiques.* Along the way, I will point out the environmental implications of these arguments in preparation for a final section on the dialogic role of the environment as a social actor. Because the relationships between population, development, and environment are dialogic and not deterministic, I will argue that it is possible to change those relationships should we see problems in the current situation.

But before we wade into all that, we should consider the cultural factors that make population a perennially contentious and emotional issue.

POPULATION AS CULTURE

Population is more than just numbers. "*Population* means *people*," as the Independent Commission on Population and Quality of Life, which conducted a five-year international study of population issues, observed in its 1996 final report. A South African witness in the hearings convened by the commission across the world put it this way: "Women have children; they do not have population."[19] Children are one of the most important sources of meaning and purpose in human life; they are central to our cultural values.

Population issues can fundamentally challenge these central values. I'll discuss six ways:

First, many people sense a hint of misanthropy in Malthusian arguments. People have inherent value, inherent rights of existence, most of us believe. People are also the source of most of our central interests in life. To say that we should have fewer people sounds to some like people hating.

Second, population issues rapidly connect to issues of racial, ethnic, national, and religious pride. For some people, controlling population means diminishing the group. If our population shrinks, the feeling sometimes goes, our country will become less important in the world. And within a country, subgroups sometimes feel a sense of what the psychologist Dorothy Stein terms "demographic competition."[20]

Third, the techniques of population control confront some religious values. Conception and birth are processes that even in a scientific age still evoke awe and a feeling of mystery. Many people look to religion for a framework of understanding these mysteries. All the major world religions emphasize the sanctity of life, of course, but they interpret this sanctity in various ways; in some cases, interpretations conflict with particular means of population control. Most notable is the contemporary Catholic Church's rejection of contraception as a means of population control. (The Catholic Church does not reject population control, however—just contraception as a means of achieving it.) Moreover, population control threatens the sheer number of the faithful, a fact that many religious leaders have no doubt pondered.

Fourth, population issues are fundamentally related to sex. To talk about population control is to talk about sex and sometimes to talk about controlling sex. You do not have to be a deep student of social life to recognize that issues relating to sexuality will likely be highly controversial. Moreover, because sex is a subject many find embarrassing or even immoral to talk about openly, mere discussion of contraception and other issues relating to population control can make some people anxious.

Fifth, population issues are necessarily gender issues. Reproduction lies at the center of conceptions of appropriate gender relations and gender identities, with all the implications that these relations and identities have for social power. Population control can threaten social power relations built around gender by undermining the basis on which many people legitimize these relations.

Finally, family is a central source of social identity and feelings of transcendence. It is from family relations, in part, that we understand who we are. Most of us live through most of our adult years as parents, and we thereby gain a deep sense of who we are and who we should be. Without someone to fill the role of a child, you cannot be a "mom" or a "dad." Through children, we also gain a sense of transcendence over the confines of our own individual life, a kind of immortality. Although we have other sources of transcendental values—such as religion, art, and the sense of having made a contribution to society through our work—children remain a particularly direct and accessible source. For many people, to suggest controlling population is to infringe on their principal solution to the problem of mortality: family.

These reactions are common, but they are not cultural necessities. Rather than misanthropy, population control could be seen as an enlightened form of being pro-people, for it may improve the quality of human life. Instead of diminishing the group, population control could be seen as a way to strengthen the group by making it more ecologically secure. As for religious values, our various traditions have a wide range of responses to population issues; for example, some accept contraception while others do not. Our level of comfort with sexuality is equally variable; plenty of people feel little difficulty in openly discussing sexual matters. As for gender relations, changes in the balance of power between women and men can be seen as liberating rather than threatening. And instead of compromising family identity and transcendence, population control can be seen as a more sure route to improving the life chances of our families and children.

I raise these counterpoints to illustrate the diversity of possible cultural responses to the issues often raised by population control. Significantly, all these responses have moral implications. It therefore seems unlikely that any of us can evaluate population issues in a morally neutral way. Nor should we try to, for it is these implications that, in large part, make population issues so significant for us. But even though moral neutrality is not possible, we can still evaluate population issues in a reasoned way.

Being conscious of our own moral values seems a surer route to reason than falsely assuming that we have an unbiased perspective. With our moral passions in mind—including any opinions we may have concerning sustainability, environmental justice, and the rights and beauty of nature—let us now evaluate Malthusianism and the critiques of it.

THE INEQUALITY CRITIQUE OF MALTHUSIANISM

Looking around the world, we can see an indisputable association between high levels of population growth, poverty, a wide range of environmental problems, and declines in per capita food production. For example, Africa has the highest overall rate of population growth of any continent and is simultaneously experiencing substantial declines in food production per capita as well as overgrazing, desertification, shortening fallow periods, and deforestation.

The question is why. Malthus would likely have seen diagnostic evidence in Africa for his view that population growth eventually overwhelms the productive capacity of the environment, leading to poverty and hunger. But the story is, at the very least, more complex.

A long tradition of scholars has even argued that the direction of causality should be reversed. It is not population growth that causes environmental decline and ultimately poverty and hunger; rather it is poverty and hunger that cause environmental decline and population growth as the poor struggle to gain their living. To understand the origins of poverty we should look not to population pressure, goes this counterargument, but rather to the history of international development and the social and economic inequality it has fostered between (and within) the countries of the world.

The Development of Underdevelopment

We sometimes forget, or at least overlook, that a scant century ago most of the poor countries of today were the colonial possessions of most of today's rich countries. As recently as 1950, only three countries in Africa—Egypt, Ethiopia, and Liberia—could claim full independence.[21] (See Exhibit 4.2) All of southern Asia, most of southeastern Asia and the Pacific Islands, and a substantial part of the Caribbean were also under the control of various empires a century ago. Much of the rest of the world was divided into spheres of influence that achieved a similar political result. Although colonization brought some benefits to the affected regions, Western Europe, Japan, the United States, and the former Soviet Union gained the most from these relationships, growing in wealth while their colonial possessions, for the most part, languished in poverty.

The period following World War II, however, saw a new global commitment to resolving these inequalities. The lessons of the war brought about a new global consciousness—a sense that we are all in this together, that the rich countries should help the poor, and that the right of self-determination applies to all countries. The United Nations was one product of this new consciousness. Partly in response to this new sense of global commitment, rich countries gave up their empires. New states sprang up everywhere as colonial powers pulled out. And in part, it must be said, the old empires folded up because the devastations of world war left few imperial countries with the financial or military means to maintain direct control over their former colonies.

But the commitment to helping poor countries was, at least in part, heartfelt.[22] Many believed that poor countries could modernize just as the West and Japan did, once they were freed from colonial control. With education, industrial infrastructure, industrialization of agriculture, modern political institutions, and lots of exports and imports to connect these countries into the increasingly global economy, the poor countries could soon join the rich at the table of modern luxury and avoid the dismal prospect of Malthusian decline.

In a word, these poor countries lacked only one thing: *development*. Modernization would bring it. This is the basic tenet of an influential perspective known as *modernization theory*, an idea associated with many thinkers in many fields; within sociology, Talcott Parsons remains the best-known advocate.

Perhaps President Harry S. Truman best stated the underlying spirit of modernization. As he proposed in his inaugural address on January 20, 1949, "We must embark on a bold new program for making the benefits of our scientific advances and industrial progress available for the improvement and growth of underdeveloped areas. The old imperialism—exploitation for foreign profit—has no place in our plans. What we envision is a program of development based on the concepts of democratic fair dealing."[23]

About this time (actually just a few years earlier, in July of 1944) delegates from forty-four countries got together in a quiet country resort in a place called Bretton Woods, New Hampshire, to chart the course of the world economy after the war. By that time, World War II seemed on its way to an inevitable close. Led by John Maynard Keynes, probably the most influential economist of the twentieth century, the Bretton Woods delegates sought to use the conclusion of World War II as an opportunity to fundamentally reshape global society and economy. Their stated intent was to make sure that such a calamity might never again occur. But as we shall see, grounds exist for a more cynical interpretation of the result, if not the intent.

Exhibit 4.2 *Colonial control of Africa: As recently as 1950, only 3 African countries—Egypt, Ethiopia, and Liberia—enjoyed complete political independence from European colonial powers.*

Source: Freeman-Greenville (1991).

Whatever the real reasons were, the delegates set up two key institutions that have had an enormous influence on the subsequent course of economic development: the International Monetary Fund (IMF) and the International Bank for Reconstruction and Development, or as it has come to be called, the World Bank. Both institutions make loans to countries for development purposes. The IMF gives mainly short-term loans to help countries balance their national budgets. The World Bank emphasizes loans for major infrastructure projects intended to have long-term effects: dams, roads, irrigation canals, schools, that kind of thing. Some of the money loaned by the "Bretton Woods institutions," as they are often called, comes from capital subscriptions from member countries, but most comes from the sale of bonds.

Since that time, several other international or "multilateral" banks have been founded, most with a regional focus, such as the Inter-American Development Bank and the Asian Development Bank. Most of the capital for international development loans comes from private foreign banks, generally in the range of 75–85 percent of the total, depending on the year.[24] But loans from multilateral banks are usually at least a part of most major development projects. Countries use the seal of approval of a multilateral loan to leverage development funds from private sources, both domestic and foreign. In addition to these sources, there has been an enormous proliferation of private international aid organizations and governmental aid agencies, which unlike the big development banks usually make gifts and not loans.

International development has become a major human activity, involving movements of capital equivalent to hundreds of billions of U.S. dollars annually. The result of a half century of international development and modernization, however, is continued disparities in wealth between countries. In fact, the gap between the rich and the poor has widened substantially.[25]

For example, between 1980 and 1992, per capita GNP in the wealthiest countries grew by 2.3 percent, but per capita GNP in the countries the World Bank defines as "low income" grew by just 1.2 percent. In the "middle-income" countries during this period, per capita GNP actually fell by 0.1 percent.

India and China are important exceptions, however. India's per capita GNP grew 3.1 percent between 1980 and 1992, and in China per capita GNP grew 7.6 percent.[26] Considering that these are by far the two largest poor nations (and by far the two largest of all nations) this is significant growth.

Nevertheless, taking a longer look shows an overall widening gap even with respect to India and China. For example, because of the United States' huge economic head start, the difference in per capita GDP between the United States and China increased by more than 30 percent between 1970 and 1992.[27] The accumulation of advantage, a process discussed in chapter 3, also works at the level of nations.

Understanding Underdevelopment. The reason for the ever-widening gap between rich and poor lies in the structure of the world economy, say a number of social scientists.

The treadmill-driven tendency to seek new markets and new places for investment has sent the capital of wealthy nations overseas. Poor nations have usually welcomed this investment, but most development funds have come in the form of loans, not gifts. Although aid and charity account for a significant portion of the capital flow, the rest has been sent with the expectation that it would be returned, with a comfortable margin for profit as well. The World Bank, for example, is a highly profitable institution and its bonds are considered unusually secure investments. As of 1993, the World Bank had cleared $14 billion in profit for its investors.[28]

Meanwhile, poor nations have become mired in debt. Although the debt crisis faced by developing countries has received much international attention, debt continues to rise. As of 1994, the external debt of developing countries was over $2 trillion ($2,066 billion, to be precise), and these countries were spending about $200 billion a year to pay it off.[29]

To put the level of international debt in perspective, economists often cite the ratio of a country's annual external debt service to the value of its annual exports, the source of the funds needed to pay off foreign creditors. In developing nations today, that ratio averages 17 percent; in several countries, it rises to over 30 percent; in Zambia it is a whopping 174.4 percent.[30] These countries therefore need to maintain at least a 17 percent profit margin on their exports (and return none of that 17 percent margin to investors within their own borders) in order to pay off their debt. This is a highly unlikely scenario. The typical rate of profit for a corporation ranges only from 2 to 12 percent.[31] Moreover, the average economic growth rate in these countries is running at only about 0.4 percent.[32] In short, most developing nations today owe far more than they can comfortably pay back without impoverishing themselves still further.

Data like these support the *world systems theory* advanced by André Gundar Frank, Immanuel Wallerstein, and others.[33] World systems theory sees the process of development as inherently unequal, dividing the world into *core* regions and *periphery* regions. Because of differences in political and economic power, wealth tends to flow to the core regions from the peripheral ones, feeding the former and bleeding the latter. Thus over time development tends to exacerbate economic differences instead of leveling them. World systems theorists also sometimes point to regions that have some of the features of both core and periphery, what they term *semiperiphery* regions. Examples of core countries would be the United States, Japan, and the wealthier nations of Europe. Peripheral countries include Uganda, Zaire, Vietnam, Bangladesh, Ecuador, Panama, and many others. Countries like Costa Rica, the Slovak Republic, and Turkey would be semiperiphery. According to world systems theorists, core, periphery, and semiperiphery relations can emerge not only between countries but within them as well.

Figures on capital flows bear out the notion that, despite their commitment to international development, the core nations have received the most benefit. Between 1982 and 1987, for example, the net movement of capital from poor countries to rich ones was $155 billion dollars. The figures vary from year to year, and in 1982 the net movement was over $20 billion the other way—that is, to poor countries.[34] But the dominant trend over the half century since the Bretton Woods conference has been much the same as it was during the period that President Truman termed the "old imperialism."

The Structural Adjustment Trap. The continued poverty of poor countries has been much exacerbated by a World Bank and IMF policy known as *structural adjustment*, a term coined by Robert McNamara, President of the World Bank from 1969 to 1981.[35] (McNamara was also U.S. secretary of defense during the beginning of the Vietnam War.) "Structural adjustment" refers to a comprehensive program of radical free-market changes, such as reducing public services, liberalizing trade, emphasizing export crops, eliminating subsidies, and curbing inflation through high interest rates and reduced wages—what is euphemistically referred to as "demand management." Structural adjustment programs have been instituted in dozens of countries since the late 1970s, from Africa to Asia to the Americas to the former Soviet Union.

The idea of structural adjustment is to help—some say to force—countries to reshape their economy so that they can pay off their mounting debts. Private banks often reschedule and in some cases write off loans, but the World Bank and the IMF have never done so out of fear of undermining their high bond ratings and thus being forced to raise the interest rates they offer investors.[36] So they encourage—again, some say force—debtor countries to adopt structural adjustment programs instead. Whether one calls it help, encouragement, or force, the two Bretton Woods institutions certainly give poor countries a compelling incentive to adopt structural adjustment: no more World Bank and IMF loans unless they do, which also means a greatly reduced ability to attract private foreign capital.

Free-market policies may not seem like such a bad idea. After all, these are the same policies most Western governments advocate for themselves these days. But the free-market policies increasingly adopted by rich countries have been put into practice without anything like the severity and inflexibility the World Bank and IMF have imposed on poor countries throughout the world. "Shock therapy" is what World Bank and IMF officials informally call the regimen. The result has been devastating for the marginal peoples of nearly every country that has taken this stern medicine. Typically under structural adjustment, basic social services such as education and health care have been sharply cut, and the price of formerly subsidized foodstuffs like bread has gone sky high, leaving the poor in often desperate circumstances.

Throughout the 1980s, the heyday of structural adjustment, "IMF food riots" plagued cities across Africa as starving people took to the streets, sometimes toppling governments.[37] And as investors have bought up farmland to produce export crops for the newly liberalized export trade, displaced peoples have moved into more marginal lands, promoting deforestation and land degradation. With less productive land growing food for local consumption, poor countries have found themselves more dependent than ever on imports to meet their basic food needs. Moreover, once displaced from their land, people in poor countries are less able to compensate for the newly increased food prices by growing their own. When you are poor, it is very risky to be dependent on money to get enough to eat.

Another result of structural adjustment is that many poor countries are in the unenviable position of exporting raw materials elsewhere, only to buy these materials back later as finished goods. Value is added elsewhere, and these poor countries must pay for that added value out of their scant stocks of foreign exchange funds, further crimping their ability to pay off foreign debts. The trade liberalization features of structural adjustment and a number of recent international treaties have also enabled companies from rich countries to come into poor countries and set up low-wage factories, later exporting the goods to places where people have enough money to buy them. The governments of poor countries, eager to attract the foreign investment needed to fulfill structural adjustment plans, often allow these companies to evade the environmental and labor laws they would have to contend with in their own countries. During the mid-1990s, for example, many lines of Nike sneakers were being assembled in Vietnam by women working twelve-hour days at twenty cents an hour to make shoes they could never afford themselves—to the embarrassment of a number of celebrities who were paid millions to endorse Nike products.[38]

• •
SOCIAL ACTION CASE STUDY
THE LOCAL CURRENCY MOVEMENT

If the world economic system tends to draw capital away from peripheral areas and toward core areas, maybe the thing to do is to make at least some capital inherently local.

At least that's what Paul Glover and hundreds of businesses in Ithaca, New York, think. In 1991, Glover established Ithaca "hours", a paper currency accepted only in Ithaca. The name hours refers to the local value of an hour's work at a fair wage. Thus the value of a "one-hour" note is currently set at $10, which Glover figures is the current average wage in the Ithaca area. Over three hundred Ithaca businesses and a credit union now accept Ithaca hours; many pay willing employees at least partially in hours, encouraging the local economy to stay local.

Hours come in five denominations: the two-hour, the one-hour, the half-hour, the quarter-hour, and the eighth-hour. While visiting Ithaca in 1996, I traded $2.50 for a blue and purple quarter-hour note. It reads "Time Is Money," "In Ithaca We Trust," and "This Note Is Useful Tender for Many Local Needs." On one side are two panels printed in a special thermal ink (invented in Ithaca) that disappears if you press the warmth of your thumb against it, foiling counterfeiters. Hours are printed on either locally produced cattail or hemp paper. To date, $62,000 worth of hours are in circulation in Ithaca, and the promoters are increasing the supply slowly to guard against inflation. (But in any event, the value of an hour is pegged against the value of local labor rather than the more speculative value of commodity exchanges.) The local district attorney has given hours the full backing of state law.

People love the idea. Here are some stories from a potluck supper held to celebrate Ithaca hours and the changes they have wrought.[1]

Ramsey sells bagels at a local bakery and accepts hours as payment. As he put it, "Hours keep people in our community employed better than dollars that leave the community. Dollars that go to large corporations do not really trickle back down. They concentrate capital, making the rich richer and the poor poorer."

Barbara has a shoe-repair business that accepts hours. As she described, "This money makes everybody more aware of what's available in the community. So it helps community development by keeping money local."

Tony sells stained glass and takes hours for payment. He agreed that, because of hours, "local businesses circulate money within the community better. Wal-Mart's profits go to Arkansas."

But perhaps even more importantly, a local currency like Ithaca hours can change money from being merely a means of anonymous exchange to a means of social connection. Bruce, a local jitterbug and swing dance teacher, explained: "Dollars come and go so many different ways that their social meaning gets lost. We're making a big cultural change with hours—back to the community meaning of money."

No one in Ithaca is saying that all local economic exchanges should be in hours. Their goal is not economic isolation. Nor is that the goal of the forty-two other communities in the United States and Canada that, as of June 1997, have started local currencies.[2] But in a world so driven by the single-minded ethic of competition, local currencies can help replenish one of our most precious economic resources: community.

Notes
1 These stories come from the Ithaca hours website,
  www.newciv.org/worldtrans/whole/ithacahours.html.
2 Ithaca hours website.

• •

Under these conditions, poor countries get the short end of the economic stick of structural adjustment. Value is added in peripheral areas, but the peripheral areas do not get to keep much of that value. Local workers are paid almost nothing, and somebody else owns the products of their labor. By opening up poor nations for increased foreign investment under such unequal terms of trade, structural adjustment assists in draining value away from the periphery and toward the core.

Structural adjustment has been widely criticized, and the prestige of both Bretton Woods institutions has been severely undermined. The World Bank itself is now rethinking the policy.[39] But the human and environmental damage has been done, reinforcing centuries of unequal exchanges between the rich and poor countries of the world.

The anti-Malthusian moral is this: The poverty experienced throughout the world is not just a population issue. (Some say it is not a population issue at all.) Poverty cannot be understood apart from the history of development, a history that has favored some regions over others. Any argument concerning the relationship between the environment and poverty needs to take this history into account.

Food for All

Malthusians point not only to poverty but also to the 840 million people who suffer from malnutrition as an indication of population pressures on the land. Anti-Malthusian critics of this position argue that, on the contrary, the world has plenty of food for everyone. The problem of food shortages is really a problem of access to food and of overconsumption of food by those who do have access. The principal names associated with this counterargument are Frances Moore Lappé and Amartya Sen.

One of the points that Lappé forcefully raises in a number of books is that there is little correlation, if any, between population density and hunger or between the amount of cropland per person in a country and hunger. The obvious example is Europe, which has some of the most densely populated countries in the world and yet very little hunger. Africa, which suffers from a far greater percentage of hunger nevertheless has a far lower population density. Of course, much of Africa is desert and cannot be farmed. But even when considering the amount of cropland per person, Lappé finds no particular relationship with hunger. Japan has about ten people for every acre of cropland and very little hunger. Tiny Singapore has 143 people for every acre of cropland and very little hunger. But Chad has 1.68 acres of cropland for every person—17 times as much as Japan and 240 times as much as Singapore—and quite extensive hunger.[40]

Lappé also argues that, even at current population levels, the world has plenty of food. Between 1990 and 1995, the world produced an average of 317 kilograms of grain per person each year, which is 1.87 pounds a day, or about 2,805 calories.[41] That's not an extravagant amount, but it is sufficient. However, 37 to 40 percent of that grain, depending on the year, is fed to livestock. As many have pointed out, much of grain's food value to humans is lost because animals eat not only to put on mass but also for energy to stay alive. Depending on the kind of livestock, it takes from 2 to 7 pounds of grain to produce a pound of meat.[42] With their high meat diet, Americans consume approximately 800 kilograms of grain each year per person. In India, which has a diet low in meat, people consume about 200 kilograms of grain per person per year.[43] Changes in the diet of the wealthy and a different distribution of food could raise the figure for India considerably.

In place of Malthusianism, Lappé (along with her colleague Rachel Schurman) advocates a *power-structures* perspective on food and population. Even though Japan and Singapore have little cropland per capita, they are wealthy countries; Chad and India have more cropland, but they are poor. And people who are wealthy have a lot more power, a lot more ability to gain the food they require, and a lot more "say in the decisions that shape their lives," as Lappé and Schurman point out.[44]

Lappé and Schurman argue that a power-structures perspective explains not only inequalities in access to food but also high rates of population growth. A lack of control over their lives leads poor people to regard children as an economic resource, they observe: "Living at the economic margin, many poor parents perceive their children's labor as necessary to augment meager family income. By working in the fields and around the home, children also free up adults and elder siblings to earn outside income."[45]

Given their lack of options, poor parents thus have a strong economic incentive to have lots of children, the inverse of Malthus's argument that population growth, through environmental decline, leads to poverty. Rather, Lappé and Schurman respond, poverty and environmental decline lead to population growth by decreasing the power people have over their lives, leading them out of desperation to seek economic security through having large families.

The Politics of Famine. Amartya Sen makes a similar argument concerning famine.[46] Famines, says Sen, are caused not by a lack of availability of food but rather by a lack of access to food. All societies have social systems of what Sen terms *entitlements* to food and other goods, such as the distribution of ownership of land to grow food and the ability to acquire food through trade, usually through the medium of money. Entitlements allow people to gain command of food and other goods. It is breakdowns in these systems that cause famines, not environmental decline.

Sen makes his case by analyzing four major famines in the twentieth century: the Great Bengal famine of 1943, the Sahel famines of the 1970s, the Ethiopian famines of 1973 and 1974, and the Bangladesh famine of 1974. He argues that in each instance sufficient food to feed everyone was on hand in the affected countries. The problem was that people could not get access to the food.

For example, in the 1974 Bangladesh famine, a series of summer floods on the Brahmaputra River largely wiped out one of the three annual rice crops and damaged a second one. But food imports and stocks of rice remaining from earlier harvests provided plenty of food throughout the crisis.[47] The real problem was that the flood threw a lot of farmers and agricultural laborers out of work. With nothing to harvest from one rice crop and no chance to plant the next because of the continuing floods, laborers could find no paid work. Farmers didn't have much money either because they had nothing to sell. Consequently, these laborers and farmers couldn't afford to buy much rice. Also, the United States chose this moment to cut off its normal food aid, because Bangladesh was exporting jute to Cuba. In anticipation of shortages due to the flooding and to the loss of U.S. food aid, the rice market went haywire. Prices for rice in Bangladesh jumped by 18 to 24 percent at a time when many people had little money on hand to make up the difference. Because of fluctuations in the labor market and the rice market, they had lost their entitlement to food. Somewhere between 26,000 and 100,000 died of starvation and malnutrition within three months.

Similar kinds of arguments have been applied to other famines, such as the infamous Irish potato famine of the 1840s. While millions starved, Ireland continued to export large quantities of wheat to England (some 800 boatloads in all) because of earlier export contracts.[48] In the recent famines in war-torn Somalia, Rwanda, and Burundi, there may not have been sufficient food from local farms nor much exporting of food. But high population density relative to cropland was still not the cause of the starvation, some argue. Rather, because of the war, people were not given access to food, nor could they plant in order to feed themselves. War broke down their systems of entitlement to food.

Sen's argument has an important practical (and political) implication. If there is food available even in the midst of most famines, then the long-term solution to hunger in the world is not the importation of more food. In the short term, in the midst of a crisis when people are dying, food imports are frequently necessary. But even if the long-term problem is the distribution of food, the long-term solution is not redistribution of food; rather it is redistribution of access to food, as Lappé and Schurman also argue. "What is needed is not ensuring food availability," says Sen, "but guaranteeing food entitlement."[49] In other words, don't give the poor food (except when they are starving). Rather, give them farms, give them jobs, and give them democracy.

Limits of the Inequality Perspective

The inequality perspective makes an important case for the significance of the social origins of poverty, population growth, and hunger. A purely Malthusian perspective, as nearly all scholars now agree, is clearly inadequate.[50]

Yet there is much that the inequality perspectives of Sen, Lappé, and Schurman cannot explain about hunger. Although Chad has a higher ratio of cropland per person than Japan and Singapore, and a roughly equivalent ratio to many European countries, not all cropland is equal in its productivity. The climate in Chad is quite dry and production per acre is quite low. Much more significant than cropland per capita is annual grain production per capita, which runs at about 120 kilograms per person in Africa and nearly 500 kilograms per person in Europe.[51] The power-structures perspective of Lappé and Schurman needs to take into account the spatial distribution of environmental productivity, not merely wave it aside. Environmental productivity is itself a source of social power.

Nor does entitlement breakdown seem sufficient to explain all famines, as a number of Sen's critics have argued.[52] Six years of warfare in Europe between 1939 and 1945 severely disrupted systems of entitlement, as has the recent strife in Yugoslavia. But the disruptions of war in Europe did not result in the widespread starvation that Rwanda, Burundi, and Somalia have suffered of late. Europe has long had far more food production per capita. It is also striking to consider the relatively minor disruptions that led to the Bangladesh famine. At the peak of the famine, the price of rice rose only 18 to 24 percent. Bangladesh, however, is very poor. And with a population of some 115 million in a region the size of Greece (which has a population one-tenth the size), the country finds itself compelled to import much of its food. Most of the people of Bangladesh live very close to the margin they need to survive.

When you live close to the edge, both environmentally and economically, even a minor disruption can have a big impact. Bangladesh and all the countries that have experienced famine in the twentieth century are poor countries with unfavorable levels of grain production per capita. They have very marginal systems of both food entitlement *and* food production.[53] This is a dangerous combination. When a country is too poor to easily command food imports and when it doesn't have much local food production to begin with, it will have less food around for its people to be entitled to—even in good times.

THE TECHNOLOGIC CRITIQUE OF MALTHUSIANISM

In October 1990, the anti-Malthusian economist Julian Simon won a much-discussed bet with Paul Ehrlich, a biologist and a prominent figure in the Malthusian tradition. Erhlich is the author of the 1968 bestseller *The Population Bomb*, which predicted widespread famine and starvation within ten years, and Simon and Erhlich have been publishing a series of counterattacks on each other since the early 1980s.[54] Simon bet that the price of five metals of Ehrlich's choosing—chrome, copper, nickel, tin, and tungsten—would fall over the next ten years, as opposed to rising in the face of Malthusian scarcity. Ten years later, the price of all five metals had actually dropped, after taking into account inflation. (They had agreed to pay each other the difference in value accrued by the market movement of $200 worth of each metal over the ten-year period. Simon would pay for all the metals that went up in price, and Ehrlich would pay for all the metals that went down. Ehrlich quite honorably sent Simon a check for the $576.07 difference.)[55]

It was a foolish bet for Ehrlich to make, even from a Malthusian point of view. Market forces are complex and reflect environmental conditions crudely at best. Many of the costs of natural resource production are externalized, disguising their true environmental (and social and economic) significance. Also, the prices of these metals have little to do with the resource scarcities—land, water, food—that would be significant to the poor and marginalized, those who are most likely to experience a Malthusian crisis, if anyone will. Even if the prices of the metals had gone up, the bet would have said little about Malthusian shortages.

A Cornucopian World?

Although the bet proved nothing, it did serve to highlight the debate between Malthusian arguments and a kind of anti-Malthusian argument often called *cornucopian*, of which Simon is the most prominent proponent. Simon controversially claims that the solution to resource scarcity is actually to increase population. People, says Simon, are the "ultimate resource." A larger number of people means more brainpower and labor to work out technological solutions to scarcity, Simon argues. When confronted with scarcity, we apply our collective brainpower and find new sources of formerly scarce resources and new techniques for extracting them. In some cases, new technology will allow us to substitute different materials for ones that have become scarce, what Simon calls the principle of *substitutability*.[56]

Simon cites a variety of evidence to support his arguments. Population has successfully continued to increase, and increase rapidly, for the roughly two hundred years since Malthus first published his book, Simon notes. As well, life expectancy has leaped to unprecedented levels, while infant mortality has declined considerably. Standards of living for many of us today are astonishing when compared with living standards of the past, suggesting to Simon that Malthusian limits are far from inescapable. The prices of most basic commodities have actually dropped over the decades, in line with the results of Simon's bet with Ehrlich. Simon also disputes the significance of acid rain, global warming, the ozone hole, and species loss, arguing either that these issues have been exaggerated by environmentalists or that they represent challenges that future technological innovation will overcome. He argues that, in fact, the state of the environment is now much improved, pointing to the drop in air pollution emissions in the United States and the many advances in public health.[57]

But Simon has many critics, and rightly so. One point that is often raised is Simon's neglect of social inequality. Although the lives of many have improved, since 1960 the percentage of the world's people who live in poverty, facing hunger and malnutrition throughout their lives, has remained the same. The sheer number living in poverty has doubled.[58] It is true that even the desperately poor are generally living longer, in part because of medical and other technological improvements, but life expectancy is still very uneven across the world. Simon paints an overly rosy picture of the world. We can do better.

Simon's argument that more people means more brainpower to work out problems is also rather dubious. Sure, two people can come up with more ideas than one (although they may also come up with the same ideas). But by Simon's argument, the Roman Empire would still be with us, continuing to expand, ever increasing the number of people enlisted into the task of solving the empire's problems. It is clearly not the sheer size of a society that makes it innovative. Innovativeness depends on social circumstances that encourage creative thinking, such as democratic discussion and a good educational system, not mere numbers of people. In fact, greater numbers of people may only increase a society's stock of misguided ideas, if that society is set up in a way that stamps everyone in the same mold. Also, the kind of improvements that Simon looks to are mainly high-tech. But the bulk of population growth currently is taking place among those who do not have the educational background to contribute to high-tech solutions.

Critics also doubt Simon's optimism about technology. As chapter 3 recounts, the pace of technological innovation seems to have slowed in recent decades. Also, there are limits to what technology can do. Technology has indeed made possible substantial substitutions in the resources we depend on, often in the face of scarcity, such as the techniques for the use of fossil fuel that resolved the fuel wood and water power shortages of early industrialism. But will technology always come to the rescue in time to prevent serious problems? This question is particularly germane as we encounter limits in resources that seem less substitutable, such as land for agriculture, habitat for biodiversity, fresh water, and clean air. And even if we come up with an innovation, new technology can bring with it unfortunate unintended consequences, such as the substitution of HCFCs, a potent greenhouse gas, for ozone-depleting CFCs. Solving one problem often contributes to another. Moreover, waiting for a shortage to stimulate innovation and substitution could put humanity on a path of crisis management in which we try to solve problems instead of avoiding them to begin with. This is a risky strategy, especially for the world's poor.[59]

The Boserup Effect

Ester Boserup has offered a closely related but more temperate argument for how population growth can, in some circumstances, stimulate technological change. In a famous study of agricultural development, Boserup suggests that population pressure is a primary factor stimulating the adoption of more productive farming practices. Malthus held that population pressure reduces food availability, but Boserup's view is that population can increase food production by giving people an incentive to switch to more intensive farming methods.

Consider a low-population-density farming practice like shifting cultivation, in which farmers cultivate a particular parcel of land for a few years and then let it lie fallow for twenty or thirty years before cultivating it again. In the interim, the forest grows back, restoring the fertility of the soil and breaking the life cycle of crop pests. This is an effective and relatively low-labor method of farming. But it supports few people per acre. So as population grows, rural people shorten the fallow periods—already a technological change—until problems with fertility and crop pests increase and population pressures rise even more. At that point, and usually reluctantly, villagers begin cropping fields annually and using small plows, fertilizers, and pesticides to maintain fertility and control pests. Where possible, and if pressures remain high, they may eventually irrigate their fields and purchase high-yielding hybrids rather than saving their own seed. In most cases, these more intensive practices require more labor and higher cash outlays, making villagers reluctant to switch to them. But eventually people do switch, if they can, as demonstrated by the dramatic increases in food output in developing countries in recent decades.[60]

But Boserup is no starry-eyed optimist. She has identified many qualifications to this process, which is now sometimes called the *Boserup effect*. First, technological change is not the same as innovation. Population pressures provide the incentive to adopt technologies that have been invented elsewhere but that may not prove attractive until population pressures override labor and financial costs. Such pressures also encourage innovation, she suggests, but the principle at work is necessity, not Simonian collective brainpower. In any case, "societies have most often advanced technologically by introducing technologies already in use in other societies," Boserup writes.[61]

Issues of inequality can also limit the influence of a Boserup effect. The investments required to increase the intensity of production may not be available in developing areas. And if farmers do attain sufficient capital to intensify their operations through mechanization, they may also put farm workers out of work, increasing poverty and inequality.[62]

Boserup further notes that in conditions of very rapid population growth, economic development may be severely limited.[63] Population density needs to be considered separate from population growth.[64] Whereas population density may provide the incentive to intensify production, rapid population growth may overwhelm the economic and social resources that are essential to intensification. Governments and local communities can be left constantly scrambling to provide a burgeoning population with education, healthcare, poverty relief, and infrastructure improvements like roads and irrigation. Rapid population growth also leads to a population with a high percentage of children requiring schooling and caregiving and thus competing for scarce funds and adult labor.

The problem of rapid population growth can be particularly pronounced in urban areas. When the population is generally poor, taxation does not yield sufficient funds to keep investing in new roads, public transportation, sewage lines, clean-water supplies, school buildings, hospitals, phone lines, and power generation. Nor will people have enough money to attract much private investment to provide these services. Government officials and police receive low pay and turn to corruption to maintain their incomes, making it even harder to coordinate rapid growth. Kickbacks increase the cost of providing infrastructure, and polluters avoid regulations through payoffs to officials.

Even when the population is wealthier, rapid growth presents a serious organizational problem. Mexico City, capital of one of the world's largest middle-income nations, is often pointed to as an example of the difficulty of planning in the midst of rapid expansion. Despite the horrendous traffic in the city, residents increasingly turn to cars, as an alternative to inadequate public transportation, only making matters worse. Public transit services simply can't keep up with the rapidly increasing demand of the rapidly increasing population. Because of these planning difficulties, the likelihood of corruption increases. Thus, as industries and car owners bribe their way around regulations limiting polluting emissions, the 22 million people of Mexico City experience the worst air quality of any city in the world. In 1995, air pollution exceeded the World Health Organization's standard on 321 days. Joggers wear facemasks. Wealthy children play indoors or inside giant glass bubbles. During one particularly bad 5-day period in 1996, the city's health care services attributed an increase of 400,000 patients and 300 deaths to air pollution.[65] Los Angeles may be a similar, albeit less extreme, example from a very wealthy country.

We need to make another important qualification to the Boserup effect. Like Simon, Boserup does not allow a big role for the environment in her theories of technological change. But the environment can significantly limit the potential of a Boserup effect. The problem of the unintended environmental consequences of technological change, mentioned with regard to Simon's theory of technological substitution, also applies to Boserup's theory. New production strategies bring new consequences. Equally importantly, because of the pressure to increase environmental yields quickly, more intensive production often proceeds by increasing the overall level of resource use rather than by increasing the efficiency of resource use. Sometimes efficiency even declines, resulting in soil erosion, soil degradation, deforestation, and water shortages.

The Case of Miracle Rice

We hardly ever know ahead of time all the consequences of a technological change, and the story of the development of the high-yielding rice varieties known as "miracle rice" is a clear example.

During the 1960s and 1970s, intensification of agriculture swept through the developing countries, a transformation often called the *green revolution*. Mechanization, irrigation, pesticides, a tenfold increase in fertilizer use, the introduction of high-yielding hybrids, rural road construction to open up new areas for clearing and cultivation—these practices allowed world grain production to increase 2.6-fold between 1950 and 1984.[66] The per capita world grain harvest rose by 40 percent.[67] Much of the gain was in rice, the centerpiece of the diet of billions. The success of "miracle rice" is a good way to assess the green revolution and our common feeling of technological optimism.[68]

The working lives of roughly a billion people are devoted to growing rice. Average worldwide consumption per capita is 145 pounds (dry weight) a year. In Bangladesh, the average person eats 330 pounds a year—almost a pound a day. The rice-dependent countries are also where much, if not most, of the world's population growth is taking place. However, these countries have little remaining land not already in paddies that could be brought into rice production. Increasing rice yields per acre and hectare is clearly an important challenge.

The success over the past forty years or so in meeting this challenge can be largely attributed to the work of the International Rice Research Institute (IRRI), which was founded in the Philippines in 1959 with the goal of increasing rice production. The approach IRRI took was to develop new rice that could accept high rates of fertilizer application and would also be suitable for mechanical cultivation. Most of the local rice varieties in use around the developing world at that time were susceptible to a problem known as "lodging," or falling over from growing too tall. This problem is not particularly significant when rice is harvested by hand, so local farmers never felt a great need to select against lodging in maintaining their local rice varieties. But this characteristic of rice had to be dealt with before combines could be used. Also, lodging tends to get worse with fertilizer use, as the plants shoot upwards in response to the easy flow of nutrients.

In rural Taiwan, some IRRI scientists found a wild variety of low-stature rice that they hybridized with conventional rice in 1966. The result was rice suitable for both heavy fertilization and mechanical harvesting. IRRI called this hybrid IR8, but it rapidly came to be called "miracle rice." Farmers across southern and southeastern Asia gave up their local varieties and bought IR8, and average yields of rice went up 30 percent between 1968 and 1981.

By the mid-1980s, though, the euphoria had pretty well worn off. A host of interrelated problems with miracle rice had emerged: increased pest damage, loss of genetic diversity, the killing of paddy fish, and increased social inequality.

Previously farmers had kept their own seed and selected it for suitability to local conditions. But with the coming of IR8, a huge percentage of rice land was soon planted with the same variety. A pest that could evolve to do well against that IR8 would have acre after acre of the same variety to flourish in. Moreover, simultaneous increases in irrigation led farmers to crop two and three times a year in areas where they had previously cropped only once or twice a year. Multiple cropping did wonders for rice output, but the old pattern of drying out fields once a year used to interrupt the life cycles of pests and help to keep them in check.

Farmers began applying the newly available pesticides, but all too soon the pests started evolving to resist the pesticides. IRRI went back to work to develop a new hybrid—and then another and another and another as new problems kept emerging. IR20 was resistant to a disease called *tungro* but an easy mark for brown plant-hoppers. IR26 could handle the plant-hoppers, but it was easily flattened by wind.

IRRI researchers checked their records and found that a wind-resistant variety had been recorded in some areas of Taiwan, the same area from which the genetic material for IR8 had come. But when the researchers went to Taiwan, they found that the wind-resistant variety had disappeared from use. All the local farmers were planting rice hybrids from IRRI, and no one had bothered to keep the seemingly outdated wind-resistant variety going. Eventually IRRI found a variety it could use, and came out with IR36. Four years later, though, the brown plant-hoppers had evolved and were again attacking the crops. In a few years IRRI was up to IR72, with more hybrid varieties to come, or so rice farmers must hope.

Unanticipated Consequences. IRRI's work has been widely praised for improving the diet and health of billions. Critics, though, point to the killing of paddy fish brought about by using the new hybrids. One of the major sources of protein in the diets of many rice farmers had been fish from their paddies. But the new pest problems associated with the use of hybrids forced farmers to apply pesticides at such high rates that the paddy fish were killed off in most areas. Consequently, some have argued, miracle rice has actually led to lower nutrition levels for local farmers at the same that it has allowed more people to be fed.

Then there are the social and economic complications. The new rice farming requires more capital per acre. Fertilizer, pesticides, hybrid seed, and combines cost money. Thus the new form of rice farming became accessible to only the wealthier members of rural villages. And soon they were producing rice so cheaply that other farmers could not stay in the game, starting a production treadmill that has thrown millions of farmers off the land.

Even wealthier farmers can manage the higher costs only if they have bigger farms. Formerly, tenant farming was very common in areas such as the Malay Peninsula. But now the landowners themselves need every piece of land to pay for tractors and other improvements, and tenants are finding it hard to keep their holdings. The political scientist James Scott has described the social implications of intensive rice production in Malaysia. He points out that the irrigation of paddies helped propel the move toward bigger rice farms. Without irrigation, landowners would never have been able to achieve the big harvests necessary to fund the switch to more intensive production.[69]

Intensification has been hardest on those who were too poor even to be tenant farmers, as Scott has described for Malaysia. These villagers used to survive as field workers, but with the coming of combines to do the harvesting and pesticides to do the pest control, they are increasingly out of work. The village poor used to have a kind of unwritten contract with the wealthy. Poor villagers would work in the fields, but they expected *zakat*—the Muslim tradition of charity—especially when times were hard. But *zakat* is disappearing now as the wealthy find they no longer really need the poor, furthering the social inequalities brought about by the intensification of agriculture and fueling the migration of rural peoples to the urban shanty towns.[70]

Since 1984, the rise in world rice yields has slowed considerably. More and more farmers are reaching the four-ton-per-hectare level that seems to be the practical maximum of current rice technology.[71] Yields in China and India have been stable since 1990 and have actually fallen somewhat in Japan.[72] Global yields are still increasing, but at a slower rate than population growth.

Worldwide per capita yield of all grain dropped 7 percent between 1984 and 1996. (See Exhibit 4.3.)[73] Researchers at the Worldwatch Institute suggest that the declining responsiveness of crops to further fertilization, as well as "soil erosion, the conversion of grainland to nonfarm uses, and spreading water scarcity" is limiting the growth of grain production.[74]

Exhibit 4.3 World grain production per person, 1950–96: Despite a record harvest in 1996, the overall trend since the 1984 peak has been persistently down.

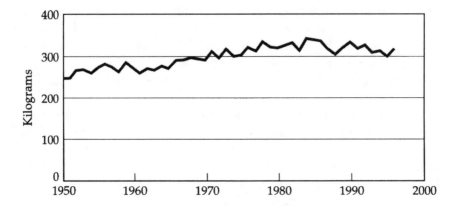

Source: Brown et al. (1997).

Will this scarcity lead to another round of technological innovation? In 1995, IRRI announced another breakthrough, a new type of rice expected to increase yields by up to 25 percent, the first significant advance in rice production in a decade.[75] And 1996 saw the first bioengineered variety of a major grain crop, Monsanto's Roundup-Ready Soybeans. The new soybeans can tolerate higher application rates of Roundup, a herbicide developed by Monsanto, without the crop itself falling susceptible to the chemical. (Monsanto, of course, makes money two ways with this new variety: soybean sales and increased pesticide sales.)

Critics worry about the environmental and moral consequences of bioengineering and other new agronomic techniques, as well as the likely continuance of patterns of social inequality. Even some bioengineers and financial analysts remain skeptical that technology can produce a "new green revolution."[76] Maybe it will. But we face the risk that it won't. And even if it does, will we be able to handle the social and environmental consequences?

THE DEMOGRAPHIC CRITIQUE OF MALTHUSIANISM

In 1945, the demographer Frank W. Notestein offered a simple model of population that has since become central to the debate over population growth. Looking over European history, Notestein suggested that development and modernization initially raise population growth rates but eventually lead to a return to a stable population, albeit at a higher level. Notestein distinguished three stages:

Stage One: In premodern times countries experience high birth rates and mortality rates that roughly cancel each other out. Because of disease, malnutrition, and accidents, average life expectancy is about thirty-five years. Children and infants are particularly hard hit because of the diseases and fragility of childhood. Parents compensate by having a lot of children, a practice supported by pro-natal social norms and social institutions as well as the common use of children as a source of household and agricultural labor.

Stage Two: With the beginning of modernization, new scientific discoveries lead to improved health and an increased food supply, and industrialization increases wealth. Mortality levels fall, but pro-natal social norms continue to promote a high birth rate. Population growth rates climb, eventually to high levels.

Stage Three: Finally, social norms and social institutions catch up with the fact that children are quite likely to survive, leading to a fall in the birth rate. Increased urbanization promotes a lower birth rate because children are no longer seen as a labor supply for the farm. And with the coming of universal schooling, children become an economic burden rather than an economic resource. Changes in social structures associated with modernism lead parents to invest more in each child. Having fewer, better-educated, better-financed children becomes more attractive than spreading a family's investment over many children.[77] Also, as a country gains wealth through industrialization, it can more easily afford social security, pensions, health care, and other social benefits, reducing the tendency for parents to see their children as their future caregivers in old age.

Notestein called this sequence the *demographic transition,* a theory that is closely related to modernization theory. Demographic transition theory is an implicit critique of Malthusianism. It suggests that, rather than expanding until environmental constraints cause it to collapse, population growth eventually levels off of its own accord. The same factors that lead to population growth—scientific advances, industrialism, and modernization—are also those that eventually lead to a return to population stability, once societies adjust to their new-found social and technological circumstances.

Exhibit 4.4 *The demographic transition: In stage 1, a stable birth rate and a fluctuating death rate roughly cancel each other out, and population remains low and stable. In stage 2, the death rate drops while the birth rate remains initially high, and population rises rapidly. In stage 3, the birth rate declines until it roughly matches the death rate, once again leading to a stable population—but at a much higher level. Scholars question the applicability of this model of population change to lower income countries.*

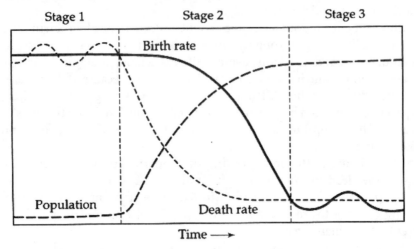

Source: Sarre (1991).

A New Demographic Transition?

Notestein based his model on the European experience. But scholars and development organizations seized on the idea that the less-developed countries might also eventually go through a demographic transition. If such an extension is correct, the solution to population problems would be for poor nations to continue down the path of modern development. Eventually, they theorize, the less-developed countries will grow out of rapid growth and the planning difficulties it causes. As a slogan that came out of the 1974 World Population Conference in Bucharest put it, "Development is the best contraceptive."[78]

The theory of demographic transition fits European history reasonably well (although there are plenty of exceptions, such as the drop in the birth rate experienced in many regions of France *before* mortality declined).[79] Yet there are substantial reasons to doubt the applicability of the demographic transition to the less-developed countries. A number of important conditions seem to set the contemporary less-developed countries apart from nineteenth-century Europe:

First, the rate of population growth currently experienced in most less-developed countries is considerably higher than the growth rate in nineteenth-century Europe. Since contemporary less-developed countries have been able to import already established medical technologies, mortality rates have declined much faster. At the same time, birth rates are far higher. Many European cultures of the nineteenth century practiced late marriage and frequent nonmarriage, as opposed to the practice of early and nearly universal marriage in most contemporary less-developed countries. High fertility and low mortality has in turn led to a young age structure throughout the less-developed world, leading to population momentum as younger generations reach their reproductive years.[80]

Second, the poverty that leads children to be regarded as a labor supply may be intractable in the face of contemporary forces of global inequality. Economic structures that channel wealth toward core countries may limit the extent to which less-developed countries will ever in fact develop, or at least may very much retard the spread of development's benefits.

Third, an increasing chorus of critics doubt the very desirability of some of those benefits. The principal doubt centers on the homogenizing tendency of development and the charge that development proceeds from a West-knows-best point of view. Critics see development not only as economic imperialism but as cultural imperialism as well. In the words of Wolfgang Sachs, "From the start, development's hidden agenda was nothing else than the Westernization of the world."[81] Hidden in the idea of "development" is the presumption that those who are "underdeveloped" or "less developed" or "developing" are missing something—that there is something inadequate about them. Western education and Western values do not liberate traditional peoples, argues Helena Norberg-Hodge, another critic of West-knows-best development.[82] Rather, they deny traditional peoples the cultural tools to function in anything but a Western economy, trapping them instead. Given that unequal relationships of economic exchange may prevent poor countries from becoming developed, or may delay development for generations, the trap is particularly tight.

Fourth, there is the environmental critique. Levels and inefficiencies of consumption associated with the European demographic transition may simply be unsustainable, and may as well compromise environmental justice and nature's rights and beauty. Even though only the wealthy few currently enjoy them, such consumption levels already seem to be compromising the environment—the situation may become far worse when the whole world tries to keep up with the Joneses. Although we must avoid the simplicity of crude Malthusianism, we must also avoid crude anti-Malthusianism. If the rest of the world is to attain development, then the meaning and the techniques of development must change.

In light of these critiques, there is increasing agreement among population specialists that if the poor countries of the world are to achieve a demographic transition, they will have to do so by different paths than European countries took.[83]

Women and Development

One vision of those different paths sees women having a key role in development. Scholars and development organizations now see improving the status of women both as an end in itself and also as one of the most significant means of reducing rapid population growth and improving the life chances of poor children.

The first two decades of development efforts, 1950 to 1970, gave scarcely any consideration to gender issues. Women were largely invisible, both as actors in and potential beneficiaries (or victims) of the development process. Ester Boserup's pathbreaking 1970 book, *Women's Role in Economic Development*, was the first work on development to highlight women, and it came as something of an academic bolt of lightening. Boserup pointed out that women in less-developed countries make vital contributions not only in the domestic sphere of reproduction but also in economic production.

In retrospect, Boserup's finding seems obvious, but at the time the official economic statistics of countries around the world consistently underestimated women's nondomestic work. For example, Egypt's national statistics for 1970 listed only 3.6 percent of the agricultural workforce as female. In-depth studies revealed quite a different picture. Half of women participated in plowing and leveling land, and three-quarters participated in dairy and poultry production.[84] A 1972 census in Peru registered only 2.6 percent of the agricultural workforce as female, whereas an interview study found 86 percent of women participating in field work.[85]

Boserup's survey found that, although there are substantial variations by region and by level of agricultural intensity, women do as much work in agriculture as men, if not more.[86] The kinds of agricultural work women and men perform do differ, however. Men tend to be more involved in the mechanized and animal-assisted aspects of production, such as plowing, and women tend to be more involved with hand operations, such as sowing seed and hoeing weeds. Contrary to stereotypes about the greater physical capabilities of men, women in fact do the bulk of the world's physical work.

Development efforts, however, were ignoring the implications of development policies for the kind of work women do and for women's status. In many rural regions in less-developed countries, particularly in Africa, women collect the bulk of fuel wood essential for cooking food—another activity dominated by women. Development policies stressing exports encouraged poor countries to convert forest lands to timber and crop production, taking little notice of their importance as a source of fuel wood. Women soon found themselves walking miles and miles each day to gather fuel. In general, the kinds of economic activity stressed by development projects emphasized men's work, underestimated the agricultural contributions of women, and almost completely ignored domestic work, seeing it as outside the money economy and therefore not really an economic activity at all.

The status of women in households and communities, as well as in politics and the economy, was not seen as a development issue at the time Boserup wrote. In the years afterward, however, issues of women's status and gender relations came closer to the center of the development debate. Scholars came to recognize that women were disproportionately represented in the ranks of the poor. Moreover, while women tended to live longer than men in the developed world, their longevity lagged considerably behind men's in the less-developed countries. The United Nations proclaimed 1976 to 1985 the Decade for Women, and now few development projects go ahead without some explicit attention to women, albeit often cursory.

One reason why "women in development" (or WID, as it is often called by development specialists) has captured so much interest is the increasing recognition of the importance of women in population issues. Demographic studies find that the status of women, measured through their education and participation in the paid economy, is the most consistent factor in fertility reduction.[87] Women frequently want to reduce fertility rates, sometimes in contrast to their male sexual partners.[88] When men come to see women as economic equals, they tend to see them more as social equals as well, and women gain more say in family planning and other family decisions. Education gives women, as well as men, a broader understanding of possibilities, eroding fatalism and building a sense of empowerment. The greater economic standing of women in paid work in an increasingly monetarized world also means that childbirth and child care can become more of an economic burden than an economic opportunity for families. As opposed to general economic development of the structural adjustment and modernization variety, improving women's standing may be one of the principal paths to a demographic transition for less-developed countries.

Some feminist critics are suspicious of this approach to development, which seems to view improving women's status as a means to the end of population stabilization, not as a moral end in itself. The emphasis should be on ending patriarchy, not on furthering women's economic development, argues Sylvia Walby.[89] Patriarchy is a system of social organization in which

women consistently receive lower status and less social power then men—
a system which, most scholars agree, still characterizes virtually all human
societies. Emphasizing women's economic development may be putting
the cart before the horse.

Part of the reason for this doubt about women's economic development
is the tendency to relegate women to lower-paid work. As less-developed
countries have tried to build their exports in order to reduce debt and
comply with structural adjustment plans, they have promoted cheap factory
work, generally performed by women. As Valentine Moghadam has put it,
women are the "new proletariat worldwide."[90]

There is considerable controversy among feminist scholars about this
phenomenon, often termed the *feminization of labor*.[91] Does it represent
the continued subordination of women in a new form, or does it represent
an opportunity for poor women to gain a better life for themselves and
their families through one of the few means available to them? Is it
empowerment or continued disempowerment?

I strongly suspect the answer is both. As other writers have argued,
improving women's status is not simply a means to population stabilization
and increased exports.[92] However it may be seen by the governments and
development agencies involved, improved status is good for both women
and their families. If nothing else, reproduction should be seen as a women's
health issue. Half a million women die each year from pregnancy-related
causes—some 200,000 through unsafe and illegal abortions and the others
through childbirth, postbirth infections, and other illnesses; 90 percent of
these deaths occur in less-developed countries.[93] Better women's health
also means better health for their children.

The persistence of patriarchy, despite improvements in women's health
and economic and social status, seems undeniable. Eliminating patriarchal
social relations is ultimately the only way to achieve equal status for women.
But the fact that attention is finally being given to women in development
(although perhaps not yet with sufficient sensitivity and commitment) should
not be seen merely as a patriarchal ploy. Rather, it may be a sign that the
world is beginning to acknowledge that improving the status of women is
good not only for women: It is good for everyone.

Family Planning and Birth Control

Another controversial aspect of population is the use of birth control in family
planning. The controversy stems partly from the coercive way that birth
control has been applied in some instances, partly from moral judgments
concerning some forms of birth control, and partly from questions about the
significance of birth control technologies in reducing fertility.

The promotion of birth control has some serious black marks on its record. One of the worst instances was India's National Population Policy of 1976, initiated during the eighteenth-month period between June 1975 and January 1977, when Prime Minister Indira Gandhi ruled as a dictator. Prime Minister Gandhi had been found guilty of election fraud, and in order to hold on to power she declared a national state of emergency. The press was censored, dissidents jailed, civil liberties curtailed. In this climate of extreme state control, the government put forth the National Population Policy under the direction of Mrs. Gandhi's son, Sanjay Gandhi. The policy emphasized sterilization—as well as health care, nutrition, and education for girls. Sterilization plans went quickly ahead, but the other aspects of the policy were more long-term and were basically ignored.

Most Indian states set bureaucratic quotas to monitor the "performance," as it was called, of the policy. Although people were paid for being sterilized, there was much coercive abuse as government officials in this strikingly undemocratic period in India's history struggled to meet their quotas. Near the capital, Delhi, the government set up vasectomy booths. People were harassed, threatened, and bribed. In about six months, some 8 million sterilizations were performed, mainly on the poor, who were vulnerable to the fees, harassment, and threats; they were probably more often targeted by the program as well. Hundreds died in the riots that broke out in protest, as well as through infections caused by the sterilization procedures. When Mrs. Gandhi finally lifted the national state of emergency, the program was quickly dropped.[94]

Instances such as this, or such as the sterilization of Native Americans that was carried out on some U.S. reservations, are intolerable. They can also lead people, in anger and suspicion, to associate all advocacy for population control with oppression. A number of critics have seen the concern about population as part of, to quote one author, a "racist eugenic and patriarchal tradition"— the fears of the rich and white about a rising darker-skinned horde, as well as an effort to control women's bodies.[95] Critics have had particular concern about the single-minded attention that some Malthusians have given to birth control as a means for reducing population growth, given that most contemporary population growth is outside the West.

Paul and Anne Ehrlich's 1990 book, *The Population Explosion*, may be a case in point. They predicted that, "the population explosion will come to an end before very long. The only remaining question is whether it will be halted through the human method of birth control, or by nature wiping out the surplus."[96]

There is nothing explicitly, and perhaps not even implicitly, racist about such a statement. Nevertheless, critics have argued that placing all the emphasis on birth control as a solution to population growth leaves intact the social inequality that is the primary cause of growth.[97] Whatever the intent of the Ehrlichs' position (and I believe the Erhlichs are in fact strongly committed to social equality), critics suggest that the effect would be the continuance of social inequality of race, class, and gender.

But just because racism, classism, and sexism have been a dimension of some birth control policies, and possibly some theories, this does not mean that birth control is necessarily racist, classist, or sexist. Indeed, preventing people from controlling births can be just as racist, classist, and sexist as any ill-conceived birth control policy. Reproduction, I believe most people would agree, is a basic human right. But so too is the right not to reproduce. Most couples around the world voluntarily seek to control and regulate—to plan—their reproduction. Limiting their ability to do so can be coercive too.

One example of a policy of coerced reproduction took place in the late 1960s in Romania under the regime of Nicolae Ceau§cescu, one of the most iron-fisted dictators of the twentieth century. In 1966, Ceau§cescu suddenly declared any form of birth control, as well as abortion, illegal. Women had to undergo gynecological exams every three months to determine if they were complying with the new law. As a result, birth rates doubled, at least initially.

Maternal mortality doubled too, with about 85 percent of these deaths due to botched abortions, illegally performed. Women across Romania also began avoiding gynecologists as much as possible, skipping appointments and failing to sign up for them, even for routine gynecological checkups. The result is that Romania now suffers from Europe's highest rate of death due to cervical cancer. Infant mortality also went up considerably (by one third) as parents neglected, abused, and even abandoned unwanted babies.[98]

Granting a right to control and plan births is not the same as approving of all forms of birth control and all national birth control policies. There is certainly extensive disagreement on the morality of some forms of birth control, particularly abortion. But one can disapprove of abortion and still support other means of controlling births.

The question remains, though, whether modern birth control technologies are effective means of reducing population growth. In detailed historical studies, scholars have noted that, at least in the European demographic transition, fertility decline generally began before modern birth control technologies were widely available. Indeed, in some places fertility declined even before industrialization began.

The point is, there is nothing new about family planning. People have been using, and continue to use, many family planning techniques other than the Pill, the diaphragm, the condom, the sponge, and other modern birth control technologies. Practices such as late marriage, extended nursing, abstinence, rhythm, withdrawal, and polyandry, among others, can be and have been effective forms of family planning.

But no doubt modern methods can be even more effective, which is one of the main reasons why so many couples across the world choose them, when they are available. The commitment to plan births is absolutely essential to the success of any family planning practice, however. If social conditions are such that people are unable or unwilling to make such a commitment, no technique can be effective. In other words, birth control and greater social equality can be complementary, rather than contradictory, social policies.

THE ENVIRONMENT AS A SOCIAL ACTOR

Malthus went too far. It is clearly incorrect to adopt a position of *environmental determinism*—the view that the environment controls our lives and that there is little we can do about it. The human population has certainly increased to unprecedented levels, despite environmental limits, and in many wealthy countries population levels have returned to stability for reasons other than environmental scarcity. Technological and social change have allowed societies across the world to increase the production of food and other resources. Although the numbers of the poor are growing, particularly in areas with rapid population growth, their poverty cannot be understood apart from the dynamics of the world economy.

But Malthus was not entirely wrong. Access to food depends not only on systems of entitlement; it also depends upon the environmental availability of food. Some resources seem hard to substitute with something else, even with the highest of technologies. And too often the risk inherent in some technologies puts the poor and marginal most in danger. Rapid population growth is also a problem in itself, apart from any environmental implications, both for organizing social benefits such as schools and a coordinated economy and for safeguarding the health of women and children. In other words, rapid growth can cause poverty, just as it is itself a product of poverty.

Moreover, because of the compounding effects of population with consumption and production, the question of growth and development is not merely one of finding enough food to feed everyone. It is also a question of whether we will ultimately be able to sustain everyone—humans and other creatures alike—if the competitive consumption and production levels of the world's rich become the ever-escalating norm.

Accepting a degree of *environmental agency*, accepting the environment's causal role in social life, is not the same as accepting environmental determinism. The role that the environment plays in our lives depends upon our interactions with it. The environment is not a given; we shape the significance it has. The environment is, in effect, a different place depending upon how we wish to use it and how we envision what it is. An environmental resource is only a resource if, because of our technical and social relations, we find it to be a resource. It is we who make resources as much as it is the environment that provides them to us. It is we who make the environment as much as it is the environment that makes us.

Perhaps the sociologist Fred Cottrel put it best: The environment limits what we *can* do and influences what we *will* do.[99] Take, for example, the process of technological change, which is often presented as constrained only by our imagination and not by the environment. Even the cornucopian vision of technological change presented by Julian Simon implicitly grants a considerable degree of agency to the environment. For Simon, environmental scarcity prompts technical innovation. Thus, the environment helps guide the directions in which we exercise our powers of imagination.

But we should not forget that the consumption and production in which the human population engages are aspects of the environment in their own right. They are not external forces that may or may not impact the environment. All human activities are part of the environmental dialogue of ecology.

One of the most important lessons to draw from that dialogue, I have tried to argue, is that population growth is a real issue in the conversation. But it is one that must always be understood within the context of consumption, production, and social inequality. Although birth rates among the wealthy are lower than rates among the poor, the consumption and production levels of the wealthy are far higher, and so are their per person environmental consequences, given current technological conditions. Social inequality—by region, class, race, ethnicity, and gender—is also in itself a principal factor in population growth, as well as growth in consumption and production. But the environmental consequences of population growth are real. And since we are a part of the environment, those consequences are necessarily consequences for us and how we may live.

Yet perhaps the most important dialogical lesson is that we can change the ecological dialogue. Changing the current dialogue of population growth seems to me to be a very good idea. Maybe we will be able to cope with the outcome of that dialogue in a way that provides general and sustainable well-being. Maybe. We're certainly not doing a great job of it now. But in order to do a better job, we need a dialogical understanding of the situation— an understanding that recognizes the complexity and interactiveness of social and ecologic life. For the problem of population is not just one of "too many people." Rather, it is also a problem of too many people with too much and too many people with not enough.

PART II

THE IDEAL

CHAPTER 5

The Ideology of Environmental Domination

No one seems to know
How useful it is to be useless.

-Chuang Tzu, third century B.C.E.

The view from Glacier Point in Yosemite National Park is one of the world's most famous. From this overlook you can see a sweeping panorama of Yosemite, which many have called the most beautiful valley in America. A number of years ago, my brother and sister-in-law, Jon and Steph, were visiting her relatives in California, and they decided to take Steph's grandmother to see Yosemite, where she had never been. An elderly woman, she did not walk well, so they took her only to sites you can get to by car. You can drive right up to Glacier Point, and they did. As Jon later recounted the story to me, they helped Steph's grandmother up to the edge and stood there for a few minutes taking it all in. Then Jon turned and asked her, somewhat hopefully, "Well, what do you think?"

She considered the question carefully, and replied, "All that forest. What a waste. There should be people and houses down there."

When two people look out on a scene, a scene of any kind, they are unlikely to appreciate it in just the same way. Faced with the same material circumstances, we each see something different. Where my brother Jon saw the beauty of wild nature in that view from Glacier Point, Steph's grandmother saw wasted resources. Such differences are a part of our individuality. They also reflect social differences in the apparatus of understanding that we use to organize our experience. There are larger social and historical patterns in the distinctive mental apparatuses we each bring to bear on the world around us. In a word, there is *ideology* at work.

In this second part of the book, we take ideal factors as the point of entry into the ecological dialogue. As we saw in the previous section, the other side of the dialogue is always close at hand, and we will find that here too. Investigation of ideal factors inevitably leads back to material questions. But the emphasis in chapters 5, 6, and 7 will be on the form the environment takes in our minds.

The independent power of ideas in our lives is well illustrated by the history of environmental ideas. The material conditions we now regard as environmental problems have long historical precedents, yet few in the first half of the twentieth century questioned the increasing per capita appetite for resources, the spread of the automobile and its sprawling land use, the invention of yet another chemical or mechanical weapon for every new instance of the environment's resistance to our desires. Articles in *National Geographic*, for example, extolled the industrial might that spawned marvel after marvel, as their titles imply: "Synthetic Products: Chemists Make a New World," "Coal: Prodigious Worker for Man," "The Fire of Heaven: Electricity Revolutionizes the Modern World," "The Automobile Industry: An American Art That Has Revolutionized Methods in Manufacturing and Transformed Transportation."

In the decades from 1960 on, though, the ideological situation changed dramatically in country after country, as chapter 6 discusses.[1] *National Geographic*, to continue with that thermometer of Western cultural values, began running articles with titles like these: "Our Ecological Crisis," "African Wildlife: Man's Threatened Legacy," "Nature's Dwindling Treasures," "Pollution, Threat to Man's Only Home," "The Tallgrass Prairie: Can It Be Saved?" A different ideology had taken more general hold, at least among the writers and editors (and, we can presume, many of the readers) of this perennially popular magazine.

Scholars have studied the role of ideology in the ecological dialogue in two broad ways, largely drawing on historical evidence. First, they have considered the ideological circumstances that make domination of the environment thinkable and tolerable, focusing on understanding Western cultural attitudes that support such a relationship to the environment. Second, scholars have considered the ideological circumstances that make such conditions and such domination increasingly unthinkable and intolerable, focusing on the social origins of the environmental movement.

Exhibit 5.1 Night falls on New Haven harbor in Connecticut: The human domination of the environment is particularly characteristic of the waterfronts of industrial port cities.

Photo: Mike Bell

This chapter considers that first role of ideology; chapter 6 the second. In this chapter, then, I examine the ideological origins of the view that human beings can and should transform the environment for their own purposes. Scholars argue that three Western intellectual traditions—Christianity, individualism, and patriarchy—have in large part provided the ideological rationale for environmental domination. These ideologies of environmental domination are by no means exclusively Western, but they are certainly heavily present in the West, which may help account for the central role of Western institutions in the industrial transformation of the earth. As well, all three of these ideologies of environmental domination have close links with ideas about hierarchy and inequality, suggesting an ideological connection between environmental domination and social domination, as we shall see.

CHRISTIANITY AND ENVIRONMENTAL DOMINATION

A common explanation for the modern urge to transform the earth is the rise of the industrial economy. But the next question to ask is, where did the industrial economy come from? As I suggested at various points in part 1 of this book, the development of economics should not be seen in purely materialist terms. Ideas of consumption, work, leisure, social status, and community infuse the economy as much as the economy infuses those ideas.

A major source of those ideas in the West is Christianity. As Max Weber argued in a famous 1905 book, *The Protestant Ethic and the Spirit of Capitalism*, Christian ideas—and, more specifically, Protestant ideas—form one of the great wellsprings of capitalist thought. It is more than accidental, said Weber, that the Protestant Reformation of the late sixteenth century immediately preceded the development of modern capitalism and the expansion of European economies all over the globe in the seventeenth, eighteenth, and nineteenth centuries. Capitalism is, in a way, a secular version of Protestantism.

The Moral Parallels of Protestantism and Capitalism

"A man does not 'by nature' wish to earn more and more money," Weber wrote, in the gendered phrasing of an earlier time, "but simply to live as he is accustomed to live and to earn as much as is necessary for that purpose."[2] So why do we work so hard to make more money than we need? A desire to maintain a place on the treadmills of consumption and production is part of it. But to leave the matter there does not answer the question of why we are on these treadmills to begin with.

The answer, suggested Weber, lies in the moral anxiety that early Protestantism inculcated in its followers. Medieval Catholicism was more forgiving, encouraging repentance and allowing last-minute, deathbed declarations of faith. If you were rich enough, you could literally buy your way into heaven by funding priests to say prayers for you and by purchasing "indulgences" from the church. But early Protestantism emphasized a kind of final weighing up of all the good and bad that a person had done in life, which made it harder to overcome one's misdeeds and made entrance into heaven less ideologically certain.

A lot of the anxiety stemmed from the idea of predestination—the idea that one is preordained either to go to hell or to be one of the "elect" who go on to heaven. Predestination was a common doctrine of early Protestants, particularly early Calvinists, and it ratcheted up moral anxiety by several notches. On the face of it, predestination seems a lousy way to motivate people, for it suggests that how you act in life doesn't matter. You are still going to go where it has been preordained that you will go. So why not lead a carefree life of sin, laziness, and gluttony? But the trick about predestination was that no one knew for sure who had grace—who was one of the elect and who was not—except through a person's worldly deeds. Those who were good, moral, upright, and successful in this life must be the elect of the next life, early Protestant creeds such as Calvinism taught.

Thus, in order to convince themselves and the community that they were among the elect, early Calvinists became ascetics, denying themselves bodily pleasures like laziness and working incredibly hard to achieve the signs of success in this life. And they began to rationalize the work process, making work more orderly and efficient, in order to maximize their worldly signs of moral worth. Basically, said Weber, early Calvinism was a competitive cult of work, denial, and rationalization.

Exhibit 5.2 John Calvin, 1509–1564: Scholars argue that Calvin's ascetic vision of Protestantism was one of the principal well-springs of the capitalist spirit and its tendencies toward environmental domination.

Source: Biblioteque Publique et Universitair de Geneve.

These same ideas still infuse economic life today, albeit without the religious framework (at least not explicitly). What has happened, Weber argued, is that we have secularized the idea that hard work and denial, rationally applied, are outward signs of how good and deserving one is. It remains one of the most basic assumptions of modern life that those who work hard are the most deserving, the most morally worthy of our admiration and of high salries. Hard workers are the elect of the heaven of social esteem. It is they who have grace.

And now we have little choice but to be hard-working rational ascetics ourselves, even if (as is likely the case) we do not follow the religious tenets of early Calvinism. The anxiety of early Protestants produced a fantastic accumulation of wealth. (If you work really hard, you are indeed more likely to achieve the worldly signs of success.) They reinvested this wealth, which led to even more wealth. And as each dedicated Protestant sought to increase his or her comparative success, the trend toward work, rationalization, and production accelerated. The treadmills of capitalism began turning ever faster. Soon one had to work hard, deny oneself, and rationalize one's life in order to attain any kind of economic foothold, for that was what everyone else was doing. Increasingly people came to accept the idea that those who worked hard deserved to get more and to gain everyone's respect; likewise they came to accept its corollary: that those who had less must not have worked so hard and therefore deserved their fate. The Protestant ethic had become the spirit of capitalism.

The history of capitalist development provides some support for Weber's thesis. Modern capitalism arose first in the dominantly Protestant countries: England, Scotland, the United States, and Germany. Within Europe even today, the least wealthy and least industrialized countries remain the least Protestant: the dominantly Catholic countries of Portugal, Spain, and Ireland, and the dominantly Christian Orthodox countries of Greece and much of Eastern Europe. France and Italy fit less well into this pattern; both are dominantly Catholic but are heavily industrialized and infused with an ascetic work ethic. However, they both industrialized comparatively recently.

Now modern capitalism is spreading well beyond the confines of dominantly Protestant countries, and even beyond the dominantly Christian countries. Religion is no longer the driving force. The capitalist spirit steadily enfolds country after country into its secularized ethic of ascetic rationalism. Economic structures have taken over from Martin Luther and John Calvin in spreading this spirit, even as this spirit dialogically propels the structures, as in the way hard work speeds the treadmill faster and faster.

Ascetic rationalism has become what Weber termed "an iron cage."[3] As Weber put it, "This order is now bound to the technical and economic conditions of machine production which today determine the lives of all the individuals who are born into this mechanism, not only those directly concerned with economic acquisition, with irresistible force. Perhaps it will so determine them until the last ton of fossilized coal is burnt."[4] In a way, we're all Calvinists now.

The Moral Parallels of Christianity, Science, and Technology

Weber is not the only scholar who has traced a connection between Western religion and social developments that greatly impact the environment. In 1967, the historian Lynn White published a short essay that remains one of the most influential and widely read analyses of the environmental predicament: "The Historical Roots of our Ecologic Crisis." White's basic argument was that environmental problems cannot be understood apart from the Western origins of modern science and technology, which in turn derive from "distinctive attitudes toward nature that are deeply grounded in Christian dogma."[5] Not only does the economy of the West have religious origins, then, but Western science and technology do as well.

Many ancient cultures participated in laying the foundation stones of science—notably China and the Islamic world. Yet, White argued, "by the late thirteenth century Europe had seized global scientific leadership."[6] The achievements of Newton, Galileo, Copernicus, and other medieval scientists were accompanied by rapid advances in Western technology. White placed particular emphasis on the development of powered machines: the weight-driven clock, wind mills, water-powered sawmills, and blast furnaces.

Even more significant, though, was the development of the mold-board plow in northern Europe during the latter part of the seventh century. The mold-board plow dramatically changed human attitudes toward the environment, said White. Previous plows had allowed farmers only to scratch at the ground. These shallow plows were adequate for the light soils of the Near East and the Mediterranean, although they restricted agriculture to being pretty much a subsistence affair, with little surplus for trade. The generally heavy soils of the North, on the other hand, required a stronger plow. The mold-board was invented to cut more deeply into the ground, loosening up the heavy northern soils. The difficult work of the mold-board plow normally took the pull of eight oxen, as opposed to the one or two used by earlier plows.

Exhibit 5.3 *A Medieval illustration of an ox-drawn moldboard-plow: According to historian Lynn White, the invention of the mold-board plow in about the 7th century radically altered European sensibilities toward environmental transformation.*

Source: Folger Shakespeare Library.

Thus the mold-board plow was essentially a powered machine. In White's words, "Man's relation to the soil was profoundly changed. Formerly man had been part of nature; now he was the exploiter of nature."[7] Formerly we had seen ourselves on a par with the natural world. Now we saw ourselves as standing above it, at least potentially.

Why this change? This exploitative and domineering attitude toward the environment, encompassing both unlettered farmers and scientific intellectuals, was so specific to one region that its origins must lie in a broad intellectual trend, White argued. The likely trend was one of the great intellectual revolutions of the Western tradition: the Judeo-Christian ethic. For at roughly the same time that northern farmers were developing the mold-board plow to handle their heavy soils, White noted, they were also giving up paganism for Christianity.

For the pagan, the world is full of spirits. Every rock and tree is potentially animated by something. Nature is alive, organic, and magical. It is cyclical, and we are part of it. Early Christianity, on the other hand, building on Judaic philosophy, saw time as linear and nonrepeating, and it saw the environment as dead and inanimate, as separate from people. For early Christianity, the spirit world of God and the saints was not *immanent* in nature—that is, suffused throughout nature, making nature a direct embodiment of spirits— but rather *transcendent* above nature.

Moreover, early Christian doctrine taught that God gave the world to human beings to exploit, to change and recreate, much as God himself could do (which is why only human beings are made in God's image, many Christians believe). Changing nature was no longer a sacrilege. Indeed, Judeo-Christianity counseled that it was God's will that we do so. In the words of Genesis, "And God said: Let us make man in our image, after our likeness; and let them have dominion over the fish of the sea, and over the fowl of the air, and over the cattle, and over all the earth, over every creeping thing that creepeth upon the earth" [Genesis 1:26]. The Judeo-Christian ethic thus gave us moral license to change the world as we see fit. As White put it, "Christianity is the most anthropocentric religion the world has ever seen."[8]

The Greener Side of the Judeo-Christian Ethic

The coincidence of the development of medieval technology and science alongside the spread of Christianity is intriguing and suggestive. The biblical license to dominate the earth likely at least facilitated the development of technology and science. The association of the Protestant Reformation with the subsequent rise of modern capitalism and the striking parallels between contemporary secular morals and the ascetic rationalism of early Protestantism also suggest an important influence of religious ideas on our material conditions.

But we cannot conclude that Judeo-Christianity unambiguously promotes science, technological progress, and capitalism at the expense of the environment. For one thing, Christianity has often been at odds with science. Consider the conflict between medieval scientists and the established Church. The inquisition of Galileo for heresy is only the most well-known example. Far from welcoming science as a way of proving that, yes, God is indeed transcendent and that nature is an inanimate machine driven forward through linear time, the Church found its authority threatened by the development of scientific thought. Even though almost all early scientists, including Galileo, presented their work as theological efforts to understand the true meaning of God, Church authorities only grudgingly accepted the argument that science was about faith. And today, many Christian religious leaders object to a range of scientific techniques, such as genetic engineering. "Dolly," the sheep that Scottish scientists announced in 1997 had been successfully cloned, was greeted by many Christians as a blasphemy.

Another sign of Judeo-Christianity's ambivalent views about environmental transformation are certain biblical passages. For example, right before the famous line in the Bible in which God tells Noah and his family to leave the ark and says, "Be ye fruitful, and multiply," which sounds rather domineering, there is a more ecological passage: "And God spoke unto Noah, saying, Go forth from the ark, thou, and thy wife, and thy sons, and thy sons' wives with thee. Bring forth with thee every living thing that is with thee of all flesh, both fowl, and cattle, and every creeping thing that creepeth upon the earth; that they may swarm in the earth, and be fruitful and multiply upon the earth" [Genesis 8:15–17].

Note that in this passage, the animals too are given the right to "be fruitful and multiply"—in fact, even before people are given that right—and Noah is ordered to help make it happen. There is an even more ecological passage later on when God promises to establish a covenant both with Noah and with "every living creature," promising not to bring on another flood: "And God said: This is the token of the covenant which I make between Me and you and every living creature that is with you, for perpetual generations: I have set my bow in the cloud, and it shall be a token of a covenant between Me and the earth" [Genesis 9:12–13].

This passage could be read as suggesting that we're not the only beneficiaries in the rainbow covenant. The covenant includes "every living creature that is with you." And when the covenant is restated half a sentence later, human beings are not even specifically mentioned. The covenant is "between Me and the earth." (And indeed, many contemporary Judeo-Christians read these lines in this more ecologically inclusive way.)[9]

Another problem with viewing Judeo-Christianity as the unambiguous source of our faith in science, technology, and progress is that Judeo-Christianity is a geographically and ideologically diverse tradition. The Eastern Christianity of Constantinople, for example, was not linked to the development of science and technology to the degree that the Latin Christianity of Western Europe was. Why not? Surely Eastern Christians had environmental constraints of their own to contend with and therefore had equal incentive to develop science, technology, and a domineering attitude toward the environment.

Thus White's focus on Judeo-Christianity may have been somewhat misplaced. The environmental ideas he discusses—linear time, an inanimate world, the dichotomy between people and nature, anthropocentrism—are certainly not explicit aspects of the Judeo-Christian religions. They do not appear in the Ten Commandments or the Sermon on the Mount, for example. And Judeo-Christianity, as we have seen, is neither exclusively Western nor unified in its teachings.

We might more accurately describe these ideas that support the domination and transformation of the environment as an underlying philosophy of the West, rather than of Judeo-Christianity alone. This does not mean that religion has no role here, though. As the principal religious tradition of the West, Judeo-Christianity must be amenable to such ideas if they are to remain widespread. Indeed, any religious tradition capable of gathering such a wide range of cultures under its tent must be amenable to a similarly wide range of interpretations. The origin of modern ideas about the relationship between humans and the environment is therefore likely more than merely religious.

Non-Western Philosophies and the Environment

Non-Western philosophic and religious traditions, however, do generally give recommendations for how humans ought to act toward the environment that are strikingly different from much Western thought. These traditions often promote a more egalitarian relationship with the earth as well as an acceptance of the environment as it is.

Taoism, for example, advises *wu-wei*, or "nonaction," as the route to contentment. Nonaction does not mean nondoing. It is working with, instead of against, nature by attempting to act without deliberate effort. (Translating Taoism into Western terms is difficult, but "nature" is certainly close to what is meant here.)[10] Here is an explanation of *wu-wei* from one the great Taoist classics, *The Way of Chuang Tzu*, which dates from the third century B.C.E.:

> Fishes are born in water
> Man is born in Tao.
> If fishes, born in water,
> Seek the deep shadow
> Of pond and pool,
> All their needs
> Are satisfied.
> If man, born in Tao,
> Sinks into the deep shadow
> Of *non-action*
> To forget aggression and concern,

He lacks nothing
His life is secure.
Moral: "All the fish needs
Is to get lost in water.
All man needs is to get lost
In Tao."[11]

Such a moral certainly does not appear to provide much license for transforming the earth to suit human concerns. Rather, Taoism counsels the forgetting of concern so as to avoid the inevitable sorrow of materialism. When one "tries to extend his power over objects, those objects gain control of him," observes the *Chuang Tzu*.[12]

Yet as the geographer Yi-Fu Tuan observed, China has long been one of the regions of the world most transformed by human action, despite the influence of Taoism and Buddhism. The ancient Chinese canal system, the extensive clearing of the land for cultivation, the formal gardening style of Chinese park land—all these represent considerable alteration of the environment. Such transformations continue today in huge projects such as the Seven Gorges Dam, accelerating urbanization, the mechanization of Chinese agriculture, and the ready adoption of a consumer lifestyle by many of China's over 1 billion inhabitants.

Nor are asceticism and rationalism new to non-Western cultures. Rationalism built ancient China's canals, agricultural system, formal gardens, cities, centralized government, and complex philosophical systems. Ascetic denial has long been a part of the training of Japanese samurai warriors as well as an important moral ideal in Japanese life.[13] The ascetic rationalism of early Protestantism was not unique to the West.

None of this proves Weber and White fundamentally wrong. It just reins them in a bit. Medieval Christianity likely did play an important role in promoting our contemporary acceptance of environmental transformation and exploitation, at least in the West. Early Protestantism similarly helped promote the train of reasoning that led to the rise of modern capitalism and the secular ideas of hard work and rationality now common throughout the West. But religion was not the only path that led to these increasingly global sensibilities.

INDIVIDUALISM AND ENVIRONMENTAL DOMINATION

Another path that has also led to environmental transformation is *individualism*, the emphasis on the self over the wider community that has long been a central dimension of the Western tradition. Individualism does not mentally prepare us to recognize how interconnected we all are with our wider surroundings, both social and environmental. With an individualistic frame of mind, we tend to ignore the consequences of our actions on those wider surroundings and therefore, because of our interconnections, sometimes on ourselves as well. Moreover, we in the West have understood that emphasis on the self in competitive and hierarchical ways. Thus we pursue our individualistic ambitions not just with "invisible elbows" that jostle others accidentally but with elbows deliberately braced for bumping and shoving aside whoever, and whatever, stands in our way.

The Ecology of the Body

One of the many scholars who has connected our Western sense of hierarchical individualism with environmental domination is Mikhail Bakhtin, a Russian social theorist. Bakhtin pointed out that individualism deeply influences the way we regard the main medium by which we are connected to the environment: our bodies. Individualism encourages us to see our bodies as sealed off from others and the natural world, with a host of consequences for what we regard as dirty, as repulsive, as polite, as scary, and as humorous. All of these cultural responses to how our bodies interact with the world have important environmental implications, as we shall see.[14]

Bakhtin based his argument on an unusual source: the quality of humor in the writings of the early French Renaissance writer, François Rabelais.[15] The novels of Rabelais are infamous for their scatological satire of French politics of the sixteenth century. They recount, in graphic detail, the outlandish and vulgar careers of Gargantua and his son Pantagruel, both fabulously obese giants. (The English word "gargantuan" derives from Rabelais's novels.) The two giants lead an outrageous life centered on feasting, drinking, excreting, copulating, giving birth, and other earthy acts. Woven through the stories are references to the political figures of the day, who usually appear in unseemly and ridiculous situations.

Rabelais's novels, published together nowadays under the title *Gargantua and Pantagruel*, caused quite a stir when they first appeared. Rabelais was often in political trouble because of them. (But he also found widespread favor, even among many of the political figures he lampooned, because even the king and his courtiers found the novels downright funny.)

The political references in Rabelais's novels no longer mean much to readers. Nevertheless, his writings remain controversial—but for a different reason: their style, a style which many modern readers find distasteful and obscene.[16] Bakhtin sought to understand why Rabelais's style of humor, rather than the subject of his humor, is now so offensive. Why is it that references to the body and all its everyday—and biologically essential— activities should be considered dirty and indecent?

Like Rabelais's novels, Bakhtin's answer caused quite a stir. His book on the subject, *Rabelais and His World*, could not be published until 1965, twenty-five years after it was written.[17] Writing during the height of Stalinist repression, Bakhtin was often in trouble with the authorities. He was denied employment and eventually forced into exile in Kazakhstan during the 1930s. After World War II he was able to regain the teaching job he had briefly held earlier at an obscure Russian university. Most other scholars still thought him dead, though. Then in the 1960s, some graduate students at Moscow's Gorky Institute rediscovered him. Now that Stalin was gone, *Rabelais and His World* was finally published, and Bakhtin's earlier works were reread and brought back into print. By the time Bakhtin died in 1975, his works were being read all over the world.

I tell the story of Bakhtin's career because it highlights the strong reactions that people often have to reminders that our own bodies perform the same basic functions as any other animal's body. But people did not always react in this way. Bakhtin says that we moderns are offended because of a historical shift in our conceptions of the body, from what Bakhtin termed the carnivalesque body to the classical body.

The *carnivalesque body* is a body of interconnections and exchanges with the social and natural environment. It is a body of openings and protrusions which connect us with other bodies and with the world around us: the mouth, the nose, the anus, the genitals, the stomach. Through these organs of connection, we exchange substances, some made by the body and some brought into the body from other bodies and from the surrounding world: air, smells, food, saliva, nasal mucus, urine, excrement, the various genital fluids, sweat, tears, mother's milk. It is also a body that relishes bodily acts and desires: eating, drinking, laziness, sleeping, snoring, sneezing, excreting, copulating, giving birth, nursing, kissing, hugging. The emphasis of the carnivalesque body is on what Bakhtin described as the body's "lower stratum." The carnivalesque body is also an ecological body, a body that is forever interacting and exchanging with natural systems.

The *classical body*, on the other hand, is a body of separation from society and nature. Most of its orifices are hidden from view. Those that are not hidden are carefully controlled through rituals that de-emphasize their openness. Food is carefully introduced into the mouth with a fork, and the mouth is quickly closed again. The nose is blown into a kleenex or handkerchief, and the mucus is carefully kept out of sight. The classical body does not belch, pass wind, cough or sneeze on others, eat with an open mouth, sweat, cry, or experience sexual desire. Excretory acts are kept strictly private. Openly discussing any of these activities is considered rude and immature, unless carried out under the strict linguistic supervision of "polite" language, such as I am using here. Emphasis is on the body's upper stratum. And the body's means of ecological connection become shameful.

The Carnivalesque Body. Bakhtin drew the term "carnivalesque" from the annual pre-Lenten festival of carnival, once one of the most important dates on the medieval calendar but which survives today in only a few places. Carnival traditionally was the people's holiday, often lasting for days. It was a time of merriment, feasting, parades, dancing, music, and general indulgence. It was a time for the outrageous.

But most importantly, carnival was a time of connection. In carnival, the community becomes all one flesh. (The *carn* in carnival means "flesh.") Everyone, high status and low, joined together in celebration. It was a time of social "uncrowning," as Bakhtin termed it, a time when the high and mighty were brought back down to earth, the people's earth. By partaking of food and drink together, by dancing together, by joking together (often through references to the lower stratum of the body that we all have, and through references to the substances that pass though that lower stratum), by celebrating the earth's abundance with feasting and indulgence, people celebrated their connections with each other and the world. Through these constant references to the bodily connections we all share—the need for food, the pleasures of leisure, the desires of the flesh, the substances that pass from and through bodies—even the famous and highly esteemed were brought down to a common level.

These carnivalesque pleasures are what we find described in Rabelais's novels, said Bakhtin.

Bakhtin makes a crucial distinction between the carnivalesque and bodily references that are merely gross and degrading, however. In carnivalesque humor, the subject of the joke is not brought beneath the tellers of the joke. Rather, it is egalitarian humor that seeks to unite everyone on the same earthy, bodily, social plane. We laugh not just at the subject of the joke but at ourselves too. Carnivalesque humor is not mere mocking; it is, as Bakhtin put it, "also directed at those who laugh."[18] It is laughter that joins us all together in the joke, renewing community. Degrading jokes, on the other hand, create hierarchy and separation. They seek to lower others without bringing them into the same common earthy community of bodily life.

Exhibit 5.4 This painting from 1498—Piero di Cosimo's The Discovery of Honey—*celebrates the festive and open-mouthed character of what theorist Mikhail Bakhtin calls the "carnivalesque body." As in di Cosimo's painting, such a body relishes exchanges and interactions with society and the natural world, rather than presenting itself as a sealed-off monad.*

Source: Worcester Art Museum.

Bakhtin wrote in defense of the carnivalesque. But he worried that bodily humor had become, "nothing but senseless abuse . . . Laughter [has been] cut down to cold humor, irony, sarcasm. It [has] ceased to be a joyful and triumphant hilarity."[19]

He also wrote to make a historical point. Why do we moderns have such trouble distinguishing between the carnivalesque and the merely gross? Why do we so often find any references to the body to be offensive and shameful? Because, Bakhtin argues, social mores have changed from medieval and early Renaissance times, in tandem with the modern rise of hierarchical individualism.

The Classical Body. Thus, a work like *Gargantua and Pantagruel* is generally offensive today not because of its politics (what offended some early Renaissance readers) but because of its affront to bodily individualism (what virtually all early Renaissance readers found deliciously funny.) Today we find individualism a lot harder to laugh at. We are ashamed at references to our bodily connections with the world. Nature itself has become offensive.

This change is evident not only in humor but in modern codes of politeness, cleanliness, and privacy. Today we eat with cutlery, particularly in formal situations. Medieval people ate with their fingers. Today we find it impolite to eat with an open mouth or with slurping noises. Medieval people were not so troubled. We have historically astonishing standards of cleanliness for our homes and bodies. We confine most bodily acts to the privacy of the bedroom and bathroom. In fact, the bathroom has become a kind of modern shrine to the individual, and expensive modern homes often include one for every member of the family, plus one for any guests—four- and five-bathroom homes have become the standard in exclusive housing developments. And we medicalize birth, death, and all the stages in between of the body's growth and interactions with life. We keep the environment as much at a distance from our bodies as we can. Again, medieval people were not so troubled.

Why do we do all these things? Because, Bakhtin argues, they are rituals of individualism and social hierarchy. In order to be elite, you need to separate yourself from the common people. Separation from nature and bodily functioning is a particularly convincing way to make that distinction. As Thorstein Veblen noted, elites try to remove themselves from environmental concerns in part because doing so indicates social power. Bakhtin would add that such environmental separation also entails showing oneself to be above bodily concerns. It requires what Weber would recognize as a kind of ascetism, a denial of bodily existence.

Having servants and machines to handle dirt, trash, and bodily excretions; being able to get through the day wearing the most impractical of clothes; traveling by means other than one's own bodily locomotion; maintaining impeccable standards of cleanliness for one's home and body; having a house and workplace big enough for separate rooms for private acts, and separate kinds of rooms for each kind of act—to acquire these forms of ecological and social separation requires power. It requires money and status. Such separation is far harder for those without money and power, thus clearly establishing who is on top and who is on the bottom.

Our desires for social distinction are thus intimately connected with our desire to distance ourselves from the body, from the earth, and from ecological reality. We cannot admit that we are connected to the earth, for doing so would undermine the very feeling of separation and distinction that modern life seeks. Seeking to live the life of the individual, we model ourselves after the classical image of the body and find references to carnivalesque connection dirty and threatening. We pretend that we have no need to heed nature's call.

Balancing the Ecological Self and the Ecological Community

As often happens when someone hits upon a new idea, Bakhtin probably overstated his case. His portrayal of medieval and early Renaissance life seems filtered through a romantic mist.[20] This period was not a golden age of unending feasting, merrymaking, and communalism. There was much hierarchy then too, as well as grinding poverty, poor sanitation, and disease. Bodily connections with society and with the environment can be fatal, a point that surely was significant to medieval people. (But so too can be attempts to deny such connections.) Thus we cannot pass off the modern interest in sanitation and medical intervention as merely the product of raging individualism.

We also need to be cautious about seeing the rise of a classical conception of the body and its implication of ecological separation as a purely Western phenomenon. Rather, it is characteristic of elites the world over. Nearly all elites adopt refined lifestyles that insulate them from the dirty, sweaty, smelly consequences of being a human animal. Bakhtin would have readily accepted this point, in fact. And he would have added that common people have long responded to the pretensions of the world's elites with carnivalesque humor. In Bakhtin's words, "Every act of world history was accompanied by a laughing chorus."[21]

Finally, we need to keep a sense of balance with respect to the carnivalesque and the classical. I for one am not prepared to lead a life of the purely carnivalesque. Besides, even during medieval times carnival was not an everyday occurence, although the spirit of carnival was no doubt a more regular presence in the lives of medieval people. Probably it ought to be in ours. But neither should we give up all forms of bodily individuality. A sense of our own difference is, after all, essential to a feeling of connection, for there must be something to connect. It's another dialogue.

Yet we also need to balance a classical conception of our selves and our bodies with a carnivalesque understanding that we are part of nature. Evidence suggests that we may be coming around to this point of view. The West has substantially changed its attitudes about the body in the fifty years since Bakhtin wrote *Rabelais and His World*. Thanks in large measure to the social changes and social movements of the 1960s, we are no longer so ashamed to speak of the body (although there are signs that such shame may be on the rise again). Hippie culture and the women's movement both emphasized the importance of being open about the body, its needs, its functions, and its realities. Hippies emphasized a more natural body style, breaking the taboos of long hair for men and leg hair and underarm hair for women, for example. Feminists helped break down the misconceptions and sense of shame long associated with women's bodies, perhaps most notably through the publication of the revolutionary book *Our Bodies Ourselves*.

These social changes suggest a connection between environmental awareness and bodily awareness. It may be no accident that the 1960s saw both an environmental movement and a body-awareness movement. In other words, accepting the importance of environmental interactions may depend in part upon accepting a more ecological—and thus less hierarchical and more democratic— conception of the body.

GENDER AND ENVIRONMENTAL DOMINATION

Another source of our domineering attitudes toward the environment is gender relations. Consider, for example, the common metaphors we in the West use to describe the environment and our interactions with it, metaphors that are strikingly sexual and militaristic. The pioneers in North America "broke virgin land" and cleared "virgin forest." Farmers have long spoken of the "fertility" of the soil, and surveyors and military commanders assess the "lay of the land." Mariners sail on the "bosom of the deep." The environment in general is "Mother Nature." We speak of abuse of the environment as "raping the land," and we speak of civilization as the "conquest of nature." The sex of the environment in these examples, sometimes implied, sometimes overtly stated, is female.

In light of the violence of some of the imagery—the "breaking," "clearing," "rape," and "conquest" of female nature—these are disturbing metaphors. They suggest, along with a range of other evidence, that there is an ideological link between the domination of nature and the domination of women. If patriarchal ideas pervade our thinking about society, then they likely influence our thinking about the environment as well for we must use the same mind, the same culture, to understand both.

The Ecology of Patriarchy

Note the common Western tendency to consider women as being closer to nature than men. Not only is nature female, but females are more natural, our traditions often suggest. We tend to associate women with reproduction—with the natural necessities of giving birth, raising children, preparing food—and with the domestic sphere, the realm of social life where we attend to reproduction and bodily and emotional needs. In contrast, we have conventionally associated men with production—with transforming nature so that it does what we want it to—and with the public sphere, the realm of rationality, civilization, government, and business.

These gendered associations imply a clear hierarchy, with men on top. Western thinkers have often considered women inferior because of their alleged closeness to nature and men as superior because of their allegedly greater skills in the allegedly higher aspects of human life. For example, the ancient Christian philosopher Thomas Aquinas thought of woman as "a necessary object . . . who is needed to preserve the species or to provide food and drink." Edmund Burke, the late eighteenth-century English philosopher, wrote that "a woman is but an animal and an animal not of the highest order." Hegel felt that "women are certainly capable of learning, but they are not made for the higher forms of science, such as philosophy and certain types of creative activities." Sigmund Freud mused that "women represent the interests of the family and sexual life; the work of civilization has become more and more men's business."[22]

The social implications of such a patriarchal hierarchy are quite troubling, many writers now argue, and so too are the environmental implications. By demeaning women for their stereotypical association with reproduction and with nature we encourage both the domination of women and the domination of the environment.

Ecofeminism. The work of these writers comes out of a new tradition of scholarly and philosophical inquiry, *ecofeminism*, which explores the links between the domination of women and the domination of the environment and argues that the domination of the environment originates together with social domination of all kinds—across not only gender but also race, ethnicity, class, age, and other forms of social difference treated as hierarchies.[23] It is common for socially dominated groups to be linked with nature, ecofeminists observe. People of color have often been associated with savagery. Lower classes have often been seen as primitive and as having inadequate control over their emotions, leading to a greater tendency toward violence and sexual licentiousness. And women have often been relegated to the realm of nature and its reproductive requirements, as opposed to reason and civilization.

It seems that when we think social hierarchy, we think natural hierarchy— and probably vice versa, too. Val Plumwood has written, the "human domination of nature wears a garment cut from the same cloth as intra-human domination, but one which, like each of the others, has a specific form and shape of its own."[24]

Environmental activists themselves have sometimes promoted the association of women with nature, for example by using the image of "Mother Earth." ("Love your mother," referring to the earth, is an ever-popular environmental slogan.) In this case, nature is being positively valued, and the activists who use the expression probably feel that it therefore positively values women as well, reversing the traditionally negative connotation of being associated with nature.

This is an ideologically dangerous strategy, say some ecofeminists. Listen to this statement from Charles Sitter, senior vice-president of Exxon, who used the image of Mother Earth to minimize the significance of the *Exxon Valdez* oil spill in Alaska's Prince William Sound, "I want to point out that water in the Sound replaces itself every twenty days. The Sound flushes itself out every twenty days. Mother Nature cleans up and does *quite* a cleaning job."[25]

This "Mom-will-pick-up-after-us" vision of the environment, as Joni Seager and Linda Weltner have termed it, is both ecologically problematic and sexist. As Weltner put it, "Men are the ones who imagine that clean laundry gets into their drawers as if by magic, that muddy footprints evaporate into thin air, that toilet bowls are self-cleaning. It's these over-indulged and over-aged boys who operate on the assumptions that disorder—spilled oil, radioactive wastes, plastic debris—is someone else's worry, whether that someone else is their mother, their wife, or Mother Earth herself."[26]

But the point of ecofeminism is not to blame men for environmental problems. Nor are all ecofeminists women.[27] Ecofeminists, like other feminist scholars, are concerned about our patriarchal system of social organization which is enacted by both men and women but results in the domination of women. What ecofeminists add to feminist theory is the notion that the domination of nature is linked to patriarchy and other forms of social domination, and vice versa. But like men, women too have been active agents in the domination of nature. Plumwood points out that, "Western women may not have been in the forefront of the attack on nature, driving the bulldozers and operating the chainsaws, but many of them have been the support troops, or have been participants, often unwitting but still enthusiastic, in a modern consumer culture of which they are the main symbols, and which assaults nature in myriad direct and indirect ways daily."[28]

• •

SOCIAL ACTION CASE STUDY
WOMEN AND ENVIRONMENTAL LEADERSHIP

Some of the most important leaders of the modern environmental movement have been women. In a perfect world this would be no cause for particular notice, but in the world we have, men still generally dominate the leadership of government, business, and social movements. Thus it is important to underline the prominence of women in modern environmentalism, women like writer and biologist Rachel Carson in the United States, former Green Party leader Petra Kelly in Germany, the writer and social critic Vandana Shiva in India, and sustainable development advocate and former prime minister Gro Bruntland in Norway. Indeed, women have been among the environmental movement's most influential global advocates.

But the global roles of these women should not overshadow the equally important roles women have played in local environmental leadership. Perhaps the best-known example of a woman leading a local environmental movement in the developed world is Lois Gibbs, founder of the Love Canal Homeowners Committee.

Incredibly, the modest neighborhood of Love Canal, New York, was built on land where Hooker Chemical Corporation had dumped 21,000 tons of chemical waste. Under the leadership of Lois Gibbs and other local women, the homeowners committee successfully lobbied the state and federal governments to take notice of the black oil oozing through basement walls, the strong chemical smells, and the death of trees, grass, and flowers in the Love Canal neighborhood. Gibbs had become particularly concerned when her son began to experience severe attacks of asthma, and even occasional convulsions, when he went to school. Eventually, the federal government bought out 700 homes in the area. In response to calls she was getting from local activists around the country facing similar problems, Gibbs later went on to found the Citizens' Clearinghouse for Hazardous Waste, which exchanges information, provides technical assistance, and coordinates national action on local toxic waste problems.

In India, the ten-year long struggle against the Narmada River dam projects has been led by a forty-year-old woman, Medha Patkar. Hundreds of thousands of people would be displaced by the dams, including some 320,000 by the project's largest dam, the Sardar Sarovar. Also, the Narmada is the holiest river in the

Hindu tradition. But World Bank funding was available to a national government hungry for the power to industrialize, and the project went ahead despite vigorous opposition from local people, and indeed from much of the world. Medha Patkar has led the nonviolent Narmada Bachao Andolan, the Save the Narmada Movement. She has testified, gone on hunger strikes, defied police orders, and been arrested numerous times. In one particularly dramatic incident, she and several other Narmada Bachao Andolan leaders threatened *jal samarpan*, suicide by drowning, in the waters already impounded by the still-under-construction Sardar Sarovar Dam. At the last moment, the Indian government conceded to most of the group's demands, and the *jal samarpan* was called off. Finally, the Indian Supreme Court suspended work on the dam in 1995, pending review.

The work of the Narmada Bachao Andolan is not over, nor is that of the Citizen's Clearinghouse for Hazardous Waste. But the strength and determination of Lois Gibbs, Medha Patkar, and thousands of women and men like them have already achieved much that millions can be thankful for.

• •

Patriarchal Dualisms. A key tenet of ecofeminism is that our cultural climate of domination has been built on *dualisms*—morally charged, oppositional categories with little gray area in between—that deny the dependency of each upon the other. Thus, man is man, and woman is woman. Nature is nature, and culture is culture. Our dualisms interlock into a larger cultural system of domination, ecofeminists such as Plumwood argue. Culture versus nature, reason versus nature, male versus female, mind versus body, machine versus body, master versus slave, reason versus emotion, public versus private, self versus other.[29] In each dichotomy, the first member of each pair dominates over the second. The core dichotomy, Plumwood writes, "is the ideology of the control of reason over nature."[30] The dominating side in each pair is culturally linked to reason, and the dominated side is culturally linked to nature.

This tendency to separate the world into antagonistic pairs, ecofeminists suggest, is a legacy of a Western us-versus-them *logic of domination.* Ecofeminists advocate a different form of logic, one that recognizes gray areas and interdependence, and one that recognizes difference without making hierarchies. They want us to be able to make categorical distinctions that respect the diversity and interactiveness of the world and that do not rely on absolutist, mechanical, and hierarchical boundaries.

Exhibit 5.5 *The dualisms of Western thought: Ecofeminists argue that an interlocking series of polarized and morally-charged categories underlie much of Western philosophy, and that these categories denigrate both women and nature.*

culture	nature
reason	nature
mind	nature
human	nature
male	female
mind	body
master	slave
reason	matter
reason	emotion
rationality	animality
freedom	necessity
universal	particular
civilized	primitive
production	reproduction
public	private
subject	object
self	other

Source: Plumwood (1994).

The Western logic of domination is not just an intellectual problem, say ecofeminists; it has all-too-real material outcomes. Under Western rationality, the dominated and naturalized "other" does not receive fair environmental treatment. Women, people of color, people in lower socioeconomic groups, nonhuman animals, the land itself—all these groups tend to experience a lack of environmental justice because our cultural orientation is to regard them as generally less important and less deserving. Women, for example, are less likely than men to receive an even share of environmental goods. Worldwide, poverty rates are significantly higher for women—making women more susceptible to environmental bads as well.

But patriarchy also leads to the environmental oppression of men, even those from favored social groups. The patriarchal vision of masculinity leads men to take foolish risks with machines, chemicals, weather, and the land. Men often die as a result, or become maimed and diseased. Thus, all of us have an interest in changing the current social order.

Gender Differences in the Experience of Nature

The dualisms of patriarchal reasoning also affect the way women and men experience the environment. Although, on the whole Western women and men experience the environment quite similarly, some significant differences suggest that we have indeed internalized some of the patriarchal stereotypes.

In the late 1980s I conducted an ethnographic study of the experience of nature in an English exurban village. Although similarities far outweighed differences, village men described their natural experiences to me using significantly more aggressive, militaristic, and violent imagery. Village women emphasized a more domestic environmental vision based on their experience of nurturing in nature.[31] For example, men spoke of the pleasures of releasing their pent-up aggressive feelings through clearing brush and engaging in visceral rural sports such as "skirmish", a mock war game played in the woods with guns that shoot paint balls. One village man described the game,

> I think when we were made, we were made with instincts to defend our tribe. . . . These instincts never get an airing. We sit in our office desks [isolated] from that danger, save-the-family type situation. . . . But when you go out there playing this game . . . it's like a dog that's been cooped up forever and then one day it's taken for a walk in the woods and it sees a rabbit. It sniffs it and all its primitive instincts come alive. . . . It's quite exciting when a ton of people are coming at you with a gun.[32]

No village woman described such pleasures. Nor did any village man relate stories of nurturing in nature such as those told to me by several village women. One village woman, for example, told a story about a family cat that helped raise two ducklings, extending nurturing feelings even across the divide of predator and prey. She tells the story best, so here it is in her words:

> We had a cat [Suzy]. We always had lots of cats. And this particular time I went to Harchester, and there were two little ducklings in a pet shop window. And like a fool I thought, well, the kids will like them. And I brought them home, didn't I? And Suzy became a mother and she got kittens, at this particular time. And of course she took the two little ducklings over, didn't she? So wherever she went with the kittens, the ducklings followed. And they used to sleep together in this cardboard box. The cat and the ducklings! . . . It's completely true. She would wash and cuddle the ducklings, just like they were her own. It's the mothering instinct, I suppose. . . .[33]

This is an incredible story, one that even got the family's picture in the paper, along with the cat and the ducklings. But significantly, this was a story that a woman told me. Her husband, whom I knew well, never mentioned it. This was her story, not his. Rather, he told me stories about rough weather and other hard environmental conditions and his feats of physical prowess and mental toughness in the face of these conditions.

Perhaps village men and women told these different types of stories to conform to their expectations of what a male researcher should be told, and not to express their true feelings. Even so, it is significant that their expectations ran along such gendered lines.

I must emphasize once again that the similarities between men's and women's stories far outweighed the differences, however. I must also emphasize that it is not helpful to blame men for experiencing nature in ways that I suspect most readers—both male and female—would regard as less laudable. The point of an ecofeminist perspective, as Joni Seager explains, "is *not* [to] reduc[e] environmental understanding to simplistic categories of 'wonderful women' and 'evil men.'"[34] Rather, the point is to highlight the environmental consequences for both women and men of patriarchal social structures and patterns of thinking, which both women and men bring into being.

The Controversy over Ecofeminism

Ecofeminism remains a controversial viewpoint. Much of the debate has surrounded the attempt by some ecofeminist writers to subvert Western patriarchy by reversing its moral polarity. These writers propose that women and their associations with nature should be celebrated. Reproduction, nurturing, sensitivity to emotions, closeness to nature and the body—all these things are inherently good, the argument goes. Women should embrace these qualities, not reject them. It's the other side of patriarchy's dualisms—reason, civilization, machines—that has made such a mess of things.[35]

Critics both inside and outside of ecofeminism object that such a position reifies the very social order that needs to be changed. It perpetuates the dichotomy between men and women as well as the negative stereotypes of women as irrational, as controlled by their bodies, and as best suited for the domestic realm.[36] Critics also argue that this reification is alienating and fatalistic because it implies that biological differences between men and women are at the root of patriarchy. Such a position, suggests Deborah Slicer, is best termed "ecofeminine" and not "ecofeminist."[37]

Another criticism of ecofeminist arguments is that they may exaggerate the distinctiveness of features of Western ideology such as the "logic of domination." Are Eastern cultures less patriarchal than Western ones? The evidence suggests not. Also, Eastern cultures have shown themselves to be quite capable of dominating nature. Either the "logic of domination" that infuses both our social and our environmental actions must not be exclusively Western, or the East must have its own logic of domination.

Also, in their effort to make clear the sexism that underlies some of our outlooks on the environment, ecofeminists have sometimes oversimplified their arguments. For example, the dualisms that ecofeminists have identified are not always so clear-cut. Consider the cultural association of women with nature and men with culture. In fact, the dualism often goes the other way, aligning women with culture and men with nature. Since Victorian times, one common stereotype of women has been that they are the bearers of culture and refinement and that they have responsibility for inculcating "civilization" in the next generation—and in men. One common current stereotype of men is that they are wild beasts driven by lust and violent passion, which women must tame for their own sake and for the sake of their children. Also, many of the spirits that various Western (and non-Western) traditions have sensed in the physical environment are characterized as male: Father Sky, the Greek sun god Apollo and ocean god Poseidon, the notion of a "fatherland."

Ecofeminists themselves point out, quite rightly, we need to recognize the gray areas and the interactiveness and interdependence of our categories. Unless we continually remind ourselves of the dialogics of categories, of the dialogue of difference and sameness, we easily slip into one-sided, deterministic, and hierarchical arguments. And as ecofeminists have also observed, when you survey the world with a one-sided, deterministic and hierarchical frame of mind to begin with, you are even more likely to slip in this way.[38]

However, our complaint with dualism should not be that it is wrong to create categories and draw distinctions. We need categories to recognize difference and thereby to build our theoretical and moral understanding of the world. But we also need better categories than the hierarchical, socially unjust, and environmentally destructive ones of patriarchy.

THE DIFFERENCE THAT IDEOLOGY MAKES

The various theories we have encountered in exploring the ideological roots of our current environmental and social conditions have a common theme: the central roles of inequality and hierarchy in the way we think about the environment. Whether we are talking about the competitive desire to achieve grace through work, the notion that people and their God are above nature, the achievement of individual distinction through bodily distance from the world, or the dualistic thinking of patriarchy, social inequality influences our environmental relations.

After this chapter, I hope it is clearer that social inequality has not only material but also ideological roots. This is another dialogue. Material factors structure our lives in unequal ways, leading to hierarchical visions of the world, just as ideological factors allow the material structures of inequality to develop and to persist.

Another common theme of this chapter is that, thus far, scholars have relied too much on the Western experience in formulating theories of the human transformation of the environment. Some of this neglect of the East has likely been due to a romantic view of the environmental sensitivity of that part of the world. But large-scale transformation of the environment in the East goes back thousands of years, just as it does in the West. Although this romantic view is flattering in some ways, it is also a back-handed insult, for it implies that the scientific and technological mind was beyond the ideological capabilities of the East. Like ecofeminine ideas, the idea that the East was ecologically sensitive (until corrupted by the West) may perpetuate negative stereotypes of irrationality and backwardness.

Placing more emphasis on economic factors may help us understand how the ideology of transformation arose (recalling, with Weber, that any economic pattern is as much an ideological matter as a material one). The global spread of capitalism has been propelled by the accelerating treadmills of production and consumption, bringing with it social structures and ways of thinking that increase our orientation toward transforming the earth.

But still the explanation is not complete. Environmental transformation was going on before capitalism arrived in both the East and West. Also, and perhaps even more importantly, we need to remember that the socialist economies of the former Soviet bloc and East Asia showed just as much tendency as capitalist economies to transform and dominate the earth.

In short, we do not yet fully understand the ideological origins of the transformation and domination of the earth. And it may be that even after we take into account both material and ideal factors, we still may not. One implication of a dialogical view of causality is that complete explanations are rarely, if ever, possible. The spontaneous creativity that comes out of social interaction has effects that can never be completely predicted.[39]

Nevertheless, we should still pursue the analysis of social and environmental change. It is vitally important that we try to understand the material and ideal factors that dialogically shape, if not completely predict, our actions regarding the environment—particularly if we hope to guide those actions in a different direction.

CHAPTER 6

The Ideology of Environmental Concern

Rather than love, than money, than fame, give me truth.

-Henry David Thoreau, 1854

"It is our alarming misfortune," wrote Rachel Carson in 1962, describing the indiscriminate use of chemical pesticides, "that so primitive a science has armed itself with the most modern and terrible weapons, and that in turning them against the insects it has also turned them against the earth."[1] With these words, Carson concluded *Silent Spring*, a book that came like a thunderclap in a seemingly cloudless technological sky. Because of chemical poisoning, argued Carson, it was a very real possibility—and indeed it was already true in some areas—that a time could come when spring arrives "unheralded by the return of the birds, and the early mornings are strangely silent where once they were filled with the beauty of bird song."[2] Carson carefully documented her claims with the results of hundreds of scientific studies, challenging science with science. Suddenly, the technological utopianism of the postwar period no longer seemed so utopian.

Of course, we cannot assign an absolute beginning to any historical trend; history always has precursors. But so dramatic were the subsequent shifts in public opinion that it has become conventional, with some justice, to date the start of the modern environmental movement from the publication of *Silent Spring*.[3] My own mother, who read extracts from the book in a popular magazine, recently recalled to me the heated discussions it touched off among her friends. "It really shocked a lot of people," she explained. "We didn't have any idea that pesticides could be so dangerous. Nobody used to question these things."

Today, however, millions—even billions—do. The domination of the earth has become increasingly unthinkable to increasing numbers of people in the years since 1962. Although survey results can be misleading, in a poll of forty-three nations from rich to poor conducted between 1990 and 1993, 96 percent of the respondents said that they "approved" or "strongly approved" of the environmental movement. Most said they strongly approved.[5] There can be little else that so much of the world apparently agrees on.

Exhibit 6.1 *Rachel Carson, 1907–1964: A biologist for the United States Fish and Wildlife Serivice and a brilliant writer, Carson is widely credited with helping precipitate a great change in public attitudes toward the environment, particularly with her final book,* Silent Spring.

Photo: Rachel Carson History Project.

Why this strong shift? Humans had been dramatically altering their environment for centuries without evoking a popular environmental movement. Yet even the most influential book can only crystallize concerns that must already have been held in dissolved suspension in the roiling sea of public opinion. How can we understand this ideological reorientation?

This chapter seeks sociological answers to this question. It does so through a sketch of the history of environmental concern and a review of the theories advanced by social scientists to explain the recent flowering of this concern into the modern environmental movement. I will argue that, in the face of environmental domination, counterideas have always been around. These ideas have become much more widely held in the latter half of the twentieth century for three primary reasons: the rediscovery of the moral attractiveness of nature, the increased scale of material alterations of the environment, and the spread of democratic attitudes and institutions. It is, yet again, a matter of both the material and the ideal.

ANCIENT BEGINNINGS

Environmental concern has a long history—perhaps every bit as long as the history of conscious environmental transformation. Like other creatures, humans unavoidably influence their surroundings. But the first decisions to consciously tinker with the environment likely prompted some heated debate. Is this safe? Is it moral? Perhaps even, is it beautiful? And will the gods approve? At the very least, these kinds of debates have been with us since the time of the ancient Romans, Greeks, and Chinese.

Rome

The poet Horace loved his country villa in the Sabine hills above Rome. One day in about 20 B.C.E., he took up his wax tablet and his reed stylus and scratched out the following lines to his friend Fuscus:

> Fuscus, who lives in town and loves it, greetings from one who loves The country...

> •   •   •   •   •

> You stay in your nest, I sing my lovely rural
> Rivers, and trees, and moss-grown rocks. Why drag out
> Our differences? I live here, I rule here, as soon as I leave
> Those city pleasures celebrated with such noisy gabble:
> Like a professional cake-taster I run looking for good plain
> bread, Just crusty bread, no honeyed confections, dripping sweet!

> If life in harmony with Nature is a primal law,
> And we go looking for the land where we'll build our house, is anything
> Better than the blissful country? Can you think of anything?

> •   •   •   •   •
>
> Where can we sleep, safer from biting envy?
> Is grass less fragrant, less lovely, than your African tile?
> Is your water as clear and sweet, there in its leaden pipes,
> As here, tumbling, singing along hilly slopes?
> Lord! You try to grow trees, there in your marble courtyards,
> And you praise a house for its view of distant fields.
> Push out Nature with a pitchfork, she'll always come back,
> And our stupid contempt somehow falls on its face before her.
>
> •   •   •   •   •
>
> Live happy with what you have, Fuscus, and live well,
> And never let me be busy gathering in more than I need,
> Restlessly, endlessly: rap me on the knuckles, tell me the truth.
> Piled-up gold can be master or slave, depending on its owner;
> Never let it pull you along, like a goat on a rope.[6]

Astoundingly modern-sounding sentiments all. Like countless nature writers of the current day, Horace "sings" the beauty of the countryside, of rivers and trees and moss-grown rocks. And like many in recent decades who left the city for the country, Horace praises the simple life, close to nature. He has no need for the urban contrivances of "honeyed confections, dripping sweet." Just give Horace the plain crusty bread of country living. Since "life in harmony with Nature is a primal law," the country is the best place to live, he proclaims. After all, grass can be as beautiful to walk on as Fuscus's imported African tile. The water in the country is pure and sweet, Horace says, instead of the stale piped-in stuff that Fuscus gets in town. (Although he mentions the lead in the pipes—Romans used lead extensively in their plumbing—Horace couldn't know about the added danger of lead-poisoning, as this danger was unknown at the time.)

Horace praises not only the naturalness of rural living but also the social consequences. A country life frees one from the "biting envy" of the city. Horace doesn't want to live a life devoted to "gathering in more than I need," being pulled along "like a goat on a rope" by the pursuit of money and material possessions, and he warns Fuscus of these dangers. In the poem's most famous lines, Horace chastises those who contemptuously attempt to avoid these social and environmental truths by trying to "push out Nature with a pitchfork." Nature will "always come back," he warns.

That contempt was very evident in the Rome of 20 B.C.E. At that time, Rome was probably the largest city ever known, with close to a million inhabitants, the product of spectacular feats of technology and engineering. A vast system of aqueducts and pipes carried more than 200 million gallons (about a billion liters) of water a day in from the surrounding countryside. The resulting urban effluent poured into the Cloaca Maxima, an underground sewer large enough to accommodate a small sailboat, and thence into the badly abused River Tiber.[7] Wealthy Romans enjoyed running water in their homes, even showers, as well as central heating. Common people lived in *insulae*, apartment buildings the size of a full city block and sometimes as much as seven stories tall. Roman legionnaires had hot baths and flush toilets in their military camps. (Flush toilets are in fact even older; the Minoans had them at the Palace of Knossos a millenium earlier.) Showers, baths, flush toilets, and seven-story apartment buildings, two thousand years ago—and a technology, economy, and empire capable of supporting it all: mighty pitchforks against Nature.

Exhibit 6.2   *Roman aqueduct, Segovia, Spain: Although among the most elegant engineering structures of all time, these triple-arched stone aqueducts are a demonstration of the remarkable power of Roman technology to transform the environment. Horace wrote his poetry about the importance of nature and rural life in reaction to this transformative power.*

Photo: David Gradwohl.

The sentiments that Horace expressed were, we cannot doubt, in some measure formed in reaction to these new environmental transformations— transformations that also had social meaning for him. It was a culture of money and power that produced the technological pitchforks. The urban, commercial life of empire brought with it a widespread feeling that everything was becoming political—that social life was moved not by virtue but by self-serving desires for power, influence, and material possessions. Greed was overwhelming the Roman landscape and lifescape. And if all social motivations derived from the pursuit of interests, of materialist desire, where might one encounter an alternative?

For Horace, in nature. And what made nature so attractive to Horace still makes nature attractive today. Concern about nature cannot be separated from concern about social interests and how these shape our moral understandings.[7] Part of the attraction of nature stems from our struggles with the oldest of moral problems—the balance of power between us— and the oldest of moral critiques—that interests underlie what we say, do, and believe. We look to nature for a moral base that lies outside ourselves, outside human power structures, and therefore outside the potential that we may have manipulated morality for our own ends. To experience nature is to experience an interest-free foundation upon which to build our motivations. To experience nature is to experience a point of rest from the constant charges that we act as we do because we seek power. To experience nature is thus to experience social innocence.

Horace felt that innocence in a country life. By living in harmony with nature, Horace believed, he could remain free of city dwellers' relentless pursuit of personal gain and their biting envy over others' piled-up gold. In nature Horace felt he had discovered a moral realm that lies beyond the reach of the pollution of human interests and materialist desire. The search for this realm of innocence is a kind of conscience, what I term a *natural conscience*, and it is fundamental to our moral thought.[8]

Yet was Horace truly above the pursuit of self-interest himself? Had he really put "biting envy" behind him through his celebration of a natural life? One way to read his famous epistle to Fuscus is that Horace was trying his best to build a bit of biting envy in his friend—envy for Horace's lifestyle in his country villa. Wealthy Romans loved country living and established country villas for themselves across the empire. The country house was already a positional good two thousand years ago. Which is perhaps why, despite his opening avowal, Horace's epistle goes on very forcefully to in fact "drag out our differences."

The discovery of a natural conscience does not mean that one has truly escaped the moral problem of interests. It only means that one is grappling with the issue.

Horace was not the first to grapple with this problem, though. The search for a natural realm of moral innocence has frequently accompanied the rise of a complex, urban-dominated political life, and the growing wealth and social inequality that have so often been associated with such a life. For that we must begin even earlier, with the ancient Greeks, and, in a few pages, with the ancient Chinese.

Greece

Nature is an old and powerful idea. Words are not the same as ideas, of course; the same boat can carry many different loads. But it is illuminating to trace the origin of the word *nature* and the historical sequence of conceptual loads it has been asked to carry.

The boat of nature was first loaded up in Greece. The English word *nature* is a rendering of the Latin *natura*, which first appeared in the third century B.C.E. But *natura* was itself a Roman translation of the older Greek word *phÿsis*.[9] (*Phÿsis* also makes its way into English, serving as the root for physics, physician, physical, metaphysical, and so on.) *Phÿsis*'s own roots are in the Greek *phÿ*, meaning simply "to be," and *phÿein*, "to give birth." Although we can't be certain when *phÿsis* was coined from *phÿ* and *phÿein*, the word was nevertheless in use by the eighth century B.C.E. to connote the permanent, essential aspects of an object by which it might be forever known—a meaning which was apparently derived from an earlier use of *phÿsis* to mean "birth mark."[10]

By the end of the fifth century B.C.E., however, *phÿsis* had come to take on a wider and more significant meaning. The fifth century was a period of enormous change in Greek society, a period of fantastic growth in the power, size, and wealth of the city-states. After 480 B.C.E., when the Greeks defeated the Persians, to whom they had previously paid tribute, their economy began to expand mightily. The economic expansion brought wealth and urban growth. Athens grew to a size never seen before. Perhaps as many as 275,000 people lived there in 431 B.C.E.[11]

In such a place, and in such a time, it was hard not to be impressed with an urban truth: Money and politics, not the gods and other lofty concerns, moved the world of everyday life. At least that was the message of the Sophists, a group of itinerate philosophers known for their cynical and relativistic teachings about the reach of self-interest into all human affairs and beliefs. "It is for themselves and their own advantage," declared the Sophist Callicles, "that they make their laws and distribute their praises and censures."[12] Not the gods, but "man is the measure of all things," thought Protagoras. Human laws are "designed to serve the interest of the ruling class," Thrasymachus observed. In his view, "the actual ruler or governor thinks of his subjects as sheep [and] his chief occupation, day and night, is how he can best fleece them to his own benefit."[13]

What the Sophists were saying is that the moral order, including religion, is based upon mere convention—*nomos*, to use the Greek word—not some principle external to human interests, such as God, justice, or what we have come to call science. Many Sophists were famous for their rhetorical skills, which they used as proof of their view that morality is just a kind of con game. Indeed, their practice of lecturing only for a fee (which Plato complained about in *The Republic*) was itself a kind of demonstration of the ultimate Sophist point: Even truth has a price on it.

The Sophists are often considered the bad guys of ancient Greek philosophy because of their apparent anything-goes vision of morality. If morality is human-derived, it follows that morality is whatever any human wants it to be and can force it to be, many Sophists argued. But the Sophists in fact were very concerned about social inequality and sought to expose hypocrisy. Their teachings fit well with the ambitions of the students who came to hear the latest Sophist to come to town. These were mainly young or disadvantaged citizens and free noncitizens eager to acquire the rhetorical skills essential for getting ahead in the city.[14] For them, the Sophist message was comforting and hopeful: The social order is not preordained.

The Sophist argument was ultimately circular, however, for if all morality is mere rhetoric and *nomos*, so too must be Sophism itself. There had to be somewhere else to stand. *Phÿsis* suddenly sprang into widespread use as a word that might provide that foundation, a word that could root truth in something outside of human manipulation, rhetoric, bias, materialist desire, and self-interest—a word that could be a source of moral guidance in a jealous world of wealth and power. Hippocrates advised doctors that *phÿsis* was the only true calling of medicine (and thus the term "physician").[15] In the middle of the fourth century, Aristotle wrote several books on *phÿsis*, most notably the *Physics*, and went on to use it as his proposed foundation for a just society in the *Politics*.

Plato was a bit cautious about the word, though, perhaps because the Sophist opponents in his dialogues often based their arguments on *phÿsis*. For example, the Sophist Callicles claimed (or so Plato says) that might makes right was a truth "nature herself reveals."[16] So Plato sought a different solution than *phÿsis*—but one that was equally an effort to discover a moral realm beyond interest. He agreed that the Greek pantheon of gods had become a philosophical shambles. So he proposed a new kind of god, a great ideal or "form" that he claimed governed the order of things: the Good.

Plato argued that the Good was the divine agent of the world, what he called the Demiurge. As pure goodness, the Demiurge could not suffer from a materialist sin like envy. And herein lies the origin of the world, as Plato explained in the *Timaeus*: "Let us therefore state the reason why the framer of this universe of change framed it at all. He was good, and what is good has no particle of envy in it; being therefore without envy he wished all things to be as like himself as possible."[17]   So the Demiurge created the material world, using as a blueprint "his" own ideal goodness. In other words, the primal act of the universe was the denial of envy, of materialist desire. As a consequence, the whole world is good, and goodness is the whole world.

Thus was born a new manner of god. Not the jealous God of the Old Testament. Not the quarreling, querulous sort of gods that populated the old Greek pantheon. But a god who cannot sin and whose very power stems from being separated from the back-stabbing ways and moral sleight of hand of human society.

Aristotle apparently thought the Demiurge story was a bit silly, and he did not repeat it. Aristotle's distinctive moral contribution was to answer questions of interest and power in terms of nature, of *phÿsis*. But he agreed that the ultimate motor of the world, the "final cause" and "unmoved mover" of *phÿsis*, was "the Good."[18] Nature was not, as the Sophists had concluded, a source of anything-goes morality. It was, in effect, itself the Demiurge, and thus following nature was following the Good. Now nature was cured of materialist desire and could become a source of moral guidance in a world of envy and greed. The Greeks had discovered the natural conscience.

China

The classical Greeks were not the first ancient people to critique materialist desire. *The Song of the Harper*, an Egyptian text of circa 2600 B.C.E., had this to say: "Remember it is not given to man to take his goods with him. No one goes away and then comes back."[19] Similarly, the Egyptian sage Ptahhotep admonished "Beware an act of avarice; it is a bad and incurable disease."[20]

But few pursued this line of thinking with the philosophical vigor of the classical Greeks and another group of ancient thinkers: the Taoists. By the fifth century B.C.E., about the same time as the Greeks, Taoist philosophers began to take a rather skeptical view of the human world. In China, as in Greece, this was an age of commerce and empire in which power and self-interest seemed greater truths about the way the world worked than earlier religious views. Taoist writings of the time abound in criticisms of the self-centered money interests overtaking ancient Chinese society. This critical impression grew into full-fledged doubt about the materialistic underpinnings of social life in general.

Lao Tzu (or rather the writer of the *Lao Tzu*, who is not known for certain) is famously direct on the topic: "There may be gold and jade to fill a hall, but there is none who can keep them." You can't take it with you—clearly a reminder that many through the ages have seen fit to give. "To be overbearing when one has wealth and position," the *Lao Tzu* goes on, "is to bring calamity upon oneself."[21] Lao Tzu taught that "the sage desires not to desire and does not value goods which are hard to come by."[22] "Is this not because," Lao Tzu asks in a different passage, "[the sage] does not wish to be considered a better man than others?"[23] The *Lao Tzu* makes the point most plainly in the allegory of the "uncarved block," the simple, unadorned state it counsels people to emulate: "The nameless uncarved block is but freedom from desire." The secret to contentment is to "have little thought of self and as few desires as possible."[24]

Similarly, the *Lieh-Tzu*, another early Taoist work, taught the uselessness of the fancy art objects made for the aristocracy. One story in this book is of a certain Prince of Sung who commissioned an artisan to carve a morphologically correct leaf out of jade. When the artisan returned with the jade leaf after three years' labor, it was so perfect that no one could tell it from a real leaf, and the Prince was overjoyed. But when Lieh Tzu heard about it, he replied "If nature took three years to produce one leaf, there would be few trees with leaves on them!"[25]

These critiques had a deep resonance, and we find them in many later ancient Chinese writings. The *Lü-shih Ch'un Ch'iu*, a compendium of useful knowledge put together for a third-century B.C.E. prime minister, portrayed commerce as a potentially corruptible tangent from the simple ways of agrarian society.[26] Writing about the same time, Chuang Tzu counseled against giving in to "desire," materialism, and ambition, as in this passage from "The Empty Boat":

> Who can free himself from achievement
> And from fame, descend and be lost
> Amid the masses of men?
> He will flow like Tao, unseen,
> He will go about like Life itself
> With no name and no home.
> Simple is he, without distinction.
> To all appearances he is a fool.
> His steps leave no trace. He has no power.
> He achieves nothing, has no reputation.
> Since he judges no one
> No one judges him.
> Such is the perfect man:
> His boat is empty.[27]

Chuang Tzu also extolled the virtues of simplicity in the story of a Taoist sage, Hsu Yu, who, when offered the rulership of a kingdom, exclaimed, "When the tailor-bird builds her nest in the deep wood, she uses no more than one branch. When the mole drinks at the river, he takes no more than a bellyful. . . . I have no use for the rulership of the world!"[28]

Materialist skepticism in ancient China, like Sophism in Greece, proceeded so far that many Taoists, particularly Lao Tzu, came to be deeply suspicious of all knowledge. The sage "learns to be without knowledge," wrote Lao Tzu.[29] "One who knows does not speak; one who speaks does not know."[30] Like the Sophists, the Taoists sharply criticized the deceptiveness of language. Here is Lao Tzu again: "Truthful words are not beautiful; beautiful words are not truthful. Good words are not persuasive; persuasive words are not good." The passage goes on to return to the problem of knowledge more generally: "He who knows has no wide learning; he who has wide learning does not know."[31]

But unlike the Greek Sophists, the Taoists had an alternative to self-interest, an alternative that provided a natural conscience they believed to be free from materialist ambition. The Taoists found their natural conscience in the *tao*, or "the way." *Tao* is the principle that underlies things we in the West would term "natural"—in agrarian society, in the nests of tailor-birds, in moles and rivers, and in the leaves of trees. As the historian Fung Yu-Lan put it, *tao* is "the unitary first 'that' from which all things in the universe come to be." It is "the all-embracing first principle of things," what Aristotle would have recognized as the "unmoved mover" of the world.[32] *Tao* is unaffected by human doings, but people do best when they allow themselves to be guided by it, and not by human desire.

Through the *tao*, each thing obtains its *te*, its individual essential quality. *Tao* is within humans as well, and each human therefore has a *te*. We can allow *te* to express itself through *wu wei*, acting without deliberate effort.[33] Acting deliberately, what Taoists call *yu wei*, would inevitably lead one away from the *tao*. Empty your boat, advise the Taoists, and drift along with the natural conscience of the *tao*.

THE MORAL BASIS OF CONTEMPORARY ENVIRONMENTAL CONCERN

In the centuries that followed, nature remained a central pillar of the natural conscience. But nature was often tied in with other concepts—religion, science, conceptions of bodily difference such as race and gender, and many other ideas and institutions that similarly claimed at least a partial foundation in "nature." Such ideas and institutions have been strongly criticized in recent years. Critics have argued, like the Sophists once did, that human interests do indeed motivate these sources of moral judgment.

In an era of unprecedented growth in wealth, inequality, environmental domination, and political conflict, it seems apparent to many that, rather than lying above power, our basic moral ideas and moral institutions are the products of power.

Consider race, once widely seen as a "natural," and therefore perfectly moral, basis on which to allocate social rewards and social position. Increasingly—and quite correctly, I think—people see the idea of race as a way those in power have sought to stay that way. Race is rapidly losing its former status as an interest-free fact of "nature." (Chapter 7 explores this criticism in more detail.)

It is a common fate of every widely accepted formulation of a natural conscience that it is subsequently subjected to careful critical scrutiny to see if it really does rise above the problems of human interest and the balance of power. (Indeed, we should welcome such scrutiny, I believe—although we often do not.) The scrutiny of various visions of the natural conscience have been unusually intense in recent decades, though, and it is the defining feature of a cultural change often called *postmodernism*. Although skepticism about human motivations is certainly not wholly new, as we have seen, the moral dilemma is particularly strong today: If all that motivates us is power and self-interest, is there then no truly moral place to stand?

These questions had already begun to occur with some force to Henry David Thoreau in the middle of the nineteenth century, as he walked through the woods near Walden Pond. He was by no means the only one to whom such questions occurred at this time. Many worried about the direction and motivations behind the social and environmental transformations brought about by the burgeoning industrial revolution. And the moral resolution that many found was the same: a return to a purer vision of nature—nature as "nature;" as woods and winds, farms and fields, grazing sheep and flitting butterflies; as the nonsocial world. A few decades earlier, Beethoven had penned the *Pastoral Symphony*. A few decades later, Bierdstadt would paint *The Last of the Buffalo*. Cities were establishing parks, zoos, and botanical gardens, and the rich were taking up second homes in the countryside. Natural historians were reveling in the wonders of a nature beyond society, and the theory of natural selection was slowly accumulating evidence on Darwin's desk, even as the coming of industrialism was radically transforming those wonders. Thoreau was a leading exemplar of this broad cultural change.

Thoreau loved walking. Thoreau walked "four hours a day at least," he tells us in the essay "Walking."[34] And when he walked, he found himself inevitably drawn to the west. "Eastward I go only by force," he explained, "but westward I go free."[35]

Exhibit 6.3 *Henry David Thoreau, 1817–1862. Nearly a century and a half after his death, millions still find inspiration in this quiet man's eloquent writings about the moral value of wild nature. His concerns remain our concerns.*

Henry David Thoreau

From his cabin on Walden Pond, the west led away from Boston and into the open countryside. The freedom he felt in this direction was a social freedom—that is, a freedom from the social. "Man and his affairs, church and state and school, trade and commerce, and manufactures and agriculture, even politics, most alarming of them all,—I am pleased to see how little space they occupy on the landscape," Thoreau exalted. "In one half-hour I can walk off to some portion of the earth's surface where a man does not stand from one year's end to another, and there, consequently, politics are not, for they are but as the cigar-smoke of a man."[36]

Instead of the cigar smoke of politics, to the west Thoreau found the Wild. As he put it in the most famous line he ever wrote, "The west of which I speak is but another name for the Wild; and what I have been preparing to say is, that in Wildness is the preservation of the World."[37]

We can hear in Thoreau both a critique of power and interests and an alternative place to stand (or, rather, walk). What alarms Thoreau about society and the east is the play of human politics—the interest-laden "affairs" of church, state, school, trade, commerce, manufactures, and agriculture.

But to the west Thoreau found release from power and self-interests. The vital serenity of the wild was, for Thoreau, the serenity of a realm without social conflict, for in the wild was no society with which to conflict. It was the serenity of what I call a *natural other*—a vision of an interest-free realm upon which to base a natural conscience.

Like the Taoists and the Sophists, Thoreau carried his critique of material desire and self-interest into a suspicion of knowledge itself, especially the useful and arrogant knowledge of the technological ethos. Like the Taoists (but not the Sophists, as far as I have read), he praised ignorance and a recognition of how little we know:

> We have heard of a Society for the Diffusion of Useful Knowledge. It is said that knowledge is power; and the like. Methinks there is equal need of a Society for the Diffusion of Useful Ignorance, what we will call Beautiful Knowledge, a knowledge useful in a higher sense: for what is most of our boasted so-called knowledge but a conceit that we know something, which robs us of the advantage of our actual ignorance? ... Which is the best man to deal with,— he who knows nothing about a subject, and, what is extremely rare, knows that he knows nothing, or he who really knows something about it, but thinks that he knows all?[38]

It is the power behind knowledge that worried Thoreau the most, I believe. He saw in knowledge no authentic route to truth and self. That route was to be found in going west and opening oneself up to the wild— but without deliberate effort, again echoing Taoism. In Thoreau's words, "I believe that there is a subtile [sic] magnetism in Nature, which, if we unconsciously yield to it, will direct us aright." This sounds to me like *wu wei*.

Through this unconscious yielding to the natural other of the wild, Thoreau counseled, we can find our real selves, and even our real names, as opposed to the "cheap and meaningless" names we receive from society. "It may be given to a savage who retains in secret his own wild title earned in the woods," thought Thoreau. "We have a wild savage in us, and a savage name is perchance somewhere recorded as ours."[39] In that wild savage within, and in that savage name, Thoreau found a *natural me*—the truer, more authentic self that the natural other sees in us, as opposed to the me that society sees.

Thoreau's formulation of the natural conscience was very influential and is still a touchstone for environmental thought today. Thoreauvian *wu wei* can be found in the voluntary simplicity movement in all its many manifestations. His natural other can be found in the wilderness preservation movement and in the restful, yet exhilarating joy that so many find walking in their own wild wests, imagining freedom from social conflict, social constraint, and social power. His critique of materialist desire can be found in the environmentalist's condemnation of waste, pollution, corporate irresponsibility, state inaction, and the greed seen to underlie it all. Thoreau's natural me can be found in the environmentalists' self-conception that they are motivated by the interests of something outside themselves, and perhaps their self-conception that they are less artificial people.

If it is not Thoreau's own *wu wei*, natural other, natural me, and materialist critique that inform contemporary environmental concerns, then it is something of close resemblance, whether arrived at through direct moral descent from Thoreau or through moral convergence with Thoreau.

A number of years ago, while doing research in England for a book about attitudes toward nature and the countryside, I had a memorably Thoreauvian conversation with a thoughtful, committed young man, very concerned about the environment. Nigel, as I'll call him, was also very concerned about the situation in Northern Ireland, and one evening we discussed the complexities and contradictions of that bitterly contested land. We found that we agreed that fault lay on both sides. There was a pause in the conversation, as we both let that thought sink in. And then Nigel said, "That's why I think I'm interested in the environment. You *know* what's right. It's clear where one should be standing. It's never that way with politics."[40]

I have no idea if Nigel had read Thoreau. Most of the 96 percent of respondents from that 1990–1993 world poll who supported the environmental movement almost certainly had not read Thoreau. Nor had they likely read the many environmental ethicists who followed Thoreau— such as John Muir, Henry Salt, Rudolf Steiner, Lewis Mumford, Arne Naess, Mahatma Gandhi, and Aldo Leopold—let alone those who preceded him, like Horace, the Sophists, Aristotle, and Lao Tzu. They don't have to have read these classic works. The ideas they represent are part of the cultural waters in which we all swim.

Which doesn't mean, however, that we are all cultural clones of Thoreau. We reinvent the natural conscience as much as we borrow it from our cultural history. We do this because such an idea continues to help us contend with the ideological conditions of our lives. Thoreau is admired today because we see our ideas in him as much as (if not more than) we experience his ideas in us. The modern natural conscience is thus as much a new invention as it is a reinvention—as much a new discovery as it is a rediscovery.

THE MATERIAL BASIS OF CONTEMPORARY ENVIRONMENTAL CONCERN

The natural conscience is not all there is to environmental concern and its expansion into a broad popular movement in the last half of the twentieth century, however. In this section, I'll argue that perceived environmental decline is an important factor in its own right. That is, there is an important material basis to the ideology of environmental concern.

This point may seem self-evident. But a number of scholars and critics of environmentalism have raised two potential counterarguments: First, that environmentalism is a passing flavor-of-the-month kind of issue and that people will rapidly lose interest, and second, that environmentalism is mainly an elite issue. Either counterargument, if true, would lessen the significance of the material origins of environmental concern.

The Persistence of Environmental Concern

In support of the flavor-of-the-month argument, it is important to note that the intensity of environmental concern varies considerably from person to person. This is something we all know from our personal interactions with others, and it also expresses itself in survey results.

Recall again the 1990–1993 poll of forty-three countries in which 96 percent of respondents expressed their approval of the environmental movement. That 96 percent figure needs to be interpreted with care. For example, in that same poll only 65 percent indicated that they were willing to pay higher taxes to prevent environmental pollution. This still is a significant percentage, but the idea of having to pay to prevent pollution did dampen the enthusiasm of many. And when presented with the statement "The government has to reduce pollution but it should not cost me any money," 55 percent of the sample agreed—meaning that only 45 percent were willing to pay to prevent pollution. Thus, the intensity of world support for environmental concerns dropped from 96 to 65 to 45 percent, depending upon how the pollsters put the question.[41]

Moreover, we need to note that this world survey was taken around the time of the Earth Summit, a period in which environmental issues received wide coverage in the media. Public concern for most issues follows a pattern that the political scientist Anthony Downs once called the "issue-attention cycle."[42] The vogue term for it these days is "compassion fatigue." Through the combined effects of boredom, the media's restless search for the new and novel, a realization that relieving the problem would entail significant costs, and maybe a sense that government must now be taking care of things, public interest tends to wane over time. Perhaps this survey was merely tapping into public interest at the peak of environmental attention, before the inevitable onset of compassion fatigue.

And perhaps not. Public concern for the environment has in fact shown remarkable staying power, and a general upward trend, over the past thirty years.[43] True, it has had its ups and downs. After a dramatic upswing in the late 1960s, environmental concern peaked shortly after the first Earth Day in 1970 and declined throughout the 1970s. As early as 1972, Anthony Downs was already predicting that interest in environmental problems would soon follow the issue-attention cycle into the shadows.[44] For a decade, it looked like he might be right. However, the 1980s brought a resurgence of concern, reaching the unprecedented levels recorded by surveys in the early 1990s.[45]

Even if public concern fades again, as it may have already done, at least in some countries, environmentalism has shown itself over thirty years to be more than a passing fad.[46] Concern will experience periodic downturns, to be sure, but environmentalism now seems likely to remain a persistent topic of public discussion for the foreseeable future. Scholars now generally agree that environmental concern is widespread and long lasting, although variable in intensity over time and from person to person.

Social Status and Environmental Concern

Now let's inspect the common suggestion that environmentalism is an elite movement of the liberal, the white, and the comfortably well-off.

Public opinion polls in the West show that, in fact, these social factors have relatively little influence on the level of environmental concern. A 1979 British survey found that supporters of the environmental movement did tend to be drawn from middle class service professions: teachers, social workers, doctors, and the like. But the strongest opponents of environmental views—business leaders—had even higher incomes on the whole. And many lower income people and trade unionists showed strong support for environmentalism.[47]

A more comprehensive 1992 American study, drawing on eighteen years of national surveys conducted between 1973 and 1990, showed similar results.[48] Income had only a minor effect on a person's level of environmental concern, even during recessions. People who were younger, liberal, members of the Democratic party, well educated, urban and who did not work in primary industries like farming and forestry did tend to be more supportive of environmentalism. But again, these effects were slight; plenty of older, conservative, Republican, less-educated, rural, and primary industry-employed people professed environmental support.

In the polls from a few years, a person's race had a slight influence on responses. Yet contrary to the argument that environmentalism is an elite movement, whites in those years showed *lower* levels of environmental concern than minority groups. Also, gender had a slight influence in a few years' polls, but again the less socially empowered group—women—showed higher levels of concern. In any event, across all these social groupings, differences were small.

Moreover, there is abundant evidence of considerable environmental concern among the world's poor, as the Indian environmental sociologist Ramachandra Guha has forcefully pointed out. Consider the struggles of the Penan people of Malaysia fighting the logging of their forest home; the similar struggles of the Chipko ("hug the tree") movement of villagers in northern India; the hard-fought, and tragic, campaigns in Brazil and Nigeria that led to the murders of two of the world's most important environmental leaders, Chico Mendes and Ken Saro-Wiwa. Environmentalism has become a significant feature of political debate in the world's poorest countries too.

The character of the "environmentalism of the poor," as Guha terms it, often differs significantly from the environmentalism of the rich. "First and foremost," Guha has written, "it combines a concern with the environment with an often more visible concern with social justice."[49] This heightened emphasis on environmental justice has also been central to the environmentalism of the poor in rich countries, as the thousands of community-level groups that have sprung up in the United States since the late 1980s demonstrate. These groups usually focus on the unequal distribution of environmental "bads," such as the location of toxic waste disposal sites and heavily polluting industrial facilities, blending environmental and social justice concerns, particularly over race and class.[50]

There is, then, little empirical support for the allegation of Lester Thurow and others over the years that, to quote Thurow, "poor1 countries and poor individuals simply aren't interested" in environmentalism.[51] The form of and basis for environmental concern may well differ between rich and poor, but not the level of concern. As Stephen Cotgrove concluded some years ago, "the main clue [to understanding the level of environmental concern] is to be found not in demographic variables [like age, gender, and income] but in various measures of social and political beliefs and values."[52] In other words, level of environmental concern is less a matter of who you are, of social status, then it is a matter of what you believe and value.

Postmaterialism

But why do we believe and value what we do? The political scientist Ronald Inglehart has provided an important analysis of the material basis of environmental concern—the first of three that I'll compare. Inglehart's analysis, as we shall see, moves beyond the elitism critique of environmentalism while at the same time returning to it in a way.

Since the early 1970s, Inglehart has been documenting a broad intergenerational cultural shift in wealthy countries across the world, what he terms a turn from materialist to *postmaterialist* values. Along with his colleague Paul Abramson, Inglehart argues that younger generations are shifting away from "concerns about economic and physical security, toward a greater emphasis on freedom, self-expression, and the quality of life."[53] Older generations were socialized in times when worries about money, health, and natural threats were much more of a concern. Drawing on Maslow's theory of the hierarchy of needs (which I discussed in chapter 2), Inglehart argues that economic improvements have allowed younger generations to focus instead on issues of aesthetics and self-actualization, such as freedom and quality of life.[54] Increased concern for the environment, argues Inglehart, is one product of this "postmaterial" socialization. Basically, Inglehart says that we're better off now—all of us, not just the elites—and can afford to worry about the environment.

Inglehart and his collaborators have assembled an impressive array of survey evidence to back up their claim that a shift to postmaterial values is under way in countries across the globe. As older generations die off, Inglehart argues, the overall proportion of postmaterialists will increase, with far-reaching implications for politics and lifestyle choices. Inglehart has been conducting periodic surveys over the last twenty-five years to determine whether the proportion of postmaterialists is actually on the rise. (The 1990–1993 survey of environmental values in forty-three countries that I discussed previously was in fact only a small part of a larger survey led by Inglehart to test the postmaterialism hypothesis.)

In these surveys, Inglehart categorizes people as postmaterialist, materialist, or "mixed" by asking them which two of the following four choices should be their country's top goals:

1. Maintaining order in the nation
2. Giving people more say in important government decisions
3. Fighting rising prices
4. Protecting freedom of speech

Goals 1 and 3 are the materialist responses, and goals 2 and 4 are the postmaterialist ones. Any other combination is scored as mixed.

Inglehart finds that a substantial shift is indeed underway. For example, in 1972 in the United States, 9 percent of those surveyed gave postmaterialist responses, and 35 percent registered as materialist. But by 1992, postmaterialists were up to 18 percent and the materialists were down to 16 percent. The proportion of mixed had also gone up, from 55 to 65 percent, also indicating a shift in a postmaterialist direction.[55] Inglehart has documented similar changes in Britain, France, West Germany, Italy, the Netherlands, Denmark, and Ireland, as well as a slight postmaterialist shift in Belgium.[56]

Inglehart has demonstrated a correlation in these surveys between postmaterialist values and support for environmentalism. For example, in one 1986 survey conducted in twelve European countries, 53 percent of postmaterialists strongly approved of the environmental movement, but only 37 percent of materialists did.[57] In that same survey, Inglehart notes, countries with more postmaterialists were also those which had taken more actions to protect the environment, indicating that postmaterialism also translates into environmental action. This is compelling evidence, and many researchers have applied this analysis to understanding the rise of the environmental movement in countries across North America and Europe.[58]

Questioning Postmaterialism. As compelling as this evidence for a change toward postmaterialist values may be, however, there is reason to doubt Inglehart's interpretation of its link to rising environmental concern.

To begin with, postmaterialism cannot account for the environmentalism of the poor, as Guha has pointed out.[59] The bulk of people in poor countries cannot be said to have postmaterialist values, and yet environmentalism is an increasingly central political issue in these countries—and for strong materialist reasons (among others): Threats to the environment threaten human well-being. Inglehart himself has recently noted the existence of environmentalism in poor countries and has suggested that its origin must lie in materialist concerns, rather than postmaterialist ones—a considerable concession. (But we also need to be careful not to presume that the poor are incapable of anything other than materialist concerns. For example, some of the broadest visions of the environment are the holistic traditions of many native peoples.)

We also have grounds to doubt a postmaterialist explanation for environmentalism in the rich countries. When you consider it carefully, it is evident that Inglehart's explanation rests on the idea that environmental issues are not real material concerns for the West. Environmentalism seems to represent for Inglehart the idyllic musings of a gilded society.

Many environmentalists, however, would no doubt respond that ecological threats are far from being issues of postmaterialism—of Maslovian aesthetic self-actualization. Ecological threats are *material* threats. Not that there isn't an important aesthetic (and moral, as I previously argued) dimension to environmentalism. But there are also important material considerations involved—considerations that concern both the rich and the poor. In other words, Inglehart may be falsely repeating, in more sophisticated terms, the old elitism charge against environmentalism.

The Risk Society

The German social theorist Ulrich Beck has offered a different analysis of the material considerations behind environmentalism, the second of the three I'll compare. Beck suggests that modern society is turning into what he terms a *risk society*—a society in which the central political conflicts are not class struggles over the distribution of money and resources but instead non-class-based struggles over the distribution of environmental and technological risk. We in the West are moving, says Beck, from conflict over the distribution of goods to conflicts over the distribution of bads.[60] But we are not escaping material concerns: Goods and bads are equally material issues.

Significantly, many of the bads of modern society—pollution, technological hazards, ugly development—are hard to escape; they affect everyone. We are increasingly subject to a perverse new form of equality, an "equality of risk," Beck calls it. Therefore risk is fast becoming the central political issue of our times. In Beck's words, "The driving force in the class society can be summarized in the phrase: *I am hungry!* The movement set in motion by the risk society, on the other hand, is expressed in the statement: *I am afraid!*"[61]

Part of this fear is the public's pervasive sense that science is out of control, and that scientists are too. This sense, of course, increases the risk that people feel. It also leads people to question and doubt science. Our faith in the technological god has been shattered by pesticides in our food, by toxins in our water, by Chernobyls in our air, and by scientists in our news media who can't agree with each other. A risk society is not an optimistic society.

Yet Beck sees potential signs of hope. If the public can wrest back control over science, it may lead to a development he terms *reflexive modernization*—that is, a form of modernism in which we think critically about where technology and science are going and engage in democratic debate over how best to proceed. But if not, we may plunge into a period of escalating fear and conflict over risk.[62]

Indeed, risk is fast becoming global. "Risk society," says Beck, "means world risk society."[63] It remains to be seen whether the global dimensions of risk result in new global coalitions or in new global conflict.

Beck's ideas have gained a lot of attention in recent years from environmental sociologists as well as political sociologists. His suggestion that risk is fundamentally reshaping the politics of our times has caused many scholars and (at least within Germany, where Beck is from) many politicians to reconsider the significance of environmentalism. For many years, political commentators have generally viewed environmentalism as just another issue, one more demand on our political attention. If Beck is right, environmentalism is, or is fast becoming, the defining political issue of our time.

In a couple of respects, Beck and Inglehart offer similar analyses. Both the theory of the risk society and the theory of postmaterialism describe a close connection between the affluence of modern society and the rise of environmentalism. Both also see a major transformation in politics as a result of increased affluence. But from there, their visions depart significantly.

In a risk society, environmental issues are serious material matters, even in wealthy countries. Although struggles over economic survival no longer have the same political importance they once did, modern technology has produced large quantities of both goods and bads, instead of leading to a life of carefree postmaterial abundance. The ozone hole is real, and really worrisome. This and other material environmental threats have major ideological and political implications, yet that doesn't mean environmentalism is only ideology and politics.

Questioning the Risk Society. Although the idea of a risk society has been getting a lot of attention, it has also received considerable criticism.[64] Much of the criticism has focused on the notion of the perverse equality of risk society compared with the class inequalities of industrial society. "[P]overty is hierarchic, smog is democratic," Beck has written.[65] To be sure, smog affects everyone, rich and poor. So do global warming, the ozone hole, species loss, landscape destruction, pesticide residues in food, and the like. But we cannot doubt that the rich are in a far better position to avoid the worst consequences of all these threats. The distribution of environmental bads (as well as environmental goods) is far from equal. It is true that even the wealthy must contend with environmental bads, and in this fact lies some hope for building political coalitions that cross the lines of race and class and nation. Still, that doesn't mean the rich bear the risks equally with the poor. Wealth remains an important cleavage in environmental politics, unfortunately.[66]

Because of the way it understates this cleavage, the idea of a risk society is of little help in understanding the environmentalism of poor countries. One of the central driving forces of political conflict in poor countries originates very much from the feeling that "I am hungry." Yet poor countries have vigorous environmental movements, as I have discussed, just as the poor of rich countries have developed vigorous environmental movements. These movements are heavily based on class conflict—which is not to say that risk isn't involved. Disruptions in the environmental resources upon which you depend are particularly risky when you're poor. Environmental risk is not something you start experiencing only after you become comfortably well-off. We have been living in risk societies for a long, long time.

Also, it may be that Beck's risk society theory fits his native Germany better than it fits most other wealthy countries.[67] The spectacular success of the German Green Party is, well, spectacular. No other country has seen the environmental agenda take such a central political role. Although the German Greens are still a minority party, their success has prompted the other major parties in the country to address many environmental issues and concerns. Meanwhile, environmental issues have a lower, in some cases far lower, political profile in most other Western nations. Beck is right, though, to point to the frequent centrality of risk issues when green concerns do receive attention, such as the recent debate over "mad cow" disease in Britain.

But the main difficulty with both the theory of the risk society and the theory of postmaterialism is that they overstate the degree to which we have overcome economic anxiety and economic conflict. Wealth creation remains the central political goal of every country in the world, rich and poor. Meanwhile, recent years have seen a great increase in economic inequality both between and within nations, reversing the equalizing trend that had prevailed during the middle decades of the twentieth century. Despite the responses people give to Inglehart's four-item test of leading goals, even in wealthy countries people remain thoroughly caught up in the desire for economic gain and in worries about whether they will attain it. Economistic, materialist thinking seems on the rise, if anything.

But something else has also been on the rise, something that both the theories of risk society and postmaterialism point to in a way. That something, as I'll come to in a few pages, is democracy.

Paradigm Shift

Before I get to the influence of democracy, however, we need to consider one more research tradition that traces the relationship between the material and the rise of environmental concern: the *paradigm shift* thesis. This theory suggests that, in response to discrepancies between the evidence of environmental threats and ideologies that do not consider environmental implications, people are slowly but steadily adopting a more environmentally aware view of the world. People are becoming more aware of the real material effects that industrial life has on the environment, and their ideologies are beginning to change to match this new understanding. It's a deceptively simple theory, originally proposed by the sociologists Riley Dunlap, William Catton, and Kent Van Liere in the late 1970s, and by Stephen Cotgrove and Lester Milbrath in the early 1980s.[68]

I say deceptively simple in part because measuring environmental awareness turns out to be quite difficult. Paradigm shift researchers have generally approached the question by distinguishing between two paradigms, one old and one new. Under the old paradigm, humans are exceptional creatures that face few ultimate environmental limits, and the basic goal of human society is technological mastery over nature for the purpose of wealth creation. Researchers have variously termed this view the "dominant social paradigm," the "human exceptionalism paradigm," and the "technological social paradigm." Under the new paradigm, humans are a part of nature and need to maintain a sense of balance and limits in an interconnected world. Researchers have variously termed this latter view the "new environmental paradigm," the "alternative environmental paradigm," and the "ecological social paradigm."[69] Based on this contrast, paradigm shift researchers have devised batteries of survey questions to assess how strongly a person adheres to one paradigm or the other.

The next measurement complexity is assessing why people's ideas might change from one paradigm to another. In a 1982 survey of the State of Washington, a research team from Washington State University approached this issue by distinguishing between *environmental beliefs* and *environmental values*—between how a person thinks the environment is and how she or he thinks the environment ought to be. For example, the researchers assessed environmental beliefs by asking people how much they agreed with a battery of statements such as "The earth is like a spaceship, with limited room and resources." They appraised environmental values with statements like "People should adapt to the environment whenever possible."

It might be expected that beliefs and values would correspond fairly closely, but the Washington State survey found considerably stronger support for environmental beliefs than environmental values. Although 78 percent of Washington residents expressed some degree of an "ecological social paradigm," 57 percent of the respondents were what the researchers called "strong believers," and only 25 percent were "strong valuers."[70] The Washington State researchers argue that what is at work is the slow process of people's values catching up with their beliefs about external material realities—such as rising levels of pollution, the disappearing wild, technological failures like Chernobyl and Three Mile Island.

Similar to Thomas Kuhn's theory of scientific revolutions, the Washington State team's conclusions suggest that we tend initially to hold on to our paradigms even in the face of contradictory evidence. But eventually we seek to bring the two—paradigms and evidence of the external world—into better correspondence, leading to paradigm change. As the Washington State team wrote, "Our analysis suggests that shifts in social paradigms are influenced primarily by external discrepancies."[71]

Questioning the Paradigm Shift. But we must be cautious in interpreting these survey results too. To begin with, there is the obvious problem of reducing such a complex matter as environmental ideology to only two categories. Such reduction may obscure ideological complexities more than it clarifies them.[72] A lot more may be going on.

A closely related problem is deciding which particular ideology represents the environmental ideal. There are likely as many environmentalisms as there are people. Whose environmentalism, then, does one choose as the standard? Paradigm shift researchers have tried to draw this standard from the works of leading environmental writers.[73] But writers do not represent everyone (or there would be no need to conduct a survey), nor do they always agree (or they probably wouldn't bother to write). Inevitably, researchers have had to draw on their own understandings of environmental writers and environmentalism. There is thus a danger that paradigm shift researchers are only assessing the degree to which the rest of the world agrees with them about what environmentalism is.

Survey-based research also doesn't give respondents a chance to explain why they answered the survey questions in the ways that they did. Survey researchers have to presume ahead of time the kind of phrases and questions that might reflect the way people see things. But there is no opportunity on a survey to determine if a person interprets a question quite differently from the way the researchers intend. For example, I might reject the notion that "the earth is like a spaceship, with limited room and resources" because I don't like the mechanical and technological image of a "spaceship." I might see the earth more as an organism. In other words, I might disagree with the statement even though I agree with the belief the statement is meant to assess.

Finally, there is the difficulty of assessing long-term ideological change with surveys of current public opinion. The kind of ideological change that paradigm shift researchers hope to evaluate may be taking place over too long a time for surveys to document. The problem is, you can't go back and administer a questionnaire to the people of the past. Thus, survey research needs to be balanced with historical research.

These critiques do not invalidate paradigm shift research, however. Measuring and understanding public opinion is an inherently difficult task. All survey-based research faces these measurement problems. Without some simplifying assumptions, the question of ideological change probably could not be researched, particularly with the kind of large-scale public opinion polls that paradigm shift researchers have emphasized. And even a grainy image of the overall state of the public mind is useful and important to have.

Moreover, it seems hard to deny that material factors must have ideological consequence. If our patterns of thought, our mental reflexes, had no bearing on our material conditions we would likely not last long. Or, to put it another way, if you keep stubbing your toe when you kick the environment, chances are you will eventually stop to reconsider why you were kicking it in the first place. And maybe that's what we're finally starting to do.

THE DEMOCRATIC BASIS OF CONTEMPORARY ENVIRONMENTAL CONCERN

But if a mind is not already attuned to the implications of "external discrepancies," and if information about the existence of these discrepancies is not heard by that mind, ideological change is likely to be slow—even in the face of substantial material threats to the environment. In the late nineteenth century, as the industrial revolution was still gathering steam, relatively few people would have been aware of the way the new industries were polluting. And even if they had been aware, few people would have been deeply concerned, so strong was the faith in technological progress. But a hundred years later, people are both much more attuned to environmental concerns and much more likely to hear about discrepancies between their values and reality. Both this attuning and this hearing have been given ears by the spread of democracy, its sensibilities, and its institutions.

Democratic Sensibilities

"It is impossible," the historian Keith Thomas suggests, "to disentangle what the people of the past thought about plants and animals from what they thought about themselves."[74] A less-hierarchical ordering of human relations is historically associated with a less-hierarchical ordering of human-environmental relations. I don't want to overstate the point: There are plenty of exceptions. But the rise of democratic sensibilities in the social realm does seem to be generally associated with the rise of parallel sensibilities in the environmental realm.

Consider the rise of environmental concern in the eighteenth and nineteenth centuries, what is often termed the "first wave" of environmentalism.[75] This is the period of the first national parks and the first environmental pressure groups, Henry David Thoreau and Ralph Waldo Emerson, Gilbert White and William Wordsworth, and so many more important figures in environmental thought and so many more important "firsts" in environmental protection. Strikingly, this period also saw the rise of new ideas about how human society should be arranged. In 1690, John Locke published his *Two Treatises of Government*. In 1754, Jean-Jacques Rousseau published his *Discourse on the Origins of Inequality*. Inspired in part by the ideas in such books, the United States declared its revolutionary independence from Britain in 1776, and France had its own revolution in 1789. Country after country in the nineteenth century went on to make their own democratic reforms.

These new sensibilities concerning the rights of each human were accompanied by, or soon led to, similar concerns about what constituted decent treatment of the nonhuman aspects of creation. To a democratic mind, environmental exploitation just didn't feel right. Of course, the democratic mind had a long way to go (and still does). Slavery, colonization, racism, sexism, classism and the rest had hardly disappeared, nor had the "environmental movement" as we understand it today begun. (Nor is the environmental movement always democratic, as the next chapter discusses.) But beginning in the eighteenth century and continuing throughout the nineteenth century, a broadening conception of human rights was accompanied by a broadening conception of natural rights and a greater valuation of both.[76] It is likely no accident that the great early writers for environmental reform were often important figures in social reform as well, such as John Ruskin, William Morris, and Henry Salt, not to mention Thoreau.

Steadily throughout this period, democratic concern grew not only for the rights (and beauty) of nature, but also for the equitable distribution of environmental goods and bads. This was also, of course, the beginning of the industrial age. But the material threats that industrialism posed to the environment were not by themselves enough to evince a concern for environmental justice. Democratic concern played a key role.

A voice of democratic concern for environmental justice is heard in this 1845 description of conditions in Manchester, England, the center of the young industrial revolution:

> Looking down from Ducie Bridge, the passer-by sees several
> ruined walls and heaps of *debris* with some newer houses. The
> view from this bridge, mercifully concealed from mortals of
> small stature by a parapet as high as a man, is characteristic of
> the whole district. At the bottom flows, or rather stagnates, the
> Irk, a narrow, coal-black, foul-smelling stream, full of *debris* and

refuse, which it deposits on the shallower right bank. In dry weather, a long string of the most disgusting, blackish-green, slime pools are left standing on this bank, from the depths of which bubbles of miasmatic gas constantly arise and give forth a stench unindurable even on the bridge forty or fifty feet above the surface of the stream. Above the bridge are tanneries, bonemills, and gasworks, from which all drains and refuse find their way into the Irk, which receives further the contents of all the neighbouring sewers and privies... [H]ere each house is packed close behind its neighbour... The whole side of the Irk is built in this way, a planless, knotted chaos of houses, more or less on the verge of uninhabitableness, whose unclean interiors fully correspond with their filthy external surroundings. And how could the people be clean with no proper opportunity for satisfying the most natural and ordinary wants? Privies are so rare here that they are either filled up every day, or are too remote for most inhabitants to use. How can people wash when they have only the dirty Irk water at hand? ... Everything which here arouses horror and indignation is of recent origin, [and] belongs to the *industrial epoch*."[77]

That voice of democratic concern was a young Friedrich Engels.

A short while later, George Perkins Marsh, a scholar and diplomat from Vermont, began questioning the long-term sustainability of industrialism's rapacious appetite for resources. In his 1864 book, *Man and Nature, or, Physical Geography Modified by Human Action*, Marsh argued that humans had unknowingly become a geological force in their own right—clearing forests, altering climate and the flow of rivers, shifting the pace of erosion—often to the detriment of human interests. Vast areas of Michigan's forest, for example, had disappeared in a few short decades of unrestrained cutting; Marsh's own Vermont had suffered the same fate. The result was soil erosion and more severe seasonal floods, since the forests were no longer there to absorb rainwater. Marsh's main goal was "to point out the dangers of imprudence and the necessity of caution in all operations which, on a large scale, interfere with the spontaneous arrangements of the organic or the inorganic world." We must now ask "the great question," concluded Marsh: "whether man is of nature or above her."[78] This, perhaps, was the most difficult democratic question of all.

Exhibit 6.4 *The Spread of Democracy.*

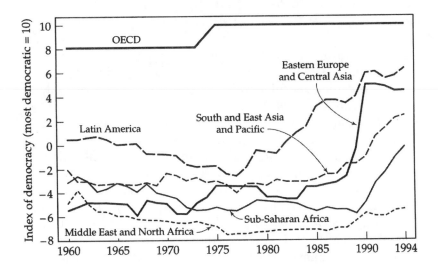

Source: World Bank

The same association between democratic and environmental sensibilities may be behind survey results showing an association between "postmaterialist" values and environmental concern. As I argued earlier, there is good reason to doubt that postmaterialism is closely linked with environmental concern, despite the association surveys have found. The reason for this association may be that Inglehart's four-item materialism/ postmaterialism scale measures democratization, not a shift toward postmaterialism. In fact, Inglehart deliberately chose the two postmaterialist items on his scale—"giving people more say in important government decisions" and "protecting freedom of speech"—to reflect democratic attitudes, as he regarded such attitudes to be one feature of postmaterialism.[79] Furthermore, a low ranking of "maintaining order in the nation" (one of his two "material" items in the scale) may reflect democratic concern about authoritarianism—and not lack of material worries. And given that inflation is no longer a major economic issue in most wealthy countries, "fighting rising prices" (the other of his two "material" items) may not be an accurate gauge of material worries either.

In other words, we are left with three items in Inglehart's scale that potentially tap democratic sensibilities and one item that is probably irrelevant. Thus the correlation Inglehart found between what he called "postmaterialism" and environmental action may actually show instead that in the twentieth century democratic sensibilities continue to influence environmental ones.

• •

SOCIAL ACTION CASE STUDY
THE ANIMAL PROTECTION MOVEMENT

Alongside rising sensibilities of concern for the environment have been similar sensibilities about the condition of animals. The spread of democratic thinking has led people to consider not only the needs and rights of the environment but of animals as well. "If a being suffers," wrote the Australian philosopher Peter Singer in his 1975 book, *Animal Liberation*, "there can be no moral justification for refusing to take that suffering into consideration, and, indeed, to count it equally with the like suffering . . . of any other being."[1]   Animals have also served as a source of moral innocence, of natural conscience, for humans searching for a moral realm free of politics and social interests. Moreover, human domination of the environment has been accompanied by a parallel domination of animals—for food, clothing, sport, research subjects, and expansion of human habitat.

Thus, because of the material domination of animals, the moral attractiveness of animals, and the spread of democractic attitudes toward animals, the modern environmental movement has developed alongside the modern *animal protection movement*. Sometimes the two movements have marched hand-in-hand, but often relations have been uneasy. Where environmentalists have sought to preserve species and habitats, animal protectionists have emphasized the condition of individual animals. Frequently these concerns have overlapped, as in the common environmental view that a vegetarian diet can help protect the environment by reducing the need for land to raise animal feed. But many environmentalists have regarded animal protection as a relatively trivial concern, and animal protectionists have regarded such environmentalists as narrow-minded.

The animal protection movement has two principal strands. *Animal welfare* activists work for the humane treatment of animals. *Animal rights* activists take a more radical view, arguing that the rights of animals stand on a par with the rights of humans. The two are sometimes confused, for they come together in protest over many issues, such as the raising of livestock in factory farms and the unregulated use of animals in medical research. But where animal rights activists generally reject meat eating and animal-based research, animal welfarists generally accept the eating of meat and the use of animals in experiments as long as the animals are treated humanely.

Like the environmental movement, public support for animal protection is high. People identify democratically with animals, they find moral value in animals, and they are concerned for the treatment of animals. However, few support the idea that animals have rights equal to those of people, and few follow related practices such as a vegan diet and refusing to wear leather. There is far more public support for the animal welfare position than the animal rights position. But however one ultimately comes down on the moral and material questions of animal rights and animal welfare, a democratic mind will almost inevitably find itself pondering these issues.

Notes
1 Singer (1996 [1975]), 9.

• •

Democratic Institutions

The institutions of democracy have been no less important to environmental concern than have democratic sensibilities. For instance, the free press has played an absolutely central role in alerting the public to environmental problems, in creating environmental "hearing." And without democratic rights to assemble, to protest, to vote, and to establish political parties that challenge the existing order, environmentalism would likely never have developed into a popular movement anywhere. No popular movement of any kind is likely without such abilities, as authoritarian governments have long recognized.

Consider how long it took for environmentalism to gain attention in the state socialist countries of the former Soviet bloc. Environmental problems went so long unattended that these countries now face some of the world's worst local environmental conditions.[80] When Mikhail Gorbachev came to power in the Soviet Union in 1985, bearing his policy of *glasnost*, which allowed a degree of political expression unprecedented in the Soviet bloc, its environmental movement suddenly came of age. Indeed, concern over environmental conditions was one of the major political forces behind the 1989 revolutions. The importance of this concern is reflected in the striking name of a Bulgarian environmental group that emerged in 1990: *Ecoglasnost*. As Guha observes, this name "bears testimony to the inseparable link between democracy and environmentalism."[81]

Ecoglasnost has also been an important factor in the development of the environmentalism of the poor countries of the Southern Hemisphere. Poor countries are often—indeed are usually—authoritarian ones. If environmental concern in poor countries has sometimes been hard to discern, in part this has been because the absence of democracy's freedoms has prevented the expression of such concern. Those with the courage of a Ken Saro-Wiwa are rare. As Guha has also observed, "It is no accident that one of the more robust green movements in the South is to be found in India, a democracy for all but two of its fifty years as an independent republic."[82]

And perhaps democracy is the real source of the "risk society." The questioning of science and technology that Beck describes as characteristic features of this society may not represent the new anxieties of the newly affluent. Instead, concern over global warming, the ozone hole, tainted food, and radioactive fallout may represent the freer communication and freer protest that democracy makes possible. It is not that we feel more at risk today than we did in the nineteenth century. The widespread poverty and high mortality rates of that time were very risky. Rather, because of the *ecoglasnost* that increasingly we all experience, we no longer feel that we have to put up with a risk society—particularly an imposed risk society. We feel we can publicly ask the question that the American folksinger Charlie King once asked in a 1970s song about nuclear power plants: "The risks are all 'acceptable'—'acceptable' to whom?"[83]

COMMUNITY, INEQUALITY, AND THE DIALOGUE OF ENVIRONMENTAL CONCERN

Environmental concern is both new and old. Much of what makes this concern so constant are enduring moral issues: namely, social inequality and the challenges it poses to community. The desire to find a moral realm outside the reach of power and self-interest—the desire to find a natural conscience—represents another manifestation of the role social inequality plays in social-environmental relations, a role that has been one of the principal themes of this book. Democracy, both in its sensibilities and its institutions, is another way that we try to deal with the challenges inequality poses to us.

Another enduring source of environmental concern is the constancy of material environmental threats. Industrialization and urbanization have brought with them an enormous range of benefits, of environmental goods. But the costs, the environmental bads, have not been inconsequential. These material threats have continually confronted us with the moral threat of inequality—of the power of some to impose on others—and thus with the question of how we are to define and organize human communities, including that biggest community of all.

Exhibit 6.5 *A model of the rise of environmental concern: Material and ideal factors shape each other, leading to change in environmental concern—which in turn reshapes the original material and ideal factors.*

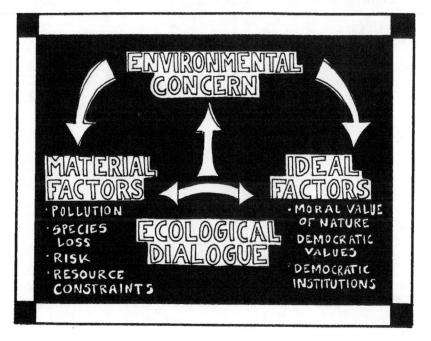

Not only has the material shaped the moral, though. Our moral sensibilities concerning the importance (or lack of importance) of democracy and a natural conscience have shaped our ability to conceptualize environmental problems as problems—yet another dialogue between the material and the ideal. In other words, material threats to the environment are thus closely intertwined with idealogical threats of environmental inequality.

The modern environmental movement can be described as a diolgue that connects the natural conscience, the condition of democracy, and the material state of the environment. Because of this dialogue, we have come to see the environment as morally attractive, morally compelling, and morally threatened. Raising our concerns in so many ways, the environment has become one of the leading moral issues of this or any day.

Yet does the ecological dialogue go further? If our ideological inclinations shape our ability to conceptualize material threats as threats, can these threats be said to have any independent existence apart from our perception of them? Indeed, can nature itself be said to have such an independent existence? These questions point to a material threat of another kind—a threat to the very existence of the material realm, or at least to how we have traditionally conceived of that realm.

But that is the subject of the next chapter. It's time for a breather.

CHAPTER 7

The Human Nature of Nature

When I hear that nature is a ruthless competitive struggle I remember the butterfly, and when I hear that it is a system of ultimate mutual advantage I remember the cyclone.

-Raymond Williams, 1972

My family's favorite brand of ice cream claims to contain something it calls "natural vanilla" flavor. I never really thought about it much until recently, when my son Sam asked me what was natural about it.

"Natural products are things people have done less to—you know, less manufacturing and processing," I told him. "Artificial vanilla flavor comes from a chemical made in a factory, and natural vanilla flavor comes from ground-up beans from vanilla plants," I said, pointing out the dark flecks in the ice cream. (I'm not even sure that's true, but it is what I said.)

Then I got to thinking that a heck of a lot of processing must go on in making "natural" vanilla flavor. Processors probably dry the beans in one machine, grind them up in another, and package them with yet a third. To grow the beans, farmers likely use a crop variety that scientists have specially developed for the purpose. No doubt they grow it in a field cleared from a tropical forest with machines, kept clear of weeds and insects with machines, and harvested with machines—not to mention the generous use of farm chemicals at several points along the way. Suddenly those beans didn't seem so "natural" anymore.

I tried to explain all this to Sam, which was probably a mistake. Soon I found myself in a major philosophical wrangle with an eight-year old. "Everything's natural," Sam said, defending the ice cream we were both licking up.

There are a number of difficulties with such an all-encompassing view, and I tried to describe them.

"Then maybe nothing's natural," he suggested before I got very far. That's not exactly what I think either, but before I could explain why, a lightbulb turned on somewhere in Sam's brain.

"Dad, I know. Everything that comes from the earth is natural, and everything else isn't." He paused for a moment to work this thought through. "That means that solar power isn't natural because it comes from the sun and not the earth."

Such are the hazards of having an environmental sociologist for a father.

But Sam was only trying to deal with some central philosophical issues that have beset environmentalism from its earliest beginnings in the ancient world through to the current day. They are central sociological issues too, for our philosophical resolutions have laid the moral foundations of environmental concern. In this chapter we explore the sociological origins and implications of the resolutions we have sought to Sam's dilemma: What is nature?

Whatever else it may be, nature is without a doubt one of the most powerful of human concepts. Some of the most noble and selfless things that people have ever done have been in the name of nature. Consider the Greenpeace activists who have gone out on the open seas in small rubber boats to put themselves between dolphins and a careless tuna industry. Or consider the protesters in England who barricade themselves in hand-dug tunnels underneath proposed highways in order to prevent the movement of heavy-construction machinery. People have often put their lives on the line—and sometimes over the line, with fatal results—in defense of nature. They have sought to defend not only nature in the environmental sense but also nature as a democratic ideal. The notion of the "natural" rights of every person to a healthy, happy, fulfilling life in freedom has moved nations, governments, and their citizens to revolutionary acts of kindness and goodness.

But we also have to recognize that nature is one of the most dangerous of human concepts. The cultural history of nature is far from uniformly noble. For example, ideas of natural differences between humans—differences of sex, of race, of ethnicity, of talent and skill—have led to the enslavement of millions, the outright slaughter of further millions, and the oppression and mistreatment of still millions more. We ignore this other side of nature at our peril.

Considering the difficult cultural history of nature, we would do well to exercise every critical caution in evaluating the uses to which we put the idea. To say that something is natural or to counsel that the appropriate course of action is to follow nature is to suggest something of immense significance for our moral values, for our identities, for our everyday lives, and thus for our politics. The previous chapter introduced the concept of the natural conscience, our common search for a realm that lies beyond the taint of social power and human interests and that might serve as an unbiased and external source of moral value and identity. But is such a realm possible? Can we truly escape the influence of our interests? This chapter takes a critical look at the relationship between ideas of nature and human interests and the implications of this relationship for the moral and political claims we make.

These are difficult issues, which challenge us all. But since these issues are central to how we constitute our human community and our ecological community, it is crucial that we accept the challenge.

THE CONTRADICTIONS OF NATURE

"Can and ought we to follow nature?" the environmental philosopher Holmes Rolston once asked.[1] Answering this question depends upon resolving a basic contradiction in the idea of nature, the contradiction between what can be termed *moral separatism* and *moral holism*.[2]

Think of the contradiction this way. One of the truisms of the contemporary environmental movement is that people are part of nature and that environmental problems have emerged because we have tried to pretend otherwise. This is a holist moral point of view. But if we are a part of nature, there is no need to advise us to follow it, for we must already be doing so. How could we do anything but follow it? Under moral holism, "follow nature" is superfluous advice.

If people are separate from nature, the moral situation is no better. Since nature is different from us and is moved by different principles, it has no meaning for us. In fact, we probably *can't* follow nature, no matter how hard we try. Under moral separatism, then, "follow nature" is irrelevant advice.

As the sociologist Kai Erikson once observed, a moral value requires "a point of contrast which gives the norm some scope and dimension."[3] It has to give us a way to make moral distinctions. Otherwise, it will be a superfluous value. A moral value also requires a point of connection, however, if it is to be relevant to our actions. For nature to serve as a source of value that we can "follow," it has to be conceived in ways that provide points of both contrast and connection.

The contradiction between separatism and holism extends into the problem of power and interest, which is so central to the natural conscience. A natural conscience depends upon a belief in a moral realm that lies beyond the reach of social power and the possibility that we might manipulate social values to suit the interests of some more than others. Such a realm requires separation from society if it is to be free from social influence, and it requires holist unity if it is to be relevant to social issues. But that unity immediately reintroduces the possibility that human interests may have been tinkering with what we conceive nature to be.

Any successful philosophy of nature must offer some kind of solution to these moral contradictions if it is to serve as a basis for a natural conscience.[4]

Ancient Problems, Ancient Solutions

The earliest philosophers of nature were well aware of the problems of holist superfluousness and separatist irrelevance. Aristotle, for example, worried about the "monism," as he termed it, in ideas like Plato's view that Goodness created the whole world and that, therefore, the whole world was good. Under such a philosophy, Aristotle wrote, "the being of the good and the being of the bad, of good and not good, will be the same, and the thesis under discussion will no longer be that all things are one, but that they are nothing at all."[5]

Aristotle suggested a way that we could distinguish the natural and the not-natural without falling into the problem of monist holism. That which comes into being "by nature," Aristotle argued, was that which had its "source of change" within itself.[6] Examples might be the movement of wind, the growth of plants and animals, the dynamics of fire. Since humans have an internal source of change—our body's processes of growth and development—much that humans do is also according to nature. But something whose source of change is outside of itself is not due to nature, said Aristotle. So anything that humans make is not due to nature, although the materials humans use may well be. Aristotle gave the example of a wooden bed. Wood grows according to natural principles of growth internal to the tree, but the shape it takes as a bed is the result of an external source of change: humans. So wood is natural but a bed is not.

This is a clever solution to the contradictions of nature. Humans are a part of nature because they have a source of change inside themselves. But when humans use that source of change to alter something outside themselves, they are not acting in accordance to nature. Aristotle thereby provided points of both moral connection and contrast.

Aristotle also argued that nature is the result of the workings of "the Good" (an idea he retained from Plato, as Chapter 6 describes). Appealing to this godlike ideal allowed Aristotle to claim that nature was interest-free—that nature had been created by something that was removed from human influence—thus allowing him to establish a natural conscience.

This was not a perfect solution, however. Maybe we're acting in accordance with our internal source of change when we do something like construct a bed or build a particular form of society or foster certain societal-environmental relations. Who is to say? We may do unnatural things for natural reasons. Aristotle's approach also could not distinguish beds made by humans from dams made by beavers and hives made by bees. A beaver dam must be as unnatural as anything humans make, for it equally has its source of change outside itself—in beavers. In fact, every action of every creature induces changes in the world around it and must therefore be unnatural, collapsing the point of moral contrast Aristotle hoped to establish.

The ancient Taoists offered a solution of their own. Recall from chapter 6 the Taoist distinction between *wu wei*, acting without deliberate effort, and *yu wei*, acting deliberately. *Wu wei* guides one along the lines of *tao*, and *yu wei* leads away from it, a clear moral contrast. And because *tao* is something larger and prior to humans, it lies beyond the taint of human interests and desires, thereby serving as a basis for a natural conscience. Taoists found a point of moral connection by suggesting that *tao* is the underlying first principle of everything, including humans. *Tao* gives everything a *te*, its essential qualities. People can ignore their *te* and act *yu wei* or they can encourage *te* by acting *wu wei*—a separatism within a holism.

This solution, though, was not without problems either, and later Taoist philosophy tried to grapple with some of these dilemmas. One problem was that acting without deliberate effort seemed a contradiction in terms. Taoism seemed to be counseling people to make a deliberate choice to act without deliberation, to desire to be without desire. Thus, in order to adopt the Taoist solution you unavoidably introduce desire and interest, undermining its value as a source of a natural conscience.

Perhaps more problematic, though, is the issue of how one is to know when one is acting according to one's *te* and when one is not. Perhaps my *te* is to construct buildings and bridges. Perhaps my *te* is to be ruler of the world—not because I myself actually desire it but because my *te* just happens to flow along such lines. In fact, it would be going against *tao* not to exercise such a *te* to the fullest, suggested Kuo Hsiang, a "rationalist" Taoist from the first century C.E. Of course, practically any human action can be justified on such grounds, and thus the Taoist point of moral contrast also collapses.

Later thinkers offered solutions to these problems. For example, a standard Taoist response to the problem of deliberately choosing to be undeliberate is that it's a matter of getting things going, like setting afloat down a river on a raft. You do have to make the choice to get on the raft, to be sure, but after that the river of *tao* takes over.[7] But the fact that later thinkers found it necessary to offer solutions highlights the centrality of the problem of nature's moral contradictions.

The Contradictions of Contemporary Environmentalism

These contradictions continue to confront us, and contemporary environmentalism is continually rethinking its solutions to them.

Take the very idea, so pervasive in environmentalism, that nature is good, and that it is best to do things the "natural" way—to use natural materials like cotton and wood and paper, instead of nylon and concrete and plastic, for example, or ground-up vanilla beans instead of "artificial" vanilla flavoring. The word *natural* here sets up a clear moral contrast between good and bad. But what law of nature does nylon, concrete, or plastic break? These substances are in fact derived from the materials of nature and the earth: petroleum for nylon and plastic; sand, water, limestone, and other crushed rock for concrete; and whatever it is they use to make artificial vanilla flavor.

Sometimes people say that the difference is that materials like nylon, concrete, and plastic have seen more processing and refining (the basis for distinguishing the natural that I initially suggested to my son). They are more the product of human actions than are cotton, wood, paper, and "natural" food. This is an empirically dubious claim, though, as anyone familiar with what goes on in the growing, harvesting, and processing of cotton, wood, paper, and "natural" food can attest to.

The moral claim being made is also dubious. Such an argument rests on a distinction similar to Aristotle's: Things that come about through their own internal source of change (or more through their own internal source of change) are natural (or more natural) and not the product of human desires and interests. But are not humans a part of nature? Is that not also one of the great moral arguments of environmentalism? Anything humans do must therefore be natural, including making plastic—as well as cities, automobiles, toxic waste, and even atomic bombs. Indeed, what human has ever broken a law of nature? If it were a law of nature, how could a human have broken it? By this logic, nothing could be more—or less—natural than an atomic bomb.

Or take the idea of wilderness, which is often seen, particularly among North Americans, as the fullest expression of the true ends of nature and environmentalism. Thoreau sought in wilderness a restful release from the pollution of politics, and millions still do today. And what is wilderness? At least as the political process has defined it, wilderness is national parks and other areas of land set aside from deliberate human interference. But isn't the very setting aside of land a deliberate human action, thereby making wilderness the product of human intention rather than the result of its absence?

Perhaps the Taoist response applies here—that establishing a national park is like setting a raft afloat. But then a critic might ask, if humans are natural, why should we exclude houses, roads, open pit mines, and McDonald's from wilderness areas? And why should we see cities and farms as less wild and less in need of the attention of environmentalist concern?

The moral problem is that environmentalism needs to establish the relevance of nature to humans by arguing for our unity with it and, at the same time, to contrast humans and nature in order to set aside a realm that is free from the pollution of human interests. Upon this basic moral contradiction modern environmentalism uneasily rests.

NATURE AS A SOCIAL CONSTRUCTION

The point I've been leading up to is one that virtually all environmental sociologists recognize today: Whatever else nature might be, it is also a *social construction*.[8] Nature is something we make, as much as it makes us. How we see nature depends upon our perspective on social life. And as this perspective changes across time and place, history and culture, nature changes with it.

The British sociologist Raymond Williams, in a classic 1972 essay, put it this way: "The idea of nature contains an extraordinary amount of human history. What is often being argued, it seems to me, in the idea of nature is the idea of man; and this not only generally, or in ultimate ways, but the idea of man in society, indeed the ideas of kinds of societies."[9] (Williams, writing in an earlier day, uses *man* to mean all people.)

Williams's point is that we look at nature through social categories formed by human interests. Our image of nature depends upon *social selection* and *social reflection*. We tend to select particular features of nature to focus upon, ignoring those that do not suit our interests and the worldview shaped by those interests. Moreover, the categories we use to comprehend nature closely reflect the categories we use to comprehend society; social life is so fundamental to our experience that all our categories reflect our social perspectives. Because of social selection and social reflection, "nature" is an inescapably social—and political—phenomenon.

I'll give several extended examples in a moment. But first let me point out that such a perspective on our perspectives of nature is itself a perspective on nature—one perhaps best labeled *postmodernist*. Since the 1960s, an increasing number of social theorists have been arguing against the objectivist notion of a world in which there is only one truth about any one thing, the truth that best represents "the way things really are." Such a simplistic view is characteristic of the technological and scientific faith of modern society, say postmodern theorists. Truth is socially relative. What you see depends on *who* you are and not just on the character of the world "out there," postmodernists argue. And so too for an idea long associated with our conceptions of truth: nature.

• •

SOCIAL ACTION CASE STUDY
BRINGING NATURE TO THE CITY: URBAN AGRICULTURE

We often regard the city as the polar opposite of nature. Cities symbolize for us the interest-laden realm of politics and greed, and nature represents a point of moral contrast from urban grime, physical and social. Cities seem both physically and socially polluted; nature seems physically and socially clean.

Perhaps for these reasons, the environmental movement has concentrated much of its efforts on wildlife and wilderness protection—establishing national parks, protecting endangered species, saving essential habitats, mostly in places far from cities. But in recent years, a new urban environmentalism has been emerging that complements the goal of protecting the distant wild. Urban environmentalists are campaigning for maintaining cleaner cities, for seeing cities as a kind of ecosystem, for using cities as an opportunity for a more environmentally-attuned lifestyle through the greater resource efficiency dense populations can make possible. Urban environmentalists are also campaigning for protection of urban wildlife habitat and open space. Cities, they argue, can be as "natural" as any other place.

One feature of the new urban environmentalism is a renewed interest in growing food in cities. *Urban agriculture* may seem like a contradiction in terms, but in fact fully a third of the world's food is produced in urban areas, according to a 1996 United Nations study. Some 800 million people worldwide raise vegetable gardens, fruit, dairy cows, and small livestock such as chickens inside urban boundaries. In all, some one-third of the world's urban land is under cultivation, raising food both for home consumption and for sale.[1]

Most urban agriculture takes place in poor countries, but there is also a strong agricultural tradition in the urban areas of wealthy countries. Some 40 percent of the dollar value of U.S. agricultural production comes from metropolitan areas, mostly on the semiurban fringe. Millions are also involved in agriculture in the urban core, through such practices as the community garden "allotments" that have been a feature of British cities for decades and through cultivation of the home vegetable gardens to be found almost everywhere.[2]

In the last decade, interest in community gardens and home gardens has been growing by leaps and bounds. Thirty percent of American households now raise gardens. The city of Berlin has found space on its municipal land for some 80,000 community gardeners but still has a waiting list of 16,000. The allotment system in Britain is expanding beyond its earlier working-class associations and is attracting increasing interest from the professional classes. New York City now has over a thousand community garden sites.[3]

In 1991 I experienced the popularity of community gardening first hand. At the time, I was a volunteer with the New Haven Land Trust, an urban open-space preservation group in Connecticut. That summer, the Land Trust helped establish a community gardening program in New Haven, offering neighborhood groups free insurance for gardens and assistance in negotiating space from landowners. We began with three community gardens, including two in very rough neighborhoods. People loved the opportunity to work with soil and with plants— and also with their neighbors—in greening their part of town. The next summer there were nine gardens, the summer after that nearly thirty. Retirement homes, church groups, youth groups, and neighborhood block watches all took up the opportunity. At last count, there were over a hundred New Haven community gardening projects growing food and flowers, as well as something equally precious—community itself.

Notes
1 UNDP (1996).
2 UNDP (1996), 47.
3 UNDP (1996), 44–47.

• •

Nature and New England's Agricultural Decline

An example of a selective vision of nature, guided by social interests, is the oft-told story of a famous event in North American environmental history: The decline of agriculture in New England. (New England is the traditional name for the six most northeasterly of the United States—Maine, Vermont, New Hampshire, Massachusetts, Connecticut, and Rhode Island.) I draw this example from some of my own research.

The Traditional Story. New England, it is widely acknowledged, is a lousy place to farm. It's too rocky and too hilly, and the soil is too acid and too infertile to raise decent crops. As soon as European settlers could, they loaded up their wagons for the better lands of the American breadbasket in the Midwest and West. That chance came with the opening of the Erie Canal in 1825, which provided the first cheap means of shipping grain back to the East. Now there was a way for farms west of the Appalachians to get their products to market. Most of New England's farmland was promptly abandoned. If you walk through the region's vast woods, you can still see the miles of stone walls—the field boundaries thrown up by farmers in their back-breaking struggle to get enough rocks out of the ground to plant a few crops. No wonder the region has so little farmland today.[10]

Exhibit 7.1   Harvard Forest Diorama for 1740. "An Early Settler Clears a Homestead." This photo of the diorama, and the two that follow, illustrate the social construction of nature—the way our views of nature are shaped in part by our social perspectives.

Source: The Fisher Museum at the Harvard Forest, Petersham, Massachusetts.

This view of New England has been widely accepted by scholars. As two economic historians wrote, "In an agricultural sense it is customary to speak of New England as 'rock-ribbed,' thin-soiled, hilly, unfriendly, hardscrabbley, and other uncomplimentary terms. Yet, when one travels over the area with an eye to farming rather than history, culture, or industry, even a native of the region must admit that the unenthusiastic terms, for the most part, approach the truth."[11]

Exhibit 7.2 Harvard Forest Diorama for 1830. "The Height of Cultivation for Farm Crops." This view shows an extensively cleared landscape just at the time of the opening of the Erie Canal in 1825.

Source: The Fisher Museum at the Harvard Forest, Petersham, Massachusetts.

A series of dioramas at Harvard University's Fisher Museum of Forestry beautifully portray the "hard-scrabbly" view of New England. The dioramas show, in captivating detail, the changing landscape of New England through history, using a single portion of Harvard's own forest in Petersham, Massachusetts (where the musem is), as an example. The diorama for 1740 shows a settler clearing a homestead out of the virgin forest. The one for 1830, labeled "The Height of Cultivation for Farm Crops," shows a land almost completely cleared for farming, with fields lined mainly by stone walls. The diorama for 1850, though, shows an abrupt turnaround in New England's agricultural fortunes. It's labeled "Farm Abandonment" and displays a secondary growth of trees already starting to retake the land.

Few have ever challenged this account.[12] In fact, the notion of "abandoned New England" has become a part of the region's identity and is nostalgically promoted in tourist books, popular histories, and scenic calendars of the area. New England's rock-ribbed, thin-soiled hills are also the butt of a number of common jokes often told in (and out) of the region, including some rather clever ones. One of my favorites (and I was born in New England) is the following description of the area's land:

> Nature, out of her boundless store,
> Threw rocks together, and did no more.

Then there's this one about Maine, one of the country's leading potato-producing, states:

> Maine's number two crop is potatoes. Its number one crop is stones.

But perhaps everyone's favorite is the following one-liner:

> [I]f the United States had been settled from the Pacific coast, New England would not yet have been discovered.[13]

This last one has many variants, and sometimes ends, "New England would be a national forest."

Setting the Record Straight. It's a great story, and most people love it. But it's plain wrong. Rather than contracting after the opening of the Erie Canal, agricultural census records show that agricultural land in New England actually expanded until 1880. In fact, it experienced only a small decline until 1910, with agricultural land in the northern New England states actually continuing to expand. Only after 1910 did a sharp drop occur. The majority of the decline, some 58 percent, took place after World War II, more than one hundred years after the Erie Canal (and later the railroads) began shipping cheap grain East. True, expansion of western pioneer proportions did not occur in New England during the nineteenth century; but neither was there widespread abandonment.[14]

Moreover, crop yields in New England are comparatively high, contrary to its infertile image. New England's per acre yields of corn, oats, wheat, barley, and buckwheat actually exceeded national averages in the late nineteenth century. It's harder to make national comparisons today because agriculture is so specialized. One of the few crops still grown in most states is corn silage, and New England's yields are 30 percent above the national average—even higher than yields in Iowa, the country's most famous corn-growing state. And New England farmers use only modest amounts of fertilizer, despite their higher yields.[15]

Exhibit 7.3 Harvard Forest Diorama for 1850. "Farm Abandonment." The diorama suggests that, by this time, the effects of the Erie Canal have led to widespread farm abandonment as Western settlers began to ship cheap grain back East. Contrary to the history told by the dioramas, in most of New England, agriculture actually continued to expand for another fifty to seventy years. But because of the way it appeals to political interests, nostalgia, and the myth of technological progress, the dioramas' version of New England's history has seldom been challenged.

Source: The Fisher Museum at the Harvard Forest, Petersham, Massachusetts.

New England farms also make a lot of money. In the late nineteenth century, the southern New England states were among the country's leaders in value of farm products per acre of farmland: In 1889, Massachusetts, Rhode Island, and Connecticut ranked second, third, and fourth in the nation. A hundred years later they were doing just as well: In 1987, Connecticut, Massachusetts, and Rhode Island ranked first, third, and fifth in the nation in value of farm products per acre of farmland—ahead of even California, Florida, Iowa, and Illinois. (Total value of farm products is far higher in these bigger states, of course, but not the average per acre of farm land.) The northern New England states—Vermont, New Hampshire, and Maine—ranked considerably lower in both 1889 and 1987, because of their less intensive production and greater distance from markets. But they still ranked, and continue to rank, in the top half of the nation.[16]

Exhibit 7.4 Land in agriculture in New England over time: The thick line represents the average for New England as a whole; the other lines are for individual states. Note that the peak of agriculture for New England as a whole is around 1880, and that most of the eventual decline has come since 1950.

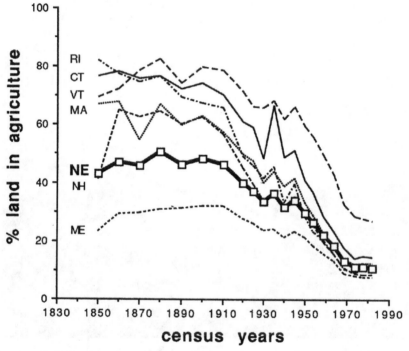

Source: U.S. Census of Agriculture.

The figures I cite above are in most cases from the national agricultural census, about as basic a source as there is. How could scholars have gotten it so wrong, then? Probably because, at some level, they wanted to—just as I, a New England native, want to set the record straight.

Social Selection and New England's Nature. The conventional view is not without evidence. It is true that rural population did decline precipitously in New England shortly after the opening of the Erie Canal. Many travel accounts written in the nineteenth century describe, usually with considerable anxiety, abandoned farmsteads all across the New England countryside. But as the historian Hal Barron has pointed out, increased mechanization allowed (and encouraged) fewer farmers to farm more land, depopulating the countryside while keeping production going.[17] The same process still goes on today in much of the West and Midwest.

Some farmland was abandoned as early as 1830, even as overall land in agriculture continued to climb in New England. One tract of early-abandoned land is the area where Harvard University now has its forest and on which the Harvard Forest dioramas are based. But these were isolated cases. Not surprisingly, this early-abandoned land now has some of New England's best forest on it, which is why Harvard chose such a site for its forest in the first place. The Harvard Forest dioramas, then, are not wrong: It's just that the history of the Harvard Forest has to be placed in a wider context.

And finally, much of New England's land is undoubtedly poorly suited to row-crop agriculture. There are definitely lots of rocks in those hills. But nineteenth-century farmers were not foolish, and they never tried to grow crops on the hilly and rocky ground. Where possible, they used it for pasture, but most of it they never cleared for farming at all. (They did cut practically all of it for timber and fuelwood, though, at least in southern New England.) At the 1880 peak of land in agriculture in New England, only a third of New England was cleared, according to the census; excluding Maine, the figure is 49 percent.[18] New England is not the Midwest. The proportion of farmable land is far lower. But the land that was farmable was, in fact, good land—at least as good as Midwestern land, and better according to some measures.

The conventional view of New England's agricultural history is not without evidence, but it depends on a selective reading of the historical record. This selection suits particular views of human society, particular social interests, as Raymond Williams would have readily recognized. I'll discuss three such views.

First, it is no accident that the conventional view of New England's hard-scrabble nature was promoted mainly by economic historians, who tend to relish anything that appears to be a victory of rational market forces. For them, New England has been the grudging bearer of the myth of technological progress and the economic glories of Western expansion.

Second, as a negative example of allegedly lower-quality farmland, the New England story has also suited some political interests. The "farm bloc," long a powerful lobby in Congress, is drawn mainly from Western and Midwestern states. Consequently, government subsidies have been structured to benefit most the crops dominated by Western and Midwestern farms. Between 1989 and 1991, for example, the proportion of economic returns to farming from direct government payments was just 0.9 percent in New England—well under the 6.5 percent figure for the whole nation. In some Western and Midwestern states, such as Montana and North Dakota, it was above 15 percent.[19]

And finally, the New England story felt right to urban and suburban New Englanders for whom it represents the loss of rural life, a loss about which they sometimes feel nostalgic and wistful. Meanwhile, the expansion of urban and suburban life—with its great demand for land and with the higher salaries that a city job generally yields—was largely responsible for the great loss of New England farmland following World War II.[20]

But urban and suburban residents, farm bloc politicians, and economic mythmakers need not take the blame, according to the traditional story of New England agriculture. The decline was due to nature itself and to the hardscrabble legacy it left New England—not to us. And in that externalization of cause, these selective views of New England's nature can perhaps offer some stony comfort.

Nature and Biology

I'll turn now to an example of both the social selection and social reflection of nature: Charles Darwin's theory of *natural* selection—the idea that species change over time as the most successful individuals pass on their distinctive traits to following generations.

When Darwin's book on natural selection, *On the Origin of Species*, appeared in 1859, it was an instant sensation, and intellectuals gave it close scrutiny and debated its implications. Among the earliest readers were, perhaps surprisingly, Karl Marx and Friedrich Engels. They immediately picked up a correspondence in Darwin's theory that irritated them considerably: It very closely resembled the economic theories of free-market capitalism that were so fundamentally altering the character of English society and, increasingly, world society. As Marx noted to Engels in a private letter in 1862, "It is remarkable how Darwin recognizes among beasts and plants his English society with its division of labour, competition, opening of new markets, 'inventions,' and the Malthusian 'struggle for existence.'"[21]

Consider some of the key mechanisms and results of natural selection that Darwin identified:

- The incredible diversity of life: To Marx, that sounded like the division of labor advocated by capitalist economists.
- The competition for reproductive success: Marx heard here the echoes of capitalist competition.
- The link between new species and the discovery of new ecological niches: This sounded suspiciously like the opening of new markets.
- The selection of the best features from the range of variation that any species exhibits: Marx saw here the idea of technological progress through new inventions.

- The struggle for survival caused by the tendency of populations to increase unless checked by external constraints: That sounded like Thomas Malthus's theory of population.

Marx's argument was that the categories Darwin used to understand evolution were originally social categories—that natural selection was social reflection. Engels later extended the point to social selection, noting that Darwin placed selective emphasis on competition in nature as opposed to cooperation, a more socialist vision of nature. Thus, the theory of natural selection appeared to be the theory of natural capitalism.

Darwin, in fact, agreed to some extent. In later writings, he described how he hit upon the theory of natural selection when, in 1838, he "happened to read for amusement Malthus on *Population*," shortly after returning from his voyage around South America on board the *HMS Beagle*.[22] (During this famous voyage Darwin made many of the observations, such as the diversity of Galapagos finches, that served as key evidence in *On the Origin of Species*). And Darwin drew additional ideas, as well as the phrase "survival of the fittest," from the writings of Herbert Spencer, a mid-nineteenth-century social theorist.[23]

Metaphors and general patterns of understanding easily flit back and forth between our theories of the realms we label "society" and "nature." Chemists talk about chemical "bonds," and sociologists talk about social ones. Physical scientists talk about natural "forces," and social scientists talk about the social kind. Ecologists talk about community, and so too do sociologists—a parallel I have repeatedly emphasized in this book. Thus, perhaps it should come as no surprise that the two scientists who first hit upon the theory of natural selection—Darwin and his lesser-known contemporary, Alfred Russel Wallace—were living in the midst of the world's first truly capitalist industrial society: 1840s and 1850s England.

The flitting back and forth of concepts between science and social life deserves special scrutiny because of the way it sometimes allows science to be used as a source of political legitimization. It was this process of *naturalization* that most concerned Marx and Engels. As Engels put it, "The whole Darwinist teaching of the struggle for existence is simply a transference from society to nature. . . . When this *conjurer's trick* has been performed . . . the same theories are transferred back again from organic nature into history and it is now claimed that their validity as eternal laws of human society has been proved."[24]

There is no evidence that Darwin himself had a conscious mission of proving the value of capitalism through discovering it in nature. But witness the way we routinely talk about the economic "forces" of capitalism, such as innovation and competition, as if they were pseudonatural processes, implying that any other arrangement would be somehow unnatural. Consider the way we often hear the marketplace described as a "jungle" in which you have to "struggle to survive." Naturalization can subtly give us the sense that the shape of our economy is inevitable and that it is foolishly idealistic to think otherwise.

We should be wary of this subtle power. Whether or not we agree with capitalism, we should expect that the argument for any economic arrangement would be made on more explicit grounds.

Nature and Scientific Racism

What may be even more worrisome, though, is the tragic history of naturalizing arguments by scientists attempting to prove inherent differences in the capabilities of human "races." The controversial 1994 book *The Bell Curve* was only the latest in a long series of such attempts.[25] But what is distinctive (and hopeful, in a way) about that book is that, unlike many earlier efforts in scientific racism, it was almost immediately widely discredited by the scientific community.[26]

Morton's Craniometry. By contrast, it was decades before scientists began to see the flaws in *craniometry*, a nineteenth-century scientific fad that compared the cranial capacities of different races. Samuel George Morton, a Philadelphia doctor of European descent, was the leading figure in craniometry. Morton spent years assembling a collection of over six hundred human skulls from all over the world—no easy feat in the 1830s and 1840s, when intercontinental travel was limited to sailing ships. He published three books on his detailed studies which, not surprisingly, showed that Europeans had the biggest brains on the planet.

This work made Morton famous. When he died, his obituary in the *New York Tribune* read, "Probably no scientific man in America enjoyed a higher reputation among scholars throughout the world, than Dr. Morton." His obituary in a South Carolina medical journal read, "We of the South should consider him our true benefactor, for aiding most materially in giving to the negro his true position as an inferior race."[27]

Morton's method was first to assign skulls to a particular race. Then he would turn the skull upside down and fill it up with mustard seed poured in through the foramen magnum, the hole at the base of the skull where the spinal cord enters. He then poured the seed back out into a graduated cylinder to determine the volume. By this method, he determined that whites had an average cranial capacity of 87 cubic inches, Native Americans 82 cubic inches, and blacks 78 cubic inches.[28]

Morton later became discouraged with using mustard seed. He noticed that, because of their lightness, mustard seeds packed poorly and gave widely variable results when the measurements were repeated. So he switched to lead shot, which gave far more consistent results. He repeated his earlier measurements, and the average volumes for all the skulls went up. But the average for black skulls went up 5.4 inches, for Native Americans 2.2, and for whites 1.8. As biologist and historian of science Stephen Jay Gould points out, "Plausible scenarios are easy to construct. Morton, measuring by seed, picks up a threateningly large black skull, fills it lightly and gives it a few desultory shakes. Next, he takes a distressingly small Caucasian skull, shakes hard, and pushes mightily at the foramen magnum with his thumb. It is easily done, without conscious motivation; expectation is a powerful guide to action."[29]

Morton still could record a comforting hierarchy of races, though, even with the new method. But the use of mustard seed was only one of many problems with Morton's work. Gould reanalyzed all of Morton's data and found them littered with statistical errors. (As a dedicated scientist, Morton was committed to empirical accuracy and published all his raw data, allowing Gould to reanalyze them a century and a half later.) Averages for whites were rounded up and for blacks rounded down; usually large skulls from nonwhite races in his collection were often excluded, without explanation, from final tabulations; and the sample itself was highly selective.[30]

Two problems with the selectivity of the sample stand out in particular. First, Morton did not consider the effect of stature on cranial capacity. Taller people tend to have bigger brains just as they tend to have bigger feet. People from different regions of the world vary in their average height. For example, a quarter of Morton's sample of Native Americans came from the graves of Peruvian Incas, a small-bodied people with correspondingly small brain sizes, but only 2 percent (three skulls) came from the Iroquois, a tall people with correspondingly large brains. Morton did note in his raw data the height of the skeletons most of the skulls came from, but he did not understand (or did not wish to understand) the influence stature had on his results.

Second, Morton did not consider the effect of gender in his sample. Women tend to be smaller then men and thus to have smaller brain sizes. Not surprisingly, Morton's sample of English skulls, the group which recorded the largest average cranial capacity, came entirely from males. His sample of black "Hottentot" skulls, which gave a very low figure, came entirely from females. Here again, Morton noted the gender of most of the skulls in his collection but did not understand (or did not wish to understand) the significance gender had for his sample.

Gould took these errors into account, recalculated Morton's averages, and found no significant differences between "races." But even if racially significant differences in cranial capacity remained, we have no basis for assuming this would indicate greater intelligence. As Gould points out, elephants have far larger brains than humans and yet we do not consider them more intelligent than us.[31] Also, given that all Morton measured in the end was differences in stature, his results would equally well demonstrate that people with the biggest feet have the biggest brains. But as foot size does not have anything like the cultural significance of skin color, Morton did not pause to consider such an interpretation.

Huntington's Environmental Determinism. Another infamous example of scientific racism was the study by Yale University geographer Ellsworth Huntington of the relationship between climate and the degree of civilization of a people, written up in his 1915 book, *Climate and Civilization.*

Huntington attempted to determine this relationship by the supposedly objective method of sending out a questionnaire to "about fifty geographers and other widely informed men in a dozen countries of America, Europe, and Asia," and asking them to rate the level of civilization in their locale.[32] Huntington compared these results with the level of what he called "human energy on the basis of climate," by which he meant the effect of the local climate on people's ability to get up and do the things that need to be done (to borrow a line from *Praire Home Companions,* the popular U.S. radio show). Climates that are too warm, Huntington reasoned, encourage laziness; too cold, lethargy—and so on for factors such as rainfall, sunshine, and cloudiness. Huntington then drew up a global map of the level of human energy, another for the level of civilization, and compared them.

Lo and behold, he found just what he was likely looking for—that the climate of Europe and the northeastern United States was associated with the highest levels of civilization. Europe and the northeastern United States were, of course, predominantly white regions of the world, and Huntington himself was white. (It is perhaps also worth noting that Yale University is in the northeastern city of New Haven, Connecticut.) And on this basis, Huntington concluded, "the climate of many countries seems to be one of the great reasons why idleness, dishonesty, immorality, stupidity, and weakness of will prevail."[33]

Exhibit 7.5a Environmental determinism: Using a Eurocentric standard, the geographer Ellsworth Huntington, argued that the amount of "civilization" across the world could be related to the amount of "human energy" created by different climatic regions. Below, Huntington's map of "civilization."

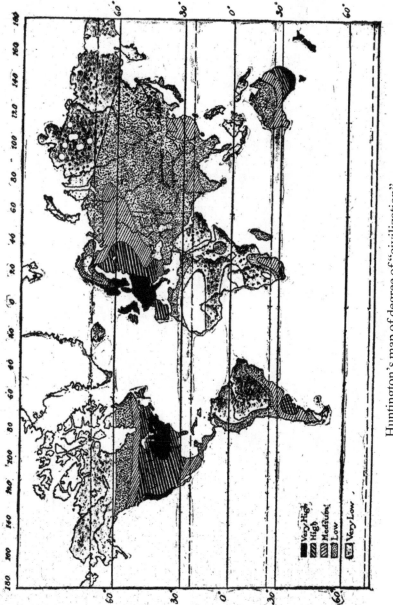

Huntington's map of degree of "civilization".

Exhibit 7.5b *Environmental determinism: Ellsworth Huntington's map of "human energy according to climate."*

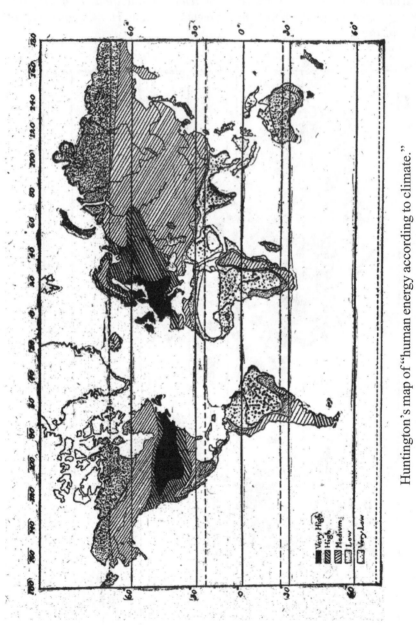

Huntington's map of "human energy according to climate."

Source: Huntington (1915).

This study was intended to be serious science, and Huntington was a famous man. Today, his method seems ludicrously biased. Huntington's "geographers and other widely informed men" almost certainly rated the level of civilization of a place on the basis of what their own experience told them was "civilization." Most likely, they saw lives similar to their own as civilized and ones dissimilar as uncivilized and filled out their questionnaires accordingly.

Of particular interest here is Huntington's environmental argument. Although extremes of cold and heat definitely create difficult circumstances for humans—which is why few people live in the Sahara Desert or at the Arctic Circle—the influence heat and cold have on matters like "idleness," "stupidity," and "weakness of will" is far from certain. In fact, one could easily reverse Huntington's line of reasoning and argue that difficult climates might actually produce peoples with the *greatest* strength of will, the least idleness, and highest intelligence, for otherwise they could not survive such extreme conditions. And indeed, the technological (not to mention the cultural) achievements of the Inuit in the Arctic tundra, the Tibetans in the high Himalayas, and the Bedouins in the deserts of the Middle East and North Africa rank, in my view, as some of the greatest in human history.

Why did Ellsworth Huntington and Samuel George Morton make these racist arguments, and why did they achieve high prominence and acceptability in their day? Probably because the socially powerful are not impervious to criticism about their dominant positions and they seek some source of ideological comfort.[34] This is part of the power—and danger—of nature as a social idea: the way we so often attempt to use it to legitimate social inequality. If nature is a realm beyond social interest, then its truths must be beyond blame and responsibility. Anything nature may apparently demonstrate about human differences can be ascribed to something external to social power. Nature can then serve as an interest-free foundation for human interests, the unmoved mover of power relations. But is it ever really that?

ENVIRONMENT AS A SOCIAL CONSTRUCTION

Nature is closely interrelated with a number of other important ways that we conceptualize the environment, and a growing body of scholarship investigates the social power relations involved. In this section we sample some of these ways, beginning with the concept of wilderness.

The Wilderness Ideal

As I discussed earlier, wilderness is a contradictory idea. The highest exemplar of the natural, it is also based on the often forcible absence of, and regulation of, one widespread aspect of the natural world: people. Most wilderness areas are routinely patrolled by rangers (frequently armed) who monitor boundaries and police human activities within. Often our wilderness parks have been created through the removal of the people who were living there previously.

As Ramachandra Guha has pointed out, such an approach to environmental protection is based on a culturally specific understanding of what the environment is and could be, one specific to North America in the main.[35] The idea of the national park originated in the United States, and the initial model was one of a wilderness region with few people. Because of its low population density and vast areas of rugged terrain, the United States had large regions with few people during the great age of park establishment in the late nineteenth and early twentieth centuries. It was relatively easy to remove the few people who were there. The native peoples had already been removed, for the most part, and the settler populations in these rugged and remote zones were thin on the ground.

Such is not the case in most of South and Southeast Asia. There, people live virtually everywhere, and setting aside any large area usually means setting substantial numbers of people aside too. Also, people and wildlife in these areas may coexist harmoniously, which is often why enough wildlife yet remains to attract interest in establishing a park. For example, when the Keoldeo Ghana bird sanctuary was established in Bharatpur, India, local villagers were told they would no longer be able to graze their livestock in the area. The villagers protested, and a battle broke out with the police in which several villagers were killed. After the grazing ban was enforced, scientists discovered that in fact bird populations declined. It turned out that grazing kept down the high grass, creating better habitat for the insects that many of the birds depended on. Nevertheless, the grazing ban remains in force.[36]

Although local villagers usually take the bulk of the blame for the loss of wildlife in their area, the more important culprits are poaching by hunters supplying primarily urban clients, earlier hunting by tourists and local elites, and the general decline in suitable habitat because of poverty-derived population growth and the spread of plantation forestry and plantation agriculture.

Paradoxically, establishing a wilderness park may actually increase the number of humans in an area by promoting tourism. In the case of Indian tiger reserves, Guha notes, the effect has been to replace local people with urban and overseas tourists and a full complement of upscale hotels, restaurants, and stores. As it takes capital and knowledge of middle-class life to set up tourist accommodations, the remaining local people often do not get much economic benefit from the establishment of a tiger reserve, aside from a few low-paying jobs.

Exhibit 7.6 *Lawren S. Harris's 1927–28 painting* Lake and Mountains: *Harris's painting shows an ideal wilderness with no trace of human activity. Such a non-human conception of wilderness sometimes leads to ecological misunderstanding, as the text describes.*

Source: Art Gallery of Ontario.

Nancy Peluso has described a similar history in southern Kenya.[37] There, the Masai tribe of migratory pastoralists has been confined to increasingly smaller reserves and "sedentarized" to make way for game and wildlife reserves, particularly for rhinos and elephants. The process began in the early 1900s, when, in response to the demands of big game hunters and conservation groups, the British colonial government established the Southern Game Reserve. At the time, however, officials did not see the Masai as a threat to wildlife, and the Southern Game Reserve was set up within the Masai reserve. But since the 1950s, a "wilderness" model of wildlife protection has taken hold. The old Southern Game Reserve has been replaced with four reserves that exclude the Masai completely and are surrounded by extensive buffer zones in which the Masai are required to adopt "group ranches" for their cattle, imposing yet another alteration of the Masai culture and economy.

There is little evidence, however, that the traditional Masai lifestyle was in conflict with the survival of rhinos and elephants. Peluso points out that, rather than being a threat to wildlife, with whom they had coexisted for thousands of years, the Masai helped maintain the savanna environment through their migratory cattle grazing. As long as it is managed properly, cattle grazing can actually increase the availability of grass for wildlife by stimulating regrowth. Grass grows most rapidly and nutritiously when it is kept short—although not so short that it has trouble providing energy to its root system. Also, cattle fertilize as they graze, providing the regrowing grass with helpful nutrients. Rather than the low-intensity cattle grazing of the traditional Masai, the main sources of rhino and elephant decline have been big game-hunters and the ivory trade.

Excluding the Masai from the new reserves in fact had just the opposite effect of what was intended. The Masai got angry and began killing some elephants and rhinos. Also, some Masai collaborated with the ivory trade in protest. Alienated from their traditional lands and traditional ways for the supposed benefit of wildlife, the Masai suddenly found themselves competing, rather than coexisting, with the rhino and the elephant. Corrupt park rangers and government officials, however, have been the main culprits in the continuing loss of wildlife to what Peluso terms the "ivory wars."[38]

Wilderness is, in the end, a state of mind more than a state of nature. Habitat provision is certainly vital for protecting biodiversity. The question is, are habitat and humanity natural opposites, or merely conceptual ones? As the environmental historian William Cronon has written, "It is not the things we label as wilderness that are the problem—for nonhuman nature and large tracts of the natural world *do* deserve protection—but rather what we ourselves mean when we use that label."[39]

Guha's, Peluso's, and Cronon's point, then, is not that the United States should invite the descendents of the Appalachian mountaineers who used to live in the area now covered by the Great Smoky Mountains National Park to move back in, or that Canada should turn Banff into a ski resort. Theirs is a more practical suggestion: that we should not universalistically, and imperialistically, promote such a culturally specific notion as a no-people vision of wilderness in places where it may lead to social injustice and may even undermine biodiversity.

For all its moral attractions as a realm free of politics, wilderness is nevertheless deeply political. There are unavoidable human consequences to the provision of habitat for wildlife—which does not mean that wildlife habitat is wrong or unimportant. It does mean, though, that we need to think through the implications for both humans and nonhumans.

Tourism and the Social Construction of Landscape

Tourism, it is sometimes said, is the largest and fastest-growing industry in the world. Such a statement is hard to verify—the definition of the tourist economy can be as narrow as hotel bookings and plane fares or as broad as the cost of the rubber one wears off one's shoes walking in the neighborhood park. But tourism indisputably has become big business.

Much of what tourists travel for is the look of a place and the occasion (or excuse) that look provides for the *culture of leisure*. Although the local culture may be part of the experience, most tourists spend the bulk of their time in the separate world of the hotel, the historical site, the beach, and the wilderness park—all places rarely frequented by local people, unless they happen to work there. In other words, tourists tend to objectify a landscape, using its visual qualities as a cultural opportunity for leisure.

To some extent, the tendency of tourists to concentrate on the look of a place is a matter of access. Local property boundaries limit physical access to those deemed to have rights to a particular area. But visual access is hard to limit in a similar way—people can't easily be confined to keeping their gaze trained only on those spots where they have been granted a specific legal right to look. The landscape can be veiled through the strategic placement of walls and roads, but these only create a different visual effect. A landscape would still exist for outsiders to "consume" through what the sociologist John Urry has aptly termed the "tourist gaze."[40]

Of course, local people experience landscape visually as well. Since their lives and work are tied up in the local land, though, their visual experience has many more levels to it. They see the land differently; it means something different to them. As Thomas Greider and Lorraine Garcovich have written, "Every river is more than one river. Every rock is more than one rock. . . . Every landscape is a symbolic environment. These landscapes reflect our self-definitions that are grounded in culture."[41] We see landscape differently, and for different purposes, depending upon who we are.

The social significance of a landscape depends as well on some things that we can never see: the social associations we experience in it. A landscape can be alive with the spirits, the "ghosts", of those we associate with it. We commonly invest a landscape with the *ghosts of place*—a sense of the presence of those who are not physically there. We build a feeling of attachment to that place through our attachment to the ghosts we sense there.[42]

A person local to an area, for example, may recall vividly events that friends and family participated in at a particular place in the landscape. He or she will likely be able to conjure up the mental images of friends and family involved in those events and to sense a connection to those places through those social attachments. The field where childhood friends used to play. The tree planted by a parent. His or her own ghost at the playground of the old school. The particularly deep sense of personal presence that generally comes with legal ownership of a place.

Tourists, of course, do not have these local associations and generally do not "see" these local ghosts—except for those conjured up, often simplistically, at historic sites, in heritage museums, and in tourism literature.[43] But tourists, too, need to "see" the landscape in some way to give it significance. The purely visual has no meaning. There is a close interrelationship between what we see and what we "see," for locals and tourists alike.

Tourism promoters play to the tourist's need to "see" by giving access to some readily accessible ghosts. As the environmental sociologist Clare Hinrichs describes, the state of Vermont in the northeastern United States has been particularly effective at giving tourists something to "see." "To speak of Vermont is to conjure up a broader vision of a balanced, beneficent rurality," Hinrichs writes.[44] This conjured ghost of rural life can then be attached to the state's mountains, ski slopes, ice cream, cheese, maple syrup, and pancake mix—even to its mail-order Christmas wreaths. "Send a bit of the Vermont woods home for Christmas," Hinrichs reports one ad as reading, allowing one to tour Vermont, to "see" it, without ever leaving home. The landscape itself becomes an exportable commodity.

Local people are often ambivalent about the consequences. Turned into postcards and advertising slogans, a landscape can bring the tourist's dollars. But often the benefits of tourism are not widely spread. The jobs are generally low paid and seasonal. Tourist dollars may also give local people the feeling that they have lost control of their community, and in the case of indigenous peoples, their culture as well. Tourism can also be an environmental disaster. Accommodations for tourists frequently burden local water supplies, eliminate sensitive habitat, and increase pollution, as well as intruding clumsily on the spirits of a place. The wilderness and rural charm that brought the tourists to begin with may soon become no more than a postcard and a slogan, even for those who live there.

Thus, the experience of a landscape—both what we see and "see"—is political. The point of critics of tourism like Urry and Hinrichs, though, is not to suggest that tourism should be banned and that tourists have no right to see or "see" the land in places where they do not live. The visual and imaginative qualities of a place are a kind of commons, something we all share. Landscape provides an important point of social connection in a world that is increasingly divided into no-go zones to which access is granted only to those with money.

But tourists and the tourism businesses they support are usually at an advantage in conflicts over landscape. Tourists tend to be wealthier than local people, and tourism businesses are often backed by corporate interests and by national and regional governments eager to generate foreign exchange and tax revenues. In such a situation of inequality, it is particularly challenging to manage a commons democratically.

Environmentalism and Social Exclusion

The final example of the relationship between conceptions of the environment and social power that I'll consider is the use of environmental arguments for social exclusion.

This is an unfortunately common phenomenon. Suburban and exurban zoning controls, for example, are often instituted with the expressed intent of maintaining open space, wildlife habitat, and the "character" of an area, among other goals. Such controls, though, can have the not-so-hidden effect of raising the cost of acquiring a residence in these areas, excluding poorer people from moving in and sometimes forcing them to move out. Moreover, rural areas in most of Europe and North America, the principal exception being the American South, are almost entirely white, and most suburban areas remain primarily so. Restrictive zoning policies help perpetuate this historical segregation—a point not lost on at least some rural and suburban residents.

In a study of an exurban Canadian village on the far commuting fringe of Toronto, Stanley Barrett found that some residents had moved "out in the country" in part to escape the multiracial and multiethnic city. One white woman who had recently moved from the city spoke very directly on the issue: "That is one thing that I like about it here—none of those people," she said, referring to blacks and Asians.[45]

Environmental arguments are also sometimes used to argue for restrictions on immigration. As a member of several national environmental organizations, I get a lot of environmental junkmail (something that ought to be considered an oxymoron). Environmental organizations I've never contacted or never even heard of will send me urgent appeals, action alerts, fake surveys of my opinion on various topics, and other grabs for my cash. A number of years ago I must have gotten into some marketer's database of people concerned about population growth, something I do believe is an important environmental issue. At the time, the U.S. Congress was considering some important immigration bills, and organizations like

Population-Environment Balance, Negative Population Growth, Zero Population Growth, and FAIR (the Federation for American Immigration Reform) used the occasion to flood my mail slot with appeals and surveys.

Their literature's frequent use of xenophobic and other dubious arguments caught my eye (and raised my ire) and I saved some of it. Here's how the letter I received in 1990 from Population-Environment Balance, signed by their "Honorary Chairman" Garrett Hardin, began:[46]

Dear Friend:

Why do so many of America's environmental problems persist despite our efforts to solve them? We Americans work hard to improve our individual lives and our country as a whole. Yet, even though we continue to make these sacrifices, we continue to suffer from worsening problems such as *environmental degradation, traffic jams, deteriorating infrastructures, and homelessness.*

The pitch here is that "we Americans" are not to blame for environmental problems, traffic jams, infrastructure deterioration, and homelessness. We work hard and sacrifice everyday. The letter continued:

... THERE IS A SOLUTION! ... But before we can discuss the solution, we must fully understand *the primary cause of these problems—overpopulation.* .... You may ask, how did we become overpopulated? Natural increase—more births than deaths—is one factor. The reality is, however, that *illegal as well as legal immigration is a major cause of population growth in the already overcrowded United States.* .... Unrestrained, the effects of this immigration-generated population growth on our environment and quality of life will continue to become more obvious and more serious.

In other words, the "SOLUTION" is getting rid of *them*. Although the letter points out in passing that "natural increase . . . is one factor" and elsewhere states Population-Environment Balance's support of birth control and sex education, nowhere does it specifically recommend smaller family size in the United States. Nor does it mention reducing the consumption levels of "we Americans" as a solution to environmental problems. Instead the letter shifts the blame onto legal and illegal immigrants, who it implies are, among other things, clogging the streets with their cars.

The letter goes on to call for a limit of 200,000 legal immigrants a year, about a third of the then-current figure of 650,000, what it calls the "replacement level" that would balance annual emigration from the United States. The letter also links population growth to a host of other issues, including crime, stress, urban sprawl, taxes, living expenses, and unemployment (but without explaining what the links might be), pushing as many "hot buttons," as marketers say, as possible.

Garrett Hardin is a widely respected environmentalist, author of one of the most famous essays of all time on environmental issues, "The Tragedy of the Commons," which I discuss in the last chapter. He is also known for promoting "lifeboat ethics"—the dubious idea that there is room for only so many, and that rather than sink the whole boat we will simply have to deny some people a place on board.[47] Here in this letter we learn who those entitled to a place in the boat are: the current citizens of the world's wealthiest and most powerful country. The basis for that decision is evidently the social power of those who already have a seat.

• •

SOCIAL ACTION CASE STUDY
ENVIRONMENTAL CLAIMS MAKING

Environmental issues are more than scientific, material facts. Environmental issues always depend upon the success of *environmental claims making*. An issue has to be popularized in order to gain the public's concern. It has to be framed in ways that the public can appreciate and that the media can turn into entertaining news—news that sells. In other words, an environmental issue is inevitably a social construction.

The environmental sociologist John Hannigan notes six factors common to public acceptance of an environmental issue:[1]

- Scientific validation of the claims
- The existence of "popularizers" who can bridge the gap between science and the public
- Media interest in the issue
- Dramatization of the problem in symbolic and visual terms
- Economic incentives for taking positive action
- Institutional sponsors who ensure both legitimacy and continuing attention to the issue

For example, acid rain emerged in the late 1970s and early 1980s as an important environmental issue in part, suggests Hannigan, because it had an appropriately scary name. "In American popular culture," Hannigan notes, "acid conjures up images of motion picture thrillers in which deranged murderers are revealed to have turned against humanity after being facially scarred for life by corrosive acids which have been hurled at them."[2] A name like "low-pH rain," a more scientifically accurate term, would hardly have been so effective at grabbing the headlines. Similarly the phrase "ozone hole" captures our attention more effectively than the more accurate phrase "thinning of the upper atmosphere ozone layer."

Environmental counter claims are equally a matter of social construction. To be effective, those who dispute the importance of an environmental issue must also be able to claim scientific authority, present their arguments in dramatic ways, devise media stunts, state their position in economic terms, secure institutional sponsors, and so on. A doubter always makes for a good story, so willing media are rarely hard to find for environmental counter claims. Also, environmentalism often confronts powerful interests, making institutional sponsors readily available for counter claims that can marshal some scientific backing.

As a result of claims making and counter claims, environmental issues experience a kind of "career," as Hannigan puts it. The success of that career does indeed depend upon science. But it depends equally on the outcome of an uncertain trial in the courtrooms of public opinion and politics.[3]

Notes
1 Hannigan (1995), 55.
2 Hannigan (1995), 132.
3 I'm adapting a line here from Hannigan (1995), 190.

• •

NATURE AND IDEOLOGY

Nature, for all the moral security we expect it to provide, is a contradictory and contested conceptual realm. Although we often see it as a source of conscience that is free of the pollution of social interests, nature is inescapably social. Nature is a social and political phenomenon as much as a physical one, as many environmental sociologists have recently argued. The French social theorist Bruno Latour even suggests that there is no such thing as nature, only "nature-culture."[48] The American environmental sociologist Bill Freudenburg and his colleagues make a similar point, arguing that we need, "to resist the temptation to separate the social and the environmental, and to realize that the interpenetrating influences are often so extensive that the relevant factors can be considered 'socioenvironmental.'[49]

It is important to recognize some limits here, though. What we have long thought of as nature is certainly a social construction. All human ideas are necessarily social constructions; we are social, and therefore so are our ideas. But is that all nature is? Is it only a social construction? Indeed, is that all *anything* is—including the very idea that ideas are social constructions?

Social constructionism is an important insight, yet it runs several theoretical dangers. To begin with, it can become a kind of universalism itself, as everything reduces to the social-constructionist perspective. This is an internally contradictory result. The moral and theoretical foundation of social constructionism is the need to recognize the existence of "truths," not truth. Second, if one conceives social constructionism as advocating a subjective point of view, it runs the danger of becoming a kind of Sophist relativism—helpful as a form of social critique about power and perspective but incapacitating for any effort to improve social and environmental conditions, lest we commit another social construction. A social constructionist might come to regard any advocacy of social and environmental reform as hopelessly intertwined with power interests and therefore might cynically retreat from any political involvement. Finally, untempered social constructionism can wallow in a purely ideal realm, unwilling to engage the material side of the ecological dialogue.

There are several responses to these potential theoretical dangers. First, we need to recognize that there is nothing wrong with committing a social construction. The value and appropriateness of a social construction depends, of course, on what the social construction is. But we also need to recognize that there is more to human experience than ideas—and more to human experience than social life. It is not only ideas, and not only society, that fill our days. There is a material side to life and to social life, and that material side interacts with our ideas and our patterns of social organization.

The point is, we are unlikely to make up whatever vision of nature we want, at least not for long. There is a certain *social inconvenience of "nature"* that will, in time, guide the kinds of social visions we take toward it. King Canute, ruler of England a thousand years ago, thought rather well of himself and supposedly once commanded the tide not to come in—with predictable results. He never tried it again.[50] Social understandings of the environment that don't work don't last long. Material consequences matter.

The history of the theory of natural selection is a good example of the interaction of the material and the ideal. The correspondence between the rise of capitalism and the theory of natural selection may suggest that society was reflected in Darwin's vision of nature. But that doesn't mean Darwin just made it all up. Rather, it could be argued that before the rise of a form of social organization like capitalism people did not have the conceptual resources—the forms of understanding—needed to envision natural selection. Before this form of social "seeing" developed, people were not able to see natural selection. A certain cast of mind is prepared to see things that other casts of mind cannot—but there has to be something there to "see." Indeed, the fossil record provides abundant material evidence in support of Darwin's basic propositions.

But the similarities in the categories we use to understand nature and society are striking. Moreover, these categories experience parallel changes. In this century, a more socialized version of capitalism than Darwin knew developed. Social services, worker protection, free education, and assistance to the poor became standard features of most democratic societies. At the same time, a more socialized understanding of nature developed: ecology, which stresses holism and mutual interdependence in the natural world. And as we have come to adopt a postmodern skepticism about "progress" in society, biologists have adopted similar views about "progress" in evolution. In place of the every-day-we're-getting-better-in-every-way implications of Darwin's ideas about competitive selection of the fittest, biologists now stress the importance of random events like the meteorite crash that doomed the dinosaurs. They also question the extent to which animals are perfectly adapted to their environments, another Darwinist idea that seemed to imply progress in evolution.

The evidence is out there for these new views of nature. Geologists are pretty sure that on the Yucatan Peninsula of Mexico they've found the crater caused by that meteorite. Such a finding, though, has social effects. For example, it probably feeds our feeling that the direction we are going in is not certain to end well—that, to echo the title of an Elvis Costello song, "accidents can happen." It fits with, and therefore promotes, our current sense of anxiety. Thus, our ideas of society reflect our ideas of nature just as our ideas of nature reflect our ideas of society. It's a two-way process, a search for a common language for understanding the conditions of our lives. It's another dialogue.

But the dynamics of these mutually supporting parallels is largely an unconscious process. I like to think of it as a kind of intellectual *resonance*. That is, we tend to favor patterns of understanding that work well across— that resonate with—the range of our experience. We feel an intuitive sense of ideological ease when a pattern we know from one conceptual realm seems to apply in another.[51] Darwin's theory of natural selection resonated with the Victorians' enthusiasm for the new capitalist way, just as the devastating crater that wiped out the dinosaurs resonates with a late twentieth century full of doubt as it faces the next millenium. It just somehow seems righter—the way a more resonant musical instrument just somehow seems to sound better—when we encounter such parallels.

The value of social constructionist arguments is that they alert us to the ideological implications of resonance and urge us to confront our intellectual ease. The results may be emotionally and politically challenging, but sometimes that's just what we need.

Maybe the best way to conclude is to go back to my philosophical wrangle with Sam. The answer to the question "What is nature?" is that everything is and that everything isn't. Both are true. Nature is an inescapably human conception, just as humans are inescapably a conception of nature. We construct nature and nature constructs us. It's a paradox, but it makes ecological dialogue possible—and necessary.

PART III

THE PRACTICAL

CHAPTER 8

Organizing the Ecological Society

There is no wealth but life.

-John Ruskin, 1863

I own a car. I admit it. And I often use it. I live in a 1,450-square-foot house with seven rooms, plus two baths. It is not a solar house. My family owns a washing machine, a television, a stereo system, an answering machine, and a clock-radio. We don't own a computer, but that's only because the one my university provides is a laptop and I regularly bring it home. I own nine pairs of footwear of various sorts; nevertheless I just bought another pair. Our closet is filled with clothes we rarely wear, and yet we buy more. And we have a second child on the way.

I'm not a complete environmental sinner, though. My wife and I do own only one car, and we put no more than eight or nine thousand miles a year on it between the two of us, roughly a third of the standard for an American household with two adults. We bicycle to work and to do most of our shopping—even in winter (which gets pretty forbidding in Iowa, where I live). We're fortunate enough to have a comparatively good bus system in our town, and we often use it. Although we own a washing machine, we use a solar-powered clothes drier—a clothes line, that is— to dry our clothes. The television lives in the closet most of the time. We watch maybe a couple of hours a month, if that. We have no microwave oven, no dishwasher, no cordless phone, no cell phone, no CD-player, no VCR, no camcorder. There is no cupboard or closet full of household poisons, except for a couple of cans of "flying insect killer," which a former occupant left behind and which we've been trying to figure out how to dispose of safely ever since. We grow many of our own vegetables during the summer, all organically, and we mow our small lawn, which is also organic, with a manual reel mower. We use energy-efficient light bulbs in much of the house, we have no air conditioning, our furnace is a high-efficiency model, and during the heating season we keep the thermostat at sixty-two degrees Fahrenheit for the day and fifty-six degrees Fahrenheit for the night. We're avid recyclers. And we do intend to stop at two kids.

I'm not a complete sinner, I think, but I'm certainly not an environmental saint either. So, am I yet another environmental hypocrite, big on the guilt trip and fairly small on action, mostly talk and little walk?

From a certain political perspective, yes, and as that is a perspective I share—the perspective of the committed environmental moralist—my environmental inadequacies often pain me deeply. Yet from a sociological perspective, my situation does not necessarily indicate some deep personal moral failing. In fact, to the extent that my situation is typical of that of others (perhaps including you) it represents some important opportunities for social and environmental change. It suggests the possibility of collective action toward making a society that more closely resembles what we say we want it to be. And indeed, the overwhelming majority of the public in both rich nations and poor are concerned about the environment, even though very few could be said to have yet put that concern into full action. This concluding chapter considers these opportunities for change, closing the dialogic circle of the material and the ideal—or perhaps, better put, opening it up—with a focus on the *practical* implications of environmental sociology.

THE A-B SPLIT

Social psychologists have long noted that there is often a sharp disjunction between what people profess to value and believe and how they actually act.[1] The *A-B split*, as it is sometimes called, standing for "attitude-behavior split," is a characteristic of probably all of us, at least to some degree. Often people consciously recognize some of these inconsistencies. We work to adjust the behavior side to fit our attitudes, and sometimes, social psychologists find, we work to adjust our attitudes to fit our behaviors. These adjustments also go on unconsciously. One classic example of this process is the way 1960s radicals often became more conservative when they started raising families and entered the world of business. They found themselves taking on the very attitudes—and enacting the very behaviors—that they had been in the streets protesting only a decade or two earlier.

But the point of the A-B split is not to suggest that these 1960s radicals are therefore hypocrites. Nor necessarily are all the rest of us who have adjusted what we believe to fit what we do, or who have gone on doing things that in fact do not fit what we believe. It is very hard to maintain a conscious sense of an A-B split. Such inconsistency strikes at the very core of our identity, our sense of who we are. Understandably, people tend to avoid conscious recognition of an ideological mismatch, if they can. But often they can't, and they try to adjust their lives and their thinking accordingly—which is also hard. In other words, an A-B split is a source of internal struggle and conflict. Contrary to the image of the complacent hypocrite, such a split is hardly something about which most people feel comfortable, at least not usually.

The sociological point here is that one of the main reasons people find their attitudes at odds with their behaviors (and often find themselves adjusting the attitudes to fit or putting the conflict out of their mind as much as possible) is social structure.[2] We do not have complete choice in what we do. Our lives are *socially organized*, with all the constraints that this implies. I own a car and use a car because the automobile-based planning of the last fifty years has led, even in my small town, to a scattering of businesses, schools, parks, and homes. Even our relatively good bus system can't make up for this structured *in*convenience, so I often feel strongly pressured to use my car.

Social organization, however, also presents us with opportunities. When we as a community consider our collective attitudes and our collective behaviors—when we consider the ideal and the material implications of the current arrangement of our social and ecological lives—we have an opportunity to reconsider them as well. The social organization of our communities may be a large part of our problems, but the *social reorganization* of our communities can be a large part of the solutions. We can create new social structures, new constraining influences that shape and guide our lives.

In other words, social structures are not necessarily bad things. It depends on what they guide us into doing. Social structures do not necessarily create the A-B split (or what is really an ideal-material split). Properly rearranged, properly reconsidered, social structures can help heal the splits in our communities—including that biggest community of all, the environment of which we are (thankfully, I say) an inescapable part.

But it's never easy.

THE PROBLEM OF COLLECTIVE ACTION

What it takes is cooperation. One does not need to consider the matter closely, however, to recognize that human groups very often fail to act for the collective good.

The Tragedy of the Commons

The biologist Garret Hardin, in a famous 1968 article, "The Tragedy of the Commons," described the problem in stark terms. Imagine you are a shepherd grazing your sheep on your village's common pastureland, back in the hills above the village. As a member of the village, you have the right to graze your sheep there, just as every other village member does. You've got only ten sheep, though, and after a while you think, "Well, I'd be a bit better off if I added a few more to my flock." Meanwhile, your fellow villagers are thinking the same thing about their own flocks. Pretty soon, as everyone adds a few more animals, there are a lot more sheep in the common pastureland.

The pastureland is only so big, though. Eventually overgrazing occurs. The grass cover gets thin, and the land starts to erode. Everybody's sheep start to die. You wind up with fewer sheep than you began with, and the eroded common land is no longer capable of supporting as many sheep as it originally could: economic and environmental disaster.

Here's how Hardin, rather dramatically, described the situation:

> [T]he inherent logic of the commons remorselessly generates tragedy. . . . [T]he rational herdsman concludes that the only sensible course for him to pursue is to add another animal to his herd. And another; and another. . . . But this is the conclusion reached by each and every rational herdsman sharing a commons. Therein is the tragedy. Each man is locked into a system that compels him to increase his herd without limit—in a world that is limited. Ruin is the destination toward which all men rush, each pursuing his own best interest in a society that believes in the freedom of the commons.[3]

Hardin intended this parable as a master allegory for all environmental problems. Three examples he mentions in the article are traffic, pollution, and overfishing. Think of streets as a kind of commons, something we all collectively own. As a member of the community, I am free to drive on my city's streets as much as I want. But what if everybody decides to get about this way? The result is traffic jams, smog, and the loss of alternatives as mass transit shuts down.

Or think of the lake where your summer cabin sits as a kind of commons. It's expensive to put in a good septic system, and it wouldn't hurt you much to flush into a shallow leaching field close to the water's edge where, as it happens, it would be the cheapest and easiest place to put the field. The lake is pretty big, and it can handle a little bit of pollution. Besides, it would be hard for anyone to determine that you're the one with the shallow leaching field close to the shoreline. Lots of cabins ring the lake. But what if everybody on the lake did what you're doing?

The oceans are a commons too. If I fish for a living, I might as well cast as big a net as I can. What I do myself won't have that much effect on overall fish stocks. Anyway, the other fishers are probably going to do the same, right? And soon the fish are gone.

Hardin's analysis is far from perfect, as I'll come to in a moment. But it is hard to ignore the fact that traffic jams are on the rise. In 1996, for example, there was a spectacular traffic jam in central London—eight hours of gridlock, involving an estimated 250,000 cars.[4] Smog is also up, and mass transit is down. Many recreational lakes have been badly polluted by their users. Fishing stocks are in terrible shape in many parts of the oceans and have simply collapsed in the Grand Banks and Georges Bank, leaving hundreds of fishing communities from Newfoundland to New England economically devastated.

These are all examples of a more general class of circumstances, what social scientists call the *problem of collective action*: In a world of self-interested actors, how can we get people to cooperate for their own benefit? Individual actors pursuing their rational self-interest often lead us to irrational collective outcomes that in fact undermine the interests of those who enact them. The result is a striking paradox of social life: We often do not act in our own interests when we act in our own interests. Or, to put it another way, when we all do what we want, it often leads to outcomes nobody wants.

WHY IT REALLY ISN'T AS BAD AS ALL THAT

Hardin's account of the "tragedy of the commons" remains one of the most discussed theories in environmental sociology, even thirty years after it was written. The phrase "tragedy of the commons" is a familiar phrase to many in the general populace. Academics regularly employ it in analyses. In a quick search of the databases at my university library, for example, I found a dozen academic articles from 1995 and 1996 that focused on the concept. In as specialized a realm as academia, this is a lot. Several of these articles extend the allegory of the commons far beyond environmental concerns, applying it to analyses of management-employee relations, prisons, and political action committees.[5]

Much of the reason for the continuing attention, though, is to point out how spectacularly oversimplified and overstated Hardin's allegory is and how it diverts attention from some fundamental social processes at work in environmental problems.[6]

To begin with, Hardin seemed to blame common ownership of resources for the tragedy. But in fact, we can find countless examples of highly successful use of commons for resource management. Grazing lands all across Africa, Asia, and South America; traditional systems of fisheries management in India and Brazil; even the private homes of modern families, which are a kind of commons in miniature and remain a highly popular form of social arrangement—these are just a few of the many examples of generally successful commons management.[7] Indeed, common ownership is the primary way that people have managed their affairs for centuries. And it has, at least until recent years, largely worked.[8]

Rather than the tragedy of the commons, Hardin's allegory is better characterized as the tragedy of individualism. For what breaks down Hardin's commons is not collective ownership itself but rather the inability (and perhaps unwillingness) of the herders to take a view wider than their own narrowly conceived self-interests.

Herders, in fact, are unlikely to conceive of their interests so narrowly, at least in traditional commons. For one thing, Hardin assumes that no one will notice the overgrazing until it is too late. But herders out there in the pasture every day with their sheep are likely to notice the condition of the grass very quickly. For another thing, Hardin assumes that the herders do not communicate with one another. More likely, as soon as the herders notice the beginnings of overgrazing, they will walk over to each other's houses in the village and have a few words about the situation. They will likely convene a meeting of some sort and try to work out an arrangement that restores the grass while following local norms about the number of sheep each herder is fairly entitled to graze on the commons.

More significant, however, is the reliance of Hardin's allegory on a rational-choice view of human motivation. People are, simply put, more complex—and thankfully so. We are moved by more than our own narrowly conceived self-interests, as chapter 2 described. Equally important are the sentiments—the norms, the feelings of affection and lack of affection for others—we have in social life. These sentiments are a crucial aspect not only of our humanity but, as we shall see, of our interests as well.

The Dialogue of Solidarities, or, Why the Lion Spared Androcles

Let me offer a counter-allegory.[9]

> There once was a slave named Androcles. His master treated him cruelly, and Androcles could bear the abuse no longer. So one day he ran away into the forest.
>
> As he was walking through the woods, Androcles came upon a lion who was roaring loudly. Androcles was frightened at first, but

then he noticed that the lion was roaring from pain. A nail had gotten stuck in one of the lion's paws. Androcles approached the lion, took the lame paw in his hands, and pulled out the nail.

The lion was so grateful for this kind act that he licked Androcles' face. As Andocles had no place to stay, the lion invited him to his cave, and there they lived with each other for some time. Every day they hunted together, using the lion's teeth and claws and Androcles's hands and wit to capture all the game they could want.

One day, however, some of the emperor's men captured them both and led them away to the Colosseum. In those days before television, people enjoyed going to the Colosseum to watch lions eat defenseless captives and to watch other gruesome sports. Androcles and the lion were to be used for this unhappy purpose.

On the day of the event, great excitement filled the air. The emperor himself was coming to watch the show. Tension mounted as the preliminary acts—foot races, weight lifting, gladiator fights—were held. Finally, Androcles was thrown into the ring, naked and unarmed. The lion, who had been starved for days, was also released into the ring. With a terrible roar, he bounded toward the poor slave.

At first, so hungry was the lion that he did not recognize Androcles. But as he approached Androcles, he saw who it was. The lion lay down in front of Androcles and licked his hand.

The emperor was astonished, and he called Androcles over to his viewing platform to explain. When Androcles told him the story, the emperor was so impressed that he set Androcles free. He also set the lion free to return to the forest. As Androcles had no education, money, relatives, or friends, he returned to the forest as well. Androcles and the lion lived out the rest of their days together, the closest of friends and companions.

And so (as the story traditionally concludes) we learn that no act of kindness is ever wasted.[10]

Why did the lion spare Androcles there in the ring? At that moment the lion could have had no idea that refusing to eat his former partner would result in freedom. Indeed, the Colosseum operators might have decided to kill this apparently hopeless lion for failing to put on a good show. (Colosseum operators were like that.)

And why did Androcles pull the nail from the lion's paw to begin with? At that moment Androcles could have had no idea that pulling the nail would result in his gaining a friend and hunting partner. (Hunting partnerships between humans and lions are, after all, rather unusual.) And neither could know that they would eventually be able to return to the forest to live out their days together.

The reason was, according to the ancient Greek storyteller Aesop, from whom I draw this tale, that the lion and Androcles were moved by more than narrow calculations of their own pure self-interest. They were moved as well by their sentiments: Androcles for a lion in pain and the lion for a friend and former companion; Androcles for reasons of commitment to certain norms of behavior and the lion for reasons of friendship, of affective commitment. These sentimental commitments in turn led—and this is a crucial point of criticism of the rational-actor model described in the "tragedy of the commons"—to the promotion of their interests, *although they could not know that at the time.* In other words, sentiments promote interests but do not reduce to them.

At the same time, interests promote sentiments. A large part of the reason Androcles and the lion liked each other is that, beginning with Androcles' act of pulling the nail and extending through the lion's refusal to eat Androcles, they had learned to rely on each other to promote each other's interests. Because they helped each other out, they liked each other and shared a sense of commitment to common norms of social behavior. And because they liked each other and shared a commitment to common norms, they helped each other out. The story is thus another example of a dialogue, this time what I like to call the *dialogue of solidarities.*

I use the plural because this dialogue is based on the interaction between two mutually supporting bases for social commitment: a *solidarity of interests* and a *solidarity of sentiments.* The interests of both Androcles and the lion were served through their relationship. But as well, they sensed the existence of sentimental ties—affection and common norms—between them. And the one constantly shaped and maintained the other.

All this emphasis on sentiment may sound a little idealistic, the kind of rare altruism we sometimes hear about in stories, or, as in this case, in an ancient fable. But sentiment is actually quite common—and quite necessary—in social relationships, at least those that endure across time and space.

Consider, for example, a domestic union of some kind, two recent college graduates perhaps. They each have interests, such as careers. They support each other through graduate school. They make their job choices with the other partner's interests in mind. They manage their home in ways that allow each to succeed at work. And thus they maintain a solidarity of interests.

However, there are always time delays involved in reciprocal and cooperative action. How does one partner know that the other will come through when it is the other partner's turn to make a career sacrifice? There are also always issues of space in reciprocal and cooperative action. The two domestic partners cannot keep each other under constant surveillance. How does each know that the other can be relied upon to coordinate shopping, to maintain monogamy (if the union is based on that understanding), to cover for each other when situations require it?

Exhibit 8.1 The dialogue of solidarities.

The answer is trust. This trust can exist because each believes the relationship to be based upon more than the narrow calculation of self-interests. Because each has affection for the other or because each has a sense of common commitment to common norms of interaction—or both—they can trust that the other will come through across the isolating reaches of time and space. Without this sense of trust that a solidarity of sentiments gives, no solidarity of interests can last long.

The process works the other way too. The persistence of a solidarity of interests is one of the principal ways that each partner comes to sense real affection and common normative commitment on the part of the other. If one partner violates that trust by not looking out for the other's interests, chances are, frankly, that pretty soon they won't like each other anymore—nor have the faith that they share some crucial norms. Trust is the essential glue of both a solidarity of interests and a solidarity of sentiments.

So, to finally return to the "tragedy of the commons," one of the main reasons why herders on a commons have usually managed to keep from overgrazing the pastures is because *they trust each other.* These are their neighbors, after all, and likely their kinfolk too. These are the people they relax with, dance with, worship with, and marry. Of course, villages sometimes fall into considerable internal conflict, and when they do, those sentimental ties may go. If so, the grass on the pastures will likely go too.[11]

The dialogue of solidarities is a kind of ecologic dialogue, a constant and mutually constituting interaction between the realm of the material (a solidarity of interests) and the realm of the ideal (a solidarity of sentiments). From this dialogue emerge solidarities of solidarities, if you will, within families, organizations, businesses, neighborhoods, villages, towns, cities, counties, provinces, states, nations, species, ecosystems, and all other kinds of commons. What I mean is, from this dialogue emerges *community*.

● ●

SOCIAL ACTION CASE STUDY
THE PRISONERS' DILEMMA

Social scientists who study "game theory" often use an imaginary situation known as the *prisoners' dilemma* to illuminate the problem of collective action.[1] The prisoners' dilemma goes like this: You and I are suspected of collaborating on a crime. The police separate us and interrogate each of us individually. They outline the same four possible outcomes to both of us. Let's consider the situation from your position:

1. If I confess and you don't, you'll get three years in jail and the police will let me off for good behavior. This is the worst outcome for you.
2. If we both confess, the authorities will look a bit kindly on each of us, but they'll still send us both to jail for two years. This is a little better for you, but not much.
3. If neither of us confesses, the police have sufficient evidence to send us each to jail for one year. This is not too bad for you (or for me).
4. If you confess and I don't, you'll be released and I'll go to jail for three years. This is the best outcome for you.

So what do you do? If you confess, you'll go to jail either for two years or for no years. If you don't confess, you'll go to jail for either three years or for one year. So you go with the lower numbers and confess.

Of course, I'll probably go through the same logic and also confess. This would lead to outcome 2, and we both go to jail for two years.

But if we could count on each other to act cooperatively, we would both refuse to confess, leading to outcome 3, only a year in jail for each of us. Unfortunately, cooperating is a dangerous strategy for purely rational social actors. What if you act cooperatively and I don't? That would lead to outcome 1, the worst result for you—and the best for me. Therefore, unless you can be sure I won't take advantage of the situation, the best strategy for you is to confess. I'll probably think things through the same way and also confess—driving us inexorably toward outcome 2, and two years in jail each.

Environmental problems often have many of the features of a prisoners' dilemma. Let's consider fishing. Let's say we have all come to recognize the unfolding tragedy of our fishing stock, and to recognize that everyone ought to be taking fewer fish. But we're each prisoners of individualism and our boats are the cells. You might make an agreement with me to reduce fishing, but why bother? You can't watch what I do on my boat. And if I haul in a few extra catches, it will lower the price of fish by increasing the supply available to the consumer. That means you'll make less money unless you also haul in a few extra catches to make up the difference. If all the other boats act likewise, the price will drop even more, increasing the pressure to over-fish, and so on. It's the treadmill of production all over again—until the fish stocks are finally depleted.

But like the "tragedy of the commons," the "prisoners' dilemma" can be criticized for over-simplifying what are inevitably complex circumstances. Both rely on a "rational choice" perspective and thus eliminate a great deal of potential behavior from the analysis, such as social sentiments. For example, if the two prisoners are relatives or good friends they may very well be able to trust that each will look out for the collective good, even if they can't communicate about it. Also, collective action problems are rarely "one-shot" situations in which there is no opportunity for communication between the parties, as the prisoners' dilemma implies. Usually we can see a collective disaster unfolding and can communicate our concerns about the problem to each other, giving us an opportunity to coordinate our actions.

Still, these models of human action are valuable because they point out the significance of social sentiments and social communication to a culture that increasingly thinks in rationalistic and individualist terms.

Notes
1 Adapted with some modification, from Elster (1989).

DIALOGUE, DEMOCRACY, AND ENVIRONMENTAL PROBLEMS

There are indications that in modern society the dialogue of solidarities is breaking down, though, and that the ecological dialogue is breaking down with it. We have considered these indications throughout the book—the challenges to sustainability, environmental justice, and the rights and beauty of nature. These challenges have material origins, such as the treadmills of production and consumption, technological somnambulism, and the interplay of population and inequality. They also have ideal origins, such as hierarchical and antidemocratic attitudes about society and the environment, and simplistic and uncritical conceptions of nature and a natural conscience. (There are, as well, important material bases to the "ideal" origins and important ideal bases to the "material" origins, as earlier chapters discussed.) All these challenges relate to issues of community— to how we socially organize ourselves; to how we envision our relations with others, both humans and others, both humans and other beings; and to how we dialogically organize our envisioning and envision our organizing.

Clearly, we need to be having a better dialogue about ecological dialogue.

Perhaps, in a perverse way, herein lies the value of Hardin's theory of the "tragedy of the commons." However historically inaccurate an allegory it may be, it does effectively portray what life might be like if we repudiate the lessons of dialogue. "Ruin is the destination toward which all men rush," gloomily wrote Hardin. If we all act individualistically, if we refuse to communicate with one another, and if we disregard the consequences for others (and thus for ourselves as well) of what we are doing, Hardin will surely be right. Such a logic, we cannot doubt, would indeed "remorselessly generate" environmental decline—as well as social inequality—which in turn would perpetuate a society desperate enough to follow such a logic to begin with.

We all know at some level that this possibility exists, it seems to me. This is why Hardin's allegory is, despite its inaccuracies, so frighteningly realistic. It reminds us of what we realize we could indeed become. This fright is a hopeful sign. It suggests that we recognize the value of broadening the dialogue of solidarities and the dialogue of ecology, even if we often fail to actually accomplish this broadness of conversation and consideration.

However, it must be said that a dialogic solidarity is not in itself a good thing: Its value depends very much on the openness and inclusiveness of that dialogue. Solidarities that gain their social power from the exclusion of others can be very destructive. Nor is ecological dialogue in itself a good thing: Its value depends very much on the extent to which we have truly considered the potential interactions of the material and the ideal. The value of both forms of dialogue depends on the extent to which we have allowed these potential "voices" to be heard. What we want is not just dialogue but broad and open dialogue.

Indeed, it could be said that the only true dialogue is a broad and open one. Otherwise, what we really have is what the theorist Mikhail Bakhtin called *monologue*, people speaking without paying attention to the response of others, be those others people or the environment.[12] One important value of true dialogue is that it encourages us to take others into account and at the same time provides the means for doing so.[13] It is hard to establish a solidarity of interests unless we know what the interests of others are. We need to communicate and to have a sentimental commitment to the value of communication. We need to have what another theorist, Jürgen Habermas, has described as "an attitude oriented toward reaching understanding."[14]

Another important value of true dialogue is that, while promoting solidarities and the congruency of the material and the ideal, it also has an essential openness to change. True dialogue doesn't begin with a preconceived end point or a final solution but rather adjusts to new ideas and new material changes that emerge from the ongoing conversation of life. As Bakhtin once wrote, "There is neither a first word nor a last word and there are no limits to the dialogic context."[15] True social dialogue and true ecological dialogue encourage new possibilities and welcome critical evaluations of what is going on and what is being said and of how we might reorganize our community life in ways more appropriate to our material conditions and our ideological orientations. Only in this way can we nourish what I take to be two of our most vital social and environmental joys: words and worlds without end.

The "Top" and "Bottom" of Social-Environmental Change

This is all rather abstract. Practically speaking, the message I've tried to convey is that environmental solutions depend fundamentally on *participation*. If we are to reorganize our communities in ways that endure, we will need to encourage as many people as possible to be involved in the discussions.

How *impractical*, you may say. All this talk, and we never get anything done! How impractical, I may say right back. All this doing without any real talk about what we really want, and really need, to get done!

The problem of doing without talking is that effective doing requires cooperation. Changes that come only from on high encourage foot-dragging on the part of those down below and encourage authoritarianism on the part of those up above. Neither seems a good route to social change. Isolated individual changes that come only from below, on the other hand, tend not to be noticed when only a few are involved and tend to be actively ignored or actively restrained when many are involved. Again, neither of these seems a good route to social change.

We are coming to recognize, I think, that a "top-down" approach—command and control" on the part of governments, corporations, and technologies—relies on unsatisfying means and produces unworkable ends. The top cannot keep the bottom under constant watch without intolerable levels of social intrusion, nor can it achieve effective policies if only the concerns of a powerful few have been taken into consideration. A "bottom-up" approach is now often advocated as the solution, and there is some wisdom in this suggestion.[16] A "bottom-up" approach is inherently based on the participation and willingness of those who enact any coordinated change. The bottom-up approach thus obviates the need for intrusive surveillance and encourages the formation of broadly based and broadly supported policies. But by itself, change coming from the bottom alone is unlikely to lead to lasting and substantial effects.

Exhibit 8.2   The "top" and "bottom" of social change

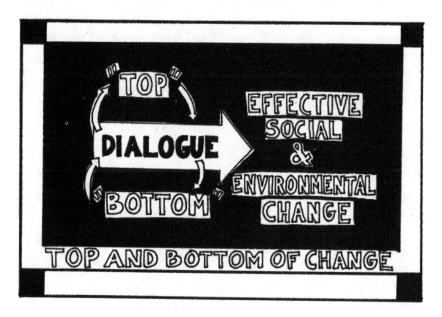

Rather, there is both a "top" and a "bottom" to effective social change, connected (yet again) by dialogue. The "top" represents our patterns of social organization based on government, the economy, technology, and other social structures. But without the participation and willingness of the bottom, these patterns of social organization cannot easily take hold. (Nor

Due to a printing error, the illustration for Exhibit 8.1, "The dialogue of solidarities," was repeated as Exhibit 8.2, "The 'top' and 'bottom' of social change." Here is the correct illustration for Exhibit 8.2, page 257

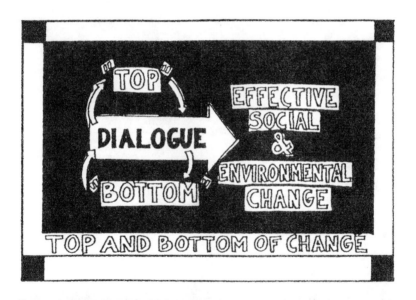

would they likely be fair.) The "bottom" represents social activism, the citizen pressure that indicates that change is desired and therefore ultimately possible. But without the participation of the "top," the "bottom" will find it hard to recoordinate its activities in the ways it desires.

What I'm talking about here, of course, is power. For the "bottom" to have power, it needs the "top." For the "top" to have power, it needs the "bottom." And for effective social reorganization to occur, they both need dialogue. That is, they both need, as Anthony Giddens has termed it, *dialogic democracy*—a democracy in which all, including the environment, are taken into account.[17]

REORGANIZING COMMUNITIES

Perhaps, in fits and starts, stumbles and leaps, we're getting there. We have managed in recent years to coordinate some important social reorganizations of environmental relations, generally through the cooperation of the bottom and the top.

Recycling in the United States

Recycling is a good example. Back in the early 1980s, some friends of mine in college lived in what they called Ecology House, a big old Victorian home owned by our university. These students lived there as a demonstration of urban environmental living. The students raised money for and installed a backyard compost bin, a composting toilet, energy-efficient lighting, a solar greenhouse for heating, and other environmental improvements. But most impressive, I always thought, was the way these roughly ten students, all of whom cooked and ate in the house, produced one lonely paper shopping bag of garbage a week. Everything else was either precycled, recycled, or reused. They didn't generate much garbage to begin with, they returned to the production stream what they did generate, and they found other uses for a lot of stuff other people would have simply pitched.

Some people thought they were crazy, though. Unless you have that kind of young idealistic zeal, who could be bothered to sort paper, metal, and glass, or to compost food scraps (let alone personal manures)? "Recycling sounds like a great idea, but almost nobody will ever do it," they were often told. The doubters had some statistics to back them up, too. As late as 1985, the recycling rate in the great throw-away society, the United States, was just 3 percent.

By 1995, the national rate was 22 percent and rising. In 1988, there were just 600 curbside recycling programs in U.S. communities; by 1993, there were 3,700. The city of Seattle now recycles 50 percent of its waste. The state of New Jersey set itself the target of recycling 25 percent of municipal waste and by 1995 had achieved 53 percent.[18]

For a while the main barrier to increased recycling was an embarrassment of recycled riches. The market was glutted, prices dropped, and a few communities were finding it necessary to send some of the materials they had collected to the landfill. But as more factories were set up to handle recycled materials, the situation rapidly reversed itself. Prices skyrocketed. In some cities, bundles of recycled newspapers were being stolen off the streets before official collection trucks could get to them.

Prices for recycled materials have dropped again since then and remain somewhat volatile, as is typical of raw materials markets. And recycling is now experiencing a political backlash—a sure sign, in a dialogic democracy, that an idea has hit prime time. Most of this backlash was unleashed in 1996 when Mayor Giuliani of New York sought to cut 38 percent from the city's recycling budget and the *New York Times* published a widely noticed (and, in my view, largely erroneous) piece criticizing recycling.[19] (At the time of this writing the political climate has moderated somewhat, although recycling remains under fire from some quarters.)[20]

Nevertheless, community recycling in the United States must be considered an astonishing success story. And why? Because people demanded it be done. They were tired of having incinerators and waste dumps foisted on their neighborhoods. And they wanted to do something good for the environment. It was a matter of their interests and their sentiments. All that was needed were the social structures that could make it possible: government action, corporate investment, and technological changes. And it happened because the top and the bottom found they had something to talk about together.

Supplying Water in a Costa Rican Village

For years, international agencies have been drilling wells, planting trees, providing new crop varieties, building dams, and promoting tourism in "less-developed" communities across the world, hoping to spur economic development. Sometimes this form of international aid has worked, but very often it has not. Local people have often looked on with pleasant smiles while the dams were put up and have shaken hands in apparent thanks when given trees to plant, only to fail to maintain the dams and the trees later. Eventually—after the development reports were filed away back at the international aid agency's headquarters—the dams crumbled and the trees died.

Astonishing as it seems in retrospect, supporters of this 1970s-style approach to development rarely bothered to ask a crucial question of local people: What do you want? Such a top-down style of development assistance not only alienated the people it was supposed to help, but, because of the development officials' lack of knowledge of local conditions, top-down approaches often resulted in increased social inequality and environmental damage.

In the early 1990s, though, development agencies began to see both the practical and the democratic value of what has come to be called *participatory development*.[21] Involving local people as equal partners and leaders in development projects ensures a sense of ownership—of sentimental commitment—to a project. It also ensures that the project is more likely to do what people want, making the project fit their interests as well. This approach is so totally obvious in retrospect that it may seem incredible that development efforts ever took another course. But early development thinking often had little respect for the views of local people, seeing them as backward and incapable of understanding all the advantages of the modern techniques that were being offered to them, while assuming (rather contradictorily) that the modern way was what everyone wanted.

In 1994, I was fortunate enough to see firsthand the results of a more participatory approach to local development. An old friend lives in Platanillo, Costa Rica, a farming village of about five hundred people in the foothills of the Talamanca Mountains. We had lost touch since meeting in the 1970s, but I happened to be in the country on university business, so I decided to look him up. The village has no phone, and I wasn't even sure he was living there anymore. So I quite literally looked him up. I took the Platanillo bus up the dirt road into the mountains on a Saturday afternoon, got some directions from the barkeeper in the local tavern, and surprised my friend as he was returning from his fields for the day. He recognized me almost immediately, even after seventeen years, and excitedly led me around his farm and the village.

One of the places he brought me to, with considerable obvious pride, was the new water-supply dam that he and some other villagers had installed earlier that year. The dam made a small impoundment on a stream up in the mountains above the village—not big enough to cause much damage should it give way some day but large enough to supply all the houses on that side of the valley with running water. Before the dam was built, everyone was drawing water by hand from household wells, often dug dangerously close to outdoor toilets. Now everyone in the neighborhood had safe running water piped into their houses.

The people in Platanillo had some outside help in building the water system. My friend mentioned that several development agencies were involved, although he didn't mention which ones. That didn't seem important. Instead, he talked about the neighbors with whom he had worked on the project, about the way the sluice gate worked, about the way they arranged for the land where the dam sat, and other local details. This clearly was the villagers' own water supply.

What really struck me, as my friend described the new system, was how much he knew about it—far, far more than I know about the water supply system in my own community. After all, my friend had helped build and design the one in his community. Should those pipes or that dam or the watershed up above or down below ever develop any problems, he and his neighbors would know what to do and would feel a sense of investment and responsibility for carrying out any repairs. Which was a good thing, I thought. In such a remote place, if the local people didn't take care of a problem, it would be a long time before anyone else would.

As I took the bus back down the valley that evening, I passed a building in the next village down the road from Platanillo with a sign on it that said "U.S. Peace Corps." I don't know if Peace Corps volunteers were involved in Platanillo's dam—my friend never said. But if they were, I thought, they sure understood the value of participation.

Growing Local Knowledge in Honduras

Jeff Bentley is not your typical social scientist. I knew that as soon as I laid eyes on him in 1993, when he gave a seminar in our department. The title of his talk was suitably academic sounding—something like "Farmer-Scientists and Integrated Pest Management in Honduras," as I recall. But rarely, even in this informal age, is a seminar delivered by someone wearing old jeans whose bottom hems are frayed from continually catching beneath the wearer's construction-style boots. He did wear a sport coat, a tweed one, but it only made his jeans and uncombed hair seem that much more incongruous in a university seminar room.

And yet Bentley held the packed room (including several conservatively dressed scientists from the entomology department) absolutely spellbound. Bentley had been employed over the past few years in the Department of Crop Protection at the Escuela Agricola Panamericana in Zamorano, Honduras, trying out a radical new way of doing research on Honduras's farm problems: working *with* the country's poor peasant farmers. In collaboration with Werner Melara, and others at Zamorano, Bentley had been going into Honduran villages and conducting entomology seminars with local farmers. "We don't tell them what to do to solve their pest problems," Bentley said. "We try to give them the intellectual tools for solving the problems themselves."[22]

Over the last forty years, the typical approach of agricultural scientists working on the problems of tropical agriculture has been to encourage peasant farmers to adopt hybrid crop varieties developed by the scientists themselves. Such varieties generally yield more but also have fewer defenses against pests. The scientists have developed an answer for that problem too, though: pesticides. (It's a package deal.) But farmers have to buy the hybrid varieties and pesticides, rather than relying on seed saved from the previous crop and on lower-cost pest control practices. And if you're a poor Honduran farmer, money is something you don't have a lot of. (Capital-intensive agriculture also promotes international economic inequality by draining scarce cash from the Honduran countryside.) Also, a high degree of literacy is required to read the label warnings on the safe and appropriate use of the pesticides. Thousands have been poisoned.[23]

Bentley's view is that any solutions farmers devise for themselves are far more likely to be relevant to their ecological, economic, cultural, and agricultural circumstances. Also, Bentley stresses the importance and validity of farmers' own knowledge about local conditions and local farming practices—their *local knowledge*.[24] Honduran peasant farmers are poor, not stupid, and they know a lot of relevant things that the scientists don't. After all, the peasant farmers live there.

University scientists do have a lot to offer local people, though, particularly concerning phenomena that are not easily observed. In Bentley's rural seminars, he helps the farmers see inconspicuous connections that the university scientists have figured out. Most local farmers don't understand insect life cycles, so he puts larvae in glass jars for several days so that people can watch caterpillars and grubs develop into adult insects. Local farmers almost never go out into their fields at night, so Bentley takes them out to watch insect activities by flashlight. And then he sits back and lets them apply the knowledge.

In one village, the local farmers had been spending quite a bit of money on pesticides to eradicate the fire ants that were infesting their fields, although they had no evidence that the ants were harming their yields. When Bentley took them out at night, though, they watched as the ants crawled up their corn plants and ate some other insects that were harming the crop. A local woman was very impressed with this observation and wondered how to encourage the ants. She recalled that ants were often attracted to the sugar in her kitchen, and she came up with the idea of mixing a dilute solution of sugar water and spraying it on infested plants to attract the ants.

This idea, suggested Bentley, has several advantages typical of local innovations. First, it's cheap, as sugar is relatively inexpensive. Second, it relies on easily accessible local materials—sugar and water. Third, it is something that the local people understand completely, which should allow them to refine the idea, generating further innovations. Fourth, it is safe, both for the environment and for the farmers. And fifth, as it is their own idea, local farmers feel a sense of ownership and are far more likely to be committed to making the idea work.

But does this idea from the bottom actually help control insect pests? Here's where the top—the scientists—can step in again, performing experiments and helping local people design their own experiments to assess the validity of the idea. With the Zamorano approach, scientists are still very important but, as Bentley and Melara explain, "We depend on farmers to help tell us what to study and to work with us in actually carrying out experiments in their fields, fine-tuning the technologies to their conditions."[25]

The point of participatory development, in other words, is not that local people always know best. Rather, the point is to get a dialogue going between local people and scientists, between local knowledge and expert knowledge. Such a dialogue encourages the respect and concern of each party for the other and perhaps even genuine friendships, as each comes to know the other better: solidarities of interests and sentiments. Participatory development is thus *dialogic development*.

REORGANIZING OUR OWN COMMUNITIES

Innovative ideas and cooperative social reorganizations are improving our ecological dialogue in communities all across the world. In this section, I'll discuss a few examples from my own community: Ames, Iowa. These are not especially noteworthy social reorganizations. They have not attracted national and international attention, nor are they likely to do so. But their significance lies in the fact that they are *not* unique: Changes like these are happening in lots of places.[26]

A Bicycle-Powered Hauling and Delivery Business

Ames is a pleasant college town of about 50,000. Its economy is based mainly on retail, government agencies, and Iowa State University, where I teach. Despite the presence of a major university, Ames is not one of those funky college towns with a lot of alternative businesses run by aging, or New Age, hippies. It's a pretty ordinary place. "Ames—the center of it all" is the Chamber of Commerce's motto for the city, and they mean that both geographically and culturally. Still, new things happen even in ordinary places.

The sight of a bicycle hauling two trailers hooked up in tandem and loaded five feet high with recycling bins and loose cardboard is one of the striking sights of Ames. Since 1992, Joan Stein and Jim Gregory have been running Fresh Aire Delivery, a bicycle-powered hauling and delivery service in Ames. Bicycle delivery services can be found in most major U.S. cities now. The hauling side of Fresh Aire is distinctive, though. Most of their hauls consist of recycled materials collected from households, businesses, and the university. Ames has a city-operated trash incinerator. With little need to put waste in landfills, the city has instituted only a rudimentary recycling program. Joan and Jim sought to correct the problem. Using trailers they design and build themselves, they have expanded the business to the point where it employs twenty riders, including Jim and Joan. I see one of their riders almost every day.

"A lot of people just look, just stare," Joan explained to me one morning when I came over to interview them in their small but comfortable house. "And to be quite frank, it's worked to our advantage. It's kind of like a free form of advertising."

"I've hauled over a thousand pounds," said Jim. "You don't want to do that too much. You feel *real* tired!"

"And you thank the lord that Ames is flat," added Joan, laughing.

They both used to own cars, but neither does now. Joan's brother trashed hers four years ago. "I was thinking about getting rid of it anyway," she says. "So it worked out for the best. . . . It's been very liberating to live without one." Jim hasn't owned one in eleven years, although in high school he used to fix up trucks and sell them. "When I finally got into college, I guess I kind of outgrew that stage," he says.

Why did they start this business? Not because they're anti-technology. They own a computer, a telephone, and a microwave oven. And I've watched Jim mow a lawn pushing a reel mower in one hand—they also run a non-power lawn mowing service—while holding a cell phone up to his ear with his other hand.

"People assume that doing things by bike is backward. I don't think it's that at all. I think it's just *appropriate*," Jim reasons.

Exhibit 8.3 *Jim Gregory of Fresh Aire Delivery with his double-tandem bike trailers loaded up: Fresh Aire's bike trailers are a familiar sight in Ames, Iowa.*

Photo: Joe Lynch

And what makes bikes appropriate for Jim and Joan are their social and environmental consequences. "People view being inside the car as being inside their own body armor where they feel safe," Jim told me. "And I'm not sure that's the best way to go. You want to feel you're part of your environment as much as possible."

On a bike, Joan added, one stays "tuned in to the environment. And you don't abuse it so much if you're out there in the elements."

"Living this way for the past decade," agreed Jim, "I can't imagine not knowing there are kids playing, because you can hear them outside."

Maybe Joan put it best: "I just think our lifestyle keeps you accessible to other people. . . . It gives a feeling of openness."

It's the feeling of dialogue—social and ecological.

• •

SOCIAL ACTION CASE STUDY
CONNECTING THE "BOTTOM" AND THE "TOP"

Although I certainly am no environmental saint, people often compliment me and my family on the way we integrate environmentalism into our personal lives. Friends are genuinely impressed that we manage two careers with one car, that we buy much of our food locally and raise a little bit ourselves, that we don't have air conditioning, that we bicycle everywhere. "I admire your sacrifices," people have often told me.

I often find myself oddly disillusioned after people give me this compliment, though. I think we don't do nearly enough in my household, and it depresses me to think that people would find our small steps toward environmental living worth commenting on. And even more, we don't do a thing that we don't want to do. I mean, I bike because I *like* biking. We have only one car because we don't like cars, and we wish we had the courage to sell the one we've got. We prefer the fresh taste of locally-grown food and we love gardening. We dislike the noise and closeted feeling of air conditioning. It's true that I really don't particularly enjoy sorting paper for recycling, but this seems a very small sacrifice to make. So, if I pretty much only do the environmentally-attuned things that I like to do, how can I expect that anyone else will change to a more environmentally-attuned style of life?

I've gone through this thought pattern enough that it's becoming predictable, with a sequence of typical stages. And the next stage is that I realize something very hopeful: The fact that I feel I don't make any real sacrifices in living as I do means that environmentalism does not have to be a sacrifice. If one is able to organize one's life appropriately—for example, by choosing a home that is within bicycling distance of most of your major destinations, such as work and shopping—and to organize one's mind appropriately—for example, by giving up on a commercialized vision of the good life—a more environmentally-attuned life is readily accessible.

If one is able . . . and that's where the "top" of social change comes in. We can help all of us to lead more environmentally sound lives without a sense of sacrifice if we promote the appropriate ways to reorganize society. Then maybe I'll find I don't even need courage to sell my car. I'll just need to sell it.

• •

Community Supported Agriculture

That same feeling of dialogue underlies another new organization in our town: the Magic Beanstalk CSA. The acronym "CSA" stands for "community supported agriculture" projects, partnerships between farmers and consumers to support local agricultural production. Typically, consumers pay a set amount at the beginning of the season for a share in the farms' yield and get the produce directly from the farms. The idea began in Japan where local food partnerships called *teikei* have existed since the 1960s. In Britain, they're called "box schemes," as the produce usually comes once a week in a big box. And since the late 1980s, about a thousand "CSAs" have sprouted across the United States.[27] Iowa's first CSAs started in 1995, and the Magic Beanstalk is one of the three that began that summer. As of 1997, some ten local farms were producing vegetables, honey, wool, pork, beef, chicken, eggs, flowers, whole grains, and cider—all following sustainable and humane farming methods— for about one hundred Magic Beanstalk households.

Shelly Gradwell, then a twenty-five-year-old graduate student at Iowa State University, was one of several people who were key to getting the Magic Beanstalk going. Sitting under a pine tree on Iowa State's central campus, she explained to me why: "Our closest connection to the environment is through what we eat three times a day. That's our most close, direct, and intimate connection with the land. And that was totally missing in 1990s environmentalism."

Shelly used to work for the U.S. Park Service, doing environmental education, and she got frustrated with the contradictions she saw in some wilderness-preservation enthusiasts. "They talk all about conservation and preservation of wilderness, jump in their Saabs on the weekends, and drive up into the mountains and bag peaks—and buy all that expensive gear and petroleum-based clothing. . . . It almost seemed to me like an extractive kind of use, even though they were total wilderness preservationists. They only seemed to think about the environment on the weekends."

CSAs, on the other hand, decrease energy use by promoting a local food supply. Typically, CSAs use sustainable (usually organic) and humane methods, and yet they deliver the food at a competitive price. The elimination of retailing allows farmers to claim a bigger share of the food dollar and still keep prices low, making sustainable, organic, and humane produce affordable. Thus, CSAs are not necessarily Saab-and-Goretex environmentalism. (The Magic Beanstalk, like many CSAs, also has a special program to make food more affordable for lower-income households.) CSAs provide a way for people to connect symbolically with the land, as Shelly described, as well as a way for urban people to connect with rural people and vice versa. CSAs are about more than food; they are also about community, social and ecological.

A CSA clearly depends in part upon a solidarity of interests. By committing to a price up front, consumers share in the risk of agricultural production. Farmers have guaranteed sales, which is a great comfort when you are about to sink a lot of money and time into the ground. Consumers' interests are served by getting a good product at a good price. Each side gets something they are interested in.

Exhibit 8.4 *Picking peas and weeding onions at the Magic Beanstalk CSA: Members of a community supported agriculture project sometimes help out with the chores on a volunteer basis.*

Photos: Shelly Gradwell

The success of a CSA depends as well upon a solidarity of sentiments—at least the Magic Beanstalk does. Both producers and consumers share a commitment to a common norm: promoting sustainable community. This common desire is central to the group. Producers and consumers interact socially through harvest festivals, field days, kids' days, cooking and canning classes, short chit-chats when the produce is delivered, and more. They *like* each other, and the group wouldn't operate so smoothly if that weren't the case.

All of these solidarities were severely threatened during the Magic Beanstalk's first year, though. The spring of 1995 was very wet and cold in Iowa. People had signed up expecting weekly vegetable deliveries to start in mid-May, but the main producer's fields were under several inches of water. By mid-June, not a leaf of lettuce had been delivered—a rather inauspicious beginning. The organizers were panicked, convinced the CSA was about to collapse before it had really even begun. But no customer called to complain. The producers sent out letters offering a full refund to anyone who wanted out. No one did. Because of normative and affective commitments, the solidarity held across this trust-busting moment. And when regular vegetable deliveries finally began in the first week of July, a loud collective whoop could be heard in central Iowa. They had done it. They had created a lasting community.

Here's how one Iowa CSA producer described the dialogical bonds a CSA depends upon: "My shareholders are friends of mine; they trust me." Shareholders and friends; interests and sentiments. Here's another producer: "Before we started working together in the CSA, we didn't know each other at all. . . . [Now] we respect each other and know that we will help each other." Respect and helping each other; sentiments and interests. Here's a CSA member: "We became members because we enjoy fresh vegetables and because we really believe in the philosophies behind CSA." Fresh vegetables and philosophies; interests and sentiments.[28]

The Magic Beanstalk takes its name from the traditional story "Jack and the Beanstalk," in which Jack, a poor starving farm boy, grows a huge beanstalk from a magic bean in order to steal some food from the airborne castle of a giant. For the Magic Beanstalk CSA, the giant represents modern agriculture and its efforts to take away the market of small, local farms. Jack represents the courage of local farms trying to get back some of that market. As Shelly explained, "In the version that we have, the giant gets his head cut off. The beanstalk doesn't get cut down. It's the victory of local agriculture over the military-agricultural complex."

That image of a "military-agricultural complex" describes a depressingly frequent feature of market developments: social and environmental fragmentation. But markets do not have to develop in that way. Instead of being a site of pure competitive individualism, a production and consumption treadmill, a market can be a place of cooperation and connection. It all depends on whether a market is conceived of as a solidarity or as a "solo"-darity. The Magic Beanstalk CSA demonstrates that the former is possible—and preferable.

The New Urbanism

Suburban sprawl isn't as bad in Ames as it is in a lot of places. Because of the farm crisis of the 1980s, the population of Iowa actually dropped during that decade. Money was tight, so there wasn't a lot of development. "We have a real opportunity to avoid some of the mistakes that were made elsewhere," says Joe Lynch, a local Ames activist for sound urban planning.

But sprawl is nevertheless well under way in Ames, promoting automobile dependency, isolating people and neighborhoods, and leading to what Joe calls "retail strip mines"—strip developments of huge stores that close down local businesses, mine a community's economy, and ship the profits to an out-of-town corporation. Ames has a couple of big strip malls now, and our recent residential development has followed the standard separationist model in which housing types are segregated and kept far removed from commercial development, forcing people to drive to work and shops. This approach has come to be what people in town generally expect now. Commercial development today always seems to bring cars, traffic, and parking lots, so understandably no one wants that near their homes—which only promotes greater use of cars and more ugly "retail strip mines."

Exhibit 8.5 A street in Kentlands, Maryland, the best-known "new urbanism" development: Note the space-saving close-together houses with small front yards and the community-building presence of porches. Although this view shows single-family homes, Kentlands has a wide variety of housing types—as is characteristic of new urbanism developments.

Photo: Mike Bell

Joe has been one of a number of Ames residents who in the last few years have tried to change the town's vision of development. He goes to city council meetings, he writes occasional guest columns in a local paper, he reads up on what is going on in other communities, and—perhaps most importantly—he talks to people. Time and again he engages townspeople in conversation, describing the importance of what he calls "relationships" and the need to "look at systems in comprehensive ways." He stops them in the streets. He goes into local stores and chats with the owners and workers. His principal message is, as he explained to me one afternoon on the deck of his self-built solar home, "You don't solve pollution problems by worrying about what comes out at the end. You solve pollution problems by looking at the system and redesigning what people need."

The vision that Joe and other activists in town are advocating is what is often called the *new urbanism*.[29] The basic idea of new urbanism is to model new developments on the kind of traditional neighborhoods that cities routinely turn into historic districts. If we think such areas are nice enough to make special efforts to preserve them and to visit them as tourists, new urbanists ask, why not design all our neighborhoods that way? New urbanism is thus in many ways the traditional urbanism, the urbanism of a time when cities were built for people rather than cars.

New urbanism designers typically recommend the following guidelines for people-friendly development: Build houses up, not out, so lots can be narrower. Bring back the front porch, the sidewalk, and the alleyway, all zones of interaction between neighbors. Make most streets through streets so all the traffic doesn't get channeled onto a few trunk roads, causing traffic jams even in suburbs. Bring back the corner shop. Provide a diversity of housing types within a neighborhood so that people with all kinds of household situations can live there, from singles, to families with children, to the elderly. Don't mix stores and housing types higgledy-piggledy, but instead institute far more detailed zoning plans than the current big-blob style of zoning with huge areas devoted to a single type of use. Following these guidelines increases density, making walking and public transit more realistic options. Stores and schools and workplaces are located near homes—and without the traffic and parking lots that make most commercial life so unappealing and environmentally unsound today.

Ames's developers and city planners thought the whole idea was completely unrealistic at first. Also, they interpreted Joe and other planning activists as antibusiness. "I'm not against commercial activity," responds Joe, who is a small business person himself. (He runs an energy-efficiency consulting business, among other activities.) "That's not the issue. The issue is how can we design commercial activity so that it doesn't destroy our communities and our neighborhoods."

Through a long series of meetings and discussions over several years, often heated, and finally culminating in a one-day seminar at which some of the United States's leading new urbanism designers spoke, local developers and city officials and activists began to see that they had a lot in common. Some developers and officials, it turned out, didn't particularly like putting in the same old sprawling developments. It's expensive to construct and maintain the necessary roads, sewer lines, and power lines and to provide police, fire, and emergency services to spread-out developments. Moreover, some members of the local business community were worried about the problem of retail strip mining too. They just thought that's what people wanted.

Exhibit 8.6 *A street in Providence, Rhode Island, developed in the 1890s: New urbanism takes as its model "old urbanism" developments like this one. Note here too the close-together houses, the small yards, the front porches. Also note the mixing of single-family homes with the duplex in the foreground.*

Photo: Mike Bell

The result is that Ames's next development, it's biggest in years, is going to follow many features of the new urbanism approach. Lot sizes will be smaller. There will be front porches, sidewalks on both sides of the streets, and some alleyways. It will have a wide range of housing types, from apartments to townhouses to detached single-family homes. And there will be a small main street with the parking in the back, multistory commercial buildings, and stores that front directly on the sidewalk. If it works, it will be the kind of place where parents feel safe sending their children to the corner store for milk, where people walk to work or to the bus stop, where neighbors know each other a little bit better, and where fewer resources are demanded from the environment.

In other words, the activists and developers and city officials built a solidarity of solidarities, across interests and sentiments, from bottom to top, and made a change. The process was not without conflict. The parties still don't always trust one another, and the plan does not follow the new urbanism model in some ways that the activists and the designer hired by the developers regard as crucial. (The designer was upset enough to ask to have his name removed from the project.) Yet they still managed to make enough connections, social and environmental, to achieve a small but significant reorganization of the pattern of life in Ames.

As Joe says, "It's a matter of relationships, all these relationships. That's what nature teaches us." He paused and then asked me, nodding toward my tape recorder, "Did you turn that thing off?" I shook my head, and he repeated with a grin, leaning toward the machine, "That's what nature teaches us— THE VALUE OF RELATIONSHIPS. I hope that's what your book teaches."

I hope so too.

REORGANIZING SOCIETIES

Finally, we need to reorganize the larger societies of which we are all a part. Here too there is a "top" and a "bottom" to social change, as well as interests and sentiments that must be gathered together into the interactive solidarities of dialogic democracy.

To begin with, we need better sources of communication about the environment so that we will better understand what our interests really are. The basic political thermometer of social health remains growth in GNP (gross national product) per capita (although there have been moves to switch it to the closely related GDP—gross domestic product).[30] But as the environmental economist Herman Daly has noted, GNP is often a perverse measure of environmental health.[31] For example, under current accounting, a disaster like the *Exxon Valdez* oil spill shows up as a positive contribution to GNP because it stimulates so much economic activity in cleaning up the spill. So, too, for cleaning up hazardous waste sites, removing asbestos and lead paint from old buildings, and paying any medical costs incurred from environmental contamination. Moreover, depletion of nonrenewable resources shows up as income under GNP calculations instead of what it really is: an irreplaceable withdrawal from our ecological bank account. In other words, as far GNP is concerned, environmental degradation is good for the economy because, at least in the short run—and the short run is all GNP measures—it creates jobs and gives us spending money.

Daly's ideas have recently been used to devise a new thermometer, the GPI—the genuine progress indicator, a complex index of over twenty different economic factors. These factors include measures of environmental health such as pollution, resource depletion, and long-term environmental damage, as well as measures of social health such as crime and income distribution. The GPI gives a very different picture of how we're doing than does GNP. For example, in the United States GNP per capita has shown continuous gains since World War II, whereas GPI has steadily declined since 1970. The GPI dropped 1 percent in the 1970s, 2 percent in the 1980s, and 6 percent in the 1990s through to 1995.[32] Unfortunately, a lot more of us have heard of GNP than have yet heard of the GPI.

Another way to increase environmental communication is by putting the environment right where we're all sure to notice: in costs. Currently, many environmental consequences of our economic activity are external to the costs of goods and services. One way to internalize the environment in our economic thinking is through *green taxes*, sometimes called *Pigouvian taxes* after Nicholas Pigou, the English economist who proposed the idea in the early 1900s. Green taxes are an attempt to make the price of goods and services reflect their true costs and to shift the burden of government revenue generation away from regressive taxation schemes like sales taxes and value-added taxes. Finland, for example, now has a carbon tax aimed at internalizing the costs of global warming and other pollution issues associated with fossil fuel use. Britain has a landfill tax. The Netherlands and several Scandinavian countries now have energy taxes. Iowa has a tax on pesticide purchases, which is used to fund the Leopold Center for Sustainable Agriculture—the idea being that if pesticides are used less, the Leopold Center will also be needed less, and conversely.

Green taxes offer a lot of possibilities, but like any taxation scheme they have to be handled with great care. Taxes are perhaps the most hotly contested of any issue these days. If they are not supported by public sentiment, and if they harm public interests, perhaps by being instituted in regressive ways, green taxes will be a political disaster. Also, powerful interests often get the upper hand in taxation debates, as when Belgium instituted a pesticide tax that exempted farmers and when the early versions of energy taxes in Scandinavia exempted some energy-intensive industries. But perhaps we can learn the lessons of these early experiments and use green taxes to help build an economy that reflects what things really cost.

There is also increasing excitement these days among business leaders about what is increasingly called *industrial ecology*: treating industry as a part of ecologic systems as opposed to a means of dominating ecologic systems.[33] The key principle of industrial ecology is regarding pollution as a sign of inefficiency in an industry. Waste products should be regarded as wasted opportunities, not leftovers to be gotten rid of in the cheapest and faster and least conspicuous way possible. "Closing the loop" is the way advocates of industrial ecology often describe the greener approach. By greening business, we can prevent environmental problems instead of having to ameliorate them. Environmental standards such as ISO 14,000, the green business guidelines of the International Organization for Standardization, alert industry to places where the loop is perhaps not yet closed and opportunities are being wasted. Industrial ecology thus advises business to see environmental standards and environmental regulation as business opportunities rather than obstructions to be fought or dodged.

Environmental sociologists refer to this process of greening business, and greening consumers, as *ecological modernization*.[34] Rather than the old big-smokestacks-and-big-technology-that-nobody-controls vision of modernity, ecological modernization takes a greener view of modernity's potential. Is ecological modernization a contradiction in terms? It is perhaps too soon to tell. But without a more participatory and dialogic vision of modernization—a vision that includes the participation of the "top," the "bottom," and the environment itself—we may never get a chance to find out.

Exhibit 8.7 Ecological modernization: World wind generating capacity and world sales of photovoltaic cells. With technologies such as these, industrialism can become more a source of environmental solutions and less a source of environmental problems, argue ecological modernization advocates.

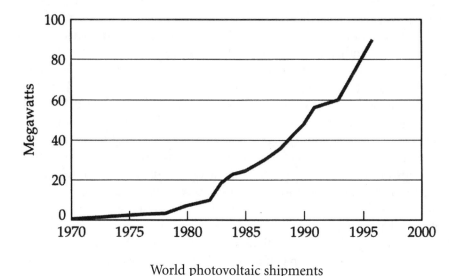

World photovoltaic shipments

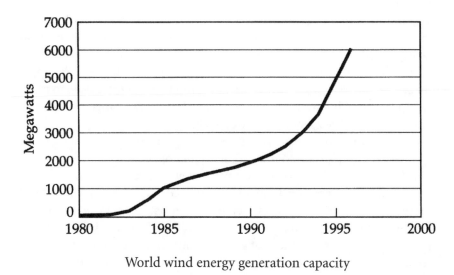

World wind energy generation capacity

Source: Brown et al. (1997).

And to get that chance we need to recognize that, among other things, there is still a crucially important place for law and good government in organizing the ecological society. We need regulation and regulatory agencies; we need laws and legislatures; we need international treaties and international treaty organizations. But we also need them to be more participatory than they have generally been in the past. As the political scientist Elinor Ostrom has observed, "In contemporary conceptions of social order, the 'government' often is seen as an external agent whose behavior is exogenous to the situation."[35] This conception of an external government has, of late, been equally characteristic of some elected officials and some of those who elected them, or have chosen not to participate in the electoral process. The us-versus-them view of the relationship between the government and the people will have to be repaired. For the government is, or rather should be, us.

REORGANIZING OURSELVES

We are, however, unlikely to work to change our local communities and the bigger communities that whole societies represent unless we have personally committed to change. Reorganizing our communities also involves reorganizing ourselves.

It's important to recognize the interaction, the dialogue, between reorganizing community and reorganizing ourselves. We are more likely to regard the environment in environmentally appropriate ways when our community life is organized to encourage such regard. But we can't simply wait around for that community reorganization to happen; we need to make it happen. Individuals are the agents of community change as much as communities are the agents of individual change.

In other words, our personal values and actions do matter. There is a crucial ethical dimension to our ecological dialogues.

Which brings us back to community, for ethical ideas are always ideas about community relationships. Aldo Leopold put it well in "The Land Ethic," probably the twentieth century's most influential essay on environmental ethics: "All ethics so far evolved rest upon a single premise: that the individual is a member of a community of interdependent parts."[36] But how we draw the boundary of community membership shapes (and is shaped by) our sense of with whom we feel interdependent, and thus for whom we feel a sense of moral concern. (Moral concern and interdependent parts—it's the interplay of sentiments and interests again.) Our fellowship with others implies that they are entitled to our moral concern, just as we are entitled to their moral concern.

My point is that in the idea of community is the idea of equality—and inequality. There is a constant tension between community and inequality, between commitment to those included within the community's boundaries and lack of commitment, and consequent inattention, to the troubles of those excluded from the community. Ideas of community, inequality, and the boundaries of moral concern are thus closely intertwined.

Each of the three central issues of environmentalism—sustainability, environmental justice, and the rights and beauty of nature—challenges a different dimension of these boundaries of concern. Sustainability considers how we draw boundaries of concern between present and future generations. Environmental justice considers how we draw boundaries of concern between human groups. The rights and beauty of nature considers how we draw boundaries of concern between humans and the rest of creation.

This last boundary is perhaps the most difficult. How can we form a sense of community with the ecosystem, something we're not even sure is an intentional actor? How can we form a solidarity of interests and sentiments with something we're not even sure *has* interests and sentiments? Would not such an "ethical extension," as Leopold termed it, be mere anthropomorphism—treating the inherently nonhuman as the human—and therefore highly unstable?

Environmental sociology can help us here, I think. We must begin by recognizing that all communities are imagined.[37] This is why trust is so important. We cannot get into the mind of the other, so we are always guessing, trusting, and closely watching for the signs of solidarity.

The same may be the case for human-environmental interactions. We need to imagine this form of community too. And this imagination is what the environmental movement has long promoted, at least as I interpret the two sides of what has long been the main debate in environmental ethics: anthropocentric environmentalism versus ecocentric environmentalism.

Anthropocentric environmentalism suggests that we consider our own interests first in our interactions with the environment—interests in sustainability and environmental justice—and also that we need to consider the environment's interests in order to gain our own. (That last clause, I should point out, is what distinguishes anthropocentric environmentalism from what might be termed anthropocentric nonenvironmentalism.) In other words, anthropocentric environmentalism says treat the environment well and it will treat us well in return: hence, a solidarity of interests.

Ecocentric environmentalism, on the other hand, suggests that we consider the environment as a moral entity in its own right and with its own beauty and that we see ourselves as a part of that moral entity. It argues that we need to go beyond questions of calculated human interest and recognize the importance of what the environmental philosopher Paul Taylor, for example, termed "respect for nature."[38] But we are part of that beautiful nature for which respect is due: hence, a solidarity of sentiments.

As with purely human communities, the solidarity-of-sentiments side of environmental ethics has always been the harder argument to make. This difficulty stems, we cannot doubt, from the individual and instrumental thinking so characteristic of our time and place. The challenge of imagination is particularly hard here because the environment does not speak, at least not directly. Which may in part be why anthropomorphism, as in the story of Androcles and the lion, is such a popular way to think about the environment: It helps us imagine the voice of the other in the ecological dialogue.

But I believe the environmental movement is right to try to make the case for a solidarity of environmental sentiments. Even though it is a hard case to make, the evidence suggests to me that it is a vital case. Moments that threaten to bust the glue of trust are too frequent. Also, we can't always wait to figure out what part of the ecosystem is crucial to our interests before we act, and sentiments may add some efficiency here. If for no other reason than they are good for our interests, we need to have sentimental bonds with the ecosystem as well. But the bonds of sentiment are unlikely to last unless they are also good for our interests—which, I believe, they are. Thus, the wise anthropocentrist is also an ecocentrist and vice versa, not one or the other.

If the paradox of collective action is that people often do not act in their own interests when they act in their own interests, the solution is clear: Also act on your sentiments. But consider those sentiments and those interests broadly and openly. We need each to participate in the maintenance of the dialogue, the ecological dialogue, over what our sentiments and interests—our ideals and our material conditions—in fact are.

Maintaining this dialogue is the basic work of the democratic community, from the smallest to that biggest community of all. It is also the sustainable, just, right, and beautiful thing to do.

Photo: Shelley Gradwell

NOTES

Chapter 1 Notes

1 For an introduction to the literature on the realist-constructionist debate see, on the realist side, Benton (1994), Dickens (1996), Dunlap and Catton (1994), Martell (1994) and Murphy (1994a and 1994b), and, on the constructionist side, Cronon, ed. (1995), Dupuis and Vandergeest, eds. (1996), Hajer (1995), Hannigan (1995), and Yearley (1991 and 1996). Within the United States, there has been considerable debate over whether the position of Buttel, a leading figure in the field, is constructionist (for example, Buttel [1992] and Taylor and Buttel [1992]; see the discussion and critique in Dunlap and Catton [1994]). Recently, however, there have been a number of attempts to reconcile the two sides, for example Bell (1997a), Burningham and Cooper (1997), Buttel (1996), and Metzner (1997).

2 For a recent example, see Seidman (1994).

3 For a skeptical view of the seriousness of environmental problems, see Bailey (1995).

4 Brown et al. (1995), 64 and Brown et al. (1977), 63.

5 Brown et al. (1997), 62.

6 Brown et al. (1997), 63.

7 Bell (1985), 168.

8 Seneviratne (1995) and Field (1995).

9 C. Bullard (1997).

10 Buie (1995), Funk (1995), MacKensie (1995).

11 Hileman (1995).

12 Figures from Brown et al. (1997), 17–18. Linden (1994) writes that "According to Franklin Nutter, the president of the Reinsurance Association of America, 'global warming could bankrupt the industry.'" Also see Stix (1996).

13 Stevens (1997).

14 The standard reference in the field is the 1996 report of the Intergovernmental Committe on Climate Change of the United Nations, an unusually accessible document that summarizes the views of climatologists as a whole. One prominent skeptic is Richard S. Lindzen, a climatologist at MIT who argues that the computer models used in global warming predictions are not accurate enough and that scientists have not taken adequate account of the role of atmospheric water vapor (Stevens, 1996).

15 There is skepticism even here, however. This skepticism is based mostly on the argument that recent measurements are biased by the increased "heat-island" effect of expanding urban areas, where most weather stations are situated. Rural weather stations show less of a warming trend. However, there is also abundant evidence of glacial retreat in mountain systems across the world, indicating global warming in even these most rural and remote of regions, as well as satellite data showing earlier springs and later falls in northern climates. See Stevens (1997).

16 Graham-Campbell (1994), 174-179.

17 Schatten and Arking (1990).

18 Schatten and Arking (1990), v.
19 Imbrie and Imbrie (1979), 179, fig. 43.
20 Intergovernmental Committe on Climate Change (1996). Quoted in C. Bullard (1997), 5M.
21 Quoted in C. Bullard (1997).
22 *New York Times* (1997).
23 Imbrie and Imbrie (1979), 178.
24 Unless, of course, your local utility uses nuclear or hydroelectric power. But these have problems of their own.
25 Brown et al. (1995).
26 On increases in ultraviolet radiation, see Stevens (1995).
27 Kerr (1995b).
28 Miller (1994), 581.
29 Miller (1994), 232.
30 Chameides et al. (1994).
31 Suplee (1995).
32 Suplee (1995).
33 In June of 1997, President Clinton announced support for new standards that would finally regulate particles smaller than 10 microns, although as of August, 1997, the U.S. Congress had yet to ratify the standards.
34 Pearce (1995).
35 Freemantle (1995).
36 Brown et al. (1995), 86–87.
37 Miller (1994), 324.
38 My calculations based on figures from Pimentel et al. (1995).
39 Brown et al. (1995), 118–119.
40 Miller (1994), 332.
41 Anderson (1995).
42 Anderson (1995).
43 Miller (1994), 347.
44 Miller (1994), 351.
45 Brown et al. (1995), 123
46 Brown et al. (1995), 122.
47 Brown et al. (1995), 123.
48 Meadows et al. (1992), 56.
49 Meadows et al. (1992), 54–56.
50 Miller (1994), 362; Brown et al. (1995), 41.
51 American Farmland Trust (1994).
52 Brown et al. (1995), 43. For an extended discussion of the difficulty of maintaining rice yields, see chapter 4.
53 Brown et al. (1991), 26–27.
54 Vidal (1995).

55 Sachs (1996).

56 Sachs (1996).

57 Sachs (1996).

58 Shell Oil, belatedly, also agrees and has now modified its statement of business principles to include specific reference to human rights (Beavis and Brown, 1996).

59 Here I am following, in modified form, the distinction Beck (1996) makes between "goods" and "bads." Beck's emphasis, however, is actually on the increasing equality he sees in the distribution of "bads," which is a central feature of what he terms the "risk society" of late modern societies. I critique this conclusion in chapter 6.

60 Hilz (1992).

61 Institute for Agriculture and Trade Policy (1995).

62 There is a voluminous literature on this topic. For an introduction, particularly to the debate over whether race is a factor over and beyond class, see Anderton et al. (1994), Boerner and Lambert (1995), R. Bullard (1994a), Commission for Racial Justice (1987), Goldman (1996), Goldman and Fitton (1994), Heiman (1996), Krieg (1995), and Mohai and Bryant (1992).

63 For an account of this pain, see Erikson (1994).

64 World Bank (1997), table 1.

65 World Bank (1997), table 1, based on the figures for "purchasing power parity."

66 UNDP (1994), figure 2.6.

67 UNDP (1994), figures 2.6 and 4.3. 1991 data.

68 Korten (1995), 39.

69 Durning (1992), p. 50, table 4-1.

70 To use the economic term, the demand for some of these items is "inelastic"—that is, there are limits to how much it can fluctuate and it probably does not increase at the same rate as wealth.

71 Brown et al. (1995), 146–147.

72 On shelter, see Brown et al. (1995), 142; on population, see Brown et al. (1996), 88.

73 UNDP (1994), figure 2.4.

74 World Bank (1995), table 1.

75 UNDP (1994), tables 18 and 40. Brown et al. (1995), 145. Note the gape between countries may have narrowed recently due to the explosive growth in the economy of China, home to nearly a fifth of the world. However, income differentials within countries have increased in most countries, particularly in China and the countries of the former Soviet bloc.

76 UNDP (1994), 98–101.

77 UNDP (1994), figure 5.6.

78 There are signs, however, that the quarter-century-long trend toward wealth concentration at the top may be waning in the rich countries. For example, between 1990 and 1995 in Britain the share of the nation's total income gained by the poorest tenth remained static at 2.5 percent rather than continuing to decline (Timmins, 1996). In the U.S., however, the poorest fifth of the population continues to grow poorer (Holmes, 1997).

79 Thurow (1996), 22; figure for 1993.

80 The Economist (1994), 19; figures for various years from the early 1980s onward.
81 Wolff (1995), 21. The figures Wolff gives for the 1920s are for inequality in wealth, rather than income, presenting some problems of comparability with the figures I cite above for the 1990s. In general, wealth inequalities are greater than income inequalities. However, the societies that are high in one are almost always high in the other, allowing the historical comparison to be made.
82 Brown et al. (1995), 142.
83 Brown et al. (1995), 143.
84 Brown et al. (1995), 143.
85 Brown et al. (1995), 146.
86 UNDP (1994), figure 5.4.
87 Korten (1995), 108.
88 Athanasiou (1996).
89 Leopold (1966 [1949]), 262.
90 Miller (1994), 421.
91 Myers (1995).
92 Hawken (1993), 29.
93 Miller (1994), 263.
94 UNDP (1994), 132.
95 Bell and Laine (1985).

CHAPTER 2   NOTES

1 Kearney (1995).
2 Cited in Guha (1995).
3 Marx (1972 [1844]) 58; emphasis in the original.
4 Marx (1972 [1859]), 4.
5 In his more considered moments, Karl Marx recognized this interplay as well, offering the term *dialectics* to describe it. Drawing on Hegel, Marx described dialectics as an endless cycle of movement from thesis to antithesis to synthesis, with any synthesis becoming the thesis to which the next antithesis responds. Such an account, however, over-polarizes the explanation of social change. The concept of dialogue, which I take from the writings of the Russian social theorist Mikhail Baktin, is an improvement because it emphasizes the mutual conditioning of social factors—a process which is not necessarily oppositional and polarized. For a more detailed critique of the concept of dialectics and a fuller explanation of the analytical advantages of dialogue, see Gardiner (1992). See also the closely related views of Weber (1958 [1904-1905], 277, footnote 84).
6 For a review, see Parker (1996).
7 Maslow (1970 [1943]).
8 Maslow (1970 [1943]), 38.
9 Maslow (1970 [1943]), 100.
10 This point is also made by Inglehart (1977) and (1990). For a detailed critique of Inglehart's particular application of this point, however, see chapter 6.

11 Sahlins (1972).

12 Sahlins (1972), 11.

13 Sahins (1972), 27.

14 Sahlins (1972), 4.

15 Gusinde (1961), 86-87; cited in Sahlins (1972), 13.

16 Sahlins (1972), 11.

17 Sahlins (1972), 37.

18 For more on the social creation of the concept of being poor, see Norberg-Hodge (1991).

19 Veblen (1967 [1899]).

20 Veblen (1967 [1899], 83.

21 Hirsch (1977), 20.

22 Twain (1991 [1876]), 20.

23 See Katz (1994) and Wilson and Yaro (1988).

24 Streeter (1996).

25 Streeter (1996).

26 For a discussion of the relationship between the ideas of Durkheim, Weber, and Tönnies on these points, see Bell (1998a).

27 Csikzentmihalyi and Rochberg-Halton (1981).

28 I take this and the following three paragraphs, in modified form, from Bell (1998a).

29 Bell (1998a).

30 I draw much of the section that follows from Bell (1997b).

31 I take this quotation (which also appears in Bell [1997b]) from Mauss (1990 [1950]), 11. I have also translated into English a few words left in Maori in the original, and put back into Maori one word originally left in English.

32 Mauss (1990 [1950]), 20.

33 Douglas and Isherwood (1979)

34 There is a huge debate on just how effective ads are and how they are interpreted by the public. The classic work that refutes a Pavlovian response to ads is Schudson (1984).

35 Schudson (1984).

36 I quote this ad from an issue of the *International Herald Tribune* from sometime in the fall of 1996.

37 From a 1996 *Seventh Generation* catalogue.

38 For example, see Anthanasiou (1996).

39 Wachtel (1983), 62, 64.

40 Schor (1992), 45.

41 Schor (1992); on other industrialized countries, see Economist (1996a).

42 Schor (1992), 29.

43 Schor (1992), 32, 82 (Table 3.2).

44 See Durning (1992), 131-132.

45 On decline in voluntary organizations, see Putnam (1996); for the rest, see Durning (1992), 43 and 132, citing surveys by others.

46 On work time, see *The Economist* (1996a); for the rest, see Knight and Stokes (1996).

47 Schor (1992), 2.

48 For example, Douglas and Isherwood (1979).

49 For an account of class-bounded patterns of fellowship in Britain, see Bell (1994a); for the U.S., see Rubin (1994).

50 Warr and Payne (1982); cited in Argyle (1987), 92.

51 Argyle (1987), 93, summarizing several studies.

52 Easterlin (1974), table 6. Most of the this data is from the early 1960s.

53 Schor (1992), 115, summarizing many surveys.

54 I take the widely used metaphor of a treadmill from Wachtel (1983) Durning (1992), 39, and Schor (1992), 125; the phrase, however, is mine.

55 Gallup (1989), cited in Schor (1992), 126.

56 Unpublished research, Department of Sociology, Iowa State University.

57 Erikson (1976).

58 Erikson (1976).

CHAPTER 3 NOTES

1 Hill (1988); cited in Irwin (1995), 2.

2 Schudson (1984) is the best account of our resistance to advertising, although he overstates our ability to resist because he concentrates on resistance to individual ads as opposed to the cumulative impact of being surrounded by ads constantly.

3 Korten (1995), 37.

4 Jacobs (1991).

5 Merton (1973 [1968]).

6 Douthwaite (1992), 18.

7 Closely related ideas can be found in the work of Schnaiberg (1980), Schnaiberg and Gould (1994), Galbraith (1958), Cochrane (1958), and others.

8 See chapter 1 for a discussion of growing inequality.

9 Morin and Berry (1996).

10 Novek (1995) and Walker (1989).

11 Jacobs (1991), 25.

12 United States Department of Agriculture (1994), state summary table 15.

13 Lynch (1995) and John Lawrence, Department of Economics, Iowa State University, personal communication.

14 For a review, see *Successful Farming* (1995).

15 D'Aoust et al. (1992), for example, found "disturbing" levels of antibiotic-resistant salmonella in the food chain.

16 For an example of scientific skeptics, see Korsrud et al. (1996). This research team fed twenty-four hogs three times the recommended dosage of several common antibiotics and found that residue levels in the hogs dropped below "recommended guidelines" eight days after the dosage ceased. But of course, the "recommended guidelines" for most chemicals

and drugs have a long history of being revised in more stringent directions in the face of subsequent evidence.

17 For example, see Cannon (1995).

18 Yepson (1995).

19 However, at the time of this writing (May, 1997), there is considerable controversy over one Iowa county, Humboldt County, which passed local ordinances controlling hog lots and then won a district court challenge to the ordinances. Hog-lot interests attempted to have a new state law passed that would override the district court's decision, but were unable to assemble a sufficiently strong political coalition to do so in the final weeks of the state legislature's 1997 session. The issue is sure to return in future legislative sessions.

20 Smothers (1995).

21 Lowe (1995).

22 Bell (1995).

23 For example, see Cochrane (1958) and Rifkin (1995).

24 Warner and England (1995).

25 Brown et al. (1997), 74–75.

26 MacKensie et al. (1992), 1.

27 Durning (1992), 80–81.

28 Brown et al. (1997), 74; Brown et al. (1996), 84.

29 Brown et al. (1996), 84.

30 Brown et al. (1994), 132–133; and National Safety Council figures.

31 *The Times* (1996) and Chris Mead, British Ecological Society, personal communication. Mead estimates the road deaths of British birds to be between three and sixty million, but with the likely total somewhere in the upper half of that range.

32 Royal Commission on Environmental Pollution study, cited in *The Economist* (1996).

33 Brown et al. (1997), 74.

34 Chris Mead, British Ecological Society, personal communication, and Reijnen et al. (1995).

35 MacKensie et al. (1992).

36 I calculated the per car figure by dividing the $300 billion by the 190 million fleet size, yields $1,578.95 per car. I calculated the per gallon figure by dividing the 2 trillion miles Americans annually drive by the fleet size, yielding 10,526.3 miles a year. Dividing this figure by 25 yields an average annual fuel use of 421.1 gallons. Dividing 421.1 into $1,578.95 yield $3,7496.

37 Yago (1984), 56–69.

38 Yago (1984), 60.

39 Merton (1957 [1949]).

40 Winner (1986), 10.

41 Gimpel (1995).

42 Kahn and Wiener (1968); cited in Gimpel (1995), 9.

43 Mumford (1934), 365.

44 Mumford (1934), 6.

CHAPTER 4 NOTES

1 Malthus (1993 [1798]).
2 Engels (1987 [1844]), 104.
3 For example, Wichterich (1988); cited in Duden (1992), 157. See discussion below.
4 Becker (1986). Similar views have been expressed by Simon (1981 and 1995); Boserup (1965) represents a more moderate position. See later discussion in this chapter.
5 See, for example, Brown and Kane (1995) and Meadows et al. (1992).
6 Brown et al. (1996), 89, and Independent Commission on Population and Quality of Life (1996), 11.
7 Crossette (1996), reporting on a new survey by the United Nations.
8 Brown et al. (1997), 81.
9 Independent Commission on Population and Quality of Life (1996), frontispiece.
10 Brown and Kane (1995), 51. Because of annual fluctuations, a more precise figure is not possible.
11 Brown and Kane (1995), 52, table 3-1.
12 World Bank (1997), table 4; figures based on growth between 1990 and 1995.
13 Brown and Kane (1995), 50.
14 World Bank (1997), table 6.
15 Crossete (1996).
16 Independent Commission on Population and Quality of Life (1996).
17 See chapter 3.
18 Lappé and Schurman (1988).
19 Independent Commission on Population and Quality of Life (1996), 15. See that report for a more extensive discussion on this issue.
20 Stein (1995), 133.
21 Barraclough (1982), 102, and McEvedy (1995).
22 For a more cynical, and I believe less accurate, interpretation, see Sachs (1992).
23 Quoted in Esteva (1992), 6.
24 Brown et al. (1995), 72.
25 For details, see chapter 1.
26 World Bank (1994), table 1.
27 World Resources Institute (1996), 162.
28 George and Sabelli (1994), 14.
29 Brown et al. (1995), 73, and World Bank (1997), table 17.
30 World Bank (1997), table 17; figures for 1995.
31 See chapter 3.
32 World Bank (1997), table 1; figure is the 1985–1995 average.
33 For an introduction, see Hopkins et al. (1982) and Frank (1969). For a recent summary, see Hall (1996).
34 Hewitt et al. (1995), 57.
35 George and Sabelli (1994), 55.

36 Brown et al. (1995), 72.

37 Walton (1994).

38 Herbert (1997).

39 See, for example, Bruno and Squire (1996), an op-ed article by two high-ranking members of the World Bank's staff arguing that inequality slows economic growth.

40 Lappé and Schurman (1988), 12, table 1.

41 Lappé, writing in 1977, used the figure of 2 pounds of grain or 3,000 calories a day, but things have changed since then. See below. I use figures derived from Brown et al. (1997), 27.

42 Brown and Kane (1994), 66–67.

43 Brown and Kane (1994), table 4-1.

44 Lappé and Schurman (1988), 14.

45 Lappé and Schurman (1988), 21.

46 Sen (1981).

47 Sen engages in a little sleight of hand here, in my judgment. Because the third rice harvest, the *aman* harvest, lasts from November to January, it is difficult to decide how to divide its production between the two years. This is an important issue because Sen bases his food-availability figures on annual grain production. Unaccountably, however, Sen includes the *aman* crop entirely in the year in which the January part of the harvest falls, despite the fact that two-thirds of the harvest period is in the previous year. (See Sen [1981], 137.) This allows him to effectively extend the size of the 1974 harvest by including the entire 1973–1974 *aman* crop in 1974 and displacing the entire 1974–1975 *aman* crop, which was badly damaged by the floods, into 1975. As a result, his figures for food availability in 1974 are suspiciously high.

48 Kinealy (1996).

49 Sen (1981), 129.

50 For example, see Devereux (1993) and Sarre and Blunden (1995), and even such well-known neo-Malthusians as Meadows et al. (1992).

51 Brown and Kane (1994), 56; 1993 figures.

52 See Devereux (1993), 76–82, for an overview.

53 Stewert (1982), cited in Devereux (1993), 79.

54 Ehrlich (1968).

55 See Sarre and Blunden (1995), 70–71, for a full account.

56 Simon (1981). See also Simon and Kahn (1984) and Simon (1995).

57 See Simon (1995).

58 See chapter 1 for details.

59 As James Scott (1976) has argued, the poor tend to be adverse to risk because their margin is already so tight to begin with.

60 Boserup (1965).

61 Boserup (1981), 3.

62 See Scott (1986) for a study of the displacement of labor and subsequent impoverishment through agricultural intensification in Malaysia.

63 Boserup (1965), 118.
64 Devereux (1993) makes this point very well.
65 Moore (1996).
66 Brown and Kane (1995), 22.
67 Brown and Kane (1995), 38.
68 The following account is drawn from Visser (1986).
69 Scott (1986).
70 Scott (1986).
71 Brown and Kane (1995), 136.
72 Brown and Kane (1995), figure 10-3.
73 Brown et al. (1997), 27.
74 Brown et al. (1996), 24.
75 Goodno (1995).
76 For example, bioengineer Donald Duvick, cited in Brown and Kane (1995), 139–140; see also the skeptical view of the *Financial Times* in Green (1996).
77 Schultz (1981).
78 Stein (1995), 10.
79 Teitelbaum (1987), 31.
80 For a more detailed account of all of these, see Teitelbaum (1987).
81 Sachs (1992), 3–4.
82 Norberg-Hodge (1991).
83 For a similar conclusion, see Teitelbaum (1987) and Sarre and Blunden (1995).
84 Pietila and Vickers (1994), 14.
85 Pietila and Vickers (1994), 15.
86 Boserup (1989 [1970]), 35.
87 Lappé and Schurman (1988), 25–26.
88 Stein (1995).
89 Walby (1996).
90 Moghadam (1996), 1.
91 Joekes (1987) and Standing (1989); cited in Moghadam (1996), 1.
92 Stein (1995), Moghadam (1996), Pietila and Vickers (1994).
93 Stein (1995), 46; Lappé and Schurman (1988), 27.
94 I take this history from Stein (1995), 129–146, who should be consulted for a more detailed account.
95 Wichterich (1988); cited in Duden (1992), 157.
96 Ehrlich and Ehrlich (1990), 17. A similar emphasis on birth control can be found in Ehrlich (1968).
97 For examples of this critique, see Mamdani (1972) and Hartmann, (1987); cited in Duden (1992), 156.
98 I take this account from Stein (1995), 20.
99 Cottrel (1955), 2. I have paraphrased Cottrel to eliminate his gender-specific usage.

CHAPTER 5 NOTES

1 Guha (in press).
2 Weber (1958 [1905]), 60.
3 Weber (1958 [1905]), 181.
4 Weber (1958 [1905]), 181.
5 White (1967), 1207.
6 White (1967), 1204.
7 White (1967), 1205.
8 White (1967), 1205.
9 For examples, see Northcott (1996) and Van Dyke (1996).
10 Fung (1966 [1948]).
11 Merton (1965), 65; my emphasis.
12 Merton (1965), 136.
13 Bellah (1969).
14 The following account is largely drawn from Bell (1994) and Gardiner (1993).
15 Bakhtin (1984 [1965]).
16 Rabelais (1931 [1532–1552]).
17 Bakhtin (1984 [1965]).
18 Bakhtin (1984 [1965]), 12.
19 Bakhtin (1984 [1965]), 28, 38.
20 On this point, see both Bell (1994) and Cresswell (1996), 128.
21 Bakhtin (1984 [1965], 474.
22 For these quotations, see Plumwood (1994a), 19, citing Morgan (1989).
23 For a recent review, see Warren (1996).
24 Plumwood (1994a), 13.
25 Quoted in Seager (1993), 221.
26 Quoted in Seager (1993), 221.
27 The leading male ecofeminist writer is Jim Cheney. See, for example, Cheney (1994).
28 Plumwood (1994a), 9.
29 Plumwood (1994a), 43.
30 Plumwood (1994b), 74.
31 Bell (1994), 210–224.
32 Bell (1994), 218.
33 Bell (1994), 219–220.
34 Seager (1993), 9.
35 For examples, see Plant (1989) and Diamond and Orenstein (1990).
36 See Seager (1993), Plumwood (1994b), Biehl (1991), and Slicer (1994). Biehl has been a strong critic from outside ecofeminism. The other three are from within ecofeminism. Buege (1994) is a critique of Biehl for tarring all ecofeminist writers with the same essentialist brush.
37 Slicer (1994).

38 Hierarchical categories also dialogically promote a hierarchical frame of mind.
39 See Bell (1998).

CHAPTER 6 NOTES

1 Carson (1962), 261–262.
2 Carson (1962), 97.
3 See, for example, Guha (1998). Guha also notes that *Silent Spring* stayed on the *New York Times* best-seller list for thirty-one weeks, sold a half million copies in hardback alone, and was soon published in a dozen countries.
4 Inglehart (1995).
5 Horace (1983), 215–216; Epistle I, 10.
6 Clare (1993), 48.
7 In making this argument, I draw heavily upon the analysis contained in Bell (1994) and Bell (1997a).
8 See Bell (1994) for more detail.
9 Collingwood (1960 [1945]), 45.
10 Lovejoy and Boas (1935), 104.
11 Finley (1963), 55. Burenhult (1994), 152, gives a figure of only 75,000 for the fifth century B.C.E., and 250,000 for Athens and its hinterlands, which is still a remarkable total.
12 Plato (1952), 483.
13 Plato (1987) 338e and 343b.
14 Rommen (1947 [1936]).
15 See Lovejoy and Boas (1935).
16 Plato (1952), 483.
17 Plato (1965) *Timaeus* sec. 4, 29.
18 See Aristotle (1987), *Parts of Animals*, I.1, 639b:20 and *Politics* I.1, 1252a: 0–5.
19 Bartlett (1980), 3.
20 Bartlett (1980), 3.
21 Lao Tzu (1963), verse 23.
22 Lao Tzu (1963), verse 156.
23 Lao Tzu (1963), verse 185a.
24 Lao Tzu (1963), verses 43a and 81.
25 Lieh Tzu (1960), 135–136.
26 Fung (1966 [1948]), 18–19.
27 Merton (1965), 115.
28 Chuang Tzu (1968), 32–33.
29 Lao Tzu (1963), ch. 54; 126.
30 Lao Tzu (1963), ch. 56; 117.
31 Lao Tzu (1963), ch. 81; 143.
32 Fung (1966 [1948]), 177, 284. For a constrasting view, see Peerenboom (1991).
33 Fung (1966 [1948]), 101.

34 Thoreau (1975 [1862]), 164.
35 Thoreau (1975 [1862]), 176.
36 Thoreau (1975 [1862]), 170–171.
37 Thoreau (1975 [1862]), 185.
38 Thoreau (1975 [1862]), 203–204.
39 Thoreau (1975 [1862]), 200–201.
40 Bell (1994), 147.
41 Inglehart (1995).
42 Downs (1972).
43 Dunlap (1992).
44 Downs (1972).
45 Dunlap (1992).
46 There has been no source of global comparison since the 1990–1992 World Values Survey, cited above, but concern likely has dropped in some countries and gone up in others, since then (Riley Dunlap, personal communication, 1997).
47 Cotgrove (1982).
48 Jones and Dunlap (1992).
49 Guha (in press).
50 For examples, see Bullard (1993, 1994a, and 1994b), Hofrichter (1993), and Taylor (1989).
51 Cited in Guha (in press).
52 Cotgrove (1982), 18.
53 Abramson and Inglehart (1995), 1.
54 Inglehart modifies Maslow, however, arguing that there is no particular order to the salience of the needs above the physical; see Inglehart (1990).
55 Abramson and Inglehart (1995), 19; table 2-2.
56 Inglehart (1995), Figure 5.
57 Inglehart (1995), 68.
58 For a summary, see the debate over the application of postmaterialism to environmentalism in the Spring 1997, issue of *Social Science Quarterly*.
59 Guha (in press).
60 Beck (1996), 8. I draw the distinction between "environmental goods" and "environmental bads," which I have been using throughout the book, from Beck.
61 Beck (1992), 49.
62 I am indebted to the work of Maurie Cohen (unpublished) for this interpretation of Beck.
63 Beck (1996), 1.
64 Buttel, Renn (1997), Alexander (1996).
65 Beck (1992 [1986]), 36.
66 Beck (1992 [1986]) 35–36, does see that risk is unequally distributed, but he does not take into account the political significance of this inequality.
67 Buttel (1997).
68 Catton and Dunlap (1980), Cotgrove (1982), Dunlap (1980), Dunlap and Van Liere (1978,

1983), Milbrath (1984).

69 Not to mention the "transindustrial paradigm," the "metaindustrial paradigm," and the "ecological paradigm." See Olsen et al. (1992) for a complete review.

70 Olsen et al. (1992).

71 Olsen et al. (1992), 137.

72 For an example of research in this general tradition that uses a far more complex array of categories, in this case in relation to attitudes toward animals, see Kellert and Berry (1982).

73 Beus and Dunlap (1991) and Dunlap and Van Liere (1978).

74 Thomas (1983), 16. Throughout this section I draw heavily on Thomas's argument, but I depart in arguing for the importance not only of material comforts to the new sensibility of nature but also new democratic feelings toward human social relations.

75 Guha (in press) and Mol (1995).

76 I depart here from what may appear to be the superficially similar argument of Nash (1989). My argument is not for a history of ethical extension through various social boundaries and thence into the natural world, but rather of the interactive development of both. Indeed, in many cases extension of rights into nature preceded extension of rights into society. For example, the Royal Society for the Prevention of Cruelty to Animals was founded some one hundred years before the foundation of the Royal Society for the Prevention of Cruelty to Children. It is, yet again, a matter of dialogic causality.

77 Engels ([1973] 1845), 89–92.

78 Marsh (1965 [1864]), 3, 465.

79 Inglehart (1990).

80 Bridges and Bridges (1996).

81 Guha (in press).

82 Guha (in press).

83 The song is called "Acceptable Risks" and can be found on King's 1979 album, *Somebody's Story,* Rainbow Snake Records, RSM 002.

CHAPTER 7 NOTES

1 Rolston (1979), 9.

2 Bell (1994 and 1997). The distinction I am drawing has some parallels in what Rolston (1979) describes as "following nature in an absolute sense" versus "following nature in an artifactual sense" but differs in that Rolston does not consider issues of power and interest.

3 Erikson (1966).

4 The solution Rolston (1979), 12, offers is what he calls the "relative" sense of following nature in which "we may conduct ourselves more or less continuously or receptively with nature as it is proceeding upon our entrance." I have elsewhere (Bell 1994a) described this as the "pastoral" solution, which places human ways on a gradient between the natural and the unnatural.

5 Aristotle (1987) *Physics* 185b:15–25.

6 In Aristotle's words, "A thing is due to nature, if it arrives, by a continuous process of change,

starting from some principle in itself, at some end." Aristotle's *Physics* II.8, 199b:15–20.

7 I thank a colleague from Hong Kong whose name I do not recall for this observation, made over beer at an Oxford pub.

8 See, for example, Beck (1996), Bell (1996), Cantrill and Oravec (1996), Cronon (1995), Dupuis and Vandergeest (1996), Eder (1996), Ellen and Fuhui (1996), Evernden (1992), Greider and Garcovich (1994), Hannigan (1995), Haraway (1991), Latour (1993), Soper (1995), Yearley (1991). There is also a large older, largely nonsociological, literature that discusses the social construction of nature, for example Collingwood (1960 [1945], Hubbard (1982), Lovejoy (1936), Lovejoy and Boas (1935), Mill (1961 [1874]), Williams (1980 [1972]), 70–71. This older literature is often ignored by more recent writers, but I have found it enormously clarifying.

9 Williams (1980 [1972]), 70–71.

10 The standard sources for this version of New England are Allport (1990), Black (1950), Raup (1967), and Wilson (1967 [1936]), among hundreds of others.

11 Haystead and Fite (1955), 29. Even environmental historians have accepted this view, for example Merchant (1989).

12 The few sources that have include Barron (1984), Destler (1973), French (1911), Higbee (1958).

13 See Bell (1996) for the sources for these.

14 Bell (1996).

15 Bell (1996), 41–44, tables 2-1 and 2-4.

16 Bell (1996), 43, tables 2-2 and 2-3.

17 Barron (1984).

18 Bell (1996), 50.

19 Bell (1996).

20 Bell (1989) and Bell (1996), 50–53

21 Meek, ed. (1971), 195.

22 Darwin (1958), 42-43; cited in Hubbard (1981), 24.

23 Hubbard (1981), 24.

24 Cited in Schmidt (1971), 47; see also Engels (1940 [1898]), 208.

25 Herrnstein and Murray (1994).

26 For example, Fraser (1995).

27 Cited in Gould (1996 [1981]).

28 Gould (1996 [1981]), table 2.1.

29 Gould (1996 [1981]), 97.

30 Gould (1996 [1981]).

31 Gould (1996) [1981]), 93.

32 Huntington (1915).

33 Huntington (1915).

34 Scott (1990).

35 Guha (1989) and Guha (1997).

36 Guha (1997), 15.

37 Peluso (1996).

38 Peluso (1996).

39 Cronon (1995), 81.

40 Urry (1990) and Urry (1995).

41 Greider and Garcovich (1994), 1.

42 Bell (1997b).

43 For extensive critiques of heritage tourism, see Lowenthal (1997 and 1985).

44 Hinrichs (1996), 259.

45 Barrett (1994), 256.

46 The letter also lists Linus Pauling, the two-time Nobel Prize winner, and Stewart Udall, former United States Secretary of the Interior, as members of the National Advisory Board of Population-Environment Balance.

47 Hardin (1977).

48 Latour (1993).

49 Freudenburg et al. (1995).

50 This story is also sometimes told in a way that is more flattering to Canute, namely that he ordered the tide to stop as a deliberate lesson in the limits of the power of kings compared to the power of God.

51 See Bell (1994), chapter 1.

CHAPTER 8 NOTES

1 In this paragraph, I am passing at great speed over an enormous amount of scholarly work. The "attitude-behavior relationship," or "A-B split" as I am terming it here, is assuredly one of the most researched topics in social science. For a recent review, see Kraus (1995).

2 This is a point that most of the scholarly literature on the relationship between attitudes and behaviors misses. Social psychological theories like Festinger's (1962 [1957]) "cognitive dissonance" and Ajzen and Fishbein's (1980) "reasoned action" tend to individualize the question, to see it as a "micro" issue rather than placing it within a wider social context. For an environmental account of the attitude-behavior split as an effect of social structure, see Ungar (1994); my argument parallels his in several regards.

3 Hardin (1968).

4 See Cooper (1996). The tie-up was caused when a truck became stuck after trying to go under a bridge that was too low. For the driver's safety, the morning papers the next day declined to give his name.

5 See Burton and Dunn (1996), Conybeare and Squire (1994), Polakowski and Gottfredson (1996).

6 For example, see Argyle (1991); Bromley (1992); Feeny et al. (1996); Hinde and Groebel (1992); Ostrom (1990); Roberts and Emel (1992); Stevenson (1991); Thompson and Wilson (1994).

7 On grazing land, see Thompson and Wilson (1994), and Mearns (1996); on fisheries in India, see Gadgil and Guha (1995), 81–84; on fisheries in Brazil, Begossi (1995).

8 See Argyle (1991) and Ostrom (1990).

9 The following account is based heavily on Bell (1998a).

10 I have drawn this version of "Androcles and the Lion" from Black (1991, 22–24), with some modification. The story is also told as "The Lion and the Mouse," and I draw the last line from a telling of this version, cited in Bartlett (1980), 66.

11 For empirical support of this argument in actual commons, see Begossi (1995) on the role of kinship in the management of Brazilian fisheries and Petrzelka (1997) on the importance of collective events like daily communal dancing for Berber herders in Morocco.

12 Bakhtin (1986). For an insightful application of the concepts of dialogue and monologue to our environmental condition, see Gardiner (1993).

13 On the notion of dialogue as "taking others into account," see Bell (1998b).

14 Originally Habermas (1984); my citation, however, is from Habermas (1989), 157 Although I cite Habermas, and my argument is informed by him, I depart from Habermas in some significant ways here. Most notably, Habermas's argument is rooted in a purely rational model in which communication, or "communicative action," as Habermas terms it, is one of two types of rational social action, the other being "strategic action." Communication, for Habermas, is a rational motivation in itself. Rather, I see communication as a means of achieving the ends of both a solidarity of interests and a solidarity of sentiments, instead of a rational end in itself. I also view social action as equally "rational," that is, oriented toward interests, and "nonrational," that is, oriented toward sentiments. The two, interests and sentiments, constitute each other. See Bell (1998a and 1998b) for more detailed explanations.

15 Bakhtin (1986), 170.

16 See, for example, Brecher (1994), Johnson (1992), Whitley (1992).

17 On "dialogic democracy," see Giddens (1994); on the process of "taking into account," see Bell (1998b).

18 All figures from Easterbrook (1995).

19 The *New York Times* piece is by Tierney (1996). Several news organizations published copycat pieces in the months that followed, for example Budianski (1996) and Seligman (1996).

20 See, for example, DiConsiglio (1997).

21 For a sample of the extensive literature on participatory development, Brohman (1996), Ghai and Vivian (1992), Hobley (1996), and Stiefel (1994).

22 See Bentley and Andrews (1991), Bentley and Melara (1991), Bentley (1994), and Bentley et al. (1994).

23 For a compelling history of agricultural poisoning in Latin America, see Wright (1990).

24 There is a huge, and growing, literature on local knowledge. For useful introductions, see Brush and Stabinsky (1996), Campbell and Manicom (1995), Geertz (1983), Hassanein and Kloppenburg (1995), Nazarea-Sandoval (1995).

25 Bentley and Melara (1991), 43.

26 The interviews for this section were conducted in July of 1997.

27 Gradwell et al. (1997), 1–2.

28 All quotations from Gradwell et al. (1997).

29 See Katz (1994), Kunstler (1993 and 1996), and Langdon (1994).

30 GNP counts the earnings a domestic company makes abroad as income; GDP does not. But GDP counts the earnings made by foreign companies as income, even though the profit goes elsewhere, a common occurrence in poor countries. Thus, GDP tends to overstate the national income of a poor country and correspondingly understate the national income of a rich country.

31 See Daly and Cobb (1989) and Daly (1991).

32 Cobb et al. (1995a) and Cobb et al. (1995b).

33 For an introduction, see Ayres and Ayres (1996), Graedel and Allenby (1995), or the new *Journal of Industrial Ecology*.

34 For the best introduction to ecological modernization, see Mol (1995).

35 Ostrom (1990), 215.

36 Leopold (1961 [1949]), 239.

37 This point was famously made by Anderson (1991 [1983]).

38 Taylor (1986).

REFERENCES

Abramson, Paul R. and Ronald Inglehart. 1995. *Value Change in Global Perspective*. Ann Arbor: University of Michigan Press.

Ajzen, Icek and Martin Fishbein. 1980. *Understanding Attitudes and Predicting Social Behavior*. Englewood Cliffs, NJ: Prentice-Hall.

Alexander, Jeffrey C. 1996. "Reflexive Modernization: Politics, Tradition and Aesthetics in the Modern Social Order." *Theory, Culture and Society* 13(4): 133-138.

Allport, Susan. 1990. *Sermons in Stone: The Stone Walls of New England and New York*. New York and London: Norton.

American Farmland Trust. 1994. *Farming on the Edge: A New Look at the Importance and Vulnerability of Agriculture Near American Cities*. Washington, DC: American Farmland Trust.

Anderson, Benedict. 1991 (1983). *Imagined Communities: Reflections on the Origin and Spread of Nationalism*. Rev. ed. London and New York: Verso.

Anderson, Ian. 1995. "Australia's Growing Disaster." *New Scientist* 147, July 29, pp. 12-13.

Anderton, Douglas L., Andy B. Anderson, John Michael Oakes, and Michael R. Fraser. 1994. "Environmental Equity: The Demographics of Dumping," *Demography* 31(2): 229-248.

Anthanasiou, Tom. 1996. *Divided Planet: The Ecology of Rich and Poor*. Boston: Little, Brown.

Appiah, Anthony. 1985. "The Uncompleted Argument: Du Bois and the Illusion of Race." In *"Race," Writing, and Difference*, ed. Henry Louis Gates, Jr. Chicago: University of Chicago Press.

Argyle, Michael. 1987. *The Psychology of Happiness*. New York and London: Methuen.

Argyle, Michael. 1991. *Cooperation: The Basis of Sociability*. London: Routledge.

Aristotle. 1987. *A New Aristotle Reader*. Edited by J. L. Ackrill. Princeton, NJ: Princeton University.

Ayres, Robert U. and Leslie W. Ayres. 1996. *Industrial Ecology: Towards Closing the Materials Cycle*. Cheltenham, UK ; Brookfield, VT: E. Elgar.

Bailey, Ronald, ed. 1995. *The True State of the Planet*. New York: Free Press.

Bakhtin, Mikhail. 1981. *The Dialogic Imagination: Four Essays*. Austin University of Texas.

Bakhtin, Mikhail. 1984 (1965). *Rabelais and His World*. Bloomington Indiana University Press.

Bakhtin, Mikhail. 1986. *Speech Genres and Other Late Essays*. Trans. Vern W. McGee. Minneapolis: University of Minnesota Press.

Barraclough, Geoffrey, ed. 1982. *The Times Concise Atlas of World History*. London: Times Books.

Barrett, Stanley R. 1994. *Paradise: Class, Commuters, and Ethnicity in Rural Ontario*. Toronto: University of Toronto Press.

Barron, Hal S. 1984. *Those Who Stayed Behind*. Cambridge: Cambridge University Press.

Bartlett, John. 1980 (1855). *Familiar Quotations*. Edited by Emily Morison Beck. Boston: Little, Brown.

Beal, Peter. 1997. "Runaway Tunnel Protester Brought to Safety." *Press Association Newsfile*, June 16.

Beavis, Simon and Paul Brown. 1996. "Shell Oil Has Human Rights Rethink." *The Guardian*, November 8, p.1.

Beck, Ulrich. 1992 (1986). *Risk Society: Toward a New Modernity*. London: Sage.

Beck, Ulrich. 1996. "World Risk Society as Cosmopolitan Society? Ecological Questions in a Framework of Manufactured Uncertainties." *Theory, Culture, and Society* 13(4): 1-32.

Becker, Gary S. 1986. "The Prophets of Doom Have a Dismal Record." *Business Week*, Jan. 27, p. 22.

Begossi, Alpina. 1995. "Fishing Spots and Sea Tenure: Incipient Forms of Local Management in Atlantic Forest Coastal Communities," *Human Ecology* 23: 387-406.

Bell, Michael M. 1985. *The Face of Connecticut: People, Geology, and the Land*. Hartford, CT: State Geological and Natural History Survey of Connecticut.

———. 1994a. *Childerley: Nature and Morality in a Country Village*. Chicago: University of Chicago Press.

———. 1994b. "Deep Fecology: Mikhail Bakhtin and the Call of Nature." *Capitalism, Nature, Socialism,* 5(4): 65-84.

———. 1995. "The Dialectic of Technology: Commentary on Warner and England," *Rural Sociology* 60(4): 623-632.

———. 1996. "Stone Age New England: A Geology of Morals." In *Creating the Countryside: The Politics of Rural and Environmental Discourse*, ed. Melanie Dupuis and Peter Vandergeest, pp. 29-64, Philadelphia, PA: Temple University Press.

———. 1997a. "Natural Conscience: A Theory of Environmental Morality." Paper presented at Social Theory and the Environment conference of the International Sociological Association, Zeist, The Netherlands.

———. 1997b. "The Ghosts of Place." *Theory and Society*, forthcoming.

———. 1998a. "Culture as Dialog," in *Bakhtin and the Human Sciences: No Last Words,* ed. Michael M. Bell and Michael Gardiner. London: Sage. Forthcoming

———. 1998b. "The Dialectic of Solidarity, or, Why the Lion Spared Androcles." *Sociological Focus*, forthcoming.

Bell, Michael and Edward Laine. 1985. "Erosion of the Laurentide Region of North America by Glacial and Glacio-fluvial Processes." *Quaternary Research*, 23: 154-174.

Bellah, Robert. 1969. *Tokugawa Religion: The Values of Preindustrial Japan*. New York: Free Press.

Bentley, Jeffery W. 1994. "Facts, Fantasies, and Failures of Farmer Participatory Research." *Agriculture and Human Values* 11(2/3): 140-150.

Bentley, Jeffery W., G. Rodriguez, and A. Gonzalez, 1994. "Science and People: Honduran Campesinos and Natural Pest Control Inventions." *Agriculture and Human Values* 11(2/3): 178-182.

Bentley, Jeffery W. and Keith L. Andrews. 1991. "Pests, Peasants, and Publications: Anthropological and Entomological Views of an Integrated Pest Management Program for Small-Scale Honduran Farmers." *Human Organization* 50: 113-24.

Bentley, Jeffery W. and Werner Melara. 1991. "Experimenting with Honduran Farmer-Experimenters." *ODI Newsletter* 24:31-48.

Benton, Ted. 1994. "Biology and Social Theory in the Environmental Debate." In *Social Theory and the Global Environment,* ed. Michael Redclift and Ted Benton. London: Routledge.

Beus, Curtis E. and Riley E. Dunlap. 1991. "Measuring Adherence to Alternative vs. Conventional Agricultural Paradigms: A Proposed Scale." *Rural Sociology* 56(3): 432-460.

Biehl, Janet. 1991. *Rethinking Ecofeminist Politics*. Boston, MA: South End Press.

Black, Fiona. 1991. *Aesop's Fables*. Kansas City: Andrews and McMeel.
Black, John D. 1950. *The Rural Economy of New England*. Cambridge, MA: Harvard University Press.

Boerner, Christopher and Thomas Lambert. 1995. "Environmental Injustice." *The Public Interest* 95(118): 61-82.

Boserup, Ester. 1965. *The Conditions of Agricultural Growth: The Economics of Agrarian Change Under Population Pressure*. London: George Allen and Unwin.

Boserup, Ester. 1981. *Population and Technology*. Oxford: Basil Blackwell.

Boserup, Ester. 1989 (1970). *Woman's Role in Economic Development*. London: Earthscan.

Bourdieu, Pierre. 1984. *Distinction*. Translated by Richard Nice. Cambridge, MA: Harvard University.

Brecher, Jeremy. 1994. *Global Village or Global Pillage: Economic Reconstruction from the Bottom Up*. Boston: South End Press.

Bridges, Olga and Jim Bridges. 1996. *Losing Hope : The Environment and Health in Russia*. Aldershot, UK: Avebury.

Brohman, John. 1996. *Popular Development : Rethinking the Theory and Practice of Development*. Oxford; Cambridge, MA: Blackwell.

Bromley, Daniel W., ed. 1992. *Making the Commons Work: Theory, Practice, and Policy*. San Francisco: ICS Press

Brown, Lester R. and Hal Kane. 1994. *Full House: Reassessing the Earth's Population Carrying Capacity*. New York: Norton.

Brown, Lester R., Michael Renner, Christopher Flavin. 1997. *Vital Signs 1997: The Environmental Trends That Are Shaping Our Future*. New York and London: Norton.

Brown, Lester R., Christopher Flavin, and Hale Kane. 1996. *Vital Signs, 1996: The Trends That Are Shaping Our Future*. New York and London: Norton.

Brown, Lester R., Hale Kane, and David Malin Roodman. 1994. *Vital Signs, 1994: The Trends That Are Shaping Our Future*. New York and London: Norton.

Brown, Lester R., Nicholas Lenssen, and Hale Kane. 1995. *Vital Signs, 1995: The Trends That Are Shaping Our Future*. New York and London: Norton.

Bruno, Michael and Lyn Squire. 1996. "The Less Equal the Asset Distribution, the Slower the Growth." *International Herald Tribune*, September 30, p. 12.

Brush, Stephen B. and Doreen Stabinsky. 1996. *Valuing Local Knowledge: Indigenous People and Intellectual Property Rights*. Washington, DC: Island Press.

Budiansky, Stephen. 1996. "Being Green Isn't Always What It Seems," *US News and World Report* 121: 42.

Buege, Douglas J. 1994. "Rethinking Again: A Defense of Ecofeminist Philosophy." Pp. 42-63 In *Ecological Feminism*, ed. Karen Warren, London and New York: Routledge.

Buie, Elizabeth. 1995. "Global Warming Question Has Scientists Under High Pressure." *The Herald (Glasgow)*, August 2, p. 6.

Bullard, Charles. 1997. "Study Seeks Cut in Carbon Dioxide." *Des Moines Register* April 28, pp. 1M and 5M.

Bullard, Robert D. 1993. *Confronting Environmental Racism: Voices from the Grassroots*. Boston: South End Press.

———. 1994a. *Dumping in Dixie: Race, Class, and Environmental Quality*. 2nd ed. Boulder, CO: Westview Press.

———. ed. 1994b. *Unequal Protection: Environmental Justice and Communities of Color*. San Francisco: Sierra Club Books.

Burenhult, Göran, ed. 1994. *Old World Civilizations: The Rise of Cities and States*. San Francisco: HarperCollins.

Burningham, Kate and Geoff Cooper. 1997. "Misconstructing Constructionism: A Defense of Social Constructionist Approaches to Environmental Problems." Paper presented at Social Theory and the Environment conference of the International Sociological Association, Zeist, The Netherlands.

Burton, Brian K. and Craig P. Dunn. 1996. "Collaborative Control and the Commons: Safeguarding Employee Rights," *Business Ethics Quarterly* 6:277-88.

Buttel, Frederick H. 1992. "Environmentalization: Origins, Processes, and Implications for Rural Social Change." *Rural Sociology* 57:1-27.

———. 1996. "Environmental and Resource Sociology: Theoretical Issues and Opportunities for Synthesis." *Rural Sociology* 61:56-76.

———. 1997. "Classical and Contemporary Theoretical Perspectives and the Environment." Paper presented at Social Theory and the Environment conference of the International Sociological Association, Zeist, The Netherlands.

Campbell, Angus, Philip E. Converse, and Willard L. Rodgers. 1976. *The Quality of American Life: Perceptions, Evaluations, and Satisfactions.* New York: Russell Sage Foundation.

Campbell, Marie and Ann Manicom. 1995. *Knowledge, Experience, and Ruling Relations: Studies in the Social Organization of Knowledge.* Toronto; Buffalo: University of Toronto Press.

Cannon, Geoffrey. 1995. *Superbug: Nature's Revenge: Why Antibiotics Can Breed Disease.* London: Virgin.

Cantrill, James G. and Christine L. Oravec, eds. 1996. *The Symbolic Earth: Discourse and Our Creation of the Environment.* Lexington: University Press of Kentucky.

Carson, Rachel. 1962. *Silent Spring.* Greenwich, CT: Fawcett Crest.

Catton, William R. and Riley E. Dunlap. 1980. "A New Ecological Paradigm for Post-Exuberant Sociology." *American Behavioral Scientist* 24:15-47.

Chameides, W. L., P. S. Kasibhatla, J. Yienger, and H. Levi. 1994. "Growth of Continental-Scale Metro-Agro-Plexes, Regional Ozone Pollution, and World Food Production." *Science* 264:74.

Cheney, Jim. 1994. In *Ecological Feminism*, ed. Karen Warren. London and New York: Routledge.

Chuang Tzu. 1968. *The Complete Works of Chuang Tzu.* Translated by Burton Watson. New York: Columbia University.

Clare, John D., ed. 1993. *Classical Rome.* San Diego, CA; New York: Harcourt Brace.

Cobb, Clifford, Ted Halstead, and Jonathan Rowe. 1995a. "If the GDP is Up, Why is America Down?" *Atlantic Monthy* 276 (Oct.): 59-78.

Cobb, Clifford, Ted Halstead, and Jonathan Rowe. 1995b. *The Genuine Progress Indicator: Summary of Data and Methodology.* San Francisco: Redefining Progress.

Cochrane, W. 1958. *Farm Prices: Myth and Reality.* Minnesota: University of Minnesota Press.

Collingwood, R. G. 1960 (1945). *The Idea of Nature.* London: Oxford University Press.

Commission for Racial Justice. 1987. *Toxic Waste and Race in the United States: A National Report on the Racial and Socioeconomic Characteristics of Communities with Hazardous Waste Sites.* New York: United Church of Christ.

Conybeare, John A. C. and Peverill Squire. 1994. "Political Action Committees and the Tragedy of the Commons: The Case of Nonconnected PACs," *American Politics Quarterly* 22:154-74.

Cooper, Glenda. 1996. "An Undying Love That is Driving Us to Distraction," *The Independent* (UK), December 12, p. 5.

Cotgrove, Stephen F. 1982. *Catastrophe or Cornucopia: The Environment, Politics, and the Future.* Chichester, UK; New York: Wiley.

Cottrel, Fred. 1955. *Energy and Society: The Relation Between Energy, Social Change, and Economic Development.* New York: McGraw-Hill.

Cresswell, Tim. 1996. *In Place/Out of Place: Geography, Ideology, and Transgression.* Minneapolis; London: University of Minnesota Press.

Cronon, William. 1995a. "The Trouble with Wilderness, or, Getting Back to the Wrong Nature." In *Uncommon Ground: Toward Reinventing Nature*, ed. William Cronon. New York: Norton.

———, ed. 1995b. *Uncommon Ground: Toward Reinventing Nature.* New York: Norton.

303

Crosette, Barbara. 1996. "World Population Growth Has Slowed, UN Survey Shows." *International Herald Tribune*, November 18, p. 2.

Csikzentmihalyi, Mihaly and Eugene Rochberg-Halton. 1981. *The Meaning of Things: Domestic Symbols and the Self*. Cambridge: Cambridge University Press.

Daly, Herman E. 1991. *Steady-State Economics*. 2nd ed. Washington, DC: Island Press.

Daly, Herman and John B. Cobb. 1989. *For the Common Good: Redirecting the Economy Toward Community, the Environment, and a Sustainable Future*. Boston: Beacon.

D'Aoust, J. Y., A. M. Sewell, E. Daley, and P. Greco. 1992. "Antibiotic Resistance of Agricultural and Foodborne Salmonella Isolates in Canada: 1986-1989." *Journal of Food Protection*. 55(6): 428-434.

Darwin, Charles, 1958. *The Autobiography of Charles Darwin*, ed. Frances Darwin. New York: Dover Pulications.

Destler, Chester M. 1973. *Connecticut: The Provisions State*. Chester, CT: Pequot Press.

Devereux, Stephen. 1993. *Theories of Famine*. New York and London: Harvester/Wheatsheaf.

Diamond, Irene and G. F. Orenstein, eds. 1990. *Reweaving the World: The Emergence of Ecofeminism*. San Francisco: Sierra Club Books.

Dickens, Peter. 1996. *Reconstructing Nature: Alienation, Emancipation and the Division of Labour*. London: Routledge.

DiConsiglio, John M. 1997. "Rethinking Recycling," *Scholastic Update*. 129:10-11.

Douglas, Mary and Baron Isherwood. 1979. *The World of Goods: Towards an Anthropology of Consumption*. New York: Basic.

Douthwaite, Richard. 1992, *The Growth Illusion: How Economic Growth Has Enriched the Few, Impoverished the Many, and Endangered the Planet*. Devon, UK: Green Books.

Downs, Anthony. 1972. "Up and Down with Ecology: The Issue-Attention Cycle." *Public Interest* 28:38-50.

Duden, Barbara. 1992. "Population." In *The Development Dictionary: A Guide to Knowledge as Power*, ed. Wolfgang Sachs, pp. 146-157. London; Atlantic Highlands, NJ: Zed Books.

Dunlap, Riley E. 1980. "Paradigmatic Change in Social Science: From Human Exemptionalism to an Ecological Paradigm." *American Behavioral Scientist* 24:5-14.

———. 1992. "Trends in Public Opinion Toward Environmental Issues: 1965-1990." In *American Environmentalism: The U.S. Environmental Movement, 1970-1990*, ed. Riley E. Dunlap and Angela G. Mertig. Philadelphia: Taylor and Francis.

Dunlap, Riley E. and Kent D. Van Liere. 1978. "The New Environmental Paradigm: A Proposed Measuring Instrument and Preliminary Results." *Journal of Environmental Education* 9:10-19.

Dunlap, Riley E. and Kent D. Van Liere. 1983. "Commitment to the Dominant Social Paradigm and Concern for Environmental Quality: An Empirical Examination." *Social Science Quarterly* 65:1013-1028.

Dunlap, Riley E. and William R. Catton. 1994. "Struggling with Human Exemptionalism: The Rise, Decline, and Revitalization of Environmental Sociology." *The American Sociologist* 25:113-135.

Dupuis, Melanie and Peter Vandergeest, eds. 1996. *Creating the Countryside: The Politics of Rural and Environmental Discourse*. Philadelphia, PA: Temple University Press.

Durkheim, Emile. 1964 (1893). *The Division of Labor in Society*. Trans. George Simpson. New York: The Free Press.

Durning, Alan T. 1992. *How Much Is Enough? The Consumer Society and the Future of the Earth*. New York: Norton.

Easterbrook, Gregg. 1995. "Good News from Planet Earth," *USA Weekend*, April 14-16, pp. 4-6.

Easterlin, Richard A. 1974. "Does Economic Growth Improve the Human Lot? Some Empirical Evidence." In *Nations and Households in Economic Growth: Essays in Honor of Moses Abramovitz*, ed. Paul A. David and Melvin W. Reder. New York; London: Academic Press.

Economist. 1994. "Inequality: For Richer, for Poorer." Nov. 5, pp. 19-21.

Economist. 1996a. "Traffic: Not Bothered." Sept. 7, pp. 25-26.

Economist. 1996b. "Undue Diligence." August, p. 24.

Eder, Klaus. 1996. *The Social Construction of Nature: A Sociology of Ecological Enlightenment*. London; Thousand Oaks, CA: Sage.

Ehrlich, Paul R. 1968. *The Population Bomb.*

Ehrlich, Paul R. and Anne H. Ehrlich. 1990. *The Population Explosion*. London: Hutchinson.

Ellen, Roy and Katsuyoshi Fuhui. 1996. *Redefining Nature: Ecology, Culture and Domestication*. Oxford, UK; Washington, DC: Berg.

Elster, John. 1989. *Nuts and Bolts for the Social Sciences.* Cambridge; New York: Cambridge University Press.

Engels, Friedrich. 1940 (1898). *The Dialectics of Nature*. Translated by Clemens Dutt. New York: International Publishers.

Engels, Friedrich. 1973 (1845). *The Condition of the Working Class in England, from Personal Observations and Authentic Sources*. Moscow: Progress Publishers.

Engels, Friedrich. 1987 (1844). "Outlines of a Critique of Political Economy." *In Perspectives on Population: An Introduction to Concepts and Issues*, ed. Scott W. Menard and Elizabeth W. Moen, pp. 104-105. New York; Oxford: Oxford University Press.

Erikson, Kai T. 1966. *Wayward Puritans: A Study in the Sociology of Deviance*. New York: John Wiley.

Erikson, Kai T. 1976. *Everything in Its Path: Destruction of Community in the Buffalo Creek Flood*. New York: Simon and Schuster.

Erikson, Kai T. 1994. *A New Species of Trouble: Explorations in Diaster, Trauma, and Community*. New York: Norton.

Esteva, Gustavo. 1992. "Development." In *The Development Dictionary: A Guide to Knowledge as Power*, ed. Wolfgang Sachs, pp. 6-25. London; Atlantic Highlands, NJ: Zed Books.

Evernden, Neil. 1992. *The Social Creation of Nature.* Baltimore: Johns Hopkins University Press.

Feeny, David, Susan Hanna, and Arhur F. McEvoy. 1996. "Questioning the Assumptions of the 'Tragedy of the Commons' Model of Fisheries," *Land Economics* 72:187-205.

Festinger, Leon. 1962 (1957). *A Theory Of Cognitive Dissonance*. Stanford, CA: Stanford University Press.

Field, Michael. 1995. "Global Warming Worries Atoll Leaders, But Scientists Uncertain." *Agence France Presse*, March 24.

Finley, Moses I. 1963. *The Ancient Greeks*. New York: Viking.

Frank, Andre Gundar. 1969. "The Development of Underdevelopment." In *Latin America: Underdevelopment or Revolution*. New York; London: Monthly Review.

Fraser, Steven, ed. 1995. *The Bell Curve Wars: Race, Intelligence, and the Future of America*. New York: Basic Books.

Freemantle, Michael. 1995. "The Acid Test for Europe." *Chemical and Engineering News* 73(18): 10-17.

French, George. 1911. *New England: What It Is and What It Is To Be*. Boston: Boston Chamber of Commerce.

Freudenburg, William R., Scott Frickel, and Robert Gramling. 1995. "Beyond the Nature/Society Divide: Learning to Think About a Mountain." *Sociological Forum* 10:361-392.

Fung, Yu-lan. 1966 (1948). *A Short History of Chinese Philosophy*, ed. Derk Bodde. New York: Free Press.

Funk, John. 1995. "Summer Chills Out: Seaon Had It All: Hot, Wet, Dry—But It's Fall Now." *The Plain Dealer*, September 23, p. 1a.

Gadgil, Madhav and Ramachandra Guha. 1995. *This Fissured Land: An Ecological History of India*. Delhi: Oxford University Press.

Galbraith, John Kenneth. 1958. *The Affluent Society*. New York: New American Library.

Gardiner, Michael. 1992. *The Dialogics of Critique: M. M. Bakhtin and the Theory of Ideology*. London: Routledge.

———. 1993. "Ecology and Carnival: Traces of a 'Green' Social Theory in the Writings of M. M. Bakhtin," *Theory and Society*. 22(6): 765-812.

Geertz, Clifford. 1983. *Local Knowledge: Further Essays in Interpretive Anthropology*. New York: Basic Books.

George, Susan and Fabrizio Sabelli. 1994. *Faith and Credit: The World Bank's Secular Empire*. Harmondsworth, UK: Penguin.

Ghai, Dharam Ghai and Jessica M. Vivian, eds. 1992. *Grassroots Environmental Action: People's Participation in Sustainable Development*. London; New York: Routledge.

Gibbs, Geoffrey. 1997. "Swampy the Star Returns to His Hole." *The Guardian* (UK), March 4, p. 5.

Giddens, Anthony. 1984. *The Constitution of Society: Outline of the Theory of Structuration*. Cambridge, UK: Polity Press.

Giddens, Anthony. 1994. *Beyond Left and Right: The Future of Radical Politics*. Cambridge, UK: Polity Press.

Gimpel, Jean. 1995. *The End of the Future: The Waning of the High-Tech World*. London: Adamantine.

Glacken, Clarence. 1967. *Traces on the Rhodian Shore*. Berkeley: University of California Press.

Goldman, Benjamin A. 1996. "What Is the Future of Environmental Justice?" *Antipode* 28(2): 122-142.

Goldman, Benjamin and L. J. Fitton. 1994. *Toxic Wastes and Race Revisited*. Washington, DC: United Church of Christ Commission for Racial Justice.

Goodno, James B. 1995. "A Job for Super Rice." *Technology Review,* August/September, pp. 20-22.

Gould, Stephen Jay. 1996 (1981). *The Mismeasure of Man,* 2nd ed. New York: Norton.

Gradwell, Shelly, Jerry DeWitt, Ricardo Salvador, and Diane Mayerfeld. 1997. *Iowa Community Supported Agriculture: Resource Guide for Producers and Organizations*. Ames: Iowa State University Extension.

Graedel, T. E. and B. R. Allenby. 1995. *Industrial Ecology*. Englewood Cliffs, NJ: Prentice-Hall.

Graham-Campbell, James, ed. 1994. *Cultural Atlas of the Viking World*. Oxfordshire, UK: Andromeda Oxford.

Green, Daniel. 1996. "Biotechnology: Long Way from Maturity in Spite of the Promises." *Financial Times*, Nov. 26, Special Section, p.1.

Greider, Thomas and Lorraine Garkovich. 1994. "Landscapes: The Social Construction of Nature and the Environment," *Rural Sociology* 59(1): 1-24.

Guha, Ramachandra. 1989. "Radical American Environmentalism and Wilderness Preservation: A Third-World Critique." *Environmental Ethics* 11:71-83

———. 1995. "Mahatma Gandhi and the Environmental Movement in India." *Capitalism, Nature, Socialism* 6(3): 47-61.

———. 1997. "The Authoritarian Biologist and the Arrogance of Anti-humanism: Wildlife Conservation in the Third World." *The Ecologist* 27(1): 14-19.

———. In press. *The Global Environmental Movement: A Cross-Cultural History*. New York: Prentice-Hall.

Habermas, J_rgen. 1984. *The Theory of Communicative Action*. 2 vols. Boston: Beacon Press.

———. 1989. *J_rgen Habermas on Society and Politics: A Reader*, ed. Steven Seidman. Boston: Beacon Press.

Hajer, Martin. 1995. *The Politics of Environmental Discourse*. New York: Oxford University Press.

Hall, Thomas D. 1996. "The World-System Perspective: A Small Sample from a Large Universe." *Sociological Inquiry* 66 (4): 440-454.

Hannigan, John A. 1995. *Environmental Sociology: A Social Constructionist Perspective*. London; New York: Routledge.

Haraway, Donna Jeanne. 1991. *Simians, Cyborgs, and Women: The Reinvention of Nature*. New York: Routledge.

Hardin, Garrett. 1968. "The Tragedy of the Commons," *Science* 162: 1243-1248.

———. 1977. *The Limits of Altruism: An Ecologist's View of Survival*. Bloomington: Indiana University Press.

Hartmann, Betsy. 1987. *Reproductive Rights and Wrongs: The Global Politics of Population Control and Contraceptive Choice*. New York: Harper.

Harwood Group. 1995. *Yearning for Balance: Views on Consumption, Materialism, and the Environment*. Merck Family Fund.

Hassanein, Neva and Jack R. Kloppenburg, Jr. 1995. "Where the Grass Grows Again: Knowledge Exchange in the Sustainable Agriculture Movement." *Rural Sociology* 60: 721-740.

Hawken, Paul. 1993. *The Ecology of Commerce: A Declaration of Sustainability*. New York: HarperCollins.

Heiman, Michael K. 1996. "Race, Waste, and Class: New Perspectives on Environmental Justice." *Antipode* 28(2) :111-121.

Herbert, Bob. 1997. "Nike's Boot Camps." *New York Times*, March 31.

Herrnstein, Richard and Charles Murray. 1994. *The Bell Curve: Intelligence and Class Structure in American Life*. New York: Free Press.

Hewitt, 1995. *Industrialization and Development*. Oxford: Oxford University Press and the Open University.

Higbee, Edward. 1958. *American Agriculture: Geography, Resources, and Conservation*. New York: John Wiley.

Hileman, Bette. 1995. "Scientists Warn That Disease Threats Increase as Earth Warms Up." *Chemical and Engineering News* 73(40): 19-20.

Hilz, Christoph. 1992. *The International Toxic Waste Trade*. New York: Van Nostrand Reinhold.

Hinde, Robert A. and Jo Groebel, eds. 1992. *Cooperation and Prosocial Behavior*. Cambridge: Cambridge University Press.

Hinrichs, C. Clare. 1996. "Consuming Images: Making and Marketing Vermont as Distinctive Rural Place," in *Creating the Countryside: The Politics of Rural and Environmental Discourse*, E. Melanic DuPuis and Peter Vandergeest, eds. Philadelphia: Temple Universtiy Press. Pp. 259-278.

Hirsch, Fred. 1977. *Social Limits to Growth*. London: Routledge.

Hobley, Mary. 1996. *Participatory Forestry: The Process of Change in India and Nepal*. London: Overseas Development Institute.

Hofrichter, Richard, ed. 1993. *Toxic Struggles: The Theory and Practice of Environmental Justice*. Philadelphia: New Society Publishers.

Hopkins, Terence K. and Immanuel Wallerstein. 1982. *World Systems Analysis: Theory and Methodology*. Beverly Hills, CA: Sage.

Horace. 1983. (C. 20B.C.E.) *The Essential Horace*. Translated by Burton Raffel. San Francisco: North Point Press.

Hubbard, Ruth. 1982. "Have Only Men Evolved?" In *Biological Woman: The Convenient Myth*, ed. Ruth Hubburd, Mary Sue Henifin, and Barbara Fried. Cambridge, MA: Schenkman.

Huntington, Ellsworth. 1915. *Civilization and Climate*. New Haven, CT: Yale University Press.

Imbrie, John and Katherine Palmer Imbrie. 1979. *Ice Ages: Solving the Mystery*. Short Hills, NJ: Enslow.

Independent Commission on Population and Quality of Life. 1996. *Caring for the Future: Making the Next Decades Provide a Life Worth Living*. Oxford; New York: Oxford University Press.

Inglehart, Ronald. 1977. *The Silent Revolution: Changing Values and Political Styles Among Western Publics*. Princeton, NJ: Princeton University Press.

———. 1990. *Culture Shift in Advanced Industrial Society*. Princeton, NJ: Princeton University Press.

———. 1995. "Public Support for Environmental Protection: Objective Problems and Subjective Values in 43 Societies." *PS: Political Science and Politics* 28(1): 57-72.

———. 1995. "Hazardous Waste Dump Plans Attacked." NAFTA and Inter-American Trade Monitor 2(27), Oct. 20.

Intergovernmental Committee on Climate Change. 1996. *Climate Change, 1995*. 3 vols. Cambridge and New York: Cambridge University Press.

Irwin, Alan. 1995. *Citizen Science: A Study of Poeple, Expertise, and Sustainable Development.* London; New York: Routledge.

Jacobs, Michael. 1991. *The Green Economy: Environment, Sustainable Development, and the Politics of the Future*. London; Concord, MA: Pluto.

Joekes, Susan. 1987. *Women in the World Economy: An INSTRAW Study*. New York: Oxford University Press.

Johnson, H. Thomas. 1992. *Relevance Regained: From Top-Down Control to Bottom-Up Empowerment*. New York: Free Press.

Jones, Robert Emmet and Riley E. Dunlap. 1992. "The Social Bases of Environmental Concern: Have They Changed Over Time?" *Rural Sociology* 57(1): 28-47.

Katz, Peter. 1994. *The New Urbanism: Toward an Architecture of Community*. New York: McGraw-Hill.

Kearney, Syd. 1995. "Liberace Museum Is Delivering the Glitz." *Des Moines Register*, October 6, p. 2t.

Kellert, Stephen R. and Joyce K. Berry. 1982. *Knowledge, Affection and Basic Attitudes Toward Animals in American Society*. Washington, DC: US Government Printing Office.

Kerr, Richard A. 1995a. "Ozone Hole Won't Worsen?" *Science* 270:376.

Kerr, Richard, A. 1995b. "Scientists See Greenhouse, Semioffically." *Science* 269:1667.

Kinealy, Christine. 1996. "How Politics Fed the Famine." *Natural History* 105(1): 33-35.

Knight, Barry and Peter Stokes. 1996. *The Deficit in Civil Society in the United Kingdom*. Birmingham, UK: Foundation for Civil Society.

Korsrud, G. O., M. G. Papich, A. C. E. Fesser, C. D. C. Salisbury, and J. D. MacNeil. 1996. "Residue Depletion in Tissues and Fluids from Swine Fed Sulfamethazine, Chlortetracycline and Penicillin G in Combination." *Food Additives and Contaminants* 13(3): 287-292.

Korten, David. 1995. *When Corporations Rule the World*. West Hartford, CT: Kumarian.

Kraus, Stephen J. 1995. "Attitudes and the Prediction of Behavior: A Meta-Analysis of the Empirical Literature," *Personality and Social Psychology Bulletin* 21:58-75.

Krieg, Eric L. 1995. "A Socio-Historical Interpretation of Toxic Waste Sites: The Case of Greater Boston." *American Journal of Economics and Sociology* 54(1): 1-14.

Kunstler, James Howard. 1993. *The Geography of Nowhere: The Rise and Decline of America's Man-Made Landscape*. New York: Simon and Schuster.

———. 1996. *Home from Nowhere: Remaking Our Everyday World for the Twenty-First Century*. New York: Simon and Schuster.

Langdon, Philip. 1994. *A Better Place to Live: Reshaping the American Suburb*. Amherst: University of Massachusetts.

Lao Tzu. 1963. *Lao Tzu: Tao Te Ching*. Translated by D. C. Lau. Harmondsworth, UK: Penguin.

Lappé, Frances Moore. 1980 (1977). *Food First: The Myth of Food Scarcity*. London: Souvenir Press.

Lappé, Frances Moore and Rachel Schurman. 1988. *Taking Population Seriously*. London: Earthscan Publications.

Latour, Bruno. 1993. *We Have Never Been Modern*. London: Harvester/Wheatsheaf.

Leopold, Aldo. 1961 (1949). "The Land Ethic." In *A Sand County Almanac*, pp. 237-264. San Francisco: Sierra Club Books.

———. 1966 (1949). *A Sand County Almanac, with Essays on Conservation from Round River*. New York: Sierra Club/ Balantine.

Lertzman, Renee. 1997. "Home and the World: A Conversation with Yi-fu Tuan." *Terra Nova* 2(1): 85-95.

Leih Tzu. 1960. *The Book of Lieh-Tzu*. Translated by A. C. Graham. London: John Murray.

Linden, Eugene. 1994. "Burned by Warming: Insurers Take Global Climate Change Seriously." *Time* 143: (Marilu): 79.

Lovejoy, Arthur O. 1936. *The Great Chain of Being*. Cambridge, MA: Harvard University Press.

Lowe, Philip. 1995. "Social Issues and Animal Waste: A European Perspective." In *New Knowledge in Livestock Odor— Proceedings of the International Livestock Odor Conference '95*. Ames: Iowa State University. Pp. 168-171.

Lowenthal, David. 1985. *The Past Is a Foreign Country*. Cambridge; New York: Cambridge University Press.

———. 1997. *The Heritage Crusade and the Spoils of History*. London: Penguin.

Lynch, Eamon. 1995. "What Price Pigs? Waste Lagoon Collapses at North Carolina Hog Farm." *Audubon* 97 (Sept./Oct.):14.

MacKensie, Debora. 1995. "Deadly Face of Summer in the City." *New Scientist* 147, September 9, p. 4.

MacKensie, James J., Roger C. Dower, and Donald D. T. Chen. 1992. *The Going Rate: What It Really Costs to Drive*. Washington, DC: World Resources Institute.

Malthus, Thomas R. 1993 (1798). *An Essay on the Principle of Population*. Edited by Geoffrey Gilbert. Oxford; London: Oxford University Press.

Mamdani, Mahmood. 1972. *The Myth of Population Control: Family, Caste, and Class in an Indian Village*. New York: Monthly Review Press.

Marsh, George Perkins. 1965 (1864). *Man and Nature*. Cambridge, MA: Belknap Press of Harvard University Press.

Martell, Luke. 1994. *Ecology and Society: An Introduction*. Cambridge, MA: Polity Press.

Marx, Karl. 1972 (1844). "Economic and Philosophic Manuscripts of 1844: Selections." In *The Marx-Engels Reader*, ed. Robert C. Tucker. New York: Norton.

Marx, Karl. 1972 (1859). "Preface to a Contribution to the Critique of Political Economy." In *The Marx-Engels Reader*, ed. Robert C. Tucker. New York: Norton.

Maslow, Abraham. 1970 (1954). "A Theory of Human Motivation." In *Motivation and Personality*, 2nd ed. New York: Harper and Row, pp. 80-106.

Mauss, Marcel. 1990 (1950) *The Gift: The Form and Reason for Exchange in Archaic Societies*. Translated by W. D. Hall. New York; London: Norton.

McEvedy, Colin. 1995. *The Penguin Atlas of African History*. Harmondsworth, UK; New York: Penguin Books.

Meadows, Donella H., Dennis L. Meadows, Jorgen Randers. 1992. *Beyond the Limits: Confronting Global Collapse, Envisioning a Sustainable Future*. Post Mills, VT: Chelsea Green.

Mearns, Robin. 1996. "Community, Collective Action and Common Grazing: The Case of Post-Socialist Mongolia." *Journal of Development Studies* 32:297-339.

Meek, Ronald L., ed. 1971. *Marx and Engels on the Population Bomb*. Berkeley: Ramparts.

Mellor, Mary. 1994. "Varieties of Ecofeminism." Capitalism, Nature, Socialism 5(4): 117-125.

Merchant, Carolyn. 1989. *Ecological Revolutions: Nature, Gender, and Science in New England*. Chapel Hill: University of North Carolina Press.

Merton, Robert K. 1957 (1949). "The Self-Fulfilling Prophecy." In *Social Theory and Social Structure*. Glencoe, IL: Free Press.

———. 1973 (1968). "The Matthew Effect in Science." In The *Sociology of Science: Theoretical and Empirical Investigations*. Chicago: University of Chicago Press.

Merton, Thomas. 1965. *The Way of Chuang Tzu*. New York: New Directions.

Metzner, Andreas. 1997. "Constructivism and Realism (Re)Considered." Paper presented at Social Theory and the Environment conference of the International Sociological Association, Zeist, The Netherlands.

Milbrath, Lester W. 1984. *Environmentalists: Vanguard for a New Society*. Albany: State University of New York Press.

Mill, John Stuart. 1961 (1874). "Nature." In *The Philosophy of John Stuart Mill*, ed. Marshall Cohen. New York: Modern

Miller, G. Tyler, Jr. 1994. *Living in the Environment*. 8th ed. Belmont: Wadsworth.

Moghadam, Valentine M., ed. 1996. *Patriarchy and Development: Women's Positions at the End of the Twentieth Century*. Oxford: Clarendon Press.

Mohai, Paul and Bunyan Bryant. 1992. "Environmental Racism: Reviewing the Evidence." In *Race and the Incidence of Environmental Hazards: A Time for Discourse*, eds. Bunyan Bryant and Paul Mohai. Boulder, CO: Westview.

Mol, Arthur P. J. 1995. *The Refinement of Production: Ecological Modernization Theory and the Chemical Industry*. Utrecht, Netherlands: Van Arkel.

Moore, Molly. 1996. "If Possible, the Air in Mexico City Just Gets Worse." *International Herald Tribune*, Nov. 26, pp. 1, 10.

Morgan, Fidelis, ed. 1989. *A Misogynist's Source Book*. London: Jonathan Cape.

Morin, Richard and John M. Berry. 1996. "As for the Economy, Public Sees Thorns: Survey Finds Americans Gloomy." *International Herald Tribune*, October 14, pp. 1, 6.

Morson, Gary Saul and Caryl Emerson. 1990. *Mikhail Bakhtin: Creation of a Prosaics*. Stanford, CA: Stanford University Press.

Mumford, Lewis. 1934. *Technics and Civilization*. London: Routledge and Kegan Paul.

Murphy, Ray. 1994a. *Rationality and Nature*. Boulder, CO: Westview.

———. 1994b. "The Sociological Construction of Science Without Nature." *Sociology* 28(4): 957-974.

Myers, Norman. 1995. "The World's Forests: Need for a Policy Appraisal." *Science* 268:823-824

Nash, Roderick. 1989. *The Rights of Nature: A History of Environmental Ethics*. Madison: University of Wisconsin Press.

Nazarea-Sandoval, Virginia D. 1995. *Local Knowledge and Agricultural Decision Making in The Philippines: Class, Gender, and Resistance*. Ithaca: Cornell University Press.
Norberg-Hodge, Helena. 1991. *Ancient Futures: Learning from Ladakh*. San Francisco: Sierra Club.

Northcott, Michael S. 1996. *The Environment and Christian Ethics*. Cambridge, UK; New York: Cambridge University Press.

Notestein, Frank W. 1945. "Population: The Long View." In *Food for the World*, ed. Theodore W. Schultz. Chicago: University of Chicago Press.

Olsen, Marvin E., Dora G. Lodwick, and Riley E. Dunlap. 1992. *Viewing the World Ecologically*. Boulder, CO: Westview.

Ostrom, Elinor. 1990. *Governing the Commons: The Evolution of Institutions for Collective Action*. Cambridge and New York: Cambridge University Press.

Parker, Barry R. 1996. *Chaos in the Cosmos: The Stunning Complexity of the Universe*. New York: Plenum Press.

Pearce, Fred. 1995. "Acid Fallout Hits Europe's Sensitive Spots." *New Scientist* 147, July 8, p. 6.

Peerenboom, R. P. 1991. "Beyond Naturalism: A Reconstruction of Daoist Environmental Ethics," *Environmental Ethics* 13(1): 3-22.

Peluso, Mancy Lee. 1996. "Reserving Value: Conservation Ideology and State Protection of Resources." In *Creating the Countryside: The Politics of Rural and Environmental Discourse*, E. Melanie DuPuis and Peter Vandergeest, eds. Philadelphia: Temple University Press. Pp. 135-165.

Petrzelka, Peggy. 1997. "Rationality and Something Else: Common Property Resources in the Imdrhas Valley of Morocco." Unpublished manuscript, Iowa State University, Department of Sociology.

Picou, Steven J. And Duane A. Gill. 1996. "The *Exxon Valdex* Oil Spill and Chrinic Psychological Stress." *American Fisheries Society Symposium* 18:879-893

Picou, Steven J., and Duane A. Gill, Christopher L. Dyer, and Evans W. Curry. 1992. "Disruption and Stress in an Alaskan Fishing Community: Initial and Contuing Impacts of the *Exxon Valdez* Oil Spill." *Industrial Crisis Quarterly* 6(3): 235-257.

Pietilä, Hilkka and Jeanne Vickers. 1994. *Making Women Matter: The Role of the United Nations*. London; Atlantic Highlights, NJ: Zed Books.

Pimentel, David, C. Harvey, P. Resosudarmo, K. Sinclair, D. Kurz, M. McNair, S. Crist, L. Shpritz, L. Fitton, R. Saffouri, and R. Blair. 1995. "Environmental and Economic Costs of Soil Erosion and Conservation Benefits." *Science* 267:1117-1123.
Plant, Judith, ed. 1989. *Healing the Wounds: The Promise of Ecofeminism*. Philadelphia, PA: New Society.

Plato. 1952. (C. 399 B.C.E.) *Plato's Gorgias*. Translated by W. C. Helmbold. New York: Liberal Arts Press.

Plato. 1985. (C. 399 B.C.E.). *The Republic*. Translated by Richard W. Sterlilng and William C. Scott. New York: Norton

Plato. 1965. (C. 360 B.C.E.). Translated by Desmond Lee. *Timaeus and Critias*. London: Penguin.

Plumwood, Val. 1994a. *Feminism and the Mastery of Nature*. London; New York: Routledge.

———. 1994b. "The Ecopolitics Debate and the Politics of Nature." In *Ecological Feminism*, ed. Karen Warren, pp. 64-87. London and New York: Routledge.

Polakowski, Michael and Michael R. Gottfredson. 1996. "The Use of Prisons as a Commons Problem: An Exploratory Study." *Journal of Research in Crime and Delinquency* 33:70-93.

Polonsky, Michael Jay and Alma T. Mintu-Winsatt, eds. 1995. *Environmental Marketing: Strategies, Practice, Theory, and Research*. New York and London: Haworth.

Putnam, Robert. 1996. "The Strange Disappearance of Civic America." *The American Prospect*, No. 24 (Winter): 34-48.

Rabelais, Francis. 1931 (1532-1552). *The Works of Francis Rabelais*, ed. Albert J. Nock and Catherine Rose Wilson. New York: Harcourt, Brace.

Raup, Hugh M. 1967. "The View from John Sanderson's Farm: A Perspective for the Use of the Land." *Forest History* 10:1-11.

Reijnen, Rien, Rudd Foppen, Cajo-Ter Braak. 1995. "The Effects of Car Traffic on Breeding Bird Populations in Woodland. III. Reduction of Density in Relation to the Proximity of Main Roads." *Journal of Applied Ecology* 32:187-202.

Renn, Ortwin. 1997. "The Demise of the Risk Society." Paper presented at the Annual Meeting of the American Sociological Association, Toronto, Canada.

Rifkin, Jeremy. 1995. *The End of Work: The Decline of the Global Labor Force and the Dawn of the Post-Market Era*. New York: Putnam.

Roberts, Rebecca S. and Jacque Emel. 1992. "Uneven Development and the Tragedy of the Commons: Competing Images for Nature-Society Analysis," *Economic Geography*. 68: 249-71.

Rolston, Holmes, III. 1979. "Can and Ought We to Follow Nature?" *Environmental Ethics* 1(1): 7-30.

Rommen, Heinrich A. 1947 (1936). *The Natural Law*. Translate by Thomas R. Hanley. St. Louis, MO: B. Herder.

Rubin, Lillian. 1994. *Families on the Fault Line: America's Working Class Speaks About the Family, the Economy, Race, and Ethnicity*. New York: HarperCollins.

Ruskin, John. 1967 (1863). *Unto This Last: Four Essays on the First Principles of Political Economy*. Edited by Llod J. Hubenka. Lincoln: University of Nebraska Press.

Sachs, Aaron. 1996. "Dying for Oil." *Worldwatch* 9(3): 10-21.

Sachs, Wolfgang, ed. 1992. The Development Dictionary: A Guide to Knowledge as Power. London; Atlantic Highlands, NJ: Zed Books.

Sahlins, Marshall. 1972. "The Original Affluent Society." In *Stone Age Economics*. New York: Aldine, pp. 1-39.

Sarre, Philip and John Blunden. 1995. *An Overcrowded World? Population, Resources, and the Environment*. Oxford; New York: Oxford University Press and the Open University.

Schatten, Kenneth and Albert Arking. 1990. *Climate Impact of Solar Variability*. Washington, DC: NASA.

Schmidt, Alfred. 1971. *The Concept of Nature in Marx*. Translated by Ben Foukes. London: New Left Books.

Schnaiberg, Alan. 1980. *The Environment, from Surplus to Scarcity*. New York and Oxford: Oxford University Press.

Schnaiberg, Alan and Kenneth Alan Gould. 1994. *Environment and Society: The Enduring Conflict*. New York: St. Martin's Press.

Schor, Juliet B. 1992. *The Overworked American: The Unexpected Decline of Leisure*. New York: Basic.

Schudson, Michael. 1984. *Advertizing, The Uneasy Persuasion*. New York: Basic.

Schultz, T. Paul. 1981. *Economics of Population*. Reading, MA: Addison-Wesley.

Schumpeter, Joseph A. 1949. *The Theory of Economic Development: An Inquiry into Profits, Capital, Credit, Interest, and the Business Cycle*. Cambridge, MA: Harvard University Press; London: Oxford University Press.
Scott, James C. 1976. *The Moral Economy of the Peasant: Rebellion and Subsistence in Southeast Asia*. New Haven, CT: Yale University Press.

———. 1986. *Weapons of the Weak: Everyday Forms of Peasant Resistance*. New Haven, CT: Yale University Press.

———. 1990. *Domination and the Arts of Resistance: Hidden Transcripts*. New Haven, CT: Yale University Press.

Seager, Joni. 1993. *Earth Follies: Feminism, Politics, and the Environment*. London: Earthscan.

Seidman, Steven. 1994. *Contested Knowledge: Social Theory in the Post-Modern Era*. Oxford; Cambridge, MA: Blackwell.

Seligman, Daniel. 1996. "Too Much Recycling?" *Fortune* 134:155-156.

Sen, Amartya. 1981. *Poverty and Famines: An Essay on Entitlement and Deprivation*. New York; Oxford: Oxford University Press.

Seneviratne, Kalinga. 1995. "Environment-Australia: Activists Denounce 'Betrayal' in Berlin." *Inter Press Service*, April 3.

Simmel, Georg. 1978. *The Philosophy of Money*. Translated by Tom Bottomore and David Frisby. London; Boston: Routledge & Kegan Paul.

Simon, Julian. 1981. *The Ultimate Resource*. Princeton, NJ: Princeton University Press.

———. ed. 1995. *The State of Humanity*. Oxford; Cambridge, MA: Blackwell.

Simon, Julian and Herman Kahn. 1984. *The Resourceful Earth: A Response to Global 2000*. Oxford; New York: Basil Blackwell.

Singer, Peter. 1996 (1975). "Animal Liberation." In *Animal Rights: The Changing Debate*, ed. Robert Garner. New York: New York University Press.

Slicer, Deborah. 1994. "Wrongs of Passage: Three Challenges to the Maturing of Ecofeminism." In *Ecological Feminism*, ed. Karen Warren, pp. 29-41. London and New York: Routledge.

Smothers, Ronald. 1995. "Slopping the Hogs, the Assembly-Line Way: Environmentalists Question a System." *New York Times*, January 30, p. A8.

Soper, Kate. 1995. *What is Nature? Culture, Politics and the Non-Human*. Oxford; Cambridge, MA: Blackwell

Standing, Guy. 1989. "Global Feminization Through Flexible Labour." *World Development* 17(7): 1077-1095.

Stein, Dorothy. 1995. *People Who Count: Population and Politics, Women and Children*. London: Earthscan.

Stevens, William K. 1995. "Study of Cloud Patterns Points to Many Areas Exposed to Big Rises in Ultraviolet Radiation." *New York Times*, November 21, p. C4.

———. 1996. "A Skeptic Asks, Is It Getting Hotter, or Is It Just the Computer Model?" *New York Times*, June 18, pp. B5, B8.

———. 1997. "A Greener Green Belt Bears Witness to a Warming Trend." *New York Times*, April 22, p. B10.

Stevenson, Glenn G. 1991. *Common Property Economics : A General Theory and Land Use Applications*. Cambridge (UK); New York: Cambridge University Press.

Stewart, F. 1982. "Poverty and Famines: Book Review." *Disasters* 6(2).

Stiefel, Matthias. 1994. *A Voice for the Excluded: Popular Participation in Development: Utopia or Necessity?* London; Atlantic Highlands, NJ: Zed Books.

Stix, Gary. 1996. "Green Policies: Insurers Cope with Global Warming." *Scientific American* 274:27-28.

Streeter, Michael. 1996. "Record Haul of Rhino Horn Is Seized." *The Independent*, Sept. 4, p. 1.

Successful Farming. 1995. "New Deals at the Packaging Plants." *Successful Farming* 93 (March): 22.

Suplee, Curt. 1995. "Dirty Air Can Shorten Your Life, Study Says: Death Rate Higher in Worst Cities." *Washington Post*, March 10, p. A1.

Taylor, Dorceta E. 1989. "Blacks and the Environment: Toward an Explanation of the Concern and Action Gap Between Blacks and Whites." *Environment and Behavior* 21 (2): 175-205.

Taylor, Paul W. 1986. *Respect for Nature: A Theory of Environmental Ethics*. Princeton, NJ: Princeton University Press.

Taylor, Peter J. and Frederick H. Buttel. 1992. "How Do We Know We Have Global Environmental Problems? Science and the Globalization of Environmental Discourse." *Geoforum* 23:405-416.

Teitelbaum, Michael S. 1987. "Relevance of Demographic Transition Theory for Developing Countries." In *Perspectives on Population: An Introduction to Concepts and Issues*, ed. Scott W. Menard and Elizabeth W. Moen, pp. 29-36. New York; Oxford: Oxford University Press.

Thomas, Keith. 1983. *Man and the Natural World: Changing Attitudes in England, 1500-1800*. London: Allen Lane.

Thompson, Gary D. and Paul N. Wilson. 1994. "Common Property as an Institutional Response to Environmental Variability." *Contemporary Economic Policy* 12:12-21.

Thoreau, Henry David. 1962 (1854). *The Variorum Walden*. New York: Washington Square Press.

———. 1975 (1862). "Walking." In *Excursions*. Gloucester, MA: Peter Smith.

Thurow, Lester C. 1996. *The Future of Capitalism: How Today's Economic Forces Shape Tomorrow's World*. New York: William Morrow.

Tierney, John. 1996. "Recycling is Garbage," *New York Times Magazine*. June 30, pp. 24-29.

Timmins, Nicholas. 1996. "Income Gap Between Richest and Poorest Ceases to Grow." *Financial Times*, November 15, p.18.

Times (London). 1996. "Roads Claim Up to 60 Million Birds a Year," September 10, p. 8.

Tinker, Irene. 1990. *Persistent Inequalities: Women and World Development*. New York; Oxford: Oxford University Press.

Twain, Mark. 1991 (1876). *The Adventures of Tom Sawyer*. Philadelphia; London: Running Press.

UNDP (United Nations Development Programme). 1994. *Human Development Report 1994.* New York: Oxford University Press.

UNDP. (United Nations Development Programme). 1996. *Urban Agriculture: Food, Jobs and Sustainable Cities*. New York: United Nations Development Programme.

Ungar, Sheldon. 1994. "Apples and Oranges: Probing the Attitude-Behavior Relationship for the Environment," *Canadian Review of Sociology and Anthropology* 31:288-304.

Urry, John. 1990. *The Tourist Gaze: Leisure and Travel in Contemporary Societies.* London: Sage.

———. 1995. *Consuming Places*. London; New York: Routledge.

Valles, Marie-Noelle. 1997. "Britain's Eco-Warriors Go to Ground in Manchester." *Agence France Presse*, June 14.
Van Dyke, Fred. 1996. *Redeeming Creation: The Biblical Basis for Environmental Stewardship*. Downers Grove, IL: InterVarsity Press.

Veblen, Thorstein. 1967 (1899). *The Theory of the Leisure Class*. New York: Funk and Wagnalls.

Vidal, John. 1995. "Black Gold Claims a High Price." *Guardian Weekly*, January 15, 1995, p. 7.

———. 1997. "Gone to Ground." The Guardian, February 22, p. T30

Visser, Margaret. 1986. *Much Depends on Dinner: The Extraordinary History and Mythology, Allure and Obsessions, Perils and Taboos, of an Ordinary Meal.* Toronto: McClelland and Stewart.

Wachtel, Paul. 1983. *The Poverty of Affluence: A Psychological Portrait of the American Way of Life*. New York: Free Press.

Walby, Sylvia. 1996. "The 'Declining Significance' or the 'Changing Forms' of Patriarchy?" In *Patriarchy and Development: Women's Positions at the End of the Twentieth Century*, ed. Valentine M. Moghadam, pp. 19-33. Oxford: Clarendon Press.

Walton, John. 1994. *Free Markets and Food Riots: The Politics of Global Adjustment*. Oxford; Cambridge, MA: Blackwell.

Ward, David. 1997. "Tunneller Vows to Stay Under as Long as It Takes." *The Guardian (UK)*, June 16, p. 7.

Warner, W. Keith and J. Lynn England. 1995. "A Technological Science Perspective for Sociology." *Rural Sociology* 60:607-622.

Warren, Karen, ed. 1994. *Ecological Feminism*. London; New York: Routledge.

———. 1996. "Ecological Feminist Philosophies: An Overview of the Issues." In *Ecological Feminist Philosophies*, ed. Karen Warren, pp. ix-xxvi. Blommington and Indianapolis: Indiana University Press.

Weber, Max. 1958 (1904-1905). *The Protestant Ethic and the Spirit of Capitalism*. New York: Charles Scribner.

Weber, Max. 1967 (1922). *Economy and Society*. Edited by Guenther Roth and Claus Wittich. Vol. 1. Berkeley: University of California.

———. 1988 (1909). *The Agrarian Sociology of Ancient Civilizations*. London: Verso.

White, Lynn. 1967. "The Historical Roots of Our Ecological Crises." *Science* 155:1203-1207.
Whitley, Richard. 1992. "Changing Organizational Forms: From the Bottom Up." In *Rethinking Organization: New Directions in Organization Theory and Analysis*, ed. Michael Reed and Michael Hughes. London; Newberry Park, CA: Sage.

Wichterich, Christa. 1988. "From the Struggle Against 'Overpopulation' to the Industrialization of Human Production." *Reproductive and Genetic Engineering* 1(1): 21-30.

Williams, Raymond. 1980 (1972). "Ideas of Nature." In *Problems in Materialism and Culture*, pp. 67-85. London: Verso.

Wilson, Harold Fisher. 1967 (1936). *The Hill Country of Northern New England*. New York: AMS Press.

Wilson, Randall and Robert D. Yaro. 1988. *Dealing with Change in the Connecticut River Valley: A Design Manual for Conservation and Development*. Amherst: Center for Rural Massachusetts, University of Massachusetts.

Winner, Langdon. 1986. *The Whale and the Reactor: A Search for Limits in an Age of High Technology*. Chicago; London: University of Chicago Press.

Wolff, Edward N. 1995. *Top Heavy: A Study of the Increasing Inequality of Wealth in America*. New York: Twentieth-Century Fund Press.

World Bank. 1994. *World Development Report 1994*. Oxford: Oxford University.

———. 1995. *World Development Report 1995: Workers in an Integrating World*. New York: Oxford University Press.

———. 1996. *World Development Report 1996: From Plan to Market*. New York: Oxford University Press.

———. 1997. *World Development Report 1997: The State in a Changing World*. New York: Oxford University Press.

World Resources Institute. 1996. *World Resources, 1996-1997*. New York; Oxford: Oxford University Press.

Wright, Angus Lindsay. 1990. *The Death of Ramon Gonzalez: The Modern Agricultural Dilemma*. Austin: University of Texas Press.

Yago, Glenn. 1984. *The Decline of Transit: Urban Transportation in German and US Cities, 1900-1970*. Cambridge, MA; London: Cambridge University Press.

Yearley, Steven. 1991. *The Green Case: A Sociology of Environmental Issues, Arguments, and Politics*. London: HarperCollins.
———. 1996. *Sociology, Environmentalism, Globalization*. London: Sage.

Yepson, David. 1995. "What about the Big Hog Lots?" *Des Moines Register*, November 27, p. 9.

INDEX

A

A-B (attitude-behavior) split, 246-47
Abramson, Paul, 191
accumulation of advantage, 68
acid rain, 15-16, 237
The Adventures of Tom Sawyer (Twain), 47
advertising
> inescapable presence of,66-67
> sentiments and, 52-54
> *See also* consumption

Aesop, 251
Africa
> colonial control of, 112
> development of underdevelopment in, 110-17
> economic role of women in, 135
> food storages of, 119
> IMF food riots of, 115
> *See also* underdeveloped countries

agricultural subsidies, 221
agriculture
> community supported, 268-71
> decline of New England's, 215-22
> environmental threats and, 18-19
> impact of global warming on, 8
> impact of mold-board plow on, 151
> impact of overirrigation of, 17-18
> local collaboration to improve, 261-64
> urban, 214-15
> water pollution and, 18

alternative environmental paradigm, 196
aman harvest, 129n.47
Ames, Iowa, 265-74
ancient Chinese environmental concerns, 181-83
ancient Greek environmental concerns, 179-81
ancient Roman environmental concerns, 175-79
Andrews, Cecile, 62
Androcles and the lion fable, 251-53
Animal Liberation (Singer), 202
animal protection movement, 202-3
animal rights activists, 202
animal welfare activists, 202
anthropocentric environmentalism, 279
Aquinas, Thomas, 164
Aral Sea (Asia), 18
Aristotle, 180, 181, 187, 210-212
ascetic rationalism, 153, 149-50

Asian Development Bank, 113
Athanasiou, Tom, 27
Australia, soil erosion in, 17
automobiles
environmental impact of, 90-91
hidden costs/subsidies of, 91-92
social organization of convenience and, 91-94
See also pollution

B

Bakhtin, Mikhail, 157-62
Bangladesh, 120, 121, 127
Bangladesh famine (1974), 120
Barrett, Stanley, 235
Barron, Hal, 220
Basel Convention (1989), 21
Bavaria, Joan, 81
beauty
of nature, 27-31
scarcity and, 48
Beck, Ulrich, 193, 194, 204
Beethoven, Ludwig van, 184
belief
environmental values and, 196
natural conscience and, 204
See also values
The Bell Curve, 224
Bell, Mike, 31, 147
Bell, Sam, 207-8, 240
Bentley, Jeff, 263-65
Bhopal (India), 21
the Bible, 154
Bierdstadt, Albert, 184
biology, 222-24
birth control, 108-9, 137-39
blind men/elephant fable (India), 4
bodily humor, 158-61
body
carnivalesque, 159-60
classical, 159, 160-61
ecology of the, 157-62
social distinction and distancing from, 161
body-awareness movement, 162
Boserup effect, 125-27
Boserup, Ester, 125, 126, 134, 135
bottom-up approach to change, 258-59, 240, 248
box schemes (Britain), 268
Branstad, Terry, 80
Bretton Woods Conference (1944), 115, 113

Bri-Bri Indians, 43
broken technological routines, 96
Bruntland, Gro, 166
Burke, Edmund, 164
Butz, Earl, 88

C

Callicles, 179, 180
Calvinism, 148-50
Calvin, John, 149, 150
Campbell, Robert H., 82
Canute, King (England), 239
capitalism
       Christianity and, 148-49
       Darwin's promotion of, 240-41, 222-23
       moral parallels of Protestantism and, 148-51
       treadmill of, 150
carbon dioxide levels, 10-12
carnivalesque body, 159-60
carnivalesque humor, 159-60
carnivalesque pleasures, 159
Carson, Rachel, 166, 173-74
Catholic Church, 108
Catton, William, 196
Ceaucescu, Nicolae, 138
Center for a New American Dream (CNAD), 63
Center for Plain Living, 63
Central Valley (California), 18
CERES (Coalition for Environmentally Responsible Economies), 81
CERES Principles, 81
CFCs, 12-13, 113
Chad, 119
Chernobyl, 193, 196
China
       economic growth of, 113
       rice yields in, 130
Chinese (ancient) environmental concerns, 181-83
Chipko ("hug the tree") movement (India), 190
Christianity
       Eastern vs. Western, 154
       modern capitalism and, 148-53
       parallels of science, technology, and, 148-51
       See also Judeo-Christian ethic; Protestantism
Chuang Tzu, 145, 182
Chuang Tzu (Taoism), 155-56
Citizen's Clearinghouse for Hazardous Waste, 166, 167
classical body, 159, 160-61
Climate and Civilization (Huntington), 226

Copernicus, Nicolaus, 151
core regions, 114
cornucopian argument, 123-25
corporate profit rate, 73
di Cosimo, Piero, 160
Costa Rican village water supply, 261-63
Costello, Elvis, 240
Cotgrove, Stephen, 190, 196
Cottrel, Fred, 140
craniometry, 224-26
Cronon, William, 232
Crutzen, Paul, 13
cultural dualisms, 168-69
culture
      ecology of the body and, 157-61
      hard work as virtue and, 83
      hierarchy of needs across, 40
      hippie, 162
      of Judeo-Christian ethic, 145-46
      non-Western, 146-47
      population control and, 108-10
      richness of primitive, 40
      technology and, 97-99
      See also values
culture of leisure, 233

D

Dacyczyn, Amy, 62
Daly, Herman, 276
Darwin, Charles, 28, 222-23
debt ratio, 1145
Decade for Women (1976-1985), 135
deforestation, 29
"demand management," 115
the Demiurge (Plato), 180-81
democracy
      dialogic, 259
      dialogue, environmental problems, and, 257-59
      institutions of, 203-4
      sensibilities of, 198-201
demographics, 131-32
      See also population
demographic transition theory, 132
development
      changing vision of Ames (Iowa), 271-72
      dialogic, 265
      participatory, 263
      three demographic stages of, 117-18
      as Western hidden agenda, 130

women and, 131-33
See also economic growth
"Development is the best contraceptive" slogan (World Population Conference, 1974), 130
dialogic democracy, 259
dialogic development, 265
dialogue
 democracy, environmental problems, and, 256-59
 ethical dimension to ecological, 278
 of solidarities, 251-56
 of technology, 89-90
disasters, 64-65
Discourse on the Origins of Inequality (Rousseau), 199
"The Discovery of Honey" (painting, di Cosimo), 160
"divided planet," 27
"Dolly" (cloned sheep), 154
dominant social paradigm, 196
Douglas, Mary, 52, 59
Douthwaite, Richard, 69
Downs, Anthony, 188, 189
dualisms, 167-68
Dunlap, Riley, 196

E

"An Early Settler Clears a Homestead" (diorama for 1740), 216
Earth Day (1970), 189
Earth Summit, 188
Eastern Christianity, 154
 See also Christianity
ecocentric environmentalism, 279
ecofeminism
 controversy over, 170-713
 described, 164-65
 See also women
Ecoglasnost (Bulgaria), 203
ecological dialogue
 changing the, 137-38
 described, 5, 37
 study of ideology and, 145
ecological modernization, 276, 277
ecological self, 162
ecological social paradigm, 196
ecology
 of the body, 268-73
 described, 1
 industrial, 247-48
 of patriarchy, 276-77
Ecology House, 260
economic growth

"Farmer-Scientists and Integrated Pest Management in Honduras" seminar (Bentley), 264
feminism, 162
feminization of labor, 136
fertility rates, 98, 106, 136
fine particulates, 15
"first wave" of environmentalism, 198
Fisher Museum of Forestry (Harvard University), 216-19
food entitlements, 120-21
food shortages
       politics of, 120-21
       population and, 119-21
Frank, Andr, Gundar, 114
Fresh Aire Delivery, 226-67
Freudenburg, Bill, 239
Freud, Sigmund, 164
Frugal Gazette, 62
Fuscus epistle (Horace), 175-76

G

Galbraith, John Kenneth, 65
Galileo, 151, 153
game theory, 254-55
Gandhi, Indira, 137, 138
Gandhi, Mahatma, 103, 187
Gandhi, Sanjay, 137
Garcovich, Lorraine, 233
Gargantua (fictional character), 157
Gargantua and Pantagruel (Rabelais), 157, 160
GDP (gross domestic product), 275
gender differences
       in environmental concerns, 189
       environmental domination and, 163-71
       in experience of nature, 169-70
       See also women
generalization of the market, 73
General Motors, 93
German Green Party, 195
Germany, 195
Ghandhi, Mahatma, 36-37
ghosts of place, 233-34
Gibbs, Lois, 166, 167
Giddens, Anthony, 259
Gimpel, Jean, 98
Giuliani, Mayor (NYC), 260
glasnost policy (Soviet Union), 203
global warming
       environmental threat of, 6-11
       weather-related natural disasters and, 7-9
Glover, Paul, 116

GNP (gross national product), 274-76
God image, 180-81
"the Good," 210
goodness, 210
goods
        community and, 57-59
        green taxes and, 276
        hau (spirit) of, 51-52
        positional, 46-49
        sentiments and, 49
        social systems of entitlement to, 120
        See also materialism
Gorbachev, Mikhail, 203
government, 277
GPI (genuine progress indicator), 276
Great Bengal famine (1943), 120
greed, 35-36
        See also materialism
Greek (ancient) environmental concerns, 179-81
green consumerism, 55-56
greenhouse effect, 10-11
green revolution, 127
green taxes, 275
"green-washing," 55
Gregory, Jim, 245-46
Greider, Thomas, 233
growth machine, 74
Gualdalcazar (Mexico), 21
Guha, Ramachandra, 21, 190, 192, 204, 230
Gujarat (India), 18

H

Hannigan, John, 237
happiness
        consumption and, 64
        prosperity levels and, 61-62
Hardin, Garret, 248, 249, 250
Hardin, Garrett, 236
hard work
        as internal treadmill, 78
        Protestant work ethic on, 150
        as virtuous, 76
Harris, Lawren S., 231
Harvard Forest dioramas, 216-19
hau (spirit of goods), 51-52
Hayes, Denis, 81
HCFCs (hydrochlorofluoroncarbons), 13, 124
"heat-island" effect, 29n.15
Hegel, Georg Wilhelm Friedrich, 164

"The Height of Cultivation for Farm Crops" (diorama for 1830), 217
hierarchy of needs, 39-40, 42, 190
hierarchy of society, 46
Hinrichs, Clare, 234
hippie culture, 162
Hippocrates, 180
Hirsch, Fred, 46, 47, 48
"The Historical Roots of our Ecologic Crisis" (White), 151
HMS Beagle, 223
hog confinement debate, 75-80, 86
Honduras, 263-64
Hooker Chemical Corporation, 166
Horace, 175-79
HOURS (Ithaca paper currency), 117-18
Hsu Yu, 183
Human Development Index (HDI), 26
human exceptionalism paradigm, 196
humor
        bodily, 158-161
        carnivalesque, 159-60
hunter-gatherer societies, 40-41
Huntington, Ellsworth, 226-29
hybrid IR8 (miracle rice), 128
hybrid IR20 (miracle rice), 128
hybrid IR36 (miracle rice, 128
hybrid IR56 (miracle rice), 129

I

Ice Age, 12
ideal factors, 203
idealists, 4
ideology
        difference made by, 171-72
        differences in, 144
        ecofeminism as, 164-65, 170-71
        nature and, 236-40
        paradigm shift thesis and, 195-97
        patriarchy as, 136, 137, 164-691, 171
        study of ecological dialogue and, 145
"IMF food riots," 116
immigration restrictions, 235-36
income inequalities, 24-27
        See also social inequalities; wealth
Independent Commission on Population and Quality of Life report (1996), 108
India
        Chipko ("hug the tree") movement of, 190
        economic growth of, 114
        Narmada River dam projects of, 166-67
        National Population Policy of 1976 by, 137-38

food supply in, 119
hard work as virtuous in, 83
rice yields in, 130
teikei of, 268
use of ascetic rationalism in, 156
Judeo-Christian ethic, 153-55
See also Christianity

K

Karin B. (West German ship), 21
Kelly, Petra, 166
Kentlands, Maryland (new urbanism), 272
Kenya, 231-32
Keoldeo Ghana bird sanctuary (India), 230-31
Keynes, John Maynard, 112
King, Charlie, 204
knowledge (local), 264-65
Kuhn, Thomas, 196
Kuo Hsiang, 211

L

labor force
    feminization of labor, 137
    miracle rice impact on Malaysian, 128-30
"Lake and Mountains" (painting, Harris), 231
land
    loss of contact with, 29
    subsidence, 18
"The Land Ethic" (Leopold), 275
landscape experience, 233-34
Lao Tzu, 182, 183, 187
Lao Tzu (Taoist work), 182
Lapp,, Frances Moore, 99, 119
The Last of the Buffalo (painting, Bierdstadt), 184
Latour, Bruno, 238
leisure class, 44-46
Leopold, Aldo, 27, 187
Liberace, Wladziu Valentine, 35
Lieh-Tzu (Taoist work), 182
lifeboat ethics, 237
Little Ice Age, 10, 11, 12
local currency movement, 117-18
local knowledge, 264
Locke, John, 199
"lodging" rice problems, 127
Logan, John, 73, 86
logic of domination, 167, 170

Lookout Point (Yosemite National Park), 145
loss of species, 28-29
Love Canal, 21
Love Canal Homeowners Committee, 166
L-shih Ch'un Ch'iu (Chinese writings), 182
Luther, Martin, 150

M

McNamara, Robert, 115-16
"mad cow" disease (Britain), 195
Magic Beanstalk CSA, 68-71
Malaysia, 129-30, 190
Malthusianism population theory
    conclusions on, 139-41
    demographic critique of, 131-39
    described, 104-5
    on food shortages, 119-21
    inequality critique of, 110-22
    limitations of, 121-22
    technological critique of, 122-31
    See also population growth
Malthus, Thomas, 103-4, 223
Man and Nature, or, Physical Geography Modified by Human Action (Marsh), 200
Maori people (New Zealand), 51
Marsh, George Perkins, 200
Marx, Karl, 36, 222-23
Masai tribe (Kenya), 231-32
Maslow, Abraham, 38-39, 40
Maslow's hierarchy of needs, 39, 40, 191
material factors, 205
materialism
    consumption and, 35-36
    ecological dialogue and, 37
    hierarchy of needs and, 38-39, 40
    of human condition, 36-42
    in hunter-gatherer societies, 40-41
    of the original affluent society, 40-41
    paradigm shift to environmental concerns from, 195-98
    See also environmental concerns; goods; postmaterialism
materialists
    categorizing people as, 191-92
    on social life, 3-4
materialist skepticism, 183
Mauss, Marcell, 51
Melara, Werner, 264
men's stories, 169-71
Merton, Robert K., 64, 93
Metalclad Inc., 21

Mexico City
  air pollution in, 14
  land subsidence in, 18
  pollution levels in, 127
  rapid population growth in, 126
Milbrath, Lester, 196
military-agricultural complex, 270
Minamoto (Japan), 21
miracle rice case, 127-29
Miser's Gazette, 62
modernization (ecology), 276, 277
modernization theory, 111
Moghadam, Valentine, 136
mold-board plow, 151
Molina, Mario, 12, 13
Molotch, Harvey, 73, 94
"Mom-will-pick-up-after-us" environment, 165
money, 67-68
monism, 210
monologue, 258
Monsanto's Roundup-Ready Soybeans, 130
Montreal Protocol (1987), 13
moral holism, 209
morality, 179-80
moral separatism, 209
moral value, 209
Morris, William, 199
Morton, Samuel George, 224-26, 229
Mother Earth imagery, 165
motivation
  interest, 49, 50
  shaped by technology/economic, 66-67
  social, 49
Muir, John, 187
Mumford, Lewis, 99, 101, 187
Murray-Darling Basin (Australia), 18

N

Naess, Arne, 187
Narmada Bachao Andolan (Save the Narmada Movement), 166-67
Narmada River dam projects (India), 166-67
National City Lines (NCL), 93
National Geographic, 99, 146
National Population Policy of 1976 (India), 137-38
Native American's sterilization, 138
natura, 179
natural capitalism theory, 223-24
natural conscience, 186
natural me, 186

natural other, 186
natural products, 212
natural resource dependent communities, 81-82
natural selection theory, 222-23, 237-38
nature
> ancient Greek concerns with, 179-81
> ancient Roman concerns with, 175-79
> biology and, 222-24
> contradictions of, 209-13
> democratic concerns for rights of, 198
> gender differences in experience of, 169-70
> ideology and, 236
> material basis within, 36-38
> modern cultural attitudes toward, 161
> moldboard plow exploitation of, 144-45
> philosophical issues of, 198-200
> respect for, 279
> rights and beauty of, 27-31, 278
> as social construction, 213-29
> social selection and New England's, 220-22
> tourism/social construction of landscape and, 233-35
> wilderness ideal and, 230-33
> women associated with, 163-64

needs
> hierarchy of, 39-40, 42, 190
> of money, 67-68

negative externalities
> described, 75
> of factory farms for Iowa hogs, 79-80

Negative Population Growth, 235
New England's agricultural decline, 218-22
New Haven (Connecticut), 147
New Haven land trust (Connecticut), 215
Newton, Isaac, 151
new urbanism, 271-74
New York Times, 260
Nigel, 186
Nigeria, 20, 21
Nike products, 116
Noah (Bible), 155-56
nomos, 180
non-Western philosophies, 140-41
Norberg-Hodge, Helena, 133
Notestein, Frank W., 131
notion of virtue, 82
> *See also* hard work
NOx (nitrogen oxide compounds), 15

O

P

prisoners' dilemma, 254-56
problem of collective action, 249-50
production
        cultural values and, 82
        dialogue of consumption and, 83-85
        treadmill of, 69-81
profit
        consumption and, 83-84
        maximizing of, 69-70
        rates of corporate, 73
Protagoras, 180
Protestant ethic, 149, 151
The Protestant Ethic (Weber), 148
Protestantism
        ascetic rationalism of, 149-50, 156
        capitalism and, 149-51
        See also Christianity
Providence, Rhode Island (new urbanism), 273
Ptahhotep, 181

Q

quality of life
        poverty and, 60-62
        wealth distribution and, 24-26

R

Rabelais, François, 157
Rabelais and His World (Bakhtin), 158, 162
race, 184-85
racism (scientific), 224-28
rainbow covenant (Bible), 154
rational choice theory, 50, 255
rationalism, 50
recipes of understanding, 104
recycling, 226-61, 265-66
reflexive modernization, 193
religious values, 108-9
respect for nature, 279
"retail strip mines," 271
rhino horn, 48
rights of nature, 27-31, 278
risk society, 204-7
River Tiber, 177
Rochberg-Halton, Eugene, 49
Rolston, Holmes, 209
Roman aqueduct (Spain), 177

Roman environmental concerns, 176-80
Romanian population policy (1960s), 138-40
Roundup-Ready Soybeans (Monsanto), 130
Rousseau, Jean-Jacques, 199
routines, 95
routinization, 104-6
Rowland, Sherwood, 12, 13
Royal Society for the Prevention of Cruelty to Animals, 48
Ruskin, John, 199, 245

S

Sachs, Wolfgang, 133
Sahel famines (1970s), 120
Sahlins, Marshall, 42, 43
Salt, Henry, 199
Sardar Sarovar Dam (India), 167
Saro-Wiwa, Ken, 17, 190, 204
Save the Narmada Movement (Narmada Bachao Andolan), 166-68
scarcity
      beauty and, 45
      causes of, 43
Schnaiberg, Alan, 75, 94
Schor, Juliet, 58
Schurman, Rachel, 120
Schutz, Alfred, 95
science
      out of control, 193
      parallels of technology, Christianity, and, 142-45
      See also technology
scientific racism, 224-29
Scott, James, 129
Seager, Joni, 165, 170
"self-fulfilling prophecy," 93
self-interests, 187
      See also interests
semiperiphery regions, 114
Sen, Amartya, 119, 120, 121,
"sensuous external world," 36
sentiments
      advertising and, 52-54
      goods and, 49
      green advertising use of, 54-56
      solidarity of, 252-53
Seven Gorges Dam (China), 156
Shell Oil Company, 20
Shiva, Vandana, 166
"shock therapy" regimen, 116

U

ultraviolet light, 12
underdeveloped countries
    demographic transition in, 132-34
    development of, 114-15
    global commitment to, 115-16
    structural adjustment trap of, 115-17
    understanding, 115-16
    women and development of, 134-37
    See also Africa; development; wealthy industrial countries
United Church of Christ's Commission for Racial Justice reports (1987), 22, 23
United Kingdom industrial emissions, 16
United Nations Decade for Women (1976-1985), 135
United Nations Development Programme, 26
United Nations Intergovernmental Panel on Climate Change, 11-12
United States
    average income in, 25
    as core country, 114
    CSAs across, 268-71
    environmental discrimination in the, 24
    GNP and GPI of the, 276
    hard work as virtuous in, 76
    impact of gasoline shortages (1970s) on, 96
    postmaterialists survey in, 192
    recycling in the, 260-61
    registered vehicles within, 90
    simplicity movement in, 62-63
    soil erosion in, 16-17
    unequal income ratio in, 26
    workweek length in the, 58
University of Massachusetts study (1994), 23
urban agriculture, 214-15
Urry, John, 233
U.S. Census of Agriculture, 220
Use Less Stuff, 62
U.S. Environmental Protection Agency, 22
use values, 74
U.S. Peace Corps, 263

V

Valdez Principles, 81
value of relationships, 274
values
    A-B (attitude-behavior) split and, 246-47
    as crucial to ecological dialogues, 278
    environmental beliefs and, 196
    environmental concerns and, 190
    of hard work, 76

Y

Z